The Reality of Budgetary Reform in OECD Nations

The Reality of Budgetary Reform in OECD Nations

Trajectories and Consequences

Edited by

John Wanna

Research School of Social Sciences, The Australian National University, Australia

Lotte Jensen

Professor of Management, Politics and Philosophy, Copenhagen Business School, Denmark

Jouke de Vries

Professor of Public Administration and Academic Director of Campus, Leiden University, The Hague, The Netherlands

Edward Elgar

Cheltenham, UK • Northampton, MA, USA

Published by
Edward Elgar Publishing Limited
The Lypiatts
15 Lansdown Road
Cheltenham
Glos GL50 2JA
UK

Edward Elgar Publishing, Inc.
William Pratt House
9 Dewey Court
Northampton
Massachusetts 01060
USA

A catalogue record for this book
is available from the British Library

Library of Congress Control Number: 2009940632

Mixed Sources
Product group from well-managed forests and other controlled sources
www.fsc.org Cert no. SA-COC-1565
© 1996 Forest Stewardship Council

ISBN 978 1 84064 689 4

Printed and bound by MPG Books Group, UK

Contents

Contributors

Xavier Ballart is Professor of Political and Administrative Sciences at the Autonomous University of Barcelona, Spain.

Ton Bestebreur is Associate Professor at Erasmus University, Rotterdam, The Netherlands and formerly the Dutch Ministry of Finance.

David Fjord is a Budget Analyst in the Danish Ministry of Finance, Copenhagen, Denmark.

Lewis Hawke is Senior Financial Management Specialist with the World Bank (Europe and Central Asia Region) and formerly in the Australian Department of Finance and Deregulation.

Alfred Tat-Kei Ho is Associate Professor and Director of the Public Affairs Program in the School of Public and Environmental Affairs, Indiana University, Indianapolis, USA.

Masahiro Horie is Professor with the National Graduate Institute for Policy Studies (GRIPS), Tokyo, Japan.

Derek Gill is Visiting Scholar with the Institute for Policy Studies at Victoria University of Wellington, New Zealand, and formerly with the Ministry of Social Development.

David A. Good is Professor with the School of Public Administration at the University of Victoria, British Columbia, Canada.

Chiara Goretti works in public finance with the Italian Senate.

Lotte Jensen is Professor in the Department of Management, Politics and Philosophy at the Copenhagen Business School, Denmark.

John M. Kim is Director of the Centre for Fiscal Analysis at the Korean Institute of Public Finance, Seoul, Korea.

Evert A. Lindquist is Professor and Head of the School of Public Administration, University of Victoria, British Columbia, Canada.

Richard Norman is Senior Lecturer in the School of Management, Victoria University of Wellington, New Zealand.

Luca Rizzuto works in public finance with the Italian Senate.

Francesco Stolfi is a Research Fellow at the School of Politics and International Relations, at University College, Dublin, Ireland.

Colin Thain is Professor of Politics in the Department of Political Science and International Studies, University of Birmingham, UK.

Jouke de Vries is Professor of Public Administration and Academic Director of Campus, Leiden University, the Hague, The Netherlands.

John Wanna is the Sir John Bunting Professor of Public Administration (ANZSOG) at the Australian National University, and Professor of Politics at Griffith University, Brisbane, Australia.

Eduardo Zapico is with the Evaluation Unit of the Directorate of the Budget, at the European Commission, Brussels, Belgium.

Abbreviations

AD	Administrative Department (Denmark)
AGBs	autonomous governing bodies (Netherlands)
AME	Annually Managed Expenditure (UK)
BAPA	Budget and Accounting Procedures Act (US)
BD	Budget Department (Denmark)
BEA	Budget Enforcement Act (US)
BRU	Budget Reform Committee (Denmark)
CASA	Civil Aviation Safety Authority (Australia)
CBAs	Central Budgetary Agencies (Australia)
CBA	cost–benefit analysis
CBA	central budget agency
CBO	Congressional Budget Office (US)
CFIS	Crown Financial Information System (NZ)
CFO	chief financial officer
CSD	Civil Service Department (UK)
CSR	Comprehensive Spending Review (UK)
DBAS	Digital Budget and Accounting System (Korea)
DEL	Departmental Expenditure Limits (UK)
DGP	Directorate General of Budget (Spain)
DGT	Dipartimento del Tesoro [Department of Treasury] (Italy)
DPEF	Economic and Financial Plan (Italy)
DPRs	Departmental Performance Reports (Canada)
DR	Danish Regions
Ecofin	Economic and Financial Affairs Council of the European Union
EDP	excessive deficit procedure
EDX	Ministerial Committee on Public Expenditure (UK)
EFPC	Economic and Fiscal Policy Council (Japan)
EMS	European Monetary System
EMS	Expenditure Management System (Canada)
EMU	Economic and Monetary Union
ERC	Expenditure Review Committee of Cabinet (Australia)
ERM	Exchange Rate Mechanism
ESEF	Economic Structure Enhancing Fund (Netherlands)
ESRC	Economic and Social Research Council (UK)

EU	European Union
FAHCSIA	Department of Families, Housing, Community Services and Indigenous Affairs (Australia)
FBO	final budget outcome
FILP	Fiscal Investment and Loan Program (Japan)
FIS	financial information system
FMCG	Financial Management Coordinating Group (UK)
FMI	Financial Management Initiative (UK)
FMIP	Financial Management Improvement Program (Australia)
GAAP	generally accepted accounting principles
GAO	Government Accountability Office (US)
GDP	gross domestic product
GFS	Government Financial Statistics (NZ)
GMRA	Government Management Reform Act (US)
GPRA	Government Performance and Results Act (US)
GRH Act	Gramm–Rudman–Hollings Act (US)
GST	Goods and Services Tax (Australia)
HRDC	Human Resources Development Canada
ICT	information and communication technology
IGAE	General Controller of Central Government (Spain)
IGR	Intergenerational Report (Australia)
IMF	International Monetary Fund
IT	information technology
JCPAA	Joint Committee of Public Accounts and Audit (Australia)
KRAs	key result areas (NZ)
LDP	Liberal Democratic Party (Japan)
LGD	Local Government Denmark
MBO	Management by Objectives (US)
MEF	Ministry of Economy and Finance (Italy)
MEH	Ministry of Economy and Finance (Spain)
MP	Member of Parliament
MPB	Ministry of Planning and Budgeting (Korea)
MPO	Management and Personnel Office, Cabinet Office (UK)
MTEF	medium-term expenditure framework (Korea)
MTFS	Medium-Term Financial Strategy (UK)
MYEFO	Mid-Year Economic and Fiscal Outlook (Australia)
MYOPs	Multi-Year Operational Plans (Canada)
NCA	National Commission of Audit (Australia)
NCA	National Court of Audit (Netherlands)
NCT	New Control Total (UK)
NFMP	National Fiscal Management Plan (Korea)
NPM	new public management

NSC	National Security Committee (Australia)
NZSF	New Zealand Superannuation Fund
OBEGAL	operating balance excluding gains and losses (NZ)
OECD	Organisation for Economic Co-operation and Development
OFFM	Office of Federal Financial Management (US)
OMB	Office of Management and Budget (US)
PAYGO	pay-as-you-go (US)
PAR	program analysis and review (UK)
PARs	Performance and Accountability Reports (US)
PART	Program Assessment Rating Tool (US)
PBB	performance-based budgeting (Korea)
PBO	Parliamentary Budget Office (Canada)
PCO	Privy Council Office (Canada)
PEEFO	Pre-Election Economic and Fiscal Outlook (Australia)
PEMS	Policy and Expenditure Management System (Canada)
PES	Public Expenditure Survey (UK)
PESC	Public Expenditure Survey Committee (UK)
PEWP	Public Expenditure White Paper (UK)
PFI	Private Finance Initiative (UK)
PMDU	Prime Minister's Delivery Unit (UK)
PMO	Prime Minister's Office
PPBS	Program and Performance Budgeting System (NZ)
PPBS	Planning, Programming, and Budgeting System
PSAs	Public Service Agreements (UK)
PSBR	Public Sector Borrowing Requirement (UK)
RAB	resource accounting and budgeting (UK)
REA	Council of Economic Advisers (Netherlands)
RGS	General Budget and Accounting Office (Italy)
RPPs	Reports on Plans and Priorities (Canada)
SABP	Self-Assessment of Budgetary Programs (Korea)
SOE	state-owned enterprise
SOI	Statement of Intent (NZ)
SRAs	Strategic Results Areas (NZ)
SSRs	Statements of Strategic Results (NZ)
TME	Total Managed Expenditure (UK)
USSGL	US Standard General Ledger (US)
VBTB	From Policy Budgeting to Policy Accounting (Netherlands)
ZBB	Zero-Base Budgeting (US)

Acknowledgements

This book builds on our previous research endeavours to analyse the significance of budgetary reform in developed economies (see John Wanna, Lotte Jensen and Jouke de Vries, *Controlling Public Expenditure*, Cheltenham, UK and Northampton, MA, USA, Edward Elgar, 2003). The previous book explored the dynamics of central agency controls within changing budgetary processes and against outcomes, while this book examines the effectiveness of the reform architecture in each chosen country. We have had support from a number of collaborative organizations and wish to acknowledge their support, including: the Department of Management, The Hague Campus, Leiden University (The Netherlands); the Research School of Social Sciences, the Australian National University (ANU) (Canberra, Australia); the Department of Politics and Public Policy, Griffith University (Brisbane, Australia); and the Department of Government, University of Copenhagen (Denmark). They all assisted in making this book possible and with administrative and financial support. The Australian Research Council, through the GovNet research network, also contributed limited financial support to the project.

We wish to acknowledge the assistance of many finance and budgetary officials who assisted the book in each country. They were important in assisting with information, providing access, giving interviews and in some cases in offering commentary and feedback. In many cases their commitment of such scholarly research meant that their involvement with this project was added to their already busy schedules. Some are specifically acknowledged in individual chapters.

Leiden University's Department of Management hosted a two-day workshop in The Hague in June 2008, bringing together academics and practitioners from the 11 OECD nations. The purpose of the workshop was to deepen the comparative analytical aspects of the country studies through dialogue and the exchange of ideas. While each country is studied separately, all chapters benefited from an emerging comparative vantage point and a detailed diagnostic from the other participants. The hospitality of Jouke de Vries and his department at The Hague Campus of Leiden University is gratefully acknowledged. Their facilities, organizational support and coverage of local costs enabled the workshop to proceed, and improved the final publication. In particular we wish to thank Charlotte Gabriel and her staff for making the event a success.

We also owe debts to others on the way who assisted at various stages. In particular, we wish to thank Dr Ben Freyens (ANU) for helping to organize the workshop and for administrative assistance; and Dr Denise Fantone from the US General Accountability Office for valuable input to the project and assistance with the US chapter. Also a number of other people gave us valuable assistance: Charles Broughton (Australian Department of Finance and Deregulation); Dr Alex Gash (Access Economics, Australia); Dr Dong Yeon Kim (Korean Ministry of Budget and Planning); Mogens Pedersen (Danish Finance Ministry); Dr Riccardo Pelizzo (Griffith University, Australia); Bridget Sullivan (NZ Treasury); Dr Ian Watt (Australian Department of Finance and Deregulation). Chris Lewis and John Butcher from the Australia and New Zealand School of Government at ANU assisted with the presentation of the final manuscript.

Finally, we extend our appreciation to Edward Elgar and his staff for their support and encouragement of research endeavours in this field, in particular Alan Sturmer.

John Wanna, Lotte Jensen, Jouke de Vries

1. Investigating the reality of reform in modern budgeting

John Wanna

> Human beings have been reforming government ever since they invented government.
>
> (Light 1997)

> Everything has been changed, but nothing has happened.
>
> (Graffiti on the Berlin Wall, 1990s)

This book is concerned with the effectiveness of budgetary reforms in a selection of developed countries. It asks how might we judge the reality of budgetary reform in these nations – in good fiscal times as well as in bad. Our intention in each country study is not to offer a synchronic snapshot reporting what exists currently, or how countries are coping with fiscal stress in the midst of the financial crisis, but to assess the reforms over a longitudinal period – say 20 to 30 years – which may differ for each country depending on the particular timelines of reform attempted or implemented. In essence, the book is fundamentally about understanding processes of change and assessing the consequences of change to budgetary systems and to the ways modern governments work. It asks whether budgetary reforms have made a difference and, if so, to what they have made a difference, and to what extent. Have they improved our forms of governance and how we are governed, or have they been of benefit to the nation and to the wider community? Despite economic difficulties are governments better placed to manage their fiscal policies and budgetary priorities into the future?

At first sight, counting the consequences of budgetary reform appears seductively simple, but in practice is inevitably complex and contextual. Judging the merits of any reform measure is problematic. So, if we wish to focus on the impacts of reform this beckons a series of further questions to provide some grounding and concreteness. For example, it would be important to know what governments set out to achieve with their reforms. Have their initial promises remained consistent, or been overtaken by other events? What then occurred, or did not occur, as a result of the reforms, and was it as a result of the reforms? Has anything been transformed as a result of reform trajectories? What have been the consequences, either intentionally or unintentionally? How have benefits or disbenefits manifested themselves? What strengths and weakness have emerged post-reform? And, is government more or less capable now as a consequence of undergoing reform – both practically and potentially? In short, we are seeking to explore whether governments have improved the ways they operate and are better able to deal with the fiscal challenges they face and will face into the future. These questions of worth and consequence are often skirted around in various literatures and international assessments, but they lie at the heart of the comparative approach of this book.

If we survey the member countries of the Organisation for Economic Co-operation and Development (OECD) we find an extensive recent history of public sector reform and reforms to the internal management of government. Most have now adopted across their public sectors various businesslike practices, management by objectives, and some devolved managerial discretion. Evidence for this can be assembled from various sources: official government reports, international comparative accounts and scholarly assessments (see OECD 2004; World Bank 1998; Pollitt and Bouckaert 2004; Halligan 2003; Christensen and Laegreid 2001). Much of the reform zeal was squeezed into the last two decades of the twentieth century and has continued through the first decade of the present century.

More specifically, many governments have attempted various types of reform to the ways their budgetary systems operate (Wanna et al. 2003; OECD various years). And again, such budgetary reforms generally date from the mid-1980s onwards, although some nations embarked on their reform journey somewhat earlier (for example, Canada from the 1960s) while some only became active much later (for example, with Korea commencing a late but ambitious flourish after 2003). Budgetary systems suddenly emerged as a topic of keen interest to governments, becoming the targets of reform and over time one of the most 'reformed' areas inside government. The intentions behind the reform initiatives varied, but they were generally promulgated to control spending and enhance the decision-making potential of governments in their annual resource plans. But why did budgetary systems and practices attract this level of attention from the 1980s? How do we account for this?

One explanation is that budgets lend themselves to reform. They are about choice and repeated choices. They are often a microcosm of government as a whole. They operate as discrete systems with their own logics, rules and norms (unlike other activities of government such as policy formulation, strategic management, implementation or personnel management). They also recur repeatedly, and in doing so their routines invite sequential reform initiatives. Another explanation may be that participants feel budgetary systems and practices are inadequate, stultifying or even counterproductive. They often aspire to make changes and 'yearn for better ways to handle these chores' (Schick 2004: 90). Just as Lenin once said about 'facts', budgets can be terribly stubborn things – hard to dismiss, harder to reinvent, though eminently manipulatory.

But other factors may have spurred and shaped reform endeavours. High debt levels and persistent structural deficits from the 1960s and 1970s caused subsequent budgetary stress. Tight budgets then forced many governments to find other ways to enhance their resource systems, often to impose greater control and fiscal discipline. Government dissatisfaction with the historical legacies of inflexible budgetary norms resulted in governments being prepared to experiment and imitate. Some governments relaxed controls over the 'smaller numbers' precisely to achieve greater overall control of the 'larger numbers'. Others attempted to strengthen the architecture of top-down controls through political or statutory mandates.

There was also a fascination with the 'new' or the 'other', and a sense at the centre of government that many other governments did things differently and perhaps better. The OECD served as an arena of 'modernity', through its regular meetings of senior budgetary officials (dating from 1980), its *Journal of Budgeting* (from 2000) and best-practice guides. It built an international epistemic community of budgetary officials interested in reform trajectories, reporting progress with reforms and occasionally attempting to outshine each other. More perceptively, Allen Schick (2004: 91) observed recently that these same budgetary officials seem generally more interested in talking only about 'the new' or their latest country reforms rather than about investigating or addressing the problems of the reform practices already attempted. They appear attracted to the 'novel', lured by the 'promises' of success associated with the next wave of change. These are no modern-day Canutes; they are international epistemic wave-makers with a global reach.

Aiming to be more proactive, governments have long sought to find ways to make their budget systems more strategic and more agile to meet changing imperatives, community demands or expectations. Frustration with the conventional allocative processes was a further stimulus to reform, as was the gradual realization that entire budgets could be 'locked in' and virtually immune from discretionary decision-making. There was the notion that budgetary reform could assist other reform platforms across the public sector and in public management generally. Intentions to impose technical efficiency through the budget process also spurred reform at times. And, there was a belief that budget reforms could perhaps shift the loci of power inside government, giving 'guardian' budget agencies more say in policy deliberations and performance review (Wanna et al. 2003).

As a result of this confluence of reform influences, most OECD member governments have been prepared to reconceptualize how they think about 'public resources' and how they use and deploy such resources in the interests of the community. They began to think differently about their 'resource interactions' with the community and how traditional budgeting expressed these relations or fitted their purposes. Budgets were no longer merely a framework for financing activities, but became much more about enhanced information exchange, enhanced performance and the achievement of policy objectives. Standing back and taking the perspective of hindsight, we can see transformations (large and small) in the ways governments treat public resources. But across these member governments there are distinct differences in approaches and paths – hence the rationale for this comparative volume.

MEANINGS OF THE TERM 'BUDGET' AND 'BUDGETARY REFORM'

Conventionally, the term 'the budget' means different things in different national settings. Hence, in a cross-national study there is considerable danger that we will not be talking about the same subject when we analyse reform to the budget. Its status and purpose can vary widely. In some nations the term 'budget' refers to a plan of intent or a government statement; in others it is a set of statements attached (loosely perhaps) to a formal appropriation bill which may only request bare numbers – what we consider as 'the budget' is really a set of appendices to a bill asking for formal approval of expenditure totals. Elsewhere, the whole budget is a proposed law, a legal statute once passed like any other, with all its components enjoying legal validity.

The contents of a 'budget' can range across a spectrum of functions. For instance, Britain refers to 'The Budget' (presented in March by the Chancellor of the Exchequer) as the annual statement of revenue required to pay for the expected spending of government. In Canada, there are really two budgets: the government's 'Annual budget' consists of a macroeconomic and fiscal statement to parliament (presented by the Finance Minister usually in February or March),[1] which includes economic projections, economic policy responses, borrowing or savings indications, and taxation measures. It is not a mandated statement, and in one year (2002) the government chose not to bring down a budget at all. A second 'budget' for the government's own purposes is spread between the 'Main estimates' of expenditure (February) and a series of subsequent supplementary estimates of spending later in the budget year. Australia, New Zealand, Denmark and The Netherlands all have composite annual budgets where the term 'the budget' refers to the main spending plan of the government for the year ahead. In these countries, the budget refers to the planned expenditures requested from parliament for the activities of government. Their documentation may include economic statements or revenue proposals – but these are subsidiary to the main purpose which is to appropriate a spending plan from the legislature.

But usually these countries have a single budget notwithstanding whatever documents are prepared or what they may contain. By contrast, the United States can have multiple budgets or partial budgets. Formally, the President must propose a budget statement requesting funds, but this often lapses in Congress and does not pass. The Congress can propose its own budget which it can seek to fund through its control over appropriations, although it will not constitute executive policy. And if budgets include revenue, debt and borrowing requirements, the budget of the US Treasury – a revenue agency – has claim to be considered part of the national budget (Rubin 1990).

To complicate matters even more, although some countries place all their demands for societal resources 'on the budget', many countries do not. These latter often have a disaggregated budget, much of which exists independently of the other components in special managed funds. Thus, many nations have placed public resources 'off-budget' so that they are not reported in annual budget papers to parliament; and these can include pension funds, health funds, infrastructure funds, debt and interest payment funds, 'future funds' for demographic pressures, and public enterprise assets. This means, for instance, that if nations claim that they have balanced or surplus budgets, we in turn need to ask what such claims include or exclude. A general government balance (or a core–residual government balance) is qualitatively different to a total public sector balance. Furthermore, we need to understand how longer-term liabilities are included in such claims: are they integrated and included, or excluded and pushed to one side? For instance, nations that choose to keep their debt or other liabilities 'off-budget' can appear fiscally virtuous when the actual story may be less flattering. This makes comparisons between nations problematic when reviewing their fiscal positions.

In this book we take 'the budget' to mean the expenditure budget and systems of expenditure management. Budgets are about choices and the authoritative allocation of resources gained from the community to meet political, social and economic imperatives. We are less directly concerned with revenues, although at times tax reform or changing magnitudes of revenue can feed into the 'success' or 'failure' of budget reforms – so we cannot ignore them entirely.

If the nature of the budget itself is variable, the nature of budget reform is even more contingent and open to debate. This is not to excite a quibble about whether all 'reforms' are desired improvements or merely changes to some pre-existing state. As we shall see in the chapters that follow, what is seen by governments as budget reform is not confined to a single category of change but can range across different levels, from radical system-transforming changes to minuscule changes in administrative practice.

We suggest that there is a sevenfold categorization of budget reforms across different domains. These may or may not be cascading and interrelated, or be discrete and operate largely exclusively. Most categories of reform exist at different levels of the decision-making process although many may in practice coexist and feed into other levels. This categorization can be depicted as follows:

- Transformational reforms: system-wide, comprehensive or programmatic reforms aimed at transforming the principles by which the system as a whole operates; these ambitious reforms are strategic recalibrations often formally expressed through fundamental laws and major change programmes.
- Component reforms: focused reforms aimed at changing some major aspects of budgetary decision-making or changing key components of the process; often these reform initiatives do not require much legislative authorization but are labelled and announced by the executive with great fanfare (often with exhortations and promotional anagrams such as Financial Management Initiative (FMI), Expenditure Management System (EMS), or From Policy Budgeting to Policy Accounting (VBTB)); medium-term economic frameworks fall within this category.
- Restraint exercises: top-down cuts to the budget base to achieve aggregate reductions. Cuts and rationing strategies can have significant impact not only in the period of actual reduction but also over future years; they can change baseline budgets, reduce forward claims, and change the politics of aggregate fiscal management. Whether they are deep or shallow cuts, or annual clawback 'dividends', restraint exercises can force changes more widely in the behaviour of claimant agencies and constituencies.

- Reallocation techniques: governments operating under fiscal constraints often want to find new ways to reallocate within existing budget aggregates. Reallocation techniques challenge existing allocative patterns that tend to be incremental or path-dependent; they create some degree of latitude for decision-making allowing for variation and the resourcing of priorities.
- Changes to internal procedures and informal rules: budgets at the micro level are structured around internal norms and rules, often promulgated by central budget agencies; most of these informal rules are imposed by executive fiat to ensure the 'integrity' of the process (as they see it). Changing or reframing these rules often changes the micro-politics of the processes (nature and timing of claims, permeability to various claims or bids, or restrictiveness of strictures or procedures).
- Technical and specialized knowledge reforms: there are constant revisions to the technical basis of budgeting and financial management (calculations, accounting techniques and standards, estimate assumptions, adjustment norms) which are often facilitated by information technology (IT) or information and communication technology (ICT) developments or professional requirements. Sequential adaptations to these techniques can lead to important changes in overall budget systems over time (as a process of technical-driven incrementalism).
- Cultural and attitudinal changes: discourses of reform can impact on both government and community expectations concerning public finance and budgetary management; attitudes to fiscal policy (tax versus spending priorities) can shift in response to government messages about the imperatives of reform. Such discourses can have demonstrable impacts on future behaviour, and this is so whether or not any actual reform initiatives espoused are actually implemented successfully.

We consider the above categorization as a comprehensive list of possible reform types or domains – it is not meant to imply that all categories will be found in every country studied or that the categories form a descending hierarchy. We do not assume that simply because a reform is launched within one domain it cannot be transposed into another or combine bits from different domains. Similarly, reforms may be announced which signal that they are conceived within one category, but in practice end up in another as time develops.

Accepting this categorization, we next face the issue of how we authoritatively attach or link actual reform initiatives to such category labels. At one level it is a practical empirical question. In most nations, governments themselves will play a significant role in nominating which type of change is intended and considered to be 'budget reform' – they use their legitimate authority to argue a case for some intended specific change, formally signifying it as 'official' policy. In describing their reform intentions they will often make claims about the objectives, scope and focus of this change. However, these same governments may be less reliable when it comes to discerning within which category of reform their initiatives appear to fall. For example, government rhetoric can give the impression that the announced reforms have a transformational character, when in reality they may resemble not much more than technical or procedure changes. Hyperbole often creeps in. For our purposes, then, the respective category of reform may sometimes be an obvious empirical labelling; on other occasions it may not be so evident.

So, self-labelling by governments is one important element in discerning what we might accept as budget reform. They get to call some of the shots. But equally, as the Danish case suggests, governments may choose not to label reforms as 'budget reforms', preferring instead to present them as more general managerial or economic reforms. They can also make changes within the corridors of administration that affect budgetary practices but which they decide not to trumpet as budget reform, for whatever reason. In reality, the decision by governments to label their budget reforms or to laud their reform credentials is itself a political one, often of symbolic value. Does it then matter whether or not governments say they are undergoing budget reform? Obviously, we should be prepared to include overt 'budget reforms' labelled as such by governments, but we should also be cognizant that some governments may be quietly reforming their practices without much fanfare. In this book we have tried to use a wide lens when focusing on what governments have done by way of budget reform.

Outside the imperatives of government, should scholars and research analysts be asked to make a convincing case to determine what counts as budgetary reform and whether announced 'reforms' are indeed real reforms? Certainly they have a legitimate voice and are not as partisan to immediate political interests as are governments when making assessments. Researchers may prefer a broader definition of budgetary reform, theoretically addressing at least one of, say, Schick's three budget functions (aggregate discipline, allocative efficiency or technical efficiency). Some may be attracted to 'big bang' transformational projects under the heading of budget reform, and there is considerable writing in this vein (see Schick 1997; 2002). But actual practice is much more complex and piecemeal, and many researchers have investigated the internalized components as significant contributors to budgetary management (see, for example, Thain and Wright 1995). Equally we cannot accept that all reforms attempted by governments automatically qualify as budgetary reforms. Our categorization above is not a catch-all template to apprehend all changes a government may decide to make.

For researchers, there is also the question of intent: was the reform under investigation meant to change the budget process or some of its parts? Here, the key is whether there was the intent to impact on resource utilization. Researchers would argue that budgetary reform must be related to some articulated objectives or intended consequences. Reforms are not just any changes that happen to appear; they are intended actions designed to reshape things differently. For analysts there is then something tangible against which to assess the changes – to measure progress or variations against a given. This means that there is no such thing as 'unintended reforms' – something approximating accidental change. Accidental changes do not constitute deliberate reforms; even those that may unintentionally bring about some benefits are better thought of as serendipitous consequences.

DISTINCT PHILOSOPHIES AND TRAJECTORIES OF BUDGET REFORM

At first glance, many OECD countries could be considered to have adopted relatively similar approaches and philosophies to budgetary reform. These would include enhanced top-down controls, a growing focus on 'total cost' approaches or accrual technologies to expenses, output-oriented budgeting and results-based performance information, programme management and devolved discretion over financial management. This suggests perhaps that the problems individual nations confronted or sought to address were similar in form and manifestation. But not all governments have shared the same set of predicaments. OECD nations had public sectors of different shapes and sizes, had different patterns of budgetary balance (or deficits), used different ways of financing public policies from contributory systems to direct taxation, and allocated resources through different norms. If reform philosophies superficially appear somewhat similar, it may be perhaps because some degree of imitation has taken place, involving deliberate processes of policy transfer or policy learning. Perhaps too, institutional and historical factors (such as legislative requirements, appropriation instruments or executive cultures) have shunted governments into certain path-dependent directions. But does this mean that once begun down a given path, countries are inextricably corralled towards a predetermined fate? We think not.

On closer inspection, budgetary reform trajectories across OECD nations display great variety. There are different take-up rates and progressions, different patterns and evolutions, different reform initiatives and instruments attempted, different timelines and milestones of implementation. Hence, we do not assume that reform trajectories have necessarily been universal, global or linear. There is great diversity in reform scenarios and we need to capture the essence of each nation's particular approach. Some nations have gone for the 'big bang' or 'take no prisoners' approach to reform; others have moved more cautiously within a strategic direction; yet others have resembled a pattern of punctuated equilibrium where reform initiatives appear haphazard if not random. There are pioneers and laggards or, as Hood and Lodge (2005) are wont to call them, 'hares and tortoises'.

So, we find that across the OECD the trajectories of budgetary reform can be episodic or systematic, ad hoc or planned, incremental or ambitious, experimental or theoretical, sequential or truncated, linear and teleological or non-linear and contingent. We ask: how and why does this pattern of diversity matter? Has the reform trajectory shaped the reform initiatives attempted? What impact has the particular approach and trajectory we observe had on outcomes or changed behaviour? Answering these questions is within the aims of this book.

We are also cognizant that any government reform process is far from complete or ended. Indeed, continual reform may be a permanent feature of modern government. As Light (1997: 2) argued in his long-wave theory of reform movements in the US administration, governments are always reforming themselves and probably always will be. In the preparation stages of this book we toyed with a working title, 'The aftermath of reform', which unfortunately conveyed the impression that many countries had undergone reform in the recent past, and that the reforms were now finished and could be dispassionately analysed. After some consideration we rejected this title as inappropriate and misleading. There is no endpoint to reform; rather we invent solutions to perceived problems which in turn then create the next wave of problems for us to consider. Yet, even if reforms are continual, we can still periodically evaluate their performance to investigate where improvements have been achieved or discover where any deterioration may have occurred.

RESEARCH QUESTIONS AND METHODOLOGY

Accordingly, the main aim of this book is to investigate the trajectories and consequences of budgetary reform in 11 advanced OECD democracies that have undertaken budget reforms of some type within the past three decades. We focus our analysis on a series of individual country-specific case studies, exploring their reform histories and assessing the consequences of reform within the jurisdiction. We then combine insights from these cases to build a comparative assessment of the impact of budgetary reform across countries to highlight similarities and differences more systematically. We are not adopting a comparative methodology in a strict sense, but drawing on cases in which we have asked similar thematic questions to construct a comparative assessment.

Initially, we provide a comprehensive overview of the budget reform processes in each country included in this study. Chapters are organized around a common thematic framework through which we ask a common set of questions. Each chapter examines what budgetary reforms were attempted, what the governments intended and eventually did, and how they did do it. Authors then ask, more importantly, what have been the impacts and consequences of such reforms. They assess whether the reforms have lived up to expectations, and fulfilled the promises made at the time of introduction. The main point of each chapter is to discover whether budgetary systems today are better than previously, whether improvements have been made, whether the system is more transparent and accountable, and easier to comprehend by various scrutiny bodies. In short, the chapters assess whether the claims of the reformers been realized in practice as economies pass through different economic circumstances. Each chapter investigates the budget reform trajectory under five thematic topics to ensure consistency of coverage and comparability. The five chosen are described below.

Historical Trajectory

Each study traces the trajectory of reform followed in the particular jurisdiction, asking when the reforms started and how they progressed. The main purpose of this overview is to provide a brief account of the 'reform narrative' pertaining to that jurisdiction. We seek to identify the original (and evolving) objectives of the approaches taken, the main events and key dates, the sequential order of reform initiatives or instruments, what was actually implemented and what was discarded or overtaken and replaced. It is important in this narrative to identify what agendas were followed, from where reform ideas and initiatives originated and how they were transmitted, and how they were adapted or modified in the jurisdiction.

Changes to Budgetary Processes

Secondly, we assess changes to the management of budget processes, asking: how have budget processes developed over the reform period?

We ask: are budgetary processes more or less streamlined now, more or less complicated and more or less top-down? What forward planning instruments are used in budget processes (annual-based projections, medium-term frameworks, forward estimates or longer-term projections)? What sequences, timelines or schedules are used by governments? What technical innovations have been attempted or implemented and how have these changed budget management (business planning, cost centres, partial accrual accounting or accrual budgeting)? What new rules have accompanied the implementation of the most recent budget reforms and have these increased the 'detail' or relaxed the 'detail' of internal regulation? Are new rules making the processes more or less transparent? To what levels, units or administrative elements are budgets allocated (to the portfolio level, individual ministries or agencies, programmes or other elements)? What scope is there for reprioritization within the budget year? Is there now more or less scope for reallocation between competing objectives, and have reforms improved or retarded the possibilities for reallocation? Do agencies self-manage to come in 'under budget'? Is there greater temporal flexibility in resource usage from budget year to budget year – are governments using carry-forwards or drawdowns more systematically or have they adopted 'non-lapsing' appropriations as a result of reform changes?

Budget Outcomes and Results

Thirdly, we investigate budget outcomes, from budgetary balances, to the ways in which results and performance reporting are treated in budgetary systems. We are interested to discover the track record of overall budgetary outcomes (surpluses or deficits) and how this pattern can be explained. Are surpluses or deficits structural or cyclical? In the past, how did governments with surpluses manage them? Did year-on-year surpluses change the way we budgeted, and what did governments do with these surpluses when they had them? Did rolling surpluses increase demands from spenders and claimants, and if so, why, or if not, why not? Were governments overly prudential in their decision-making processes, overly relying on prudence factors to underestimate revenues as a way of curtailing spending demands? As the global financial crisis emerged many nations have returned to deficit budgeting or are projected to have future deficits. Have budget reforms made their fiscal management easier or were the reforms appropriate mainly to eras of strong economic growth?

We also ask how results are captured and recorded in present-day budgets, and at what level they are reported: at the activity or programme level, or outcome, or by agency? Are performance reports integrated into the wider budgetary processes? Do governments use evaluation information in setting future budget allocations? Some of our countries have transformed their budgets away from detailed input presentations towards an outputs or outcomes framework used for budget allocative purposes. Others produce separate results-based information not used in budget formulation. It is important to know whether nominal budgetary performances (claimed outcomes or outputs) are audited for accuracy and reliability, and if so by whom. Are budgetary results largely driven by demand factors (for example, citizen usage, consumption of services, consumer demands or client satisfaction) or supply-driven (predetermined supply targets or provision contracts)?

Budgetary Communication

Fourthly, each country-based study reviews changes to budgetary communication. We ask: how do governments choose to communicate their budgets and provide information about their budgetary decisions? What channels of information are used? This includes assessing both trends in formal documentation (the scope and contents of budgetary papers), and in other information exchanges or informal communication (desktop publishing, websites, material communicated to legislatures or the media). Has budget documentation changed over the previous 30 years to the present day – and if so, what have been the main changes? Are budgets now presented in cash or accrual formats, or in terms of expenditure or expenses, departmental items and administered funds? How does budget documentation relate to the appropriation requirements? How are the budget documents produced, and who produces them, and has this changed over time? What reception do budget documents receive and from whom, and what level of scrutiny is applied to them? Are legislatures and audit offices better informed as a result of recent changes in documentation? Are documents more comprehensible and understandable to end-users or outsiders (ministers, parliaments, media, financial commentators, academics, lobbyists and interest groups)?

Budgetary Politics and Power

Finally, we gauge how power relations and the politics of the budget process have changed as a consequence of the reforms. What has occurred in budgetary politics? Have power relations changed? If so, in what ways? Which actors are now most involved, and has that changed or remained the same over time? Have the ways budget actors act or think changed? Have budget reforms impacted on the decision-making processes? Have budget reforms been integrated with other reforms – for example strategic planning, delivery options, citizen choice, joint funding arrangements. How have longer-term planning frameworks impacted on discretionary politics? Is the exchange of information at the heart of the budgetary process more or less important now? What incentive structures have changed, or has the scope for political gaming? What new forms of gaming have opened up as a result of reforms to the budgetary system and what have been closed off?

Methodology and Approach

In pursuing these five thematic topics we have adopted relatively similar methodologies. Contributors have reviewed the statutory frameworks and relevant official documentation to trace the formal aspects of their systems. They draw on historical methods, case study methods and evaluation techniques informed by multidisciplinary insights (from politics, sociology, economics, organizational studies or public finance). They have supplemented this with detailed personal knowledge and elite interviews with current government officials (budget officials, parliamentarians, agency executives). Most importantly, our approach brings together the combined expertise and perspectives of practitioners engaged in the budget process and research academics with specialist budgetary knowledge. Hence, each chapter represents a composite view; a blend of practical experience and academic evaluation. Draft chapters have also benefited from feedback and written comments from serving senior budgetary officials, some of whom agreed to be named and have been acknowledged in individual chapters.

ELEVEN COUNTRY-SPECIFIC STUDIES

The rationale for selecting our 11 OECD countries was manifold. We planned to achieve some semblance of global representation, thus allowing us to investigate budgetary reform patterns across different political and cultural settings. The countries selected include nations from continental Europe (Northern and Southern), from north-eastern Asia, and from the Anglo-American systems. This range gave us scope to explore different budgetary trajectories in different political systems with different traditions of state, law, governance and administrative cultures. Our countries include a wide variety of constitutional and institutional forms including presidential systems, parliamentary systems, single-party majoritarian governments, consensual multiparty democracies, and nations based on the principle of the separation of powers as opposed to nations where executive powers tend to be fused. Importantly, we chose countries that had some claim to be regarded as 'reformers' and had engaged to some degree with budget reforms over a number of years. Conversely, we rejected countries that had not undertaken much in the way of budgetary reform.

Interestingly, prior to the global financial crisis of 2008-09, many of the countries selected had managed to record budget surpluses over many years, with some achieving such outcomes for over a decade. These countries looked, on paper, to have 'controlled' their budgets. Some made big claims to have successfully reformed their processes (although we need to investigate more closely whether these two phenomena are causally related). Moreover, in attempting to control their budgets, all of these countries have had regular changes of party government over the past two to three decades, allowing us to gauge the impact of political complexion in our longitudinal study. Five of our nations are members of the European Union, which has imposed fiscal rules from Brussels on its member states to some effect (although the pattern of compliance and enforcement has been variable).[2] Of course, there remain enormous differences in the size of these countries, their economic strength, the size and responsibilities of government, in patterns of government spending to gross domestic product (GDP), in the provision of welfare and social expenditure, and in defence expenditure. Initiatives that may be feasible for a small unitary island economy such as New Zealand to entertain may be impossible to contemplate for a large complex nation such as the United States. The specific latitude for the national government in public finance was also contingent upon internal factors such as the scope and independence of subnational jurisdictions (provincial, regional and local governments). The particular rationales for selecting our 11 countries are sketched below.

North America

- The United States has not been a pioneer in budgetary reform at the federal level but has experimented with top-down expenditure controls and has been at the forefront in implementing performance reforms; yet its budgetary position remains parlous.
- Canada has a very long history of interest in budgetary reform but then became somewhat ambivalent about the benefits in recent years, although it has now developed a strong system of top-down 'prudent controls'.

Europe

- The United Kingdom: a cautious reformer that has undertaken reform in bursts followed by consolidation, but with an emphasis on strong central review roles with devolved agency responsibilities.
- Denmark adopted an early reform agenda in the context of high state spending patterns and high ministerial autonomy, and then achieved a record number of budget surpluses.
- The Netherlands has a variable pattern of budgetary reform and redesign, often depending on the political complexion of the government and the motivations of key stakeholders. It has attempted resource reform across many levels and while generally disappointed with the results has maintained budgetary surpluses.
- Spain has attempted statutory reforms oriented towards fiscal discipline and budget stability but of limited impact, and is still attempting to make progress with results-based budgeting and performance management.
- Italy introduced statutory reforms initially aimed at fiscal tightening and then public management and budgetary reporting, which assisted in reducing the size of the deficit although not in eliminating it. The reform drive slackened over the period 2001–06 only to be rekindled again in recent years.

Asia and Oceania

- Japan was a late reformer to its budgetary processes, but under massive pressure from fiscal stress and increasing debt is now taking reform seriously.
- Korea has recorded a long history of budget surpluses but with little budget reform until recently. As a late starter it then attempted to adopt an ambitious reform package with a 'big bang' from 2003.
- Australia was one of the early pioneering reformers, but adopted a pragmatic approach, gradually moving towards an accruals budget in an outcomes–outputs framework; although it brought its annual budget under control it is questionable how much real reform to the system has occurred.
- New Zealand: perhaps the earliest pioneer that introduced a statutory-driven budgetary reform process, theoretically driven and stark in its precepts, but produced both budgetary control and consistent surpluses until 2008.

NOTES

1. The timing of Canada's annual budget is at the discretion of the government. Budgets have been brought down as late as December and another appeared in May. Electoral cycles and the political standing of the government can affect the timing of presentation, or indeed whether one is presented or not.
2. The most notable is the Maastricht Treaty (1992) which imposes two key fiscal rules upon the EU members: that deficits should not be more than 3 per cent of GDP and public debt not more than 60 per cent of GDP.

REFERENCES

Christensen, T. and P. Laegreid (2001), *New Public Management*, Aldershot: Ashgate.

Halligan, J. (2003), *Civil Service Systems in Anglo-American Countries*, Cheltenham, UK and Northampton, MA, USA: Edward Elgar.

Hood, C. and M. Lodge (2005), 'Aesop with variations: civil service competency as a case of German tortoise and British hare', *Public Administration*, **83** (4), 805–21.

Light, P.C. (1997), *The Tides of Reform: Making Government Work*, New Haven, CT: Yale University Press.

Organisation for Economic Co-operation and Development (OECD) (2004), 'Enhancing the cost effectiveness of public spending: experience in OECD countries', in *OECD Economic Studies no 37*, authors I. Joumard, P. Kongsrud, Y. Nam and R. Price, Paris: OECD.

OECD (2000 to 2008), *Journal on Budgeting*.

Pollitt, C. and G. Bouckaert (2004), *Public Management Reform: A Comparative Analysis*, 2nd edn, Oxford: Oxford University Press.

Rubin, I. (1990), *The Politics of Public Budgeting*, Chatham: NJ, Chatham House.

Schick, A. (1997), 'The changing role of the central budget office', Organisation for Economic Co-operation and Development discussion paper 97/109, Paris.

Schick, A. (2002), 'Opportunity, strategy and tactics in reforming public management', *OECD Journal on Budgeting*, **2** (3), 7–34.

Schick, A. (2004), 'Twenty-five years of budgeting reform', *OECD Journal on Budgeting*, **4** (1), 81–102.

Thain, C. and M. Wright (1995), *The Treasury and Whitehall*, Oxford: Clarendon Press.

Wanna, J., L. Jensen and J. de Vries (2003), *Controlling Public Expenditure: The Changing Roles of Central Budget Agencies – Better Guardians?*, Cheltenham, UK and Northampton, MA, USA: Edward Elgar.

World Bank (1998), *Public Expenditure Management Handbook*, Washington, DC: World Bank.

2. Budget reforms in the United States: a 'perfect storm' for a new wave of deficit-reduction reforms

Alfred Tat-Kei Ho*

Public budgeting is composed of at least two types of decision-making: how much a government should extract from the private economy through taxation, user charges and fees, and borrowing; and how it should spend the resources to advance the social and economic good and the policy objectives desired by the decision-makers and those they represent. The first set of decisions is about the fiscal policies of a country and the second is about appropriation and management once the resources are in the hands of the government. The two sets of decisions are obviously related, because how much a government can spend depends largely on how much revenue it can raise or how much debt it is willing to incur. However, they are separate issues which often force decision-makers to ask very different questions.

Fiscal decisions are about ideologies, values, politics and economics. Different constituency groups with different ideologies and values want different things and there is often unlimited demand for public spending, but only finite resources. Policy-makers also have to balance the interests of the current and future generations and exercise self-discipline to avoid overborrowing and shifting too much tax burden to the future. Finally, fiscal decisions are influenced and bounded by the institutional rules and the distribution of power among the executive and the legislative branch, as well as the macroeconomic forces that set constraints on the latitude of fiscal choices because the government can only tax and borrow to the extent the economy can bear.

Ideologies, values and politics certainly play an important role in the second set of decisions about appropriation and spending management. The decisions of one administration have consequences for future choices. However, these decisions also contain the dimension of technical rationality and allow for more businesslike considerations, such as the analysis of the outcome, output and cost-efficiency of public programs. In a democracy, government spending should also be transparent to the public so that appropriators and government officials can be held accountable for their spending decisions.

For the past two decades, US budgetary reforms have tried to reframe and refine the institutional processes for both sets of budgetary tasks and have accomplished varying degrees of success at different times. Attempts at fiscal reform have had to struggle with the theme of how to achieve deficit reduction and spending control. Since the mid-1980s, numerous reform bills have been passed to refine the tasks and power of Congress and the President in the budgetary process. The main aim was to require policy-makers to exercise more fiscal discipline and become more constrained in spending increases. However, fiscal reforms to reduce deficits are hard to achieve because they require politically unpopular decisions, such as raising taxes or cutting programs. Conversely, initiatives that focus on managing public spending can win political support more easily because politicians are attracted to promises – as are their constituents – of painless decision-making, including identifying 'waste, fraud and abuse' or 'growing our way out of deficits'. However, even serious efforts to increase the effectiveness and efficiency of programs are far less daunting than the larger challenge of addressing fiscal control.

This partly explains why for the past few decades, several administrations and Congress have all expressed strong interest in performance budgeting and management reforms, while major budget reforms to reduce the deficit have had more ups and downs. In the following sections, I discuss the development of these reforms in the US since the mid-1980s, explain why deficit reduction reforms lost their momentum by the mid-1990s, and examine the surge of performance budgeting reforms since the early 1990s and the accomplishments and challenges faced by these reforms. The chapter concludes by examining the fiscal outlook of the US federal government and the renewed concerns about the federal deficits. It suggests that another round of major reforms by Congress and the Obama administration is necessary to restructure fiscal decision-making.

BUDGETARY REFORMS TO CONTROL DEFICITS AND SPENDING

For the past few decades, the US federal government has been battling on and off with the deficit problem. In the first 20 years after the Second World War, the problem was significantly contained and the percentage of federal deficits to gross domestic product (GDP) came down from the historical high of 30 percent in 1943 to about 1 percent in the 1950s and the

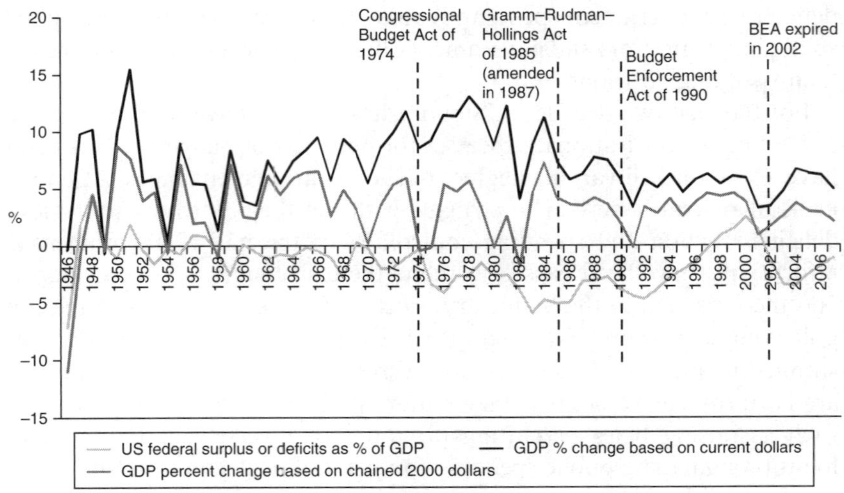

Figure 2.1 The percentage of US federal deficits to GDP, 1946–2007

1960s. Economic crises, such as the oil crises in 1973 and in the late 1970s, or the September 11 attack in 2001, certainly put extra pressure on policy-makers to come up with responsive measures, such as tax cuts to stimulate the economy and higher social spending to help the unemployed and the needy. As a result, a cyclical pattern of government deficits, as shown in Figure 2.1, resulted over the period 1946–2007. However, even during the long post-war economic boom, the US federal government continued to run a deficit except for a few years.

The mid-1970s was a turning point in the US budgetary history, not only because Congress passed the Congressional Budget Act in 1974 that established the statutory basis for the congressional budget process, but also because the deficit problem became significantly worse compared to the previous two decades. Between 1974 and 1985, the average percentage of the deficit to GDP jumped from 2 to 5 percent and the relatively higher deficit level remained unchanged until the Clinton administration in the mid-1990s. In the early 2000s, the deficit problem again resurfaced when the amount reached a historical high of more than $400 billion in 2004 (see Table 2.1). If the off-budget surplus in social security was taken out, the surge in the on-budget deficit was even more dramatic, reaching $568 billion.

The persistent US deficit problem between 1975 to 1997 and after 2002 reflected a fundamental failure of the political institutions to anticipate the problems and resolve them proactively. For example, when the economy began to recover, there was no initiative to scale back the tax cuts passed earlier or to remove tax incentives given to companies and individuals.

Table 2.1 Revenues, outlays, deficits and surpluses for the fiscal years 1985–2007 ($ billions)

	Revenues	Outlays	Deficit/Surplus			
			On-Budget	Social Security	Postal Service	Total
Under the Balanced Budget Act of 1985 (Gramm–Rudman–Hollings) and as amended by the Balance Budget Reaffirmation Act of 1987						
1985	734.1	946.4	−221.5	9.4	−0.1	−212.3
1986	769.2	990.4	−237.9	16.7	*	−221.2
1987	854.4	1004.1	−168.4	19.6	−0.9	−149.7
1988	909.3	1064.5	−192.3	38.8	−1.7	−155.2
1989	991.2	1143.8	−205.4	52.4	0.3	−152.6
Under the Budget Enforcement Act of 1990, and as amended in 1997						
1990	1032.1	1253.1	−277.6	58.2	−1.6	−221.0
1991	1055.1	1324.3	−321.4	53.5	−1.3	−269.2
1992	1091.3	1381.6	−340.4	50.7	−0.7	−290.3
1993	1154.5	1409.5	−300.4	46.8	−1.4	−255.1
1994	1258.7	1461.9	−258.8	56.8	−1.1	−203.2
1995	1351.9	1515.9	−226.4	60.4	2.0	−164.0
1996	1453.2	1560.6	−174.0	66.4	0.2	−107.4
1997	1579.4	1601.3	−103.2	81.3	*	−21.9
1998	1722.0	1652.7	−29.9	99.4	−0.2	69.3
1999	1827.6	1702.0	1.9	124.7	−1.0	125.6
2000	2025.5	1789.2	86.4	151.8	−2.0	236.2
2001	1991.4	1863.2	−32.4	163.0	−2.3	128.2
2002	1853.4	2011.2	−317.4	159.0	0.7	−157.8
2003	1782.5	2160.1	−538.4	155.6	5.2	−377.6
2004	1880.3	2293.0	−568.0	151.1	4.1	−412.7
2005	2153.9	2472.2	−493.6	173.5	1.8	−318.3
2006	2407.3	2655.4	−434.5	185.2	1.1	−248.2
2007	2568.2	2728.9	−342.2	186.5	5.1	−160.7

Note: * = between −0.05% and 0.05%.

Sources: Congressional Budget Office; Office of Management and Budget.

Policy-makers have continued to expand social and healthcare benefits and propose new programs to please their constituencies. Whether in the form of tax expenditures or as entitlement programs, these decisions have been removed from the annual appropriations process. As a result, budget priorities have shifted and spending increases have been put on 'autopilot', as shown in Table 2.2. Between 1962 and 2007, while the non-defense

Table 2.2 Outlays by Budget Enforcement Act category of a percentage of GDP, 1962–2008

Year	Total outlays		Discretionary (% of total)			Mandatory and net interest (% of total)						
	Amount ($ billions)	% of GDP	Total	National defense	Non-defense	Total	Social security	Deposit insurance	Means tested entitlements	Other	Undistributed offsetting receipts	Net interest
1962	592.5	18.8	12.7	9.3	3.4	6.1	2.5	−0.1	0.8	2.7	−0.9	1.2
1972	857.6	19.6	10.9	6.7	4.2	8.7	3.3	−0.1	1.4	3.4	−0.8	1.3
1982	1251.7	23.1	10.1	5.8	4.3	13.0	4.8	−0.1	1.6	4.9	−0.8	2.6
1992	1623.9	22.1	8.6	4.8	3.7	13.6	4.6		2.3	4.1	−0.6	3.2
1997	1684.2	19.6	6.7	3.3	3.4	12.9	4.4	−0.2	2.4	3.8	−0.6	3.0
2002	1929.2	19.4	7.1	3.4	3.7	12.3	4.4		2.7	4.1	−0.5	1.6
2007	2263.1	20.0	7.6	4.0	3.6	12.4	4.3		2.7	4.3	−0.6	1.7

Source: Office of Management and Budget, FY2009 Budget (Historical Table), US Government, Washington, DC

discretionary spending that is controllable under the annual appropriation process has remained flat at about 3–4 percent of GDP, the portion of entitlements, other mandatory programs and interest has doubled from 6.1 percent to 12.4 percent of GDP. This happened at a time when defense spending continued to decline from about 9 percent to 4 percent of GDP.

Therefore, the deficit problem demonstrated some of the deeper conflicts in budgetary decision-making, such as ideological differences among political parties with respect to the role of government, the appropriate level of taxes, and spending priorities. It also reflected the institutional challenges faced by the US Congress and the inability of the two major parties to reconcile policy differences through legislative procedures, political strategies and party discipline.

This is not to say that the US Congress has not tried to address the problem. As a result of growing economic concerns and mounting public outcry against the deficits, Congress introduced several budget reforms in the 1980s and early 1990s. In 1985, the Balanced Budget and Emergency Deficit Control Act, commonly known as the Gramm–Rudman–Hollings Act (GRH Act), was passed to impose stricter procedures and fix the burgeoning deficit estimates and impasses within Congress and between Congress and President Reagan over budget priorities. It also used the budget resolution as a tool to enforce a series of fixed annual deficit targets beginning in fiscal year 1986 and declining to zero by fiscal year 1991. The Act, with some amendment in 1987, also introduced a sequestration mechanism and an automatic across-the-board spending cut if the budget deficit exceeded the target levels.

However, the Act failed to achieve its intended effect and Congress continued to breach the deficit targets for several reasons. First, the tax cut advocated by the Reagan administration was not matched by a similar scale of spending cuts. The economic stimulating effect from the tax cut was also less than expected, thus failing to generate the necessary revenues to reduce the deficits. Finally, the deficit-cutting mechanism in the GRH Act was not enforceable. When the economy was not doing well, politicians had little incentive to raise taxes or cut spending to adhere to the deficit targets. As a result, US Congress simply ignored the GRH deficit goals and used various legislative tactics to avoid the sequestration process (Schick 1990; 2007, Chapter 2).

Realizing the failure of the GRH Act, the US Congress passed a new piece of legislation in 1990, the Budget Enforcement Act (BEA), to try to reduce the deficits. The law was originally designed to expire in FY1995, but was extended several times and finally expired in FY2002.

The BEA took a different approach by shifting from deficit targets to enforcing spending limits for discretionary programs and slowing the growth of new entitlement spending. This was to be done through two mechanisms. First, programs funded in annual appropriations Acts (referred to as 'discretionary programs') were to be controlled through caps on new authority to spend and on actual expenditures. If the amount of budget authority provided for a given year exceeds the caps, or if the actual outlays in a given year are estimated to exceed the outlay caps, then sequestration would be triggered to cut spending for programs in a defined budget category that has exceeded the spending caps, generally by some uniform percentage.

Second, spending decisions for new entitlements and other direct spending programs (those classified as 'mandatory' programs) and revenue measures were to be deficit-neutral. Any new entitlement spending or tax cut legislation would need to be fully offset in a pay-as-you-go regime known as PAYGO through reductions in other entitlement spending, new taxes or some combination of these. If this condition was not satisfied, sequestration procedures would be triggered to impose a uniform reduction of direct spending unless the programs, such as social security, interest payment and some entitlement programs, were exempt.

Evaluation of Attempts to Control Deficits and Rein in Spending

The BEA of 1990, and the related laws that followed it, generally are regarded as having been more successful than the 1985 Balanced Budget Act in controlling aggregate budget levels. Although the deficit had begun to decline as a share of GDP in the late 1980s, it was during the period that the BEA was in effect (1990 to 2002) that federal spending went from deficit to surplus. This dramatic change was due to many factors – primarily the result of a booming economy and increasing revenues. However, the procedures under the BEA, especially the spending cap on discretionary spending, were regarded by many as important contributors in instilling fiscal discipline (Penner and Steuerle 2004). The Act was also successful because it received broad political support from Congress and the Clinton administration. Furthermore, it focused on things that Congress could control, namely, appropriations and tax policy changes, rather than the deficits and the performance of the economy.

Unfortunately, the success and the fiscal regime of the BEA were short-lived. The controls that had brought discipline during a period of deficits quickly morphed into impediments under surpluses. Legislators quickly exploited the loophole in the BEA that emergency spending was exempt from the spending caps, and used the provision to introduce all kinds of new programs and spending increases. In addition, they began to ignore the PAYGO rule on mandatory spending and arbitrarily raised the spending cap on discretionary spending every year in 1999–2001 (Rubin 2006). The events of September 11, 2001, also had a profound effect on the fiscal regime designed by the BEA. The momentum to curb spending, which had already waned, was replaced with resource demands for homeland security and the wars in Iraq and Afghanistan at the same time as tax reductions were enacted. As a result, since the BEA expired in FY2002 there has been very limited enthusiasm in Congress to renew it. When PAYGO has been applied subsequently, it has been through rules adopted independently by the House and the Senate without the weight of law. The situation still prevails and recent events suggest that it is a difficult time to put in place binding spending limits, especially given the global economic meltdown triggered by the subprime loan crisis and the $700 billion bailout package for US financial institutions, as well as other bailout packages already provided or expected for other industries.

REFORMS TO MAXIMIZE SPENDING OUTCOMES AND COST-EFFICIENCY

While the reform efforts that tried to control the federal deficits have had varying degrees of success for the past three decades and politicians gradually lost interest in the efforts in the late 1990s, efforts to improve spending management and to integrate performance management with budgeting have progressed steadily. Such effort has had a long history in the US federal government, dating back to the end of the Second World War and the Hoover Commission of 1949. Although the concept of 'performance budgeting' was not clearly specified at that time, Congress enacted the Budget and Accounting Procedures Act of 1950 (BAPA) which required the President to present performance information, primarily on 'workload' (output or activity in modern terminology) and unit cost. Also, in the mid-1960s, the Department of Defense's Planning, Programming and Budgeting System (PPBS) was extended to civilian agencies. It introduced a framework for budget formulation that facilitated multiyear planning and program analysis and offered the possibility of linking outputs to long-term program objectives. Confident that management techniques could modernize the federal government, President Johnson predicted that PPBS would: 'help us find new ways to do jobs faster, to do jobs better, and to do jobs less expensively' (US GAO 1997: 35). Then in the 1970s, President Nixon introduced Management by Objectives (MBO) and President Carter introduced Zero-Base Budgeting (ZBB), both trying to emphasize the link between planning, program goals, budgeting and program output analysis.

In the following, I discuss four of these initiatives in the past two decades: the Chief Financial Officers Act of 1990, the Government Performance and Results Act of 1993, the OMB 2000 Review by the Clinton administration, and the Performance Assessment Rating Tool by the Bush administration.

The Chief Financial Officers Act (CFO) of 1990

The Chief Financial Officers Act of 1990 (P.L. 101-576), as amended by the Government Management Reform Act (GMRA) of 1994, sought to increase oversight and accountability for financial management. This act established the Office of Federal Financial Management (OFFM) within the Office of Management and Budget (OMB) to establish government-wide policies and oversight. In addition it created the position of Deputy Director for Management in the OMB to serve as the chief financial officer of the federal government as well as head of the OFFM.

A key development was the appointment in all federal departments and major agencies of a chief financial officer (CFO) responsible for developing and maintaining an integrated accounting and financial management system and overseeing all financial operations relating to the agency's programs and activities. Along with these new positions often came responsibility for the agency budget even though the Act did not expressly give the CFO a role in formulating agency budgets. This Act also created a CFO council, headed by the OMB, with agency CFO representation. The council was meant to be an advisory body that coordinated the activities of agencies relating to modernization of financial systems, internal controls, financial data and information standards. This model, although created by Congress, fitted nicely with the management style of the Clinton administration, and the council approach was used to implement the administration's management priorities in other areas.

Under the CFO Act agencies were required to develop five-year plans describing their financial management strategies, report annually on their progress, and prepare annual audited financial statements supported by relevant financial and program performance data. An amendment to the Act in 1994 gave the Government Accountability Office (GAO), formerly the General Accounting Office, responsibility for auditing the annual consolidated financial statement for the federal government prepared by the Department of the Treasury.

Over time, the CFO Act has maintained a needed focus on improving financial management systems and operations throughout the government. Although Congress required agencies to provide reliable accounting information to serve as the basis for budget requests and execution in the

Budget and Accounting Procedures Act of 1950, serious efforts to link accounting information with budget requests did not happen until the mid-1980s. The CFO Act created the necessary institutional foundation for agencies to focus on financial management improvement. The Federal Financial Management Improvement Act of 1996 built upon this and mandated agencies to record all transactions in their accounting systems using the naming convention in the US Standard General Ledger (USSGL). In the late 1990s, the Treasury's Financial Management Services further improved the system for the Federal Agencies' Centralized Trial-Balance System so that by the end of FY2001, most federal agencies could report budget execution results using the same accounting guidance with an automated system (Hoge and Martin 2006).

This is critical to the development of performance-based budgeting of the US federal government because with a more consistent and accurate system of accounting, decision-makers can be better informed when evaluating changes in the obligations, actual spending and fund balances of departments and programs. This gives rise to new possibilities of cost analysis and financial control. Although institutionally and culturally there is still a big divide between the OMB, with its lead role in budget and program policy, and the Treasury, which keeps the books and manages the government's debt, the executive branch has tried to integrate financial, budget and program performance information better. For example, Agency Performance and Accountability Reports (PARs), which bring together financial and performance information for the year just ended, are prepared promptly so that they can be used in congressional budget deliberations. This can only be done because of the legislative foundation laid down in the CFO Act and other related legislation in the 1990s.

The Government Performance and Results Act (GPRA) of 1993

The GPRA (P.L. 103-62) was another landmark piece of legislation that paved the way for performance-based budgeting reforms in the recent decade (Breul, 2007). The legislation itself was not focused on budgeting reforms, although it called for performance budgeting pilots. It was intended to address government waste and misuse of public funds (Breul 2007). However, by requiring agencies to produce a multiyear strategic plan, an annual performance plan, and an annual performance report, and by linking planning and goal-setting to the program activity structures in agency budget requests, the GPRA increased the possibility that performance information could be used directly in budget deliberations. That was why Senator John Glenn, a major sponsor of the law, remarked that the ultimate goal of the GPRA was to use performance information intentionally to guide resource allocation decisions (Glenn 1997).

There are three key reporting elements imposed by the GPRA. First, a multiyear strategic plan must be completed for every executive agency, covering five years and updated every three. The plan must include an agency mission statement and long-term general goals and objectives, describe strategies for achieving these goals, and explain the key external factors that could affect the achievement of goals. Second, an annual performance plan has to be submitted to Congress. This plan covers each program activity presented in agency budget requests, and should align annual goals with long-term strategic goals. Agencies are required to have performance measures to gauge progress towards goals and to explain how the resulting performance data will be verified. Third, an annual performance report competes the reporting cycle. Each agency must review and provide discussion of its actual performance for the prior year compared with the anticipated performance goals established in its annual performance plan. Agencies are expected to explain any differences and to provide baseline and trend data to help ensure that their performance is reviewed in context.

The OMB 2000 Review

While the US Congress plays an important role in providing the legislative foundation for the performance budgeting initiatives, successive presidents and their Office of Management and Budget (OMB) have been equally important in providing substantial guidance and leadership on how performance budgeting initiatives should be implemented. An example is the OMB 2000 Review carried out during the Clinton administration. Under the leadership of director Alice Rivlin, an economist and the first Director of the Congressional Budget Office (CBO), the OMB undertook a comprehensive two-month self-examination in 1994. At the conclusion of this effort, Rivlin reorganized the OMB to integrate staff with certain management skills into the 'budget side' of the OMB, where staff with program-specific knowledge and budget responsibilities resided.

Specifically, the new OMB structure brought together responsibilities for: (1) budget formulation, analysis and execution; (2) program effectiveness and efficiency; (3) annual, mid- and long-range policy and program analysis; (4) implementation of government-wide management policy; and (5) program evaluation. Although many OMB examiners would argue that agency and program management were always part of their responsibilities, Rivlin expected agencies to justify and OMB program examiners to explain funding requests more systematically with performance data. A bigger adjustment for the OMB as an institution and for individual examiners was the expectation that they would work more cooperatively with their agencies. This meant periodic review with agencies on agency-wide operations, such as financial management, procurement and information technology, as well as reviews of specific programs or administrative components of agency. OMB staff members were encouraged to open communications and share information (within limits) with their agencies. In turn, the results of these reviews and a new emphasis on performance measurement would be used in making resource decisions.

The Program Assessment Rating Tool (PART)

Following up on the philosophy of the OMB review that performance measurement and budgeting should be more closely linked, and building upon the legislative foundation provided by the GPRA, the Bush administration initiated the Program Assessment Rating Tool (PART). The designers of the tool wanted to push beyond the GPRA requirements because they asserted, and others agreed, that performance information from the GPRA was not helpful enough in the budgetary process. For example, the multiyear and annual performance goals at the department level were usually too broad and could not be linked easily to specific appropriations, program spending and the annual budgeting framework.

The PART is a framework consisting of about 25 questions (varying by the nature of programs) used to help assess a program's strengths and weaknesses. Divided into four sections each with its own weight, the PART questions address: (1) program purpose and design (given 20 percent weighting); (2) strategic planning (worth 10 percent); (3) program management (worth 20 percent); and (4) program results (counting for 50 percent weighting). The first three sections use a 'yes–no' format, while the last uses a four-point scale (namely, 'yes', 'to a large extent', 'to a small extent', or 'no') that allows examiners to give agencies credit for progress in achieving goals.

Once a PART assessment is completed, the program receives one of four overall ratings based on a numerical score: effective, moderately effective, adequate or ineffective. A fifth rating, 'results not demonstrated', may be given, independent of a program's numerical score, if the OMB decides that performance information, performance measures or both are insufficient or inadequate. All federal programs were included in the PART, although the scope of what activities were covered in each assessment varied greatly, and were evaluated in a five-year time-frame. Hence, the budget request for FY2008 was the first year that all programs had been evaluated at least once.

EVALUATION OF PERFORMANCE BUDGETING INITIATIVES – 1990S AND EARLY 2000s

The performance budgeting initiatives by the US federal government for the past decade have been a continuation of the long historical efforts toward linking performance measurement and analysis with budgeting. It has been a long journey because linking up performance and budget requests or appropriations is not easy and simple. While the OMB has claimed that over time it has used the PART results to propose cuts in program funding requests if programs have not been performing satisfactorily, the relationship between budget requests and performance has been complex and has not been linked mechanically (Fantone 2007). There is clear evidence that the OMB has used the PART in its budget review process to reduce proposed funding for poorly performing programs. However, there is also evidence to show that the OMB also proposed funding increases for programs that were rated 'ineffective' or could not demonstrate clear results, because extra funding might be needed to target specific weaknesses identified in a PART assessment or to pay for further evaluation if there was insufficient evidence to demonstrate effectiveness.

In addition, it is clear that the relationship between appropriations and performance rating by the OMB is very weak. As Philip Joyce (2008: 956) points out:

> the budget process is a political process . . . If the Congress wants to use the budget to dole out pork, and their constituencies re-elect them for doing so, is this necessarily wrong just because it offends our academic and expert sensibilities about what the 'rational' allocation of resources would be?

One has to remember that the US federal government is built on a system of checks and balances that makes shared power and responsibility necessary.

Performance budgeting initiatives such as the PART have not and will not be able to change the fundamental nature of the budgetary process, which is political. For example, despite some effort to communicate PART results, the OMB has had limited success in engaging Congress in the PART process (Posner and Fantone 2007). According to the US Government Accountability Office (US GAO2004), congressional staff revealed a number of issues and concerns about the design of the PART tool, results of assessments, and the way the OMB has communicated PART results. Many congressional staff of both parties expressed skepticism that the OMB's assessments could be impartial and devoid of political influence or that the PART could be anything other than an executive branch tool. Congressional staff members were unlikely to accept conclusions about a program's performance without seeing the evidence used in support, particularly when the rating was contrary to what they believed to be true about a program. Others said that it was not the right communication tool if the OMB wanted to signal the importance of PART results to Congress.

Hence, as the critics of performance budgeting initiatives have correctly pointed out, performance measurement information provided by the OMB is unlikely to make a significant impact on the appropriation decisions by Congress. Nevertheless, this does not necessarily imply that these initiatives are meaningless and have no impact on the power dynamics of different parties in the budgetary process. For example, the PART has been seen as a powerful tool in some instances for the OMB to shape agencies' strategic planning, budget requests and program performance measures. Agency officials told the US GAO (2005) that by encouraging more communication between departments and the OMB, the PART helped illuminate both how the OMB makes budget decisions and the way examiners think about program management. Since 2007, the OMB has been concentrating its efforts on institutionalizing aspects of the PART process by holding regular meetings with agency leaders ('performance improvement officers') responsible for fostering budget and performance integration in their organizations. President Bush also institutionalized this position through an Executive Order in November 2007.

Many observers of the past performance budgeting initiatives agree that these initiatives have made a considerable impact on the budgetary process beyond the appropriation stage, by influencing budget execution and program management. For example, the requirements of the GPRA have forced agencies to think more systematically about their mission, goals and performance plans. The PART by the Bush administration is also very effective in influencing agencies' program management practices. Through deliberation with agencies about the PART rating, the OMB has been able to shape agencies' strategic plans and program evaluation activities (Ho 2007; Gilmour 2008). Also, OMB managers and staff reported that the PART deliberation often stimulates richer discussions within a department or program on what a program should be achieving, whether the program is performing effectively and, if not, how program performance can be improved (US GAO 2005). Accordingly, performance budgeting initiatives like the PART have made some effective contribution to budget execution.

CONCLUSION: A 'PERFECT STORM' FOR A NEW WAVE OF BUDGET REFORMS?

For the past few decades, the US federal government had made numerous reform efforts on two trajectories: one has been to control spending and balance the budget; the other has been to manage spending better to ensure that taxpayers' money is used in an accountable, efficient and effective manner. The second theme of reforms has been pursued consistently by different administrations and party leadership. Although there are still questions about how much impact performance information has made in influencing appropriation decisions, policy-makers and reformers have continued to advocate the need for performance budgeting reforms. There is evidence that it has made some positive impact on program execution and the strategic thinking of agencies.

By contrast, the first theme of budget reforms to control spending and deficits has followed a more rugged path of fluctuating success. Its trajectory has conformed to a pattern of 'two steps forward, one step backward'. While the main statutory reforms introduced in the mid-1980s and early 1990s demonstrated some success and turned the deficits into a surplus by FY1998, the accomplishment was short-lived. Since FY2002, the federal government has been running a substantial deficit again and US Congress has abandoned the fiscal rules established under the Budget Enforcement Act of 1990.

With the global economic slowdown occurring from late 2007, it is unlikely that the Obama administration and US Congress will introduce any drastic actions to address the deficit problems in the near future. However, inaction in the long run would be unacceptable and impossible to justify. In 2006, the federal government reported a net operating cost (cost exceeding revenues) of $450 billion despite significant increases in revenues. Its cash outlays also exceeded its cash receipts by $248 billion (unified budget deficits) despite a decent economic recovery in 2004–06. According to the former US Comptroller, the current and past directors of CBO and other budget experts, the long-term fiscal outlook of the US federal government is unsustainable if current policies continue given the growing numbers of baby-boomers retiring and the expected increase in social and healthcare spending (Walker 2007). The problem is certainly beyond what performance budgeting reforms can fix, because cutting waste and making programs more efficient can only do so much when there is a structural deficit problem and a foreseeable and significant surge in mandatory entitlement spending.

The current economic crisis may help refocus attention by the new administration and Congress on the need for fiscal discipline in a way that may not have been possible in recent years. The reforms will be politically difficult because it will require politicians to make tough choices on how much money the government should get from the private economy, how much the government should pay for social security and healthcare, and how much individuals and companies should be responsible for financing these expenses. However, the Obama administration may indeed have found a 'perfect storm' to push these reforms through. There are growing public concerns about the magnitude of the foreign-owned debt, and many Democrats as well as Republican politicians have expressed concerns about the national and economic security implications caused by the deficit problems. Also, the economic sentiment in the US may have also shifted as a result of the subprime loan crisis, and there is a growing public belief that the US should tighten its belt and stop the habit of living on debt. Finally, the clear victory in the presidential election in 2008, and the growing majority of the Democratic Party in the Senate and the House of Representatives as a result of the election, may have given President Obama extra political capital to initiate tough reforms, including reforms that control social security and Medicare spending, tax increases for selective groups of taxpayers, and ways to reinstall the PAYGO mechanism in the appropriation process. Hence, it is likely that the US federal government will soon enter a new phase of budget reforms similar to those in the mid-1980s and early 1990s, refocusing on the theme of spending and deficit control.

NOTE

* The author and editors would like to acknowledge the input and assistance of Denise M. Fantone of the Government Accountability Office to this chapter and for her contributions at The Hague workshop.

REFERENCES

Breul, J.D. (2007), 'GPRA: a foundation for performance budgeting', *Public Performance and Management Review*, **30** (3), 312–31.

Fantone, D.M. (2007), 'US program assessment rating tool', in M. Robinson (ed.), *Performance Budgeting: Linking Funding and Results*, Washington, DC: Palgrave Macmillan (for the International Monetary Fund), pp. 167–92.

Gilmour, J.B. (2008), 'Implementing OMB's program assessment rating tool: meeting the challenges of performance-based budgeting', in F. Stevens Redburn, R.J. Shea and T.F. Buss (eds), *Performance Management and Budgeting: How Governments Can Learn from Experience*, Washington, DC: the National Academy of Public Administration, pp. 21–48.

Glenn, J. (1997), 'Implementation of the Government Performance and Results Act of 1993', testimony before the US Senate, Joint Committee on Governmental Affairs and Appropriations, 105th Congress, 1st Session, Washington, DC: US Government Printing Office.

Ho, A.T.K. (2007), 'The governance challenges of the Government Performance and Results Act: a case study of the substance abuse and mental health administration', *Public Performance and Management Review*, **30** (3), 369–97.

Hoge, J. and E. Martin (2006), 'Linking accounting and budget data: a discourse', *Public Budgeting and Finance*, Summer, 121–42.

Joyce, P.G. (2008), 'Does more (or even better) information lead to better budgeting? A new perspective', *Journal of Policy Analysis and Management*, **27** (4), 945–60.

Penner, R.G. and C.E. Steuerle (2004), 'Budget rules', *National Tax Journal*, **57** (3), 547–57.

Posner, P.L. and D.M. Fantone (2007), 'Assessing federal program performance: observations on the US Office of Management and Budget's Program Assessment Rating Tool and its use in the budget process', *Public Performance and Management Review*, **30** (3), 351–68.

Rubin, I.S. (2006), *Politics of Public Budgeting: Getting and Spending, Borrowing and Balancing*, 5th edn, Washington, DC: Congressional Quarterly Press.

Schick, A. (1990), *The Capacity to Budget*, Washington, DC: Urban Institute Press.

Schick, A. (2007), *The Federal Budget: Politics, Policy, Process*, 3rd edn, Washington, DC: Brookings Institute Press.

US General Accounting Office (US GAO) (1997), *Performance Budgeting: Past Initiatives Offer Insights for GPRA Implementation*, GAO/AIMD-97-46, Washington, DC: US Government Printing Office.

US Government Accountability Office (US GAO) (2004), *Performance Budgeting: Observations on the Use of OMB's Program Assessment Rating Tool for the Fiscal Year 2004 Budget*, GAO-04-174, Washington, DC: US Government Printing Office.

US GAO (2005), *Managing for Results: Enhancing Agency use of Performance Information for Management Decision-making*, GAO-05-927, Washington, DC: US GAO.

Walker, D.M. (2007), *Fiscal Stewardship: a Critical Challenge Facing our Nation*, GAO-07-362SP, Washington, DC: US Government Accountability Office.

3. Budget reform in the United Kingdom: the rocky road to 'controlled discretion'

Colin Thain*

BRITAIN'S HIGHLY POLITICAL TRAJECTORY OF BUDGET REFORM

Budgetary policy in the United Kingdom has long been dominated by the Treasury, one of the oldest state institutions in the Western world. Its story is essentially that of a ministry of finance, but it has accrued political and administrative resources that make it an amalgam not only of a ministry of finance and an economics department, but also a powerful central department, an influential policy actor in its own right, and a foreign economic policy agent. Unlike most of its comparators internationally, the Treasury gains its authority for managing and controlling public expenditure, setting tax rates, managing borrowing and setting the overall fiscal framework from convention, quasi-legal rules and precedent. Little of its authority is statute-based. It is the most political of all central departments – acutely attuned to the prevailing winds of power in Westminster and Whitehall.

In looking at the impact and consequences of budgetary reform from 1976, this chapter captures five themes in the UK case. First, the constant battle by the Treasury to maintain or regain power to control spending from the rest of Whitehall's spending departments, involving ever more complex political and administrative techniques to keep spending levels within prescribed limits. Second, the Treasury's repeated attempts since the 1970s to ground budgetary policy in a wider macroeconomic framework – from crisis measures in 1976, to monetarist experiments in the 1980s, through to the 'controlled discretion' under the Treasury of Gordon Brown. Third, a spasmodic but real tension between the Treasury and other actors at the centre of government, particularly the agencies and units surrounding the premierships of Margaret Thatcher and Tony Blair, over performance and delivery. Fourth, for most of the period there has been an almost total lack of collective Cabinet involvement in deciding the allocation within the overall envelope of total public spending, except during crises. And fifth, the context of changes affecting the way the state operates in public policy. 'Governance' has replaced 'government' as the central state has become 'hollowed out', finding itself managing increasingly disaggregated central departments, autonomous agencies, public–private contracts and regulatory structures (Rhodes 2000). This is against a background of multilevel engagement upwards with the European Union and downwards with devolved administrations in a quasi-federal state (Peters 2001).

As Table 3.1 shows, there have been five distinct phases of reform and renewal in budgetary policy:

- crisis management from 1976 to 1979;
- believing in monetarism in the period from 1980 to 1990;
- pragmatic reassertion of control from 1992 to 1997;
- controlled discretion from 1997 to 2007; and
- the onset of fiscal crisis from 2007 to the present.

During each phase there have been bursts of innovation and change, particularly in the periods 1982 to 1990, and 1998 to 2005. It is also important to distinguish reforms which were predominantly public spending-orientated: designed to gain control of public spending which was seen to be 'out of control' such as in the mid-1970s; to bring spending in line with tightened fiscal limits such as in the 1980s or from 1992; and to tighten control already achieved as in the period from 1997 to 2001. Other reforms focused on efficiency and management, and fitted more broadly into a programme for improvement in the public sector's delivery of services. In this latter sense, the Treasury was often at odds with the Cabinet Office and the Prime Minister, seeing control of aggregates or control of the agenda as more important than broader managerial reform. In practice, reforms designed to bring spending into line with plans were often complemented by initiatives which aimed to improve management, when resources available to departments and agencies were squeezed.

THE CRISIS OF SPENDING CONTROL, 1976–79

During the 1960s the UK evolved a sophisticated system for planning and controlling public spending that befitted an era of Keynesian planning (Heclo and Wildavsky 1981). The Public Expenditure Survey Committee (PESC) system combined regular surveys of public expenditure as a whole,

Table 3.1 Summary of Budgetary reform events in the UK, 1976-2008

Period	Fiscal and economic framework	Public spending timescale and methodology	Political process for spending	Central Institutional innovations	Performance and output management	Off-budget elements
1976-79	1976 IMF programme involving borrowing, spending cuts and monetary targets. 'monetarily constrained Keynesianism'	1976 annual cash limits grafted onto medium-term resource planning	Frequent bilaterals between Treasury and departments; Cabinet meetings	Chief Secretary (in charge of spending) joins Cabinet to support Chancellor		Some minor sale of assets (BP shares)
1979-90	1980 medium-term financial plan (MTFS) linking money supply targets, borrowing and public spending; followed by 1985 exchange rate target; join ERM in 1990	1982 Cash planning introduced – end of medium-term planning	Bilaterals, adjudication by Cabinet Committee (Star Chamber)	Efficiency Unit set up in Cabinet Office; Next Steps Agency team	1982 Financial Management Initiative (FMI); 1986 Running costs control; 1988 Next Steps Agencies	Privatization

Table 3.1 (continued)

Period	Fiscal and economic framework	Public spending timescale and methodology	Political process for spending	Central Institutional innovations	Performance and output management	Off-budget elements
1992-97	Following exit from ERM 1992 range of changes – new monetary framework, tightening of fiscal policy	1992 New Control Total (NCT) to tighten spending control; Fundamental Expenditure Reviews (FER) of each department	1992 Creation of Cabinet Committee (EDX); 1993 Unified Budget combining tax and spending		'Citizens' Charter' to improve public sector performance	1992 Private Finance Initiative (PFI)
1997-2007	1999 fiscal rules (code of fiscal stability) introduced as part of 'controlled discretion' including operational monetary independence for Bank of England	1998 Medium-term planning reinstated 2–3 yr Comprehensive Spending Review (CSR); 2000–1 Resource accounting introduced (RAB); DEL and AME spending aggregates	1997 Abolition of unified budget; 1998 abolition of EDX; centralized control in Treasury with aggregates negotiated with PM	Cabinet Office Social Exclusion Unit; 2001 Prime Minister's Delivery Unit (PMDU) set up to monitor performance; Treasury Office of Government Commerce	1998 Public Service Agreements (PSAs) between Treasury and departments; Foundation Hospitals; Trust Schools; Cabinet office Capability Reviews	Public-Private Partnerships (PPP) and PFI accelerated; assets register and asset sales

2007-	Pre-budget report 2008 suspends fiscal rules for duration of economic downturn.	Accelerated spending in Keynesian style stimulus; tougher spending limits after 2010	Increased use of Cabinet Committees by Brown; creation of National Economic Council to coordinate policy; increased power for Department of Business	PMDU relocated in Treasury; Treasury brings in PSA regime into PDMU	PSAs in 2007 CSR modified with fewer targets; some integration into spending decision process	Effective suspension of PFI as credit crunch bites; more private assets brought onto budget – partial public ownership and recap of banks

over a four- to five-year timescale, set against: available resources in the economy; medium-term stability in budgetary allocations; improved Treasury and departmental systems of financial control; and improved collective decision-making in Cabinet (Lowe 1997). The system appeared to overcome its first major test, the devaluation of sterling in 1967, which had involved a significant tightening of fiscal policy. Indeed, it appeared strengthened by this as spending cuts were quickly agreed, the contingency reserve was used for the first time as a control mechanism, and the Treasury began developing more sophisticated financial information systems. Ministers were prepared to accept cuts because they were publicly announced, a lesson not lost on the Treasury, which began publishing a more detailed Public Expenditure White Paper (PEWP) in 1968 that has remained an integral part of budgeting ever since.

As the system entered the 1970s, it was buttressed by the creation of a House of Commons Select Committee on Expenditure to monitor the Treasury's planning and control of spending. This in turn led to a more open approach from the department as it sought the support of parliament for improving information systems, grafting on policy analysis of outputs and effectiveness, and experimenting with programme budgeting to complement the input emphasis of the PESC. There followed some early improvements in information systems, and programme analysis and review (PAR) was introduced in the early 1970s, chiming with the desire of the new Conservative government of Edward Heath to improve the efficiency and effectiveness of the public sector. By 1973 confidence in the system was such that it was claimed to have 'reached full maturity' and was 'probably superior to that found anywhere else in the world' (Goldman 1973: 53).

Less than three years later the system was in crisis. Critics focused on the 'missing billions' of 1974–75 – the discrepancy between what the new Labour government planned to spend and what was actually spent (Wright 1977). Of the 28 per cent increase in spending between 1970 and 1975 only half could be traced to plans in the PEWP or subsequent policy announcements. The Treasury refuted the claim that spending was out of control, arguing that spending was higher not because PESC was inadequate but because of outside pressures: accelerating inflation, the oil crisis and a change in government; although it acknowledged that it had underestimated the relative price effect (the tendency for prices to rise faster in the public sector). Writing much later, the then permanent secretary of Treasury acknowledged that: 'there can be little quarrel with the proposition that the system of expenditure control which was in operation at the beginning of the 1970s was ill-suited to handle the problems which rapidly escalating inflation brought about' (Wass 2008: 326).

PESC was inadequate because governments tended to cut future planned spending when there was a crisis, and then restore these cuts when conditions improved or the political situation dictated. The five-year plans were neither guides to what was spent, nor predictions of what would happen during the survey period. A still more significant flaw was more technical: the Treasury could not control the rising monetary costs of programmes because they were based on constant prices unique to each survey, and related to the control of resources (volume terms) rather than control in cash. The Treasury lacked an information system which could produce data on what resources central and local government was consuming.

The crisis in spending control played its part in a wider economic crisis which led to the embarrassment of a request for support from the International Monetary Fund (IMF). Two alternatives were suggested: to return to more traditional Gladstonian cash controls and abandon PESC; or to introduce a financial control system into PESC creating a more positive planning system. A 'PESC-plus' system would involve grafting on cash controls together with output and effectiveness measurements and the verification of whether resources were achieving stated objectives. This would require a comprehensive information system and a means of measuring performance – themes that were to remain relevant in the 1980s and return in the early twenty-first century.

The immediate response was dictated by the exigencies of the crisis and a cash control system was introduced in April 1976. Cash limits were set for the year ahead to cover the monetary costs of roughly three-quarters of central government expenditure. They were applied to 'year one' of the survey. The Treasury continued to plan and allocate spending on the basis of constant prices related to the volume of resources available, but with greater certainty that levels of spending in cash would be controlled in the year ahead. What was required however was a more robust financial information system. Following a review led by the Treasury and including representatives from the departments and management consultants, an enhanced financial information system (FIS) was introduced in 1976–77. Monthly figures for spending were available within ten days, showing for each cash limit what had been spent and what remained to be spent in the rest of the financial year; overspending could be identified and cash flow monitored against expenditure profiles for each department.

CASH CONTROL FROM IDEOLOGICALLY DRIVEN REFORMS, 1980–90

The Labour government (1974–79) was a reluctant trimmer of public spending, and indeed after a remarkable economic bounce-back after the IMF crisis, spending plans again showed growth. By contrast the Conservative Thatcher government elected in 1979 argued in its first PEWP that 'public expenditure was at the heart of Britain's economic decline', and that 'over the years public spending has been increased on assumptions about economic growth which have not been achieved', with the inevitable result of 'a growing burden of taxes and borrowing' (HM Treasury 1979: 1).

The Medium-Term Financial Strategy

The Medium-Term Financial Strategy (MTFS) unveiled in 1980 extended this repudiation of the post-war consensus even further by signalling a change of economic policy regime (Buiter and Miller 1983). Policy was set in an explicitly medium-term nominal framework which placed monetary targets at the centre of economic policy, supported by reductions in borrowing (Public Sector Borrowing Requirement: PSBR) and an unprecedented set of plans to reduce public spending in real terms. It was a deliberate, rational set of self-imposed constraints by the Treasury, adopted to reduce its room for action. Whilst much of the development of policy was marked by 'adventurism' (Tomlinson 2007), the MTFS represented the most systematic attempt by an OECD country to incorporate monetarist tenets into budgetary policy (Thain 1985).

THE ADVENT OF CASH PLANNING

The first evidence of a change in regime under the MTFS was the abandonment of medium-term volume planning in 1981. Cash planning was the corollary of the MTFS's emphasis on nominal aggregates. In its early years it appeared as if the Treasury would determine the amount of public spending as a residual, after decisions were taken over the money supply, taxation and borrowing in a dictum that 'finance determined expenditure'. In practice, that was impossible to achieve as recession and political constraints added upward pressure on spending.

As so often with reforms in budgeting there was a mix of pressures and factors which led to cash planning, in addition to those driven by ideology. Part of that mix was a seminal report on budgeting led by a former senior civil servant, Lord William Armstrong (1980). It reported in July 1980, recommending a thorough reform of budgetary practice to produce a unified and coherent system for planning expenditure and taxation and, via a 'Green Budget', the opportunity for public and parliamentary debate about budgetary options in the autumn prior to the March Budget. The

Armstrong proposals were taken up by the House of Commons Select Committee on the Treasury and Civil Service, and the topic became the subject of its own inquiry. Together these two reports represented the most comprehensive review of budgeting since Plowden (1961), which had led to the PESC system.

The Treasury and Civil Service Committee resisted the Treasury's objections that a 'Green Budget' would be too disruptive of ministerial, administrative and parliamentary timetables and add considerably to the Treasury's workload. The committee suggested a more modest 'Green Book' incorporating information on public spending, forecasts and specific proposals for changes in tax rates. What emerged was the Autumn Statement, which was no more than an institutionalization of the less formal process by which the Treasury was required to present twice-yearly forecasts for the economy under the Industry Act 1976. It was not until the early 1990s with the unified Budget of Chancellor Norman Lamont, and in the period after 1997 when the Pre-Budget Report was introduced, that the general principles of the Armstrong Report were acted upon (we return to these issues later in the chapter).

Pressure to change to cash planning came from outside the Treasury when the Prime Minister's Policy Unit became convinced that the continuation of volume planning was effectively indexing the public sector against inflation. In technical terms this was because even though plans for 'year one' of the survey were cash-limited, volume plans in constant prices continued to be used in years 'two' and 'three' (and in 'year four' as well until 1980). This enabled departments to argue for spending levels in subsequent years on the basis of 'entrenched entitlements'. It was hard for the Treasury to resist pressure to revalue the costs of those volumes in line with changes in prices. Any squeeze in spending achieved through cash limits could be 'unwound' in subsequent negotiations, and any efficiency savings not necessarily passed on into future years. It was also difficult for the Treasury to work out whether an increase in a programme budget in real terms was the result of the increased cost of providing that service or a genuine enhancement in the quality or quantity of service provided. Measurement of output and performance were almost entirely based on inputs, not outputs. In addition the improvements in information management through the FIS, which had improved the monitoring of cash flow, could not be applied under the constant price system during the period from when a decision to spend was made until final out-turn figures were available two or three years later.

The Treasury claimed five advantages for cash planning: ministers would only discuss cash which would actually be spent and would have to be raised by taxation and borrowing; it would mean finance could determine expenditure and not expenditure finance, as had happened under volume planning; cash planning meant a more explicit consideration of public sector pay; the new system provided managers of programmes with an incentive to adjust spending in line with changing costs, and efficiency gains would be embedded in the system; and finally, there would be no need constantly to rebase spending using different indices. Traditional Treasury concerns to control spending were thus allied with demands for greater value for money in public services, as managers would now have to think about what level of service could be provided with a given level of cash. Managers would also have an incentive to assess what was being achieved in their programmes, and look for the best indicators of output – this was an adventitious benefit, almost an afterthought, and not a driving factor behind the Treasury's abandonment of the PESC system. In reality, the Treasury was prepared to trade uncertainty in planning – as departments were only given annual budgets – for greater certainty in control. Short-term control became paramount, in a reversal of the Plowden principles, which had emphasized procedures which were forward-looking. Thus ended the Treasury's brief and disastrous flirtation with planning public spending in volume terms. From 1982–83 all public spending decisions were taken in cash for the year ahead as the Treasury recommitted itself to its historic mission of containing spending levels. It was not until 1998 that the Treasury returned to planning spending for a three-year period, but under very different circumstances from the 1960s and 1970s.

FINANCIAL MANAGEMENT INITIATIVE: FINANCIAL CONTROL RATHER THAN MANAGERIAL REFORM

Budgetary reforms during the 1980s and 1990s took place against a wider international trend of 'new public management' in the public sector. This involved a raft of changes including: hands-on and heroic management; standards and measures of performance; output controls; disaggregated units in the public sector; increased competition; a move away from a public service ethos towards private sector styles of management; and parsimony in resource use. These were translated, with more pragmatism than the strong rhetoric would have suggested, by the Conservative government after 1979 into a series of initiatives which focused on the size and pay and conditions of work of the civil service, privatization and efficiency scrutinies led by a stand-alone unit reporting to the Prime Minister – the Efficiency Unit (Metcalfe and Richards 1990). The most significant innovations were the Financial Management Initiative (FMI) and Next Steps Agencies.

The origins of the FMI lay in the Rayner efficiency scrutinies and the desire by the Treasury to improve departmental financial systems sufficiently to enable it to benefit from the move to cash planning (Thain and Wright 1995). The Rayner scrutinies tended to involve one-off scrutinies and quick efficiency savings derived from ad hoc reviews of departmental activities. Rayner's unit was small and relied on support from the Civil Service Department (CSD). It had the advantage of independence from both the Treasury and the CSD and carried the Prime Minister's personal support. It showed her commitment to improving the efficiency of Whitehall; a task she felt had to be led by a businessman and could not be left to the Civil Service to tackle.

In 1981 and 1982 the Treasury led the process of financial reform, through the Financial Management Coordinating Group (FMCG). The FMCG concentrated on effective control of the cash cost of public spending programmes; and ensuring that the information available from departments matched the needs of the Public Expenditure Survey (PES) and parliamentary estimates. It also began work on separating out departmental running costs from the rest of the programme budgets, and improving information systems so that departmental costs could be broken down and some output measures derived. This was highly significant because in order to cash-limit and control running costs, not only would departments need better information systems, but budgets would have to be decentralized, making line managers responsible and accountable for their costs. The Treasury soon realized that to isolate and control running costs it was necessary to set up local cost centres within departments, and give managers budgets to cover both staff and non-staff costs. This was a step which challenged the Treasury's traditional centralized management of administrative expenditure. If the Treasury was to obtain better control of running costs, with potential savings, it would have to give departments incentives to decentralize budgetary authority, and this risked creating a more difficult task for expenditure controllers in Treasury.

By 1982 the Treasury and the Cabinet Office's Management and Personnel Office were able to build on the work done in pilot studies and invite 19 major spending departments to produce action plans for discussion. The Treasury was signalling a lack of prescription, having learned from the experience of the US with the Planning, Programming, and Budgeting System (PPBS) and the UK with PAR in the 1970s that centrally imposed systems fail. It was felt that it was better to let departments create systems appropriate to the job on the ground that had the full support of staff. Whitehall departments and agencies had varying business pressures, types of programmes, and different scales of working that meant that no one financial management system could be rolled out across central government. What was missing from the reform was a commitment by the Treasury to give departments more delegated authority for expenditure, to mirror the delegation of budgetary responsibility to line managers within departments. The Treasury baulked at the potential loss of its hard-won reassertion of control. This unwillingness to adopt a more strategic approach and the slow pace of reform were to be sources of tension between the Treasury and management reformers around the Prime Minister.

Progress implementing the FMI across Whitehall varied, although by 1984 most departments had created a top-down management information system. By 1986 some departments were able to use their systems to prepare bids for spending in the PES round. It was becoming clear that decentralized budgetary control within departments would enable them to plan, allocate and monitor their running costs, while providing the Treasury with a tighter central control on them. There was less progress on using the FMI to manage programme expenditure. It appeared that just as the Treasury was unwilling to cede control to departments, senior staff in finance and personnel divisions in departments were unwilling to delegate to policy divisions. Wider constitutional issues were raised too, as greater delegation implied greater personal responsibility for individual civil servants in a way incompatible with traditional notions of ministerial responsibility to parliament.

The slow adoption of the FMI led to increasing tensions between the Treasury and other central actors. Responsibility for reform was split three ways between the Treasury, Cabinet Office/Management and Personnel Office (MPO) and the Prime Minister's Efficiency Unit. The Treasury adopted a pragmatic stance, wanting a system grounded in practical budgetary controls. Its main interest in the FMI was as a vehicle for efficiency savings and tighter control of spending. By contrast, the Efficiency Unit was staffed by 'believers' committed to creating cultural change in Whitehall. To them, senior officials should become more like managers in the private sector, embracing management, value-for-money and results-driven approaches (Rayner 1984). The unit also had a grander strategy for promoting effective as well as efficient government. But its ability to achieve its wider agenda was hampered by its own lack of clout against the Treasury's constitutional responsibility for expenditure. The weakest of the three actors – the Cabinet Office's MPO – lacked both the support of the Prime Minister and the Treasury's operational power. It was in nominal charge of civil service efficiency, but did not have leverage over pay and manpower. The Treasury was able to control, channel and limit a reform process which had the potential to be too far-reaching. The Treasury pursued a limited financial, not managerial reform, designed to enhance departmental systems to deliver greater financial discipline, to enable the Treasury to control public expenditure more efficiently and effectively.

Such tensions at the centre of government were to remain evident in the battles over further reforms to management in the late 1980s and 1990s, particularly over Next Steps Agencies. And they were to resurface in the early part of the twenty-first century, when Tony Blair attempted to push Gordon Brown's Treasury into greater commitment to performance matters.

Controlling Running Costs

Separate budgets for the administrative expenditure of departments were introduced in 1986, as the most significant by-product of the FMI. It was an example of the Treasury's twin track approach to budgetary reform: the simultaneous desire to tighten central control of departmental spending in order to control the aggregates of public expenditure, while giving programme managers greater flexibility in how they operated their budgets. Yet what appeared to be merely a technical improvement in budgeting arrangements in fact allowed the Treasury into highly sensitive issues of departmental politics as the control regime gave entry into the departments' financial management systems and trespassed on internal personnel issues. Detailed monitoring of running costs enabled expenditure controllers in the Treasury to probe departments on the effectiveness of their internal management systems (including how they intended to deploy staff, at what cost and with what expected efficiency improvements). Running costs control limited the ability of departments to switch between programme spending and running costs. Departmental managers were allowed to move expenditure between headings within their running costs limits, but not allowed to move between running costs and capital or current programme expenditure, without Treasury agreement.

As the regime was bedded in during the 1990s, the Treasury gradually allowed more flexibility in its operation. Alongside these controls, manpower targeting was ended – a rather blunt instrument which formed part of Prime Minister Thatcher's 'Grand Strategy' for the civil service. Until the 'New Labour' government introduced manpower reduction targets following the Gershon (2004) review of public sector efficiency in the early part of the twenty-first century, departments had been relatively free from constraints on staffing numbers. From 1988 departments could justify higher staffing levels provided they were able to show efficiency gains. In practice, as most running costs were based on numbers of staff employed, the flexibility entailed was marginal.

Next Steps Agencies

The Next Steps initiative unveiled by Prime Minister Thatcher in 1988 was one of the most far-reaching reforms of the civil service in the twentieth century. By 2001, 126 agencies had been created. They were responsible for discrete areas of programme delivery and employed more than 277 000 officials, or 57 per cent of all civil servants (James 2003). The initiative was another example of reform being driven by 'managerial enthusiasts' employed by the Prime Minister, rather than by the Treasury or the Cabinet Office. Thatcher's efficiency adviser, Sir Robin Ibbs, reviewed the progress of management reform and reported to the Prime Minister. His recommendations went beyond the usual approach to efficiency matters and urged nothing less than a 'change in the British Constitution, by law if necessary, to squash the fiction that Ministers can be genuinely responsible for everything done by officials in their name' (Hennessy 1989: 620).

The Ibbs report concluded that the size, complexity, diversity, traditional structures, monolithic nature and rule-bound traditions of the civil service made it very difficult to implement a far-reaching policy of delegated budgeting. The FMI had been slow and senior officials lacked the necessary managerial skills to implement the changes. The present system was focused on providing political support for ministers, not the management of departments. The report went on to suggest three priorities:

> First: the work of each department must be organised in a way which focuses on the job to be done; the systems and structures must enhance the effective delivery of policies and services. Second: the management of each department must ensure that staff have the relevant experience and skills needed to do the tasks that are essential to effective government. Third: there must be real and sustained pressure on and within each department for continuous improvement in the value for money obtained in the delivery of policies and services. (Efficiency Unit 1988: 7)

It then recommended that separate agencies be created involving 'any executive unit that delivers a service for government'. Ministers and the permanent heads of departments would set the objectives and priorities, within a 'well-defined framework' under which the agency would be expected to operate. After ground rules for policy, budgets, targets and how sensitive political issues were to be dealt with, the agencies should be left with as much freedom as possible to deliver the service. This should include freedom over recruitment, pay and pay scales. The central departments would have to adjust to this new order. The Treasury and Cabinet Office were to be the leaders of the cultural change implied by the reform. This would mean that in future, after confidence had been established in the budgeting regime, detailed control would not be exerted by the centre; rather, it would focus on allocating resources, maintaining pressure for improvements in value for money, maintaining watch over the development of the civil service, and ensuring that standards of propriety were maintained.

The Prime Minister held off from acting on the Ibbs report because of the assault on vested interests implied by it, and not least the misgivings of the Treasury, that feared loss of control of public spending. In its responses to House of Commons committees the Treasury stressed that the changes to the PES since 1976 aimed at tight short-term control of spending could be weakened by Next Steps. The common ground between the Cabinet Secretary Robin Butler and the Permanent Secretary of the Treasury Peter Middleton, when both argued that reform should ensure proper control of spending and value for money, suggested that change would be slow. In the event, their misgivings did not stop the Prime Minister from supporting the initiative. Cabinet ratified it and the report of the Efficiency Unit on the reform was published in February 1988. Initially there was some reluctance to establish agencies because host departments were unwilling to suggest candidates for agency status. Only three agencies were created in 1988 and seven in 1989. But the initiative took off in 1990–92 when 66 agencies were launched, representing 36 per cent of all civil servants.

Whilst Next Steps showed the limits of Treasury power – it could not stop the initiative – it was able to insert a degree of caution in the pace of development, and in balancing public spending control and value for money. Institutionally, this caution was embedded in the process for agreeing candidates for agency status. The Treasury was involved throughout the whole process: in the initial stages and when a framework document was drafted covering the aims, management systems and performance targets. The Treasury also had to be satisfied, before any flexibility or delegation was granted that tasks had been properly assessed and that the agency had a high-quality financial management and budgetary system. Finally, the Treasury was involved in approving the corporate and business plans prepared by the host department and agency. Once satisfied about the rules of the game, Treasury took the initiative in subsequent developments of Next Steps.

Margaret Thatcher left office in 1990 having prodded and pushed the managerial element of budgetary reform from 1982 onwards. Her policy unit and efficiency advisers had been instrumental in a range of initiatives. The Treasury's concern was predominantly in maintaining its hard-won reassertion of control over spending, and it was prepared to slow the pace of reform if necessary before being sure that managerial innovation and improvements in policy delivery did not jeopardize this short-term control.

The Failure to Reduce Spending

One of the ironies of the Thatcher years was that despite strong rhetoric against public spending, and repeated attempts to reduce its absolute aggregate level, it rose on average by 1.9 per cent per year in real terms from 1978–79 to 1992–93, and then by 2.7 per cent in the period from 1992–93 to 1995–96. By contrast, the 1980 MTFS had planned to reduce spending in real terms by 4 per cent. The achievement of that ambitious target was immediately at risk in its first year, with spending rising 2 per cent more than planned in 1980–81. The Treasury maintained the objective but scaled down the ambition, and deferred planned reductions of 1 per cent in real terms to the end of the target period. Control was tightened following the introduction of cash planning, but overall levels of spending continued to rise as the economy was hit by recession. The 1982 White Paper made no reference to the objective of cutting spending. The goalposts were repeatedly moved during the next 11 years.

Governments usually couch their policy objectives in general terms so that adjustments can be made if circumstances change. Such a political strategy was more difficult for the Thatcher government because it had stated its objectives clearly and in the unambiguous publication of a strategy document codifying those objectives. So, it squirmed. In 1984 the difficulties of effecting cutbacks was acknowledged in a Green Paper on Expenditure and Taxation (HM Treasury 1984: 20), which noted that the aim was to hold 'spending broadly at its present level in real terms'. By 1985 a different aim was emphasized: reducing spending as a proportion of gross domestic product (GDP). This was followed in the autumn of 1986 by the acceptance of the reality of spending rising in real terms, as the aim became more modest still: 'to see to it that total public spending even without taking account of privatization proceeds, continues to decline as a proportion of GDP'.

The Treasury acknowledged that even the more modest goal of keeping spending steady could not be achieved, and that expansionary plans merely recognized reality. But it was a bystander in setting objectives or determining what was feasible. The aim of reducing spending as a proportion of GDP remained in place until the 1990s, with success claimed as spending fell during the strong growth of the 'Lawson boom'. This was not sustainable when the economy hit recession again but, as Chancellor Lamont acknowledged in 1990, even though policy was set to reduce expenditure as a proportion of GDP, this might not necessarily happen every single year and there might be periods when activity was weak and the ratio would rise. The objective shifted for a fourth time to that of a balanced budget over the medium term: a 'clear and simple rule which ensures that a prudent fiscal policy supports monetary policy in the fight against inflation' (HM Treasury 1991: 11).

Thus, from the initial objective of cutting spending in real terms, the Conservative government ended up resorting to the same broad policy objectives of the 1960s and 1970s. Changes in objectives, and in the presentation of those objectives, were part of a long learning process in which Treasury devised expedient strategies for coping with the uncontainable pressures for more public spending. Those pressures became particularly acute in the aftermath of the UK's exit from the European Exchange Rate Mechanism (ERM).

PRAGMATIC REASSERTION OF CONTROL, 1992–97

Britain quit the ERM in July 1992. The policy of tying sterling to the ERM subsequently ended in complete failure in September 1992. 'Black Wednesday' had a searing impact on the Treasury's morale. Its reputation for economic competence had to be rebuilt. This was against the background of recession, rising inflation and the need to rebalance fiscal policy through tighter control of public spending. The actions of the Chancellor, Norman Lamont, on budgetary policy were pragmatic attempts to regain control, using crisis conditions to reassert Treasury control on Whitehall.

The 1992–93 Reforms: Containing the 'Politics of Budgeting'

Lamont presented the Cabinet with a raft of reforms aimed at tightening budgetary policy. A 'New Control Total' (NCT) was introduced, profoundly changing the way in which the Treasury determined the aggregate level of spending as a quid pro quo for tougher controls. And a new Cabinet budget committee, the Ministerial Committee on Public Expenditure (EDX) was created to give ministers a say in the collective prioritization of spending. Lamont also brought together taxation and spending in a 'unified budget'.

The previous control total – the 'Planning Total' (which had excluded local government spending) – had been arrived at through an iterative process involving both 'top-down' processed (that is, Treasury attempting to reduce spending levels in line with macroeconomic objectives) and 'bottom-up' processes (departments bidding for extra spending). The reconciliation of those two usually incompatible sets of pressures was made through 'bilateral' meetings between the Chief Secretary to the Treasury (the second Treasury Cabinet minister) and the relevant departmental minister. If the Treasury remained dissatisfied with the outcome of that process, or enough ministers resisted pressure to settle, a further collective political process of adjudication was forced on Prime Minister Thatcher – the so-called 'Star Chamber'. It reflected her style of leadership which favoured small committees and 'even smaller, less formal groups of Treasury and economic department Ministers centered on the Treasury and Number 10' (Burch 1983: 411). Three or four ministers met under the chairmanship of the Deputy Prime Minister or another senior minister, with the Chief Secretary in attendance, to hear the case of ministers who had not settled their budgets. The Star Chamber was an ad hoc element in the PES system – it was not always used. It was used repeatedly in the period 1981–86 when there were concerted attempts to stick to tough spending objectives, but fell into disuse in the period 1987–91 when pressures eased or rising spending was acknowledged as inevitable.

The NCT profoundly changed the processes for determining the aggregate. Instead of accommodating bottom-up pressures, the Treasury imposed top-down limits on spending for the three years of the survey cycle, and specified limits over the PES cycle. In order for this to work, the NCT only included non-cyclical expenditure, thus separating out unemployment benefits and debt interest, which were difficult to estimate and control during a period of recession. It represented a clearer, more transparent and quantifiable objective than a ratio of expenditure to GDP or the New Planning Total. In essence the Treasury was reverting to the policy norm of the 1960s and 1970s that spending should grow in line with the productive potential of the economy. Hence, a reasonable operational target for the NCT, allowing for future trends in cyclical social security and debt interest, produced a growth rate of 2 per cent per annum for public spending as a whole. The NCT figure represented maxima, which could be lowered if GDP growth fell, if the fiscal position deteriorated or if items outside the NCT such as debt interest payments grew too rapidly.

This represented not only a considerable tightening of the budgetary envelope, but also a strong centralization of control by the Treasury in imposing feasible limits on departments. For the new regime to work, the Chancellor advocated 'sharing the Treasury's information, which was its source of power, with other Ministers' (Lamont 1999: 302). This was not popular with Lamont's senior officials. The proposal was to create a permanent feature of the PES at Cabinet level – a new EDX committee chaired by the Chancellor. Departments would no longer make bids for additional resources to the Treasury but to the committee. It would include senior and non-departmental ministers and the Chief Secretary. The aim was that by 'volunteering to share the decisions' the Chancellor hoped to 'persuade the Cabinet to be more realistic and to understand the conflicts in bids for scarce resources' (Lamont 1999: 302). The fears of senior Treasury officials were initially justified as two key members of EDX sought to extend the committee's remit to look at other linked aspects of economic policy – such as taxation and tax expenditures. It took Prime Minister John Major's support of the Chancellor to ensure that EDX focused primarily on managing the spending envelope (Major 1999: 671–2). After these teething problems, EDX appeared to work because it was packed with 'the Prime Minister's A team' and 'supposedly disinterested Ministers with small departmental budgets', so one or other of these types of minister could 'be counted on to go for a colleague's jugular' when they came before EDX (Hogg and Hill 1995: 120). EDX was to survive until 1998 when it was disbanded by Gordon Brown, thus ending an unusual five-year period of the Treasury sharing some of its decision-making power with senior Cabinet ministers, in what approximated to a form of collective decision-making on the priorities of spending, if only at the margins.

The Unified Budget 1993–97

Another of Lamont's reforms which did not survive the change of government in 1997 was the move to bring together decisions on revenue and expenditure in a 'unified budget'. Prior to 1993, spending decisions were usually announced in the autumn after bilateral meetings between the Treasury and departments, and after the operation of the Star Chamber or EDX. Decisions about taxation were made in the traditional Budget in March, just before the start of the next financial year which began in April. By committing himself to changing this, Lamont was acting on one of the Armstrong Committee's recommendations made 13 years previously. Lamont argued:

> In my view our system was not only illogical but also had a number of undesirable consequences. It could not be right to consider expenditure proposals completely unrelated to income, and thus the system . . . tended to encourage unrealistic expectations on expenditure. I also felt that the announcement of tax proposals in isolation created a tremendous pressure for gimmicks and innovative special tax reliefs . . . The old system had contributed to the extraordinarily complex tax system that we have built up over the years. (Lamont 1999: 166)

Treasury officials were hostile to the change, using arguments again that it would add to the burden of work of Treasury officials. In addition they thought it would weaken Treasury power as it would open up taxation issues to more collective Cabinet debate,[1] and risk pressure for higher spending and taxation as it was often possible to keep spending down by threatening ministers with possible unpopular tax rises in the following budget to help pay for extra bids. In the event, the first unified budget was delivered by Lamont's successor, Ken Clarke in November 1994, and repeated in 1995 and 1996. The unified budget appeared to enhance the authority of the Chancellor, who was able to range over all aspects of the government's programme, introduce eye-catching tax changes and bask in the reflected glory of increases in the expenditure of welfare programmes.

'CONTROLLED DISCRETION' AND CENTRALIZED CONTROL: 1997–2007

The advent of a 'New Labour' government in 1997 heralded a number of significant changes in the way public spending was planned. Equally significant was how a powerful Finance Minister, Gordon Brown, was able to use the malleability of the political system to change the role and scope of the Treasury. During his ten years as Chancellor he changed the rules of the budgetary game, exploiting the elasticity of an unwritten Constitution, the growing power of the Prime Minister and Chancellor, large parliamentary majorities, a strong political agenda and a relatively weakened bureaucracy. Brown's Treasury became a far more significant economics ministry, effectively sponsoring a number of policy sectors, especially Health, Work and Pensions, and International Development, in contrast to the more traditionally neutral Ministry of Finance role. Brown's love–hate relationship with the Prime Minister also created an extra twist to the sometimes fraught relationship between the Treasury and the Prime Minister and his advisers. At times the Treasury ceased to be a cooperative central department, slowing the impetus for public sector managerial reform.

Brown came to the role with a firm agenda, worked out when he was opposition spokesman on the economy with his special adviser, Ed Balls. This agenda was eventually given the overarching moniker of 'controlled discretion' (HM Treasury 2002). Economic policy granted more independence on monetary policy to the Bank of England; fiscal policy was constrained by transparent rules and a Code of Fiscal Stability; and total public spending was controlled centrally. Discretion came from creating space for the Treasury to act as a microeconomic manager freed from day-to-day monetary policy; public spending grew within the envelope provided by the fiscal rules; and departments were given more scope to vire resources through a three-year planning horizon. Allocations between competing programmes ceased to be a matter for collective decision-making but were decided by the Prime Minister and Chancellor. The rise in the power of a more activist Treasury was, for the first eight years of

New Labour, sustainable due to high rates of economic growth. Spending levels rose even though the debt-to-GDP ratio fell.

Fiscal Rules

In 1998 the Treasury set out two firm fiscal rules: a 'golden rule' that it would only borrow to invest and not for current spending; and a 'sustainable investment rule' which would hold net public debt below 40 per cent of GDP over the course of the economic cycle. Since they were introduced there has been a healthy debate about their role and operational sustainability (Kell 2001; Heald 2003). The rules depend on a backward-looking assessment of when the economic cycle begins and ends for the sustainable investment rule. In 2005 Brown was widely seen as moving the goalposts to reset the cycle for measurement purposes, and in doing so damaged their credibility as a real constraint on fiscal policy-making. But compared to previous eras, the rules have been integrated into internal Treasury policy when tax, spending and borrowing have been brought together, with the two rules providing an operational constraint. Figure 3.1 shows the trends of spending and borrowing when Brown was Chancellor. The figure shows three distinct phases: (1) cautiousness and surpluses between 1997 and 2000; (2) increased levels of spending in 2000–2007; and (3) from

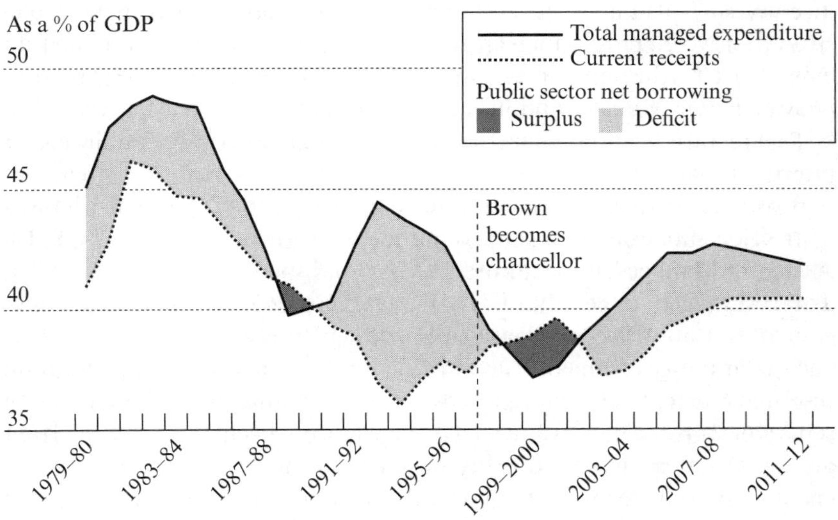

Source: Wolf (2007).

Figure 3.1 Revenue and spending, 1997–2007

2007 a slower rate of growth, a result of a tougher economic and fiscal position. Spending levels on health and education increased significantly after 2000. But one of the tensions between Brown and Blair was that after 2001 public service productivity did not match the increase in resources. To encourage improvement Blair established the Delivery Unit in 2001 (Barber 2007).

A NEW PLANNING FRAMEWORK AND COMPREHENSIVE SPENDING REVIEWS, 1998 AND BEYOND

The public spending framework unveiled in 1998 marked a return to the three-year planning of spending which had been abandoned in 1982 for cash planning. The new regime was based on four principles. First, it was intended to be consistent with plans for managing total public finances, and was set in a 'long-term, prudent and transparent' way. Second, the success of the public spending regime was meant to be based on 'policy outcomes rather than resource inputs' (HM Treasury 1998), a sign that the Treasury was finally embracing some of the principles of the managerial reformers of the 1980s. Third, as the regime covered spending over a three-year period, it was intended to give departments and their agencies incentives to 'plan over several years and plan together where appropriate so as to deliver better public services with greater cost effectiveness' (HM Treasury 1998). Fourth, rules for costing capital assets were intended to provide a framework for public investment.

The regime was based on yet another change to the definitions of public expenditure used for control purposes. The definitions chosen, however, were fairly close to those used in the NCT regime in 1992. Three elements were included: Departmental Expenditure Limits (DEL), Annually Managed Expenditure (AME), and the sum of the two totals, Total Managed Expenditure (TME).[2] DEL spending was planned and controlled on a three-year basis in Spending Reviews. To ensure consistency with the government's fiscal rules, departments were given separate resource (current) and capital budgets. The resource budget contained a separate control total for 'near cash' expenditure such as pay and current grants which can impact directly on the measure of the golden rule. To encourage departments to plan over the medium term, departments could carry forward unspent their DEL provision from one year to draw down in future years, subject to Treasury testing also whether the plans were realistic. This end-of-year flexibility removed any incentive for departments to use up their provision at the year end. The Treasury expected end-of-year flexibility to be passed down from departments to their executive agencies to benefit service delivery.

Under DEL the credibility of medium-term plans was enhanced at both central and departmental levels. DEL plans were strictly enforced and departments had budgetary certainty over the medium term. Departments were expected to prioritize competing pressures and fund these within their overall annual limits. The DEL system provided a strong incentive to control costs and maximize value for money.

The Treasury established a small centrally held DEL Reserve. Support from the Reserve was available only for genuinely unforeseeable contingencies which departments could not be expected to manage within their DEL. This replaced a far more significant policy tool – the Reserve which was in play from 1984, itself a refinement of the Contingency Allowance/Reserve from 1963 to 1984. In each successive iteration, the resources allocated to the reserve were squeezed and rules about access tightened. Rapidly rising spending during the period 2001–07 meant that there was less of a squeeze on resources, requiring fewer calls on the reserve. This is likely to be reversed in the 2008–11 period as spending is constrained by the deterioration in public finances.

AME was expenditure which could not reasonably be subject to firm, multiyear limits. AME included social security benefits, local authority self-financed expenditure, debt interest and payments to European Union (EU) institutions. AME typically consisted of programmes which were large, volatile and demand-led. It was reviewed twice a year as part of the Budget and Pre-Budget Report process, reflecting a closer integration of the tax and benefit system than previously. AME was not subject to the same three-year expenditure limits as DEL, but was still part of the overall envelope for public expenditure. Affordability was taken into account when policy decisions affecting AME were made. The only real constraint on such decisions was a self-denying ordinance not to take policy measures which were likely to have the effect of increasing social security without taking steps to ensure that the effects of those decisions could be accommodated prudently within the fiscal rules.

The first Comprehensive Spending Review (CSR) in 1998 set the principles of the new public expenditure regime, including the new control aggregates (HM Treasury 1998). It involved a comprehensive review of departmental aims and objectives alongside a zero-based analysis of each spending programme. Subsequent reviews in 2000, 2002, 2004 and 2007 were not zero-based. The CSR system extended the Treasury's top-down control over spending.

Three levels of politics characterized the Blair–Brown spending regime. First, 'high' politics involved clashes of interest between the Prime

Minister and Chancellor (over allocations for tax credits, defense, home and security). Second, 'medium' politics were decided by the Chief Secretary and departmental ministers in areas less salient to the Prime Minister or Chancellor, or where firm commitments had already been given (such as in health) for increased resources. Third, 'low' politics involved lower-priority programmes or steady state funding which could be handled almost exclusively by officials. After initially using a Cabinet committee for the 1998 CSR, Brown abandoned collective discussion of priorities. The total envelope available to departments was determined after decisions were taken about AME – and some of this was effectively pre-empted because of Brown's personal interest in tax credits. Overall DEL levels were then set with allocation between departments effectively determined by bilateral negotiations between a Treasury team and Blair's No. 10 team. For most of Brown's chancellorship there was little evidence that improved departmental performance produced meaningful additional resources, or vice versa. For the first time, the Treasury as a finance ministry was seen to be partial to certain public spending programs because the Chancellor was active as a policy agent in sponsoring spending initiatives.

Public Service Agreements

Public Service Agreements (PSAs) form one of the most far-reaching elements of 'performance management' since Next Steps. Seen by some as an 'ambitious tool of governance' (James 2004) and an innovation that is part of a 'top-down, total system approach' (OECD 2007), they also represented a significant interference by the Treasury in departmental management.

The 1998 CSR introduced PSAs with each department set clear targets in terms of the public service improvements expected. Initially, PSAs set around 600 targets and were an attempt at heavy intervention by the Treasury in departmental activity. PSAs were presented as 'contracts' to justify three-year spending allocations. They were then modified to be more output-based. Fewer targets were set – dropping from 600 to 30 – with increasing emphasis on cross-cutting performance agreements involving more than one department engaged in policy programmes, a closer alignment with departmental objectives, and increasing emphasis on devolved responsibility. But they nevertheless had little influence on spending allocations. The Delivery Unit set up in 2001 became increasingly involved in performance measurement, but its first head stressed performance cultures rather than spending discussions (Barber 2007). This meant the unit was unable to 'close the circle' linking allocations under the

PSAs to evaluations and feedback into the next CSR. As already noted, it was not uncommon for the Treasury to be more interested in squeezing spending than in management reform per se.

Resource Accounting and Budgeting (RAB)

Some budgetary reforms have had a long gestation period straddling more than one administration. Resource accounting and budgeting (RAB) is a good example of this. It was first raised in 1993 by Chancellor Clarke in the first unified budget. It took nearly nine years before departments began to use the 'full economic cost of their activities' in the RAB system, with data used both for the CSR exercises and for accountability to parliament in the supply estimates (Likierman 2003; Heald 2005). Andrew Likierman, an academic turned head of the Treasury's accounting team, drove the reform forward, suggesting that it was not just a technical matter of moving to accruals but about improved accountability and financial management across government. Resource and capital budgets were set in terms of accrual information, measuring resources as they are consumed rather than when the cash was paid. So, the resource budget included a charge for depreciation, indicating the consumption or wearing out of capital assets. But the system introduced was not a full accruals system – for example, the full costs of the off-budget Private Finance Initiative (PFI), where the private sector builds and then leases back to public bodies, were not included in the system.

Within their resource budget, departments had separate controls on near-cash spending, on resource spending which impacted directly on the Golden Rule, and on administration budgets. Administration budgets were the successor to the running costs control regime. The amount of their resource budget that departments could spend on running themselves (for example, paying civil servants' salaries) was limited by these administration budgets set in the CSR. Administration budgets were used to ensure that as much money as practicable was available for front-line services and programs. These budgets also helped drive efficiency improvements in departmental activities as they excluded the costs of frontline services delivered directly by departments. There is little research on how RAB has impacted on the overall budgetary system or on departmental cultures, but it would not be surprising if it were found to have had greatest impact on administrative spending, where the Treasury would reap the greatest benefits.

CRISIS RETURNS: DEALING WITH THE CREDIT CRUNCH AND FISCAL PRESSURES – 2007 AND BEYOND

After a brief period of calm, the change of Prime Minister and Chancellor in June 2007 coincided with the return of fiscal crisis – a seemingly persistent feature of budgetary policy for much of the last 40 years. Not only was borrowing predicted to rise to more than 8 per cent of GDP by 2009–10, but the debt budget–ratio was set to exceed the 40 per cent fiscal rule limit, rising to more than 50 per cent of GDP by 2010 (HM Treasury 2007). The UK economy proved to be particularly vulnerable to the collapse of bank lending as a result of the subprime mortgage defaults in the US.

While it may be too early to say what the impact of the financial crisis will be on the UK's budgetary system, a number of initial conclusions can be drawn. First, the fiscal rules have been suspended until the middle of the next decade (2015). Second, the period of sustained public spending growth has come to an end: the next spending cycle from 2010–11 will involve real growth substantially below the trend rate of economic growth in order to reduce public sector deficits. Third, Keynesianism has made a return, with talk of forward-loading capital spending in order to provide support for the economy as it contracts. And new forms of intervention – such as the recapitalization of major banks – have brought more private assets onto the public sector balance sheet. Fourth, there has been a return to some form of collective Cabinet involvement in budgetary policy – at least at the margins. Gordon Brown also established the National Economic Council in October 2008, to improve coordination across government.

At the same time, there have been changes in budgetary policy unconnected with crisis. One of Brown's first acts was to bring the Prime Minister Delivery Unit (PMDU) into the Treasury where its new head will report to both the Chancellor and the Prime Minister. The Treasury has integrated its PSA capability into the PMDU, creating something that more closely resembles a unit for performance management and assessment. There is some evidence that Cabinet committees now take performance management more seriously, as twice-yearly discussions of PSAs are placed on the agenda of functional committees. The Treasury has been weakened by having a Prime Minister who knows its personnel and working style, and after losing such a dominant Chancellor has had to relearn the importance of collegiality. This has coincided with a period when it will require some of the traditional skills of a finance ministry to manage the process of tighter budgets and harder choices. Yet, paradoxically, the return of fiscal crisis makes the value of a powerful Chancellor more apparent.

THE EXPLOSION OF BUDGETARY DOCUMENTATION

One theme that straddles all the periods covered in this chapter is the explosion of the amount of material published on budgetary policies and issues. This has been spawned by some mundane, though nevertheless important factors, such as the availability of desktop publishing packages, portable document format (PDF), and sophisticated websites. It is doubtful whether conventional government publishing houses could have turned round the sheer volume of material now produced. The Treasury was always ahead of the game on such information flows, pioneering the use of web-based information in the mid-1990s. Moreover, sophisticated presentation matters far more, and has become one of the tools of political communication. The Treasury has a 'mission to explain' what it is doing and how budgetary policy involves difficult choices.

There remain important questions about whether quantity has produced better quality. Although under Chancellor Brown the independent Parliamentary National Audit Office was given more responsibility to audit the assumptions behind policy – such as the fiscal rules, and economic forecasts – there is a widespread concern that official statistics are not trusted. This has led to concerns about the impartiality of National Statistics and attempts to foster mechanisms to ensure more independence from political interference. And whilst the Treasury publishes many more background papers on budgetary policy, and has been required through Freedom of Information legislation to release yet more, there remains a question about how far public debate has improved. Ultimately, information needs to be aligned with an increase in the scrutiny powers of key parliamentary committees, and a genuine sense of independence of such bodies from the executive. There is also a need to return to the debate kick-started by the Armstrong Committee in 1980, about creating a proper 'green' or consultative pre-Budget report involving more open discussion of policy options.

CONCLUSIONS: BUDGETS, PERFORMANCE AND COLLECTIVE DECISION-MAKING

This chapter has attempted to show that there are multiple paradoxes in the UK budgetary system. Increased centralization and control has coexisted alongside 'constrained discretion' allowing departments some flexibility in the operation of their own budgets. After Norman Lamont's EDX reform was shelved by Gordon Brown in 1998, there was an almost total collapse of collective Cabinet involvement in setting budgetary priorities or in the allocation of spending. Allocations were determined by fiat and negotiation between the Prime Minister and Chancellor. More recently, in the midst of the current financial crisis there has been something of a return to collective decision-making.

Whilst the technologies and techniques for appraising performance have become ever more sophisticated, there have been tensions since 1980 between the Prime Minister of the day and the Treasury over feeding information about the quality and quantity of delivery into wider budgetary decision-making. Whether this will change with a new Prime Minister and Chancellor remains to be seen. What is apparent currently is that moves toward collective decision-making and performance appraisal are taking place against the background of potentially the worse economic downturn and consequential fiscal crisis since the end of the Second World War.

NOTES

* I am grateful for the views of a large number of current and former Treasury and Bank of England officials, former ministers and journalists who have been interviewed as part of a larger current (2007–10) research project being conducted with Ross Christie on The Treasury under New Labour. I am grateful to the Economic and Social Research Council (ESRC) for its research support. Grant Number: RES-062-23-0369. The chapter also draws heavily from research conducted by Maurice Wright and I in the late 1980s and early 1990s on the Treasury and Whitehall.

1. A feature of the British system since the nineteenth century has been the near total monopoly of the Treasury on matters of taxation. Politically, only Prime Ministers have been able to press alternative proposals, and then only spasmodically and at the margins. This has meant that the UK has not followed other Organisation for Economic Co-operation and Development (OECD) states in supply-side tax cuts at the expense of borrowing. On the other hand, it has meant a potentially unhealthy lack of real debate on alternative tax policies, the consequence of which can be seen in Gordon Brown's political difficulties over the removal of the lower 10 per cent rate of income tax in 2007, which came into effect in April 2008.
2. Total Managed Expenditure is consistent with the National Accounts and represents the public sector's current and capital spending, with the public sector consisting of central government, local government and public corporations.

REFERENCES

Armstrong, Lord W. (Chairman) (1980), *Budgetary Reform in the UK*, report of committee of inquiry set up by the Institute for Fiscal Studies, Oxford: Oxford University Press.

Barber, M. (2007), *Instruction to Deliver: Tony Blair, Public Services and the Challenge of Achieving Targets*, London: Politicos.

Buiter, W.H. and M.H. Miller (1983), 'The macroeconomic consequences of a

change in regime: the UK under Mrs Thatcher', London School of Economics Centre for Labour Economics Discussion Paper no 179, London, November.
Burch, M. (1983), 'Mrs Thatcher's approach to leadership in government: 1979 – June 1983', *Parliamentary Affairs*, **36** (4), 399–416.
Efficiency Unit (1988), *Improving Management in Government: The Next Steps*, report to the Prime Minister, London: HMSO.
Gershon, P. (2004), *Releasing Resources to the Frontline: Independent Review of Public Sector Efficiency*, London: HM Treasury; accessed at www.hm-treasury.gov.uk/media/C/A/efficiency_review120704.pdf.
Goldman, S. (1973), *The Developing System of Public Expenditure Management and Control*, Civil Service College Studies, no 2, London: HMSO.
Heald D. (2003), 'Fiscal transparency: concepts, measurement and UK practice', *Public Administration*, **81** (4), 723–59.
Heald, D., 2005. 'The implementation of resource accounting in UK central government', *Financial Accountability and Management*, **21**(2), 163–89.
Heclo, H. and A. Wildavsky (1981), *The Private Government of Public Money: Community and Policy Inside British Politics*, 2nd edn, London: Macmillan.
Hennessy, P. (1989), *Whitehall*, London: Secker & Warburg.
HM Treasury (1979), *The Government's Expenditure Plans 1980–81*, Cmnd. 7746, November, London: HMSO.
HM Treasury (1984), *The Next Ten Years: Public Expenditure and Taxation into the 1990s*, Cmnd. 9189, July, London: HMSO.
HM Treasury (1991), *Autumn Statement 1991*, Cmnd.1729, November, London: HMSO.
HM Treasury (1998), *Modern Public Services for Britain: Investing in Reform: Comprehensive Spending Review: New Public Spending Plans 1999–2002*, CM 4011, July, London: HMSO.
HM Treasury (2002), *Reforming Britain's Economic and Financial Policy: Towards Greater Economic Stability*, E. Balls and G. O'Donnell (eds), Basingstoke: Palgrave.
HM Treasury (2007), *Meeting the Aspirations of the British People: 2007 Pre-Budget Report and Comprehensive Spending Review*, Cmnd. 7227, October, London: The Stationery Office.
Hogg, S. and J. Hill (1995), *Too Close to Call: Power and Politics – John Major in No. 10*, London: Little, Brown & Company.
James, O. (2003), *The Executive Agency Revolution in Whitehall: Public Interest Versus Bureau-Shaping Perspectives*, Basingstoke: Palgrave Macmillan.
James, O. (2004), 'The UK core executive's use of public service agreements as a tool of governance', *Public Administration*, **82** (2), 397–419.
Kell, M. (2001), 'An assessment of fiscal rules in the United Kingdom', International Monetary Fund Fiscal Affairs Department working paper 01/91, Washington, DC.
Lamont, N. (1999), *In Office*, London: Little, Brown & Company.
Likierman, A. (2003), 'Planning and controlling UK public expenditure on a resource basis', *Public Money and Management*, (January), 45–50.
Lowe, R. (1997), 'The core executive, modernization and the creation of PESC, 1960–64', *Public Administration*, **75** (3), 601–15.
Major, J. (1999), *The Autobiography*, London: HarperCollins.
Metcalfe, L. and S. Richards (1990), *Improving Public Management*, 2nd edn, London: Sage.

Organisation for Economic Co-operation and Development (OECD) (2007), *Performance Budgeting in OECD Countries*, Paris: OECD.
Peters, B.G. (2001), 'The United Kingdom becomes the Untied Kingdom: is federalism imminent or even possible?' *British Journal of Politics and International Relations*, **3** (1), 71–83.
Plowden, E. (Chairman) (1961), *Control of Public Expenditure*, Cmnd. 1432, London: HMSO.
Rayner, Lord D. (1984), 'The unfinished agenda', Stamp Memorial Lecture presented at University of London, 6 November.
Rhodes, R.A.W. (ed.) (2000), *Transforming British Government: Volume 1, Changing Institutions*, and *Volume 2, Changing Roles and Relationships*, London: Macmillan.
Thain, C. (1985), 'The education of the Treasury: the medium-term financial strategy 1980–84', *Public Administration*, **63** (3), 261–85.
Thain, C. and M. Wright (1995), *The Treasury and Whitehall: the Planning and Control of Public Expenditure, 1976–1993*, Oxford: Clarendon Press.
Tomlinson, J. (2007), 'Mrs Thatcher's macroeconomic adventurism, 1979–81, and its political consequences', *British Politics*, **2**, 3–19.
Wass, D. (2008), *Decline to Fall: the Making of British Macro-Economic Policy and the 1976 IMF Crisis*, Oxford: Oxford University Press.
Wolf, M. (2007), 'Virtues and vices of Mr Brown', *Financial Times*, 21 March.
Wright, M. (1977), 'Public expenditure in Britain: the crisis of control', *Public Administration*, **55** (2), 143–69.

4. Australia after budgetary reform: a lapsed pioneer or decorative architect?

Lewis Hawke and John Wanna

Australian governments were early pioneers of budgetary reform at the national level, commencing with an ambitious reform program dating from around 1982 (see Wanna et al. 2000). Over some two decades Australia's budgetary systems were transformed and its internal budgetary practices became more managerial, outcomes-focused and businesslike. Arguably, budgetary reform drove broader public sector reform and was used to underpin a wide agenda of new public management (NPM) across government. Budget discipline improved at the center, while departments imposed internal budgetary discipline so that they came in 'under budget'. Devolution and resource flexibilities meant that various traditional impediments to effective resource management were removed. Prior to the financial crisis, annual budget outcomes improved so that regular deficits became regular surpluses year after year. Budgetary documentation, fiscal plans and financial reports increased in scope, volume and regularity. As a pioneer, Australia pushed ahead with budgetary reforms, at times at breakneck speed. But of late, Australia's momentum has waned, and its enthusiasm for carrying through the reforms to deliver more meaningful performance information has diminished, despite repeated calls for change. Australia appears now to be either a lapsed pioneer searching for direction, or a jurisdiction complacent with its own investment in decorative architecture.

According to some measures, the Australian budgetary reform story appears relatively successful. Prior to the 2009 budget, the Australian budget had been in surplus for ten out of the previous 11 years. Total receipts for the national government have remained stable at between 25 and 26.5 percent of gross domestic product (GDP) since 1998. Then as the economic crisis loomed, revenues were predicted to drop to 23.6 percent by 2010. A staggering turnaround in 2008–09 saw projected surpluses fall from $21.7 billion (or 7 percent of government revenues or 1.8 percent of GDP) to a deficit of $32 billion. While net debt had fallen from 18.5 percent GDP in 1995–96 to −3.7 percent in 2008–09 it was again expected to rise to 20 percent by 2012. The government's fiscal stimulus was premised on a policy of maintaining strong expenditure growth into the future, running up 'temporary deficits' with the budget coming back into surplus sometime after 2013. In 2009 the government still delivered tax cuts, higher spending on infrastructure, and two rounds of cash payments to citizens. By contrast, spending on departments and agencies ('own-use spending') was tightened considerably with limited scope for growth in the future. So, despite the immediate financial crisis, Australia's trajectory of budgetary reform and the outcomes produced conveys the impression of historical success and increasing control.

Yet, behind the aggregate numbers the picture is more complex and an appraisal of substantial reform may be less flattering. If anything, Australia has suffered from 'reform triumphalism' which may not be fully warranted. Arguably, Australia has shown itself prepared to tackle the technical input side of budget reform, while consigning broader strategic decision-making to the margins, and being churlish in showing reluctance to tackle the harder performance-related side of the budget including 'hard' accountabilities for delivering programs. In this chapter Australia's reform path will be described and analysed in an effort to explain why it has followed this seemingly meandering route. It explores the hard questions still needing to be addressed after more than 20 years of experience with reform.

AUSTRALIA'S BUREAUCRATIC TRAJECTORY OF BUDGETARY REFORM

Australia's reform trajectory was bureaucratic, pragmatic and instrumental, with reforms largely being introduced by executive fiat (and buttressed by bureaucratic pressure) rather than mandated through statutory provisions. Unlike in many other countries, statutory provisions in Australia have tended to follow reform initiatives, not lead them. Hence, a pattern of reform emerged that was largely intermittent, incremental and piecemeal. Often when reforms were introduced, the executive was not particularly forthcoming about what it intended to achieve with any one component, preferring to talk in generalities such as greater efficiency, transparency, tighter discipline or a greater focus on results. When central budgetary agencies (CBAs) announced reform initiatives, they tended to take the form of instructions and 'rule changes' ('memoranda' to other departments) – without explicit rationale or declared objectives. Governments were reluctant to announce rationales and evaluation criteria for reform instruments against which they could be subsequently judged or measured. It is true that new governments sometimes came to office brandishing new proposals for budgetary reform.[1] But as incoming governments their reform proposals were frequently rhetorical, unclear or indeterminate; or ambitious grandiose statements were made that were then rarely revisited. Sometimes one reform initiative was announced but another was implemented, such as the Financial Management Improvement Program (FMIP) which started life as a training program and ended as a label for a series of reforms to the running costs arrangements (see Wanna et al. 2000, Chapter 8). Similarly, the Hawke Labor government (1983–91) announced that it was intending to introduce 'program budgeting', but never did and instead gradually implemented 'portfolio budgeting' (Barrett 1988). There is considerable evidence from Australia that government longevity is inversely related to budgetary reform, and that older governments tire of budget reform, manifesting complacency and seeking to prevent further changes being introduced (see Wanna 2007).

As the main spenders and taxers in the Australian federation, national governments gradually introduced budgetary reforms to impose fiscal discipline and contain structural budgetary imbalances in response to the economic constraints and fiscal stresses of the 1970s and 1980s. Annual deficits and increasing levels of public debt encouraged governments to take a closer interest in both their fiscal policy settings and internal budgetary processes (Keating 1990; Keating and Holmes 1990). Ministers agreed that if they were to be held accountable for the consequences of poor budgeting outcomes, then they ought to exert greater influence over crucial aspects of government budgeting, including aggregate-setting and new policy proposals. The political support for nascent reform measures was crucial to their development and take-up. However, while ministers gave their imprimatur they did not generally drive the reform agenda; central agency officials became the champions of reform, tinkering away when political circumstances permitted.

The reform process began (unintentionally) in the Treasury in the 1960s with the collation and extension of stand-alone 'forward estimates' that were gradually made robust and folded into budget formulation. The Coombs Royal Commission into government administration 1974–76 also gave impetus to the quest for efficiency and effectiveness. Early expenditure controls were fairly blunt and limited in their effectiveness. The Fraser government (1975–83) imposed restraint through arbitrary top-down ceiling controls, clawbacks and across-the-board cuts. A second inquiry into government management by Reid (1983) advocated the adoption of improved financial management and business practices. Reid argued that:

'the performance of the public administration has fallen below desired and acceptable standards'. The main message of his report was accepted by the Hawke government (1983–91) which shortly after issued two White Papers (*Reforming the Australian Public Service*, 1983, and *Budget Reform* 1984). The stated aims of *Budget Reform* were both budgetary and managerial. The document articulated the following aims:

- to develop better means of identifying and setting budget priorities;
- to focus attention more clearly on the goals and objectives of particular programs;
- to develop and apply . . . specific techniques aimed at improved performance and more efficient resource use; and
- set up machinery to ensure that the efficiency and effectiveness of programs was regularly reviewed. (Australian Government 1984: 1–2)

In addition, a contemporaneous 'FMIP diagnostic study' was undertaken by officials that promoted improved management, efficiency and 'greater effectiveness in implementing Government policies and programs' (Australian Government, 1984: v).

The Hawke and Keating (1991–96) governments emphasized the containment of expenditure growth, with tighter 'targeting' of benefit programs, compulsory savings (efficiency dividends), the use of co-contribution payments and user-charging devices to ration and supplement public funding. They attempted to 'force managers to manage' within prescribed resource limits set over the medium term, thereby bringing aggregate budgets under control. By the late-1980s Australia had made the transition from consecutive high deficits being reported in its final budget outcomes (FBO) to annual surpluses often exceeding budgetary forecasts. Resource management across government and in individual agencies had been brought under administrative control possibly for the first time since the parsimonious nineteenth-century era of small-government liberalism. However, the recession of 1991–92 was met with an expansionary fiscal policy with expenditure increasing by over 5.5 percent for two years (1991–93), and revenues falling over the same period. This recession contributed to seven straight years of deficit budgets (1990–97).

The Howard government (1996–2007) was initially committed to reining in the large cyclical deficit (and debt level) that it inherited from the Keating government. Its first two budgets imposed significant cuts totaling around $8 billion. The government's principal goal was to deliver annual budgetary surpluses; although to preserve some latitude the formal policy was to 'keep the budget in surplus over the economic cycle' (a three-year timeframe). The government committed itself to 'the principles of sound fiscal management' in both its annual budget statements and the Charter of

Budget Honesty (Parliament of Australia 1998) but failed to specify what this meant in practice. In 1996 the Howard government established its own National Commission of Audit (NCA) to report on the state of government finances and the role of the federal government in service provision. This commission advised the government to establish specific fiscal targets but not to set these in legislation, so as to preserve necessary flexibility and latitude for the government's desired economic policy. The NCA also advised the national government to withdraw from many areas of direct service delivery in preference to the states – advice which the government rejected.

In its first five years in office the Howard government pursued a series of reforms to resource management: the introduction of compulsory competitive tendering; outsourcing of programs and equipment; 'price-based' budgeting or costing methodologies; and a new budgetary reporting regime. The government's most significant budgetary reforms were implemented in 1999–2000 – a full accrual budgetary (and reporting) system, and an outcomes and outputs framework used for both budgetary appropriation and internal budgetary management. In the process, portfolio budgeting and centrally driven program evaluation were discontinued and agency-based budgeting was reinstalled. Thereafter, the Howard government lost interest in further budget reform apart from some minor tinkering with the machinery it had built to achieve smoother operations.

The incoming Rudd government (from 2007) began implementing Operation Sunlight, a statement of budgetary transparency conceived while in opposition (Tanner 2006). Operation Sunlight promised five major areas for budget reform: including tightening outcomes descriptions, providing program-level information, clearer reporting or estimates, better disclosure of special appropriations, and improved intergenerational reporting. In its first two budgets (2008 and 2009), the government had revised its method of financial reporting – adding goods and services tax (GST) revenue into national budget figures – and announced a series of further budget reform agendas covering the next three years (for example, outcomes reviews).

THE REFORM EDIFICE

After more than 25 years of intermittent budgetary reform, the main innovations introduced into the Australian budgetary system include:

- The institutional separation of functions between an economics ministry (the Department of Treasury) and a budget ministry (the Department of Finance) (1976).

- A consolidated budgetary decision-making process allowing comparative merits of proposals to be judged and determined by a special cabinet committee (Expenditure Review Committee, 1980s); this placed greater focus on internal political will and flexibility of action rather than any legislated targets.
- The greater involvement of cabinet in aggregate budgetary limits and setting fiscal plans or strategies (endorsing a medium-term economic framework but not public 'expenditure targets'), especially from the mid-1980s onwards).
- 'Hard' forward estimates (rolling baselines) were devised for agencies, imposing fixed resource limits on them but giving them some certainty as well.
- The gradual consolidation of input budgets to 'one-line' running costs and portfolio budgets (1980s), followed by one-line agency budgets for departmental expenses after 1999.
- Greater in-year and between-year flexibilities and managerial discretion over departmental expenses (1980s and 1990s).
- Greater emphasis on program structures in agencies and more reliance on program management.
- The imposition of productivity dividends on agencies (an annual administrative cut called the 'efficiency dividend'), and the insistence on 'offsets' (co-contributions) from departments making bids for new policy funding (a test of priority and significance).
- Corporatization and privatization of public enterprises – getting their operations off-budget and off the balance sheet, effectively reducing the budget to the government's own operations (1980s and 1990s).
- The adoption of a Charter of Budget Honesty (Parliament of Australia 1998) and an integrated set of budgetary and reporting statements.
- The adoption of sophisticated central budget information management systems complementing the financial information systems of agencies.
- The adoption of 'full-cost' budgeting through accrual budgeting and accounting, recognizing assets and liabilities (1999).
- Better asset recognition and asset management, property leasing arrangements and procurement.
- Adoption of an outcomes framework whereby appropriations are voted to outcomes (1999).[2]

We can construct this list only with the benefit of hindsight. Australia's trajectory of budget reform was not planned or linear and has occasionally zigzagged. For instance, separate agency banking was discontinued, forward estimates were unilaterally centralized, then devolved to agencies, then partially recentralized. There was no overall template or blueprint, but equally the process was not totally random. Instead, some broad principles and directions can be traced that guided executive thinking, and there was much consistency between governments of differing political suasion. The principles were more managerial than neoliberal, oriented towards doing more with less and improving 'value for money'. They were based on a presumption that program managers (spenders) would manage their own budgets better and more conservatively if allowed to do so. But such broad principles often emerged from, rather than led, the unfolding path of experimentation. Only gradually did governments come to endorse the principles of higher-level priority-setting, devolution and devolved responsibilities, and a results-based orientation to spending allocations.

There are now two competing Australian narratives explaining these changes. Triumphalists within government generally insist budget reform was intended, rational, logically anticipated and evolving as a process of progressive consolidation (DoFA 1998). As the victors in the reform process they were later able to rationalize the surviving components of budgetary reform and proselytize about them (see Keating 1990; MAB 1997; DoFA 1998). They insisted that the surviving reforms had been intended from the outset; that they knew they would work; that they were augmented and extended when successful, and then documented and if necessary legitimized through changed legislation or budget rules. Logical representations of the reforms were disseminated internationally through the Organisation for Economic Co-operation and Development (OECD) and senior budget officials' meetings (see Chan et al. 2002). Other critics inside and outside government (Wanna et al. 2000; Barton 2006; Wanna 2007) have insisted that the reform process was a hit-and-miss affair with many 'reforms' ditched along the way, some mistakes erased, and only those reforms retained that were considered effective. They point to a history of disputes and disagreements between advocates of rival directions – especially between 'central controllers' and 'devolved managers', or between advocates of 'cash' versus 'accrual' budgeting. Some actors and agencies suffered identity crises and role confusion in the process, not understanding or accepting what they were supposed to be doing as reforms unfolded (this included agencies such as the National Audit Office, Treasury, Finance and even parliament).

MORE IS LESS: BUDGETARY PAPERS AND DOCUMENTATION

The budget timetable was changed in the mid-1990s to fit the annual budget better with the financial year. Budgets are now usually presented in mid-May (not August), limiting the time available for parliamentary debates and Senate estimates hearings to little over a month. The budget is meant to be approved by both houses before the new financial year starts (1 July), although some taxing or spending matters outside the appropriation Acts may remain unresolved or lapse.

Australia uses consolidated business-style financial reporting, with cash flow statements, accrual-based operating statements, balance sheets, movements in equity and monthly financial reporting. Various changes have occurred to the accounting standards and policies underlying the budget calculations and reporting requirements. The intention has been to make the public accounts as close as practical to private business accounts and to harmonize different accounting treatments. Although these figures are meant to deliver greater accuracy and reliability, at each budget governments have often chosen a particular indicator that they prefer (which 'looks best') from at least four 'official' alternatives and then only referred to that figure (Barton 2006). This allows the government slippage room to interpret the results in the most favorable light.

There have been considerable changes to the scope and contents of the main budget papers since the early 1980s. During the 1980s governments produced longitudinal 'functional' information (for example, for health, social security) including annual changes in specific programs. Currently, separate portfolio budget statements (and detailed statements for each agency within the portfolio) contain detailed information on new allocations and new policy initiatives, but usually little on existing policy spending (the 'base'). Additional estimates are presented in November and, since the establishment of the Charter of Budget Honesty Act 1998, all new 'in-year' policy announcements are collated into a legally mandated Mid-Year Economic and Fiscal Outlook statement (MYEFO – which also updates aggregate budget balances and forward estimates). Governments are also obliged to produce Intergenerational Reports (IGR) at least quinquennially and a Pre-Election Economic and Fiscal Outlook (PEFO) within 10 days of the issue of writs for a general election.

Budget and fiscal reports are aligned with other budget reporting and agency annual reports in a 'clear-read' style. Agency annual reports are required to include not only basic financial information but also information on the agency's performance in terms of outcomes. Agency annual reports must be tabled in parliament within four months of the end of the financial year (October).

However, while these integrated reports provide greater overall consistency, they remain flawed. Important fiscal principles are not defined in law or are left vague. Executive flexibility is preferred to statutory limits, and looser 'principles' espoused rather than specific targets. Some key terms in the Charter of Budget Honesty Act 1998 are subjective and highly contextual (for instance 'sound fiscal management' is described as managing financial risks prudently having regard to circumstances). The Treasurer must release an annual 'fiscal strategy statement' based on 'principles of sound fiscal management', but the explanation of 'sound fiscal management' leaves wide scope for interpretation. The words mean what the government wants them to mean. The IGR is a stand-alone set of projections and not integrated into the budget processes. Fiscal discipline would be improved if the Act contained declared parameters or targets as guiding benchmarks against which to judge performance (for example, on expenditure targets, debt levels, deficit ratios and expenditure to GDP ratios). In the absence of specific definitions, the Act remains a set of platitudes and nice-sounding intentions.

Despite the advances in documentation there has been much criticism that more documentation offers less meaningful information. A Joint Committee of Public Accounts and Audit report on accrual budget documentation (JCPAA 2002) was critical of the opacity of much of the new information. A report by the Senate Standing Committee on Finance and Public Administration, on 'Transparency and accountability of Commonwealth public funding and expenditure' (2007) argued that multiple accounting standards were confusing, that outcome reporting was often meaningless and that much of the activity-based program data was not included, thereby reducing parliament's oversight capacities. There has also been criticism of accrual budgeting, especially over the hyped-up claims about its accuracy and benefits. In Australia's case there is criticism that budgets satisfy the form rather than the substance of accruals and that there is an ineffective operating statement and inadequate balance sheet management.

The lack of input information about programs was also highlighted in the Murray Report (2008). Senator Murray agreed to conduct an independent review of budgetary transparency, implementing Operation Sunlight (in 2006) and leading to a major 'overhaul' of practices. He advocated a single accounting standard, more readable budget papers, more accurate cross-referencing of related documents, program-level reporting in portfolio budget statements, sunset clauses for standing appropriations, that a register of 'special accounts' should be produced for parliament, and that non-lapsing 'underspends' in agencies should be reported. His review produced a comprehensive critical assessment of documentary problems and shortcomings. Similar criticisms have been made in a recent OECD review of the Australian budgetary system (Blondal et al. 2008).

THE MYTH OF OUTCOMES BUDGETING: BUDGETARY FORMAT AND MANAGEMENT

Ostensibly, Australia now budgets according to an outcomes-based framework using full accrual budgeting that is informed by a performance-oriented philosophy – or at least this is what the reformers claim (DoFA 1998, 2001; Chan et al. 2002). In practice, Australia only uses the outcomes framework for a fraction of its resource appropriations. Outcomes funding in Australia is a means of funding and protecting organizational 'base' budgets, not of prioritizing across government. Responsibility for devising and revising the outcomes and working towards them is largely devolved to individual agencies. It is evident that after almost a decade of applying the outcomes framework, the budgetary format remains a tool for the disciplined utilization of resources by agency executives and operational managers rather than more strategic allocations from the center to government priorities. Agencies have a clear incentive to deliver within budget allocations, not necessarily to maximize outputs.

The essence of Australia's budgetary system applied tight fiscal discipline and annual expenditure control at the center while allowing agencies flexibility to reallocate resources and sufficient discretion to manage. Australia never implemented program budgeting but instead used portfolio-based budgeting as a composite base budget method. This was composed of 'running costs' and 'program costs' (grants and other funding). Agencies were charged an efficiency dividend (mostly at 1.25 percent of running costs but from 2008 increased to 3.25 percent) to stimulate internal efficiencies or minor reprioritizations. The efficiency dividend has survived for more than 20 years (1987 to date) as an annual sleight-of-hand to keep administrative costs in check (unless agencies won new administrative funding with new policy proposals). This base-budgeting system was in effect rolled into the superstructure of the outcomes framework that became the decorative architecture for presentation.

The Australian parliament's capacity to influence the allocation of funds within appropriations is limited under the Constitution, which prevents the Senate from amending bills for the ordinary annual services of government that account for the majority of annual appropriations.[3] Legislation was passed in 1999 to present these annual appropriations on an outcomes basis alone. Since then top-down accrual budgets have been provided to each agency, divided into two amounts. Departmental expenses represent the total operating resources approved by parliament as a composite figure for use by an agency on any of its outcomes. Administered items consist of grants, subsidies or other program funding administered on behalf of others (not controlled by the agency). Around 17 percent of the budget goes to departmental expenses, with 83 percent in administered items. Only 8 percent of the administered items are included within the annual appropriations for outcomes (making up 25 percent of the total budget), the rest (75 percent) are appropriated under special appropriations that are not considered by parliament as part of the annual budget bills. These special or standing appropriations authorize expenditures according to the purposes defined in separate laws (but not by outcomes). They are passed as stand-alone laws and remain in effect for as long as the specified conditions are met.

Outcomes have become labels mapped onto reporting structures or organizational profiles. Agencies within the general government sector are required to identify, measure, plan and report on the basis of outcomes and sub-outcomes. The reporting on outcomes is additional to mandatory financial reporting and legal requirements for parliamentary appropriations. There are now more than 500 outcomes in total across the general government sector. The number of outcomes per agency can vary from one outcome for most bodies (including some large departments), to 14 outcomes in the Department of Health and Ageing. Output groups (to be renamed programs) can vary in size from a few million dollars to billions of dollars. The Health and Ageing department's 2008–09 estimate for its Private Health Insurance Program Management output group is $2.4 million. The estimate of the Department of Infrastructure, Transport and Regional Services for its 'Infrastructure Investment' output group in the same year is $3510 million.[4]

Internally, governments tend to make budgetary decisions at the output or program level, not at the outcome level. In this sense, 'outcome budgeting' is a misnomer. Outcomes are larger aggregates of activities that express big-picture impacts or intended directions. They are not established as allocation devices or to impose resource limits. They are not crucial parts of the strategic decision-making architecture of budget prioritization. Moreover, governments would find it difficult if not impossible to budget on an outcome basis.

Changes to outcomes and outputs occur frequently. Few of the original outcomes and output specified in the first outcome-based budget in 1999–2000 exist today. This is partly due to changes in administrative arrangements by the government, changes in legislation and refinements by agencies to align better with evolving policies and strategies. Changes to outcomes must be authorized by the Minister for Finance. Agencies have to explain their variations but are not challenged over them by cabinet or the parliament. Changes to outputs can occur in consultation with the relevant departmental minister, and no other external authorization is required. In portfolio budget statements presented to parliament for information (not authorization), departmental outputs are 'priced' and given performance indicators for quality and quantity. In practice, budget funding for departmental outputs can be used to contribute to any of the agency's outcomes.[5]

All outcomes sit within single agencies and there are no outcomes shared across agencies. At one level this introduces another fictional dimension to the system, but at another it provides a strong focus for chief executives and the management of individual agencies. Yet, the scope, precision and specificity of outcomes can vary considerably. Some agencies focus on direct impacts such as access to, and awareness of, their services. The Department of Health and Ageing nominates as one outcome that 'Australians have access to cost effective medicines'.[6] Others have chosen outcomes relating to broad economic or social change where they are only one of many contributing influences, such as sustainable government finances (Department of Finance and Deregulation), a sound economic environment (Department of the Treasury), cultural enrichment and international influence (Department of Immigration and Citizenship).

The Department of Families, Housing, Community Services and Indigenous Affairs (FAHCSIA) reports extensive details on its outputs and performance measures which are intended to contribute to top-level outcomes that are very broad, such as: 'families and children have choices and opportunities', or 'strong and resilient communities' – both of which could describe almost anything. Some agencies specify 'intermediate' outcomes to clarify and strengthen the link between outputs and outcomes. The Civil Aviation Safety Authority (CASA) describes the outcomes expected for each of its four outputs, linked to the agency's vision and the portfolio outcome for all transport and regional services agencies, as summarized in Table 4.1. The structure and composition of results shown under the outcome is open to the agency, unless specific elements are required by statute.

Under the devolved system, agencies can design performance measures for each outcome and output.[7] Central guidance on how agencies should construct their performance data was last revised in 2003.[8] There is no formal quality control by the CBAs, but budgetary officials can provide advice, on request, regarding the suitability of performance measures. There is no obligation on agencies to act on central agency advice on

Table 4.1 Outcomes and outputs for CASA, 2007–08

Output		Budget 2007–08 $000	Actual ($000)
Output 1: Aviation Safety Standards	A safer aviation community achieved through development and application of quality safety standards	24 514	25 926
Output 2: Aviation Safety Compliance	Compliance with Australian aviation safety legislation is secured through effective surveillance, education and procedurally fair enforcement	58 740	52 317
Output 3: Aviation Safety Promotion	An informed and safety-motivated aviation community is achieved	18 030	20 432
Output 4: Aviation Regulatory Services	Regulatory services provided in a timely and consistent manner, aligned with CASA's safety obligations	37 349	33 087
TOTAL		**138 633**	**131 762**

Source: CASA (2007), *Annual Report, 2007-08*, Canberra, October, accessed at http://www.casa.gov.au/scripts/nc.dll?WCMS:STANDARD:937629001:pc=PC_92588#table21.

performance measures unless directed by ministers. Agencies are only required to include outcome and output information for the budget year, not every year of the medium-term financial estimates. The Australian government requires agencies to include in those reports the indicators and targets to be used for measuring performance. The indicators and targets include effectiveness indicators and output (or output group[9]) quantity, quality and resources allocated. Resources are measured in accrual terms for budgeting and reporting of results.

There is no mandatory requirement for in-year reporting of performance results by agencies. Full-year performance results must be reported in agency annual reports. Performance results are not required to be audited by either internal or external auditors. Agencies are at liberty to decide their own arrangements for internal reporting of performance under the responsibilities delegated to each agency's chief executive office or departmental secretary.[10] Agencies have their own systems for establishing and maintaining performance information. There is no central record of agency performance and agencies generally do not incorporate non-financial performance information into their financial systems or financial reports. A common approach is for individual program managers or functional units to be responsible for establishing and maintaining data. This is done either within a common central system with standardized reporting arrangements, or within separate operational systems where data is automatically generated as part of everyday activities.

Criticisms have been voiced of the outcomes framework. There are claims that outcomes are too generic and often nebulous; that program structures are far less visible to external scrutiny; that the framework only loosely links budget allocations with performance reporting; and that outcomes may not be useful to all types of agency (more appropriate for direct service providers than central agencies, policy agencies or regulatory agencies). It is also argued that outcomes and outputs are more appropriate for state and local levels of government than at the national level. Although all agencies can present their entire organization under an outcomes template, many have not organized their activities or staff around the outcomes structure, which suggests that the outcomes framework is more cosmetic than operational.

Periodically, the great hope of the budgetary reformers was that performance evaluation would become the 'crowning glory' of the process (Uhr 1991). They were anxious to demonstrate 'value for money' and complete the Gladstonian review loop. But Australia's attempts to base resource decisions on regular performance reporting have faced the same barriers and hindrances faced by other OECD nations. Formal attempts to integrate (internal) evaluations into the budget process began in the late 1980s (including at one stage proposals for compulsory program evaluation plans every 3–5 years). Over the years many evaluation schemas have been promoted, but they have proved disappointing and have often been abandoned. Requirements for routine performance information as part of the budget formulation process collapsed in the late 1980s. Joint management reviews were focused on management issues and not budget-related. 'Appropriateness reviews' could be called by cabinet on particular programs, especially those close to termination, but they were not universalized. 'Lapsing program reviews' were promoted by the Howard government but were abandoned once the voluminous workload and minimal impact on decisions were realized. They had become a mechanical process necessary to justify continuation of funding. There is now a centrally coordinated process for 'strategic reviews' aimed at systematic examination of important areas of government activity. Rather than targeting every program or activity, strategic reviews seek to ensure that resources in selected areas are used efficiently and managed effectively to achieve government policy priorities.

REALLOCATION ACROSS SECTORS: FROM FINE-SLICING, TO SHARING THE LARGESSE, TO SHARING THE PAIN

The 1980s witnessed intense efforts by the government, spurred on by central agencies, to whittle down fiscal deficits, rein in expenditure and quarantine budget decision-making. This was achieved by establishing strong control on total spending, capping portfolio allocations and requiring internal reallocations to fund new policies and efficiency savings. Some reallocation occurred across sectors, but most of the policy churn occurred within portfolios. Mutually reinforcing control by the Treasurer and the Finance Minister, combined with the enforcement of restrictive cabinet rules and a rigorous filtering process and scrutiny of new spending through the Expenditure Review Committee of Cabinet (ERC) for every budget decision, ensured that growth in spending was carefully managed for much of the late 1980s. As the Treasurer's premonition of a 'banana republic' threat receded in the early 1990s, cracks began to emerge in the strong annual budget scrutiny process and the strict portfolio budget ceilings. This came in the form of major sectoral initiatives for education, health, child care and the labour market. The 'mini-budgets' and policy announcements outside the regular budget process became more common and had increasingly significant budgetary consequences.

The change of government from Labor to a Liberal–National Coalition in 1996 provided both a change of political philosophy and the opportunity for a new government to reassert control over spending and impose new discipline on fiscal policy. The Howard Coalition government established a National Commission of Audit to review expenditure and public administration aimed at fulfilling their electoral promises for better and more transparent financial management, and to address the '\$10 billion black hole' in the budget allegedly left by their predecessors.

In the early years of the Howard government there were indeed substantial cuts in selected areas of expenditure, notably for certain areas of indigenous affairs, education, social security, health and general public services. The defence budget was shielded from cuts. The early pruning, combined with a commitment to maintaining budget surpluses over the economic cycle, appeared to provide a dividend for fiscal prudence and allowed the government to pay down debts. This created a virtuous cycle of reducing debt and future interest and repayment obligations, allowing the government more latitude to reshape the fiscal environment. The government took the opportunity to capitalize on its positive fiscal reputation to introduce a broad-based consumption tax. This provided the justification to rationalize the tax base and fundamentally to change the basis for fiscal transfers to state and territory governments.

As federal coffers continued to expand due to a combination of strong revenue growth, shrinking debt obligations and habitual conservative revenue and expenditure forecasting by central agencies, the Howard government appeared to lose its appetite for expenditure control. On the contrary, it developed a predilection for seemingly unfettered increases in expenditure with substantial increases in new spending occurring throughout the year, entirely divorced from the discipline of the budget process. Major increases in expenditure on health and family benefits in the new millennium helped to boost total expenditure well beyond the levels of 1996 when the Howard government took over, and increasing faster than the growth in the economy. Spending grew in the last six years of the Howard government by 54 percent (or around 7 percent per annum – often twice the consumer price index). The experience of the Howard government supported the hypothesis that governments are only interested in tight budget controls, savings options and rigorous assessment of new policy proposals in times of fiscal strife.

The so-called 'hunting licence' period in the lead up to the annual budget (which was mostly about looking for final cuts, finalizing bids, or revenue adjustments) became a period of unheralded largesse. Last-minute funding approvals could be gained largely to satisfy various targeted 'demographics' or constituencies. Clearly, government budgeting is a political process about choices and plans, and politics cannot be eliminated from the process. Although growth in level of expenditure has been greatest in the areas of health and social services since 1998, all sectors experienced growth in government expenditure. Reallocation within portfolios and mandatory savings options became the exception for financing new expenditure, in stark contrast to the 1980s. There has been a huge reduction in the 'savings' measures the Howard government imposed: down from over 30 percent in 1997–98 to just 1.5 percent in 2007–08 (Laurie and McDonald 2008: 32).

Politically, the budget process has become far less consolidated than it was in the 1980s. Much slippage has crept in and the resource decision-making process is a far more open and leaky system. The approach to budget management became less about a narrow, annual priority-setting and filtering mechanism and more about regular, high-profile announcements of new initiatives. Budget decisions are now made throughout the year – not consolidated into one round where competing merits can be decided – meaning more decisions are taken outside the budgetary process. The number of budget decisions has increased from 359 in 1997–98 to 825 in 2007–08 (Laurie and McDonald 2008: 31).

FROM SURPLUS BALANCES TO FISCAL DEFICITS

Over the past 22 years Australia has produced 13 annual budgetary surpluses (with two others close to balance depending on which figures are used). Since 2002 surpluses of greater than 1 percent of GDP were achieved every year. At the time surpluses became the single most important acid test of a government's economic credentials (avoiding the 'deficit fetish'). We would argue that budget surpluses were generated by a combination of expenditure discipline (weakening in the last six years of the Howard government) and burgeoning tax receipts (that have shown strong uninterrupted growth since the recession of 1991–93). Tax payments grew by 60 percent from 2001–02 to 2007–08. A significant part of the budgetary success story in Australia is that it is one of the few OECD nations that have chosen not to index taxation rates – meaning that taxes rise through 'bracket creep'. While company tax is a flat rate of profits (30 percent), income taxation is progressive and the rates at which higher tax percentages apply are not indexed to wage or price movements.

In the era of high annual surpluses, governments faced the problem of what to do with such accumulating surplus funds, without overheating the economy. There was a steady succession of annual tax cuts announced with the budget (some multiyear). More significantly, the government sought to 'park' funds in various 'locked box' funds or virtual funds. These foundations (or sovereign funds) were to be used for parking surplus cash from the budget together with other financial assets (part of the government's share ownership of the telecommunications company Telstra). Such funds include the Future Fund (a civil and military pension fund with $60 billion), an education investment fund (with $11 billion) and a health and hospitals fund ($10 billion). Such funds can be managed entirely off-budget (as with the Future Fund), or be locked boxes where only the interest can be used annually. Alternatively, funds can be on-budget so that the principal and interest can be used for in-year approved purposes. The latter type includes the infrastructure, health and education funds which are really budget 'top-up' funds or virtual funds.

The Rudd Labor government came to office in November 2007, initially amid fears of rising inflationary pressure. Revenue was still growing sufficiently for it to introduce its promised tax cuts in 2008. As with its predecessors, the Rudd government's first budget (a mildly expansionary one) displayed a degree of prudence and careful realignment. But within months of this budget – which was premised on massive surpluses – the government along with most other OECD nations fell into deficit. New estimates of sequential deficits were produced first in the MYEFO and then in a special report in early 2009. Two stimulus packages were deliberately introduced in late 2008 and early 2009. The deficit figures were confirmed in the second budget, which included a second round of tax cuts, and provided increases to aged pensioners and for job training. The second budget coming six months into the financial crisis argued that $210 billion had been removed from the budget out-years from reduced tax receipts. Projected accumulated deficits were expected to run to around $300 billion by 2013. Although the Rudd government has greatly trimmed departmental expenses, there was not much evidence of a major reprioritization across government.

The Rudd government continued to operate the off-budget funds. During 2008 it announced the establishment of an additional infrastructure fund – the 'Building Australia Fund' (with a promise of $20 billion for nation-building projects). The government also declared that it would make further additions to these funds, but by early 2009 was forced to make significant payments from these funds as part of its fiscal stimulus. In March 2009 the Future Fund contained $58 billion, the education fund $6.5 billion, the Building Australia Fund $2.5 and the Health Fund $1 billion.

Despite trumpeting their historic surpluses, governments have avoided having their policy outcomes and outputs evaluated. Governments have been reluctant to allow the Auditor-General to audit performance information or comment on the robustness of reporting claims. Only a small number of federal departments and agencies have output-related activities or deliverables – the rest contribute to policy and facilitate funding arrangements. Moreover, intergovernmental transfers largely escape performance review. Intergovernmental transfers are not required to be audited for the performance of those delivering the intended outputs (such as other governments or non-government providers).

THE POLITICS OF THE BUDGET PROCESS

Over the Howard years (1996–2007) government budgeting went from austerity to profligacy. If the overall budget process remained disciplined, the politicians increasingly were not. Howard and his ministers took the view that they had earned a fiscal dividend (based on budget discipline) that allowed them to engage in political expediency and profligacy each year – and especially in the lead-up to elections in 2004 and 2007. They believed that due to the favourable fiscal circumstances, the government could afford to be generous with last-minute funding. The annual senior ministers' review changed its role from being the overarching 'fiscal guardian' to becoming the principal 'fiscal spender'. More than this, policy proposals voted down by the ERC would reappear a few months later through ministerial correspondence and be endorsed by the Prime Minister outside the budget process.

The new Rudd government has retained the ERC and strengthened its resolve to make cuts. It has also established a second cabinet budget committee: the strategic budget committee, consisting of the four most senior ministers. This was because the government had concerns that the ERC only rationed spending proposals rather than taking a more strategic overview of priorities. Although Treasury is leading the government's fiscal policy injections, the Finance Ministry led by Lindsay Tanner is again focusing on technical efficiency and has conducted two rounds of razor-gang reviews of agency spending. But although the government has talked tough it has not made severe cuts or realigned priorities. The new government also retained the separate National Security Committee (NSC) to focus on defence and security spending priorities, separate to the main budget round.

The Department of Finance in recent years has appeared to lose direction and become unsure of its guardian roles. After engineering much of the NPM reform agenda from the mid-1980s to the mid-1990s (see Wanna et al. 1996), Finance became introspective and was unsure how next to act. In the late 1990s it contemplated adopting a supportive, caring posture, working in conjunction with agencies to achieve value (the 'Future of Finance project'), but then abandoned this. It backtracked from its activist and 'bean-counting' roles, releasing its control over the forward estimates process (devolving their construction to agencies) and arguing that ministers would ask for 'green briefs' (costing papers that often provide critical comments on proposals) when they wanted them. It downsized substantially in the late 1990s, shedding many long-term staff whose experience in detailed monitoring of agency estimates was no longer considered necessary (Campbell 2001).

Finance also became more neoliberal and ideological, seeking to respond to the free-market approach proclaimed by the government of the day, by applying it to public administration. It sponsored the compulsory outsourcing of all information technology (IT) across government and urged the government to adopt a fiscal rule of aiming for a surplus every year (not over a three-year cycle) irrespective of the economic conditions.

The government was forced to backtrack on IT outsourcing and did not accept Finance's advice that the government should commit itself to explicit fiscal targets. Finance also spent considerable time internally debating Schick's (1997) OECD paper 'The changing role of the Central Budget Office' and his follow-up 'Does budgeting have a future?' (2001). It sought a role that was distinct from the Treasury's macroeconomic and tax policy advice role, but one that had equal or better standing, as chief financial officer and investment advisor for the whole of government (Wanna and Bartos 2003).

One of the main consequences of this uncertainty was that after its most notable achievement, namely the establishment of an accruals-based, outcome budget framework, Finance was both sidelined and to a large degree dealt itself out of many of the ongoing agendas of Howard government in its second, third and fourth terms (see Campbell 2001). The department appeared to attach less importance to rigorous and confrontational budgetary analysis than to accounting purity. Many long-time budget analysts left the department for other agencies, leaving a hole in the department's collective memory while strengthening the financial skills of line departments. They were often replaced by accountants, many from the private sector. Budgetary analysis units were reduced from 13 to four, and Finance's challenge function became far less effective. Howard and some of his senior ministers were reported to be displeased by the performance of Finance over the introduction of the initial accrual budgets (Kelly and Wanna 2004). The government became so frustrated with the quality of estimates and reporting that it called for a broad review in 2002 which resulted in a significant injection of new funding for Finance and for financial management staff in other departments.

The last three heads of Finance have attempted to steer the department in contrary directions: Steve Sedgwick attempted to make it a management consultant; Peter Boxall attempted to turn it into a merchant banker while pushing selected agendas and investing in accounting expertise; more recently Ian Watt has sought to refocus Finance on its traditional guardian role, tightening up the quality of technical budgetary advice and data analysis. This prolonged identity crisis in the CBA led one official to comment recently: 'Is Finance coming back from the dead, or has it been mortally wounded?' Finance found it difficult to serve a Liberal ministry that was deeply suspicious of its own public service, but has gradually repaired its relations with government. Under Rudd, Finance has again expanded its responsibilities: but mainly in non-budget areas. It is still not back to the proactive and reform leadership role it carved for itself in the 1980s.

The Treasury was also sidelined for many years, staying out of detailed budget allocations and interested primarily in the macroeconomic impacts of the cash budget. It resisted much of the impetus toward accrual budgeting, seeing it as unnecessarily complex and somewhat distorting. It was also overlooked when costing some significant policy measures, leading the secretary Ken Henry to complain of the Treasury being bypassed and hasty announcements leading to bad policy (Henry 2007).

CONCLUSION: THE QUEST TO EVALUATE THE MERITS OF BUDGET REFORM

So, finally, how do we assess the impacts of budget reform in Australia? Arguably, there has been no overall evaluation of the benefits of budget reform, although some local managerialists might argue that a substantial government report into management in the public service (MAB 1992) constituted an extensive review up to that point (see below). There are, however, some partial accounts that attempt to evaluate the impacts of the reforms.

Governments felt obliged even as early as the mid-1980s to present some evaluations of their reform efforts. Triumphalist officials had made some promises and commitments that their budget reform measures would result in better public management and better resource efficiencies. Various audiences (including parliament, the Auditor-General, journalists and academics) became interested in how much progress had been made and whether the reforms had worked. Demands for evaluative information on the achievements of the reforms produced a flurry of reviews in the 1980s and early 1990s. Parliament in particular was most active in calling for reviews of the effectiveness of budgetary reform (possibly because it was receiving less detailed input information in budgetary documentation).

A series of four progress reports on the FMIP were generally positive towards the initiative but remained skeptical as to actual progress. The first two FMIP reports (1986 and 1988) undertaken by the government largely sketched the evolving 'improvement program' as it was considered too early to review performance. The third report by a parliamentary committee entitled *Not Dollars Alone* (Parliament 1990) reported 'weaknesses in execution and implementation'. It argued that there had been improvements in financial management and some in general management, but that savings to the budget were impossible to quantify and it could not form a balanced view on whether service delivery improvements had been achieved (1990: 119–21).

The fourth and most substantial evaluation report already mentioned, called 'The Australian public service reformed: an evaluation of a decade of management reform' (MAB 1992) was conducted by an interagency taskforce on management improvement. It conducted extensive surveys of public service staff across a range of management topics. The review noted that an overall assessment of the reforms was problematic, but generally found strong executive support for the budgetary and financial management reforms while admitting that administrative staff often felt that the quality of services had been compromised by the reforms. This government report was written by a team of managerialists and sanctioned, though heavily edited and reworked, by senior officials.

In 1998, the JCPA commenced a review of the Department of Finance as a central resource manager in the context of devolved financial management, but although submissions were collected – some positive and some critical – this review was never completed. Other parliamentary committees subsequently conducted detailed reviews of specific financial and budgetary changes such as the 'efficiency dividend' imposition and the 'running costs arrangements'. But they were only focused on particular reform instruments, not on the whole edifice of reform. The first report (HRSCBFPA 1994) on the 'efficiency dividend' noted it was important as a cost-containment measure but argued it was inappropriate for small agencies. The second on the 'running costs arrangements' (HRSCBFPA 1995) argued that one-line budgets provided flexibility for service delivery but that running costs were continuing to grow. Further reports by the parliament have already been mentioned

Further evaluation of the budgetary system was then deferred while the new accruals, outcome-based approach was designed and implemented. After the first iteration of the new framework, Finance and the Treasury invited Michael Vertigan (from the Victorian Treasury) to conduct a review and to sort out a clash of institutional roles between the two CBAs. His report (Vertigan 1999), while supportive of the direction of change, was nevertheless critical of the 'crash-through' implementation process (see Wanna and Kelly 2004).

External assessments have been at best episodic and addressed to selected topics. The Australian Auditor-General (unlike the Canadian) has not conducted an overall inquiry into the merits of the budgetary system or budget performance, but did undertake a one-off investigation into the accuracy of central budgetary estimates which found a high degree of accuracy (ANAO 1999). This particular review was very contentious in Finance and the department initially did not wish to cooperate with the investigation. The Australian National Audit Office regularly conducts performance audits (50–60 per annum) on programs and agencies which expose strengths and weaknesses of program and financial management. It has also conducted three performance audits on performance information which reported to the Parliament in 2002, 2004 and 2007. Those audits all highlighted the widespread weakness in the quality of agency performance measures and reporting, particularly for outcomes. The Auditor-General has also on occasion chosen to investigate whether proposed savings measures have been realized in budgetary outcomes (for example, the review of the cost-effectiveness of the outsourcing of IT). Occasionally, too, academics have reviewed and commented on progress, but they remain a small group of scholars. In particular, works by Forster and Wanna (1990), Weller (1991), Zifcak (1994), Uhr (1991, 1996), Wanna et al. (2000), Wanna and Bartos (2003), Kelly and Wanna (2004) and Wanna (2006) provide commentary on the progress of reform initiatives. While there is no overall consensus on the reform project per se, there is much analysis and commentary on its various aspects.

More recently, four relatively critical assessments have appeared in close proximity that may galvanize commitment to introduce a further series of reforms. These are the ALP's Operation Sunlight (Tanner 2006), an assessment by Wanna (2007), Senator Murray's report (2008) and an OECD country report into Australian budgetary practice (Blondal et al. 2008). These assessments all made similar criticisms: the outcomes and outputs framework is too vague; the government's performance in achieving outcomes was inchoate; there are problems with multiple accounting standards; some aspects of accrual budgeting are unwarranted (for example, the appropriation of cash for non-cash items such as depreciation was described as 'peculiar'); the intergenerational data produced is not linked to the budget processes; and principles of sound fiscal management were open to political manipulation. In 2008 the Rudd government announced its commitment to address many of these critical aspects. If it does, Australia may once again become a pioneer; if it does not, Australia will be confined within the decorative architecture of previous reform efforts while the foundations remain in need of repair.

NOTES

1. See *Labor and Quality of Government* (ALP 1983); *Budgetary Reform* (Australian Government 1984); National Commission of Audit (1996) and *Operation Sunlight* [2007]. All these position papers contained intentional statements of budgetary reform, and some were implemented in the immediate years, but many of their principles or suggestions were later discarded or ignored. The Rudd government's 2008 announcement of its intentions to introduce a list of reform measures contained in Operation Sunlight but time will tell whether it will be true to its word.
2. For further details on Australia's budgetary reforms see: Wanna et al. (2000) and Wanna and Bartos (2003).

3. Section 53 of the Commonwealth of Australia Constitution Act 1901.
4. Australian Government (2008), *Portfolio Budget Statements* 2008–09, various, May, Canberra.
5. The High Court of Australia confirmed that departmental appropriations are not confined to individual outcomes in its reasons for the judgment on *Combet* v *Commonwealth* in 2005.
6. Australian Government (2008), *Portfolio Budget Statement 2008-09: Health and Ageing Portfolio, Budget related paper no.1.10*, May, Canberra.
7. Subject to consultation with their policy minister for outcomes, outputs and performance measures, and to approval by the Minister for Finance and Deregulation for outcomes.
8. The guidance is only available on the Internet at: www.finance.gov.au/budgetgroup/Commonwealth_Budget_-_Overview/the_outcomes_outputs_framewo.html, accessed June, 2008.
9. An output group is a collection of related outputs that contribute to the same outcome. It is a classification used by many agencies to consolidate and simplify reporting.
10. The laws which set out the responsibilities of agency chief executives are the Financial Management and Accountability Act 1997 and the Commonwealth Authorities and Companies Act 1997.

REFERENCES

ALP (1983), *Labor and Quality of Government*, Canberra: ALP.

ANAO (1999), 'Management of Commonwealth budgetary processes', audit report no 38, 1998–99.

ANAO (2006), 'Application of the outcomes and outputs framework', audit report, no 23, 2006–07.

Australian Government (1983), *Reforming the Australian Public Service*, Canberra: AGPS.

Australian Government (1984), *Budgetary Reform*, Canberra: AGPS.

Barrett, P. (1988), 'Emerging management and budgetary issues: the view from the centre', *Canberra Bulletin of Public Administration*, **54** (May), 52–6.

Barton, A. (2006), 'Sense and nonsense in government accrual accounting and budgetary systems', in B.S. Grewal and M. Kumnick (eds), *Engaging the New World: Responses to the Knowledge Economy*, Melbourne: Melbourne University Press, pp. 557–70.

Blondal, J., D. Bergvall, I. Hawkesworth and R. Deighton-Smith (2008), 'Budgeting in Australia', *OECD Journal on Budgeting*, **8** (2), 1–64.

Campbell, C. 2001. 'Juggling inputs, outputs and outcomes in the search for policy competence: recent experience in Australia', *Governance*, **14** (2), 253–82.

Chan, M., M. Nizette, L. La Rance, C. Broughton and D. Russell (2002), 'Australia', *OECD Journal on Budgeting*, **1** (4), 35–69.

Department of Finance and Administration (DoFA) (1998), *Specifying Outcomes and Outputs: Implementing the Commonwealth's Accrual-based Outcomes and Outputs Framework*, Canberra: DoFA.

DoFA (2001), *Australia's Outcomes and Outputs Framework*, May, Canberra: DoFA.

Forster, J. and J. Wanna (1990), *Budgetary Management and Control*, Melbourne: Macmillan.

Financial Management Improvement Program (FMIP) (1986), *Report*, Canberra: AGPS.

FMIP (1988), *Report*, Canberra: AGPS.

Hawke, L. (2008), 'Production and quality of information for performance budgeting: the Australian case', paper presented at the International Conference on Performance Budgeting, Mexico City, Mexico, 9–10 June.

Henry, K. (2007), 'Treasury's effectiveness in the current environment', speech to Treasury staff, 14 March.

House of Representatives Standing Committee on Banking, Finance and Public Administration (HRSCBFPA) (1994), *Stand and Deliver*, Canberra: AGPS.

HRSCBFPA (1995), *Keeping the Customer Satisfied*, Canberra: AGPS.

International Monetary Fund (IMF) (1999), *Code of Good Practices on Fiscal Transparency*, Washington, DC: IMF.

Joint Committee of Public Accounts and Audit (JCPAA) (2002), 'Review of accrual budgeting documentation', June, Canberra: Australian Parliament.

Keating, M. (1990), 'The processes of Commonwealth budgetary control', in J. Forster and J. Wanna (eds), *Budgetary Management and Control*, Melbourne, Macmillan, pp. 1–16.

Keating, M. and G. Dixon (1989), *Making Economic Policy in Australia, 1983–1988*, Melbourne: Longman Cheshire.

Keating, M. and M. Holmes (1990), 'Australia's budgetary and financial management reforms', *Governance*, **3** (2), 168–85.

Kelly, J. and J. Wanna (2001), 'Are Wildavsky's guardians and spenders still relevant? New Public Management and the politics of government budgeting', in L. Jones, J. Guthrie and P. Steane (eds), *Learning From International Public Management Reform*, Amsterdam: Elsevier Science.

Laurie, K. and J. McDonald (2008), 'A perspective on trends in Australian government spending', Canberra: Commonwealth Treasury.

Management Advisory Board (MAB) (1992), 'The Australian public service reformed: an evolution of a decade of management reform', report by the Task Force on Management Improvement, Management Advisory Board, Canberra: AGPS.

MAB (1997), *Beyond Bean-Counting: Effective Financial Management in the APS – 1998 and Beyond*, Canberra: MAB.

Murray, A., Senator (2008), *Review of Operation Sunlight: Overhauling Budgetary Transparency*, Canberra: Senate, pp. 1–133.

National Commission of Audit (NCA) (1996), *Report of the Commission*, Canberra: AGPS.

Organisation for Economic Co-operation and Development (OECD) (2001), 'OECD best practices for budget transparency', May, Paris: OECD.

O'Faircheallaigh, C., J. Wanna and P. Weller (1999), *Public Sector Management in Australia*, Melbourne: Macmillan.

Parliament of Australia (1990), *Not Dollars Alone*, review of the Financial Management Improvement Program, report of the House of Representatives Standing Committee on Finance and Public Administration.

Parliament of Australia (1995), *Financial Reporting for the Commonwealth: Towards Greater Transparency and Accountability*, report by the Joint Committee of Public Accounts, November, Canberra: Australian Parliament.

Parliament of Australia (1998), *Charter of Budget Honesty Bill 1996*, Bills Digest no 142 1997–98, Canberra: Parliamentary Library.

Reid, J. (1983), *Review of Commonwealth Administration*, Canberra: AGPS.
Schick, A. (1997), 'The changing role of the central budget office', OECD discussion paper (OECD/GD 97/109, Paris; also (2001), *OECD Journal on Budgeting*, **1** (1) 9–26.
Schick, A. (2001), 'Does budgeting have a future?' paper presented to 22nd meeting of Senior Budget Officials, Paris, OECD/SBO 2001/4; also (2002), *OECD Journal on Budgeting*, **2** (2).
Senate Standing Committee on Finance and Public Administration (2007), *Transparency and Accountability of Commonwealth Public Funding and Expenditure*, March, Canberra: Australian Parliament.
Tanner, L. (2006), *Operation Sunlight: Enhancing Budget Transparency*, Canberra: ALP.
Uhr, J. (1991), *Program Evaluation*, Federalism Research Centre, Canberra: ANU.
Uhr, J. (1996), 'Testing the policy capacities of budgetary agencies: lessons from finance', *Australian Journal of Public Administration*, **55** (4), 124–34.
Vertigan, M. (1999), *Review of Budget Estimates Production Arrangements*, July, Canberra: Australian Government.
Walsh, P. (1995), *Confessions of a Failed Finance Minister*, Sydney: Random House.
Wanna, J. (2006), 'Between a rock and a hard place: the nonsense of Australia's Charter of Budget Honesty Act 1998', paper to the Australasian Political Studies Association conference, Newcastle, NSW.
Wanna, J. (2007), 'Through a glass darkly: the vicissitudes of budgetary reform in Australia', Annual CPA Lecture, Canberra.
Wanna, J. and S. Bartos (2003), 'Good practice: does it work in theory? Australia's quest for better outcomes', in J. Wanna, L. Jensen and J. De Vries (eds), *Controlling Public Expenditure*, Cheltenham UK and Northampton, MA, USA: Edward Elgar.
Wanna, J. and J. Kelly (2004), 'Crashing through with accrual-output price budgeting in Australia', *The American Review of Public Administration*, **34** (1), 99–111.
Wanna, J., L. Jensen and J. de Vries (2003), *Controlling Public Expenditure*, Cheltenham, UK and Northampton, MA, USA: Edward Elgar.
Wanna, J, J. Kelly and J. Forster (1996), 'The rise and rise of the Department of Finance', *The Canberra Bulletin of Public Administration*, **82**, 53–62.
Wanna, J., J. Kelly and J. Forster (2000), *Managing Public Expenditure in Australia*, Sydney: Allen & Unwin.
Weller, P. (1991), 'Financial management reforms in Australia', *Canberra Bulletin of Public Administration*, **67**, 9–17.
Zifcak, S. (1994), *New Managerialism: Administrative Reform in Whitehall and Canberra*, Buckingham: Open University Press.

5. Discerning the consequences and integrity of Canada's budget reforms: a story of remnants and resilience

David A. Good and Evert A. Lindquist

Describing and capturing the essence of budget reform is not easy. Each budget reform is often a reaction to the failings of the previous reform. Yesterday's reforms become today's practices and today's practices become tomorrow's problems. What was promised in reform announcements rarely gets implemented in practice. Indeed, the reality of budget reform is a 'slippery and fluid phenomenon' (Lindquist and White 1994). Understanding the intentions of reform, what gets done, and what was achieved requires time and perspective, and appreciation of the flow and legacy of previous reforms.

When Canadian officials from the budget office meet annually with their counterparts from the 30 member countries of the Organisation for Economic Co-operation and Development (OECD), they talk about the 'functions of the budget office'. Using the latest language, they reflect on 'the role of fiscal rules', 'the political economy of reallocation' and 'budgeting and managing for performance' (OECD 2003). Indeed, as Schick (1997) explains: 'all budget systems – reformed and traditional – have three basic budget objectives: (i) to maintain aggregate fiscal discipline, (ii) to allocate resources in accord with government priorities, and (iii) to promote the efficient delivery of services' (see also Allen and Tommasi 2001). Part of the story about budget reform in Canada is the changing relative importance of these objectives to government and the changing ways governments have gone about pursuing them.

This chapter reviews Canadian experience with various budget reforms and assesses their effects on budget outcomes and process. The story of Canadian federal budget reform is one of reforms and remnants, and of reaction and resilience – reaction to, rather than anticipation of, emerging problems and situations, and resilience and flexibility to cope with the uncertainty of external shocks and internal tensions. The chapter starts with a brief history of the trajectory of budget reforms and their remnants from the early 1960s to the early 2000s. It then examines more disparate recent reforms since 2003. Unlike previous reforms, these have not been designed or promulgated as an integrated package, but comprise the following elements: a strong commitment to a balanced budget or better; prudence in economic and fiscal forecasting; extensive year-end budgeting; budgeting from the center of government, controlled by the Prime Minister and the Minister of Finance; limited administrative and operational reviews and reallocation; the strengthening of financial watchdogs; and a proliferation of departmental and whole-of-government performance reporting.

In Canada the budget process and its outcomes have typically been explained as a simple bilateral relationship between departmental spenders and central guardians (the Department of Finance and Treasury Board Secretariat). But in recent years the budgetary process has evolved into a more complex multilateral relationship involving not only spenders and guardians, but also priority-setters (the Prime Minister's Office and the Privy Council Office) and financial watchdogs (the Office of the Auditor General) (Good 2007). Budget reforms and their impacts will be analysed with respect to the evolving relationship among these four budget players.

BUDGET REFORMS AND REMNANTS IN CANADA: A BRIEF HISTORY

While it is difficult to build a coherent picture of recent budget reforms, it is easy to define four previous reform periods in Canadian budgeting:

1. 'rational' reform: the road to program budgeting (1960s–1978);
2. the 'grand design': policy and expenditure management system (1979–83);
3. incremental and evolving change (1984–93); and
4. 'Program Review' and prudent budgeting (1994–2003).

The literature has done a good job of reviewing Canadian budgetary reform over these periods, but there is insufficient appreciation of the extent to which some of these reforms anchor Canada's budget system to this day, and how the style of launching budget reform has changed. Many of the reforms successively emphasized different facets of budgeting, which remain relevant to this day.

All these eras of reform had distinct and clear beginnings, often occasioned by change in government or party leadership and usually trumpeted with high-profile announcements along with a label. As these reforms were put in place they displaced some elements of older reforms, but remnants persisted. Some provided platforms for further reforms, and other more transitory initiatives were brushed aside in the latest sweep of change. The triggers of reform stemmed from dissatisfaction with budgetary outcomes, the budgetary process and sometimes both. Guardians can become dissatisfied but so too can spenders, priority-setters and financial watchdogs. With a weak tradition of parliamentary scrutiny of expenditures, the trigger is ultimately in the hands of the Prime Minister, supported by the Minister of Finance and, on occasion, the President of the Treasury Board.

All the reforms were complex and multifaceted, often followed by mini-reforms that typically, but not always, re-enforced the original intent of the reform. Some reforms were comprehensive, others more cursory. Some have been more theoretical and planned, while others were practical reactions to pressing and immediate crises of the government of the day. In contrast to their inception, most reforms do not have distinct endings: they either faded away or were superseded in the fanfare accompanying newer reforms.

THE LURE OF PROGRAM BUDGETING: THROUGH TO THE LATE 1970s

Like several OECD countries, the Canadian government embraced the program budgeting approach by adopting the Planning, Programming, and Budgeting System (PPBS) in the late 1960s and early 1970s. Since Confederation in 1867, the federal government relied entirely on line-item budgeting, focusing on costs and controls, and with budget requests and allocations to departments made on the basis of standard objects of expenditure. These included tangible items like salaries and wages, postage, telephones, travel expenses, materials and supplies, and repairs and upkeep. There was no need to relate expenditures to program objectives, the services produced or results achieved. Cash line-item budgeting was simple, readily understandable to politicians and the public. The budget process was sustained by a system for recording and reporting expenditures and outstanding commitments, and included elaborate controls on financial inputs and detailed administrative procedures. The overall system was centrally driven by the Office of the Comptroller of the Treasury.

In 1966 the Treasury Board was given responsibility for managing the government's expenditure budget and formally separated from the Department of Finance. This established a new institutional foundation for expenditure management and control with its Secretariat consisting of two influential branches: the Program Branch, responsible for budget analysis and advice on departmental expenditure levels; and the Planning Branch, responsible for program evaluation and performance measurement. Together, they implemented PPBS through a set of rational tools: the setting of program objectives; systematic analysis to clarify objectives and assess alternative ways to achieve them; framing the budgetary programs to achieve objectives; future projections of program costs; plans for the year-by-year achievement of programs; and information by program to monitor the achievement of objectives and to reassess those objectives and programs. Policy and expenditure decisions were separated, with the cabinet committees theoretically deciding on the programs (what should be done) and Treasury Board deciding the expenditures (how much should be provided).

In 1968, a newly elected Prime Minister Trudeau created and chaired a cabinet committee on priorities and planning to determine government priorities, establish the fiscal framework (on the advice of the Minister of Finance), and ensure implementation of the government's plans and priorities. In 1970, the Treasury Board introduced 'A–B–X' budgets to support the PPBS program review function.[1] This became the overall framework around which departments and agencies formulated budget requests and the Treasury Board reviewed them, with the support of the Department of Finance.

PPBS attempted to shift the focus on interactions between spenders and guardians from the specifics of line-item budgets (inputs like pencils and paperclips) to the goals of program budgets (the outputs or results of surface transportation, fisheries management, military equipment and employment development). The main idea was that: 'what comes out of a program is more important than what went into it'. Coupled with this was the belief that guardians had become too strong and intrusive, using line-item budgeting to 'micro-manage' budgets. For guardians, PPBS offered the prospect of more rational policy and expenditure decisions, and for spenders, the promise of 'letting the managers manage', since it relied on information that could only come from departments and agencies (Royal Commission on Government Organization 1962).

PPBS fostered a clear division of labor between spending and guardian roles. The need to relate expenditures to programs encouraged more interaction between the Treasury Board program analysts and program administrators in spending departments. However, the enormous volume of individual programs and their complexity meant that ministers became less involved over time, usually deferring to the recommendations of officials on the size of program budgets.

PPBS worked well for spenders, but not guardians. Early on the process was largely bottom-up, focusing on allocating expenditures rather than determining and limiting fiscal aggregates, or ensuring prudent financial management. Spender and guardian interactions focused on individual programs with bargaining taking place over budgets and the exchanges over information. Spenders traded program information to secure program budgets and guardians attempted to control individual program expenditure totals, assuming this would control overall government expenditures.

Yet, total government expenditures increased significantly over time, at a rate higher than growth in the economy. To make matters worse for guardians, the government announced a major and far-reaching decision in the pre-election budget of 1974 to index the personal income tax system to adjust automatically to increases in inflation. Previously 'the Treasury' benefited from inflation since individuals were automatically bumped into higher tax brackets, providing a regular 'fiscal dividend'. This did not produce smaller deficits, but made it easier for governments to find additional revenue to fund new spending or meet the costs of increasing public debt. The government also indexed to inflation its major social transfer payments to individuals, putting additional pressure on its expenditure budget. Statutory appropriations increased significantly,[2] at a rate higher than the growth in overall spending.

The Auditor General of Canada (1976) brought public attention to the rapid growth in public expenditures through a rhetorical declaration in his annual report that 'parliament and indeed the government has lost, or is close to losing, effective control of the public purse'. This paved the way in 1977 for significantly strengthening the role of the financial watchdog through far-reaching amendments to the Auditor General's Act and a legislative basis for 'value-for-money audits' (now called performance audits). This ushered in a new era of independent performance reviews of departmental management and programs by the Auditor General, ostensibly as an agent of parliament. The Office of the Comptroller General was established in 1978 to strengthen financial management and program evaluation within government.

Guardians in government also struggled to strengthen the expenditure decision-making process of cabinet and ensure that government expenditures would increase no more rapidly than gross domestic product (GDP) growth. Previously new spending initiatives were generally first considered by cabinet committees with little regard to expenditure, then considered by cabinet and, only after that, referred to Treasury Board for resource considerations. The government introduced the 'Treasury Board referral system' to ensure that spending proposals be reviewed by Treasury Board prior to consideration by cabinet.

Finally, Prime Minister Pierre Trudeau launched a surprise government-wide \$2.5 billion expenditure reduction exercise in the summer of 1978. The 'Guns of August' initiative sought to keep growth in government spending in line with GDP increases. The Treasury Board, with the support of the priority-setters in the Privy Council Office, managed this budget-cutting exercise. Unlike the bargaining and negotiation between spenders and guardians under PPBS, there was no discussion and negotiation with departments and agencies: Treasury Board guardians focused on the most expeditious way to achieve expenditure savings, recognizing that priorities had little to do with the exercise of securing immediate and significant savings.

Extensive interaction between spenders and guardians over programs did not lead to controlled spending but, rather, to spending becoming out of control. Controlling the parts did not guarantee control of the total. When it came to budgeting, the whole was indeed more than the sum of its parts. Process discipline at the bottom was not translating into aggregate discipline. It was time to explore new approaches to expenditure management.

PEMS: THE 'GRAND DESIGN' OF THE EARLY 1980s

The Policy and Expenditure Management System (PEMS), established in 1980, marked a significant and innovative budgetary reform, lauded by international practitioners and students of budgeting.[3] Unlike PPBS, PEMS was not a separate budget reform designed and developed by the Finance and Treasury Board guardians in isolation from ministerial decision-making. Instead, it was developed as an integral part of the cabinet decision-making process and carried the weight and support of Prime Minister Trudeau.

Under PEMS the cabinet committee on priorities and planning, chaired by the Prime Minister, established a multiyear fiscal framework and ten budget envelopes. Five cabinet committees were each responsible for managing two budget envelopes. PEMS sought to have cabinet committees focus on expenditure implications of new proposals in particular policy sectors, freeing up the Priorities and Planning Committee to concentrate on top government priorities like the constitution, energy and the economy.

Not only did PEMS deal with direct expenditures but it also sought to integrate decisions on tax expenditures in the envelope budget system. As part of the 'rules of the game', the tax expenditures and off-budget financing (loans, loan guarantees and advances) of departments and agencies were taken into account when establishing envelope levels. For a few years this led to broader analysis and consideration of tax expenditure estimates by the Department of Finance and the Ministries of State, which supported the policy committees of cabinet, and by relevant spending departments. For a brief time spenders made fewer demands on Finance for tax expenditures and the Minister of Finance made fewer unilateral tax expenditure announcements.

On paper, as reflected in the 'rules of the game', the system appeared considerably more integrated. In practice there were four distinct subsystems operating, searching for overall coordination. These four subsystems and their institutional leaders, still in evidence today, were: macroeconomic management (Finance), major government priorities (Privy Council Office), ongoing expenditure management (Treasury Board) and new expenditure management (at the time, Ministries of State in support of cabinet committees) (van Loon 1983). These subsystems were momentarily linked for a brief period in 1981–82.

To implement PEMS, departments and agencies prepared Multi-Year Operational Plans (MYOPs) that set out the ongoing costs of existing programs for review by the Treasury Board. Departments and agencies prepared strategic overviews setting out the policy rationale and expenditures for new initiatives for consideration by cabinet committees. The Office of the Comptroller General (Treasury Board of Canada 1981) promoted program evaluation and published an ambitious guide to ensure that departments and agencies 'systematically gather[ed] verifiable information on programs and demonstrable evidence on their results and cost-effectiveness', and 'periodically produce[d] credible, timely, useful and objective findings on programs appropriate for resource allocation, program improvement and accountability'. However, in a time of overall government expenditure growth, program evaluation proved to have little effect on individual program expenditures.

By 1983, PEMS showed acute signs of strain. The promises of maintaining limits at the top, of linking sector priorities and budgetary envelopes at the middle, and of ensuring effective program evaluation at the bottom were not being achieved. Cabinet committees could not achieve political consensus to make real and significant savings to fund new programs. Spending ministers were just that: spenders, not guardians. When it came to allocating new money to priority sectors, the Minister of Finance was increasingly unprepared to make broad allocations by sector and leave ministers in cabinet committees to determine precise allocations to departments and programs. Instead, the Minister of Finance began earmarking new money in envelopes specifically for particular programs, departments and ministers. These 'special allocations' or 'side deals' soon evolved into 'regular allocations'. They undercut the role of cabinet committees in making allocations within their sectors and budgetary envelopes, and reduced the influence of ministers chairing the policy committees and the role of the priorities and planning committee in determining overall sector allocations.

There were increasing concerns about the large, expensive and elaborate organizational structures of the two Ministries of State (for Social Development and for Economic and Regional Development) and the 'mirror committees' of deputy ministers, which supported the 'system' and two major policy committees of cabinet. Finally, ministers were wasting enormous amounts of time participating in cabinet committee and other meetings only to learn that important priority and expenditure decisions were quietly made elsewhere; through some combination of the Prime Minister, the Minister of Finance, the Priorities and Planning Committee, or an inner circle of influential ministers.

PEMS did not provide the means for a spending-inclined government to establish and maintain fixed limits on overall expenditures. Budgeting systems cannot achieve what political will is unprepared to do. During 1979–84, real growth in expenditures outstripped real growth in the economy. Inflationary pressures intensified, interest rates skyrocketed to an unprecedented level of 19.5 percent, and an increasingly large portion of total expenditures went to pay the interest on a rapidly growing public debt. Deficits increased each year. The government regularly forecasted a balanced budget in the projected fifth year of its fiscal framework, but never came close to achieving it: each year a significant upward adjustment was made to the framework.

Guardians were not so much overwhelmed by new spenders as by past spenders whose expenditure programs were tightly entrenched through a combination of established legislative and political commitments and inflationary expectations, which could not be easily reduced even in the face of a dramatic and worsening economic situation. The promise of regaining expenditure control at the envelope and sector level proved impossible to achieve in the face of what was required – a significant and major reduction of expenditures – to remain within projected overall limits. The limits were not fixed targets to stay within, but rather planned ceilings that could be adjusted upward.

PEMS with its elaborate cabinet machinery and decision-making process did, however, allow Prime Minister Trudeau to devolve certain issues 'down and out'. Such issues could be dealt with by others while allowing him and a smaller inner circle of ministers and advisors to focus on the two dominant priorities of the day: national unity, including the patriation of the Constitution and establishment of the Charter of Rights and Freedoms; and the national energy program. Pushing things 'down and out' meant that policy committees, armed with the Ministry of State assessment reports, invariably sharply critical of any increased spending, could scrutinize the spending proposals of their fellow colleagues. To be sure, 'a few butterflies were caught, but no elephants were stopped' (Wildavsky 1974: Chapter 14), and the only major reallocation was an amount of $150 million put forward by a new and inexperienced minister responsible for housing.

PEMS was premised on fixed expenditure limits at the top in order to force policy committees of cabinet to make choices and trade-offs within expenditure envelopes at the sector level. When limits proved flexible and adjustable, sometimes through significant changes in the macroeconomy, and at other times through 'side deals' on expenditure increases between the Minister of Finance and a spending minister, the incentives to undertake difficult decisions involving nasty trade-offs within expenditure envelopes quickly disappeared. PEMS strengthened the budgetary role of priority-setters in the Privy Council Office and the Prime Minister's Office and marked the beginning of a formal fiscal and economics unit in the Privy Council Office to advise the Prime Minister on the budget. It also signaled and acknowledged the reinstatement of a major program policy role for the Department of Finance as it made more allocations directly to departments and agencies when establishing sector-wide envelope levels. The role and influence of the Treasury Board and its Secretariat waned as it focused less on new expenditure initiatives and more on adjustments to the base of approved departmental spending. It also tracked expenditure commitments made by policy committees, the Minister of Finance or Treasury Board, on the policy, program, statutory and operating reserves.

To many, the highly formalized structure of PEMS with its supporting cast of institutions and mirror committees looked too heavy and its accomplishments too light. The system was cumbersome and time-consuming especially for ministers.

INCREMENTAL AND EVOLVING CHANGE: MID-1980S TO MID-1990s

The election of the Mulroney Conservative government in September 1984 signaled a time for policy change. The day after taking office, Prime Minister Brian Mulroney launched a high-profile budget initiative: a government-wide expenditure review led by the Deputy Prime Minister, Erik Nielsen, but relying on external input from 19 joint working groups comprised of private sector leaders and senior public servants.

In expectation of positive results from this expenditure review, and with visible and seemingly strong support from the Prime Minister, the Finance Minister crafted his first budget (May 1985). It featured an expenditure reduction target of $15 billion by 1990–91.

Within days, however, the government was under intense pressure from senior citizens about the impact of the budget. On the front lawn of Parliament Hill, the Prime Minister reversed the Minister of Finance's budget cuts to pension benefits, declaring that his government would not break its 'sacred trust' with seniors.[4] This decision encapsulated the Mulroney government's approach to expenditure management: ducking the hard decisions while embracing a series of incremental and gradual adjustments – some temporary and others more lasting – to cope with escalating budget pressures.

When the expenditure review was completed in 1986, the cabinet received an extensive menu of direct expenditure cuts as well as tax expenditure reductions and eliminations of nearly $8 billion. They included eliminating subsidies to agriculture, fisheries, transportation, business and regional development, bolstered by evidence that the federal government was 'giving with both hands' – direct expenditures as well as tax expenditures. The proposals had significant regional implications, especially divisive and sensitive for a cabinet molded from strong regional interests. The government was not prepared to generate more conflict and did not implement any major recommendations.

From 1986 to 1993, expenditure management reforms were decidedly incremental, relying on a 'carrot and stick' approach and minimizing budget conflict. The carrots, building upon the Glassco mantra of 'let the managers manage', included several government-wide initiatives intended to provide departmental flexibility, authority and efficiency, and improve accountability and performance.[5] The major initiatives included: the Increased Ministerial Authority and Accountability initiative designed to strengthen departmental authority; single operating budgets for departments to increase flexibility between salary and operating budgets; elimination of person-year controls on departments; a carry-forward to the following year of up to 5 percent of departments' budgets for operating expenditures; increased retention for departments of funds raised from cost recovery; and some additional flexibility in deploying human resources. Eliminating person-year controls, to increase flexibility and efficiency in departments, negatively affected the Treasury Board Secretariat. Not only did it have less information on key aspects of departmental operations, but it had less leverage over program design.

The 'stick' was not 'big', nor did it carry the weight of the Prime Minister. Instead it was a series of little sticks, applied continuously by the

Treasury Board through centrally directed across-the-board expenditure reductions to departmental operations and programs (Savoie 1990). The reductions, sometimes dressed up as extracting a 'productivity dividend', were based upon the simple and easy-to-implement rule of 'equal sacrifice' for all. This significantly reduced budget conflict among ministers and increased the certainty that expenditure reductions, although small, would be achieved. The consequences, however, were significant and far-reaching. Information exchanges dramatically declined between spenders and guardians, and so did the quality and quantity of program and expenditure information flowing to the center and the analytic capacity of the Treasury Board Secretariat. With an increasingly uncertain economy, the five-year fiscal projections became less credible: each year the deficit was substantially higher than forecasted. Unexpected spikes in interest rates dramatically exacerbated the fiscal situation, increasing expenditure of which well over one-third went to finance the growth in public debt. Meanwhile, 'across-the-board' cuts significantly reduced the government's ability to deliver programs. An expenditure review committee of cabinet, chaired by the Deputy Prime Minister, had limited success in dealing with a few expenditure pressures, but did not curtail the growth in spending nor the ballooning deficit and debt.

As expenditures became more difficult to manage, the government shifted its focus to government organization. In 1993, Minister Robert de Cotret, a former president of the Treasury Board, undertook a major review of the organization and machinery of government at the request of Prime Minister Mulroney. The focus was on options for streamlining operations by reorganizing government departments and rationalizing or eliminating government agencies, boards and commissions. In June 1993, Mulroney's successor, Prime Minister Kim Campbell, announced a major reorganization that included: reducing the number of cabinet ministers from 40 to 24; eliminating many small departments and agencies; merging departments to create large departments such as Human Resources Development Canada and Industry Canada; folding the Office of the Comptroller General into the Treasury Board Secretariat; and developing 'ministerial portfolios' that clustered departments, agencies and commissions in order to encourage greater horizontal coordination.

This reorganization reduced the number of spenders, but did not strengthen the role of guardians, watchdogs or priority-setters. The Treasury Board continued to show confusion over its new role. Eliminating the Comptroller General's office meant that financial management watchdogs in departments and agencies had less influence and status. Finance had to deal with powerful spenders in the enlarged and newly established 'mega' departments of Industry Canada and Human Resources

Development Canada (HRDC), and priority-setters in the Privy Council and the Prime Minister's offices continued to support spenders over guardians. In a nutshell, spenders and their allies had become too strong and guardians and their allies too weak. There was a growing need to strike a new and more fundamental balance.

'PROGRAM REVIEW' – MAKING REAL BUDGET CUTS: MID-1990s TO 2003

Program Review was the flagship of the budget reforms of the Chrétien government, culminating in the 1995 budget that unveiled significantly restructured programs and dramatic expenditure reductions (Aucoin and Savoie 1998). In October 1993, the Liberal government announced its intention to reduce the ballooning deficit 'step by step', consistent with an election campaign commitment to reduce the deficit to 3 percent of GDP ($25 billion from a level of $42 billion). In the February 1994 budget, Finance Minister Paul Martin promised to 'review all government spending' and announced that Minister Marcel Massé would lead the Program Review exercise. It was broadly assumed that part of the savings would be used to fund new priorities, but by May 1994 Martin and his department knew, based upon the negative reaction to the February budget, that all expenditure savings would go to meet the deficit-reduction target.

The Privy Council Office structured the review process and identified five tests for agencies to use in reviewing programs.[6] Reflecting the seriousness of the fiscal situation and the strong need for guardianship, the Deputy Minister of Finance added the 'affordability test' comprising two questions: is the resultant package of programs and activities affordable within the fiscal constraint? If not, what programs or activities should be abandoned? These six tests underpinned a subsequent government-wide review of this work by a specially created steering committee of deputy ministers, chaired by the Clerk of the Privy Council, and the coordinating group of ministers, chaired by Minister Massé.

The Minister of Finance and his officials set notional targets for each department broadly divided into three categories: very significant reductions over 50 percent (for example, in Transport Canada); substantial reductions of about 25 percent for many departments; and smaller reductions of less than 15 percent. In the fall 1994 Economic and Fiscal Update, Martin committed publicly that 'come hell or high water' the government would achieve its target of reducing the deficit to 3 percent of the GDP ($25 billion) in the upcoming 1995 budget. The Prime Minister strongly and visibly supported his Finance Minister: special pleading for adjustments by powerful spending ministers were turned back to the cabinet committee, under strict instructions from the Prime Minister to ensure that if any relief was provided to any minister then that minister had to offset the increase elsewhere in their portfolio. In addition, all requests for new spending were immediately and flatly refused. Fears of how the Mexican peso crisis in late 1994 might negatively affect the Canadian economy strengthened the resolve of the guardians to restructure programs and achieve significant expenditure savings. Guardians now had the strong and visible support of the priority-setters, and they worked arm-in-arm against the spenders.

In parallel with increasing public anxiety about the size of government deficits and the ever-expanding costs of servicing a ballooning debt at the expense of sustained public services, Martin initiated reforms to the pre-budget public consultation process. These extensive and high-profile public consultations provided opportunities to solidify a fiscal posture of restraint and to get the public to recognize that hard choices about continuing certain programs would be required.[7] By being open and specific with the public about the expenditure decisions required to finalize the budget, and with unprecedented use of extensive public opinion surveys and focus groups, the Finance Minister shaped public expectations, reduced the likelihood of public surprise, increased support for the budget and dulled opposition attacks.

The results of Program Review were significant. The main elements were unveiled in the February 1995 budget: the achievement of a 3 percent deficit target; $29 billion worth of multiyear expenditure cuts which reduced 1996–97 program spending to 13.1 percent of the GDP (the lowest level since 1951); the elimination of 45 000 public service and military positions with incentive programs put in place for early retirement and early departure; significant restructuring of many federal programs (particularly in the areas of transportation, employment insurance and job training, defense and foreign aid, agricultural, industrial and regional subsidies); the elimination of several boards, commissions and advisory agencies; and significant reductions in transfer payments to provincial and territorial governments by creating the Canada Health and Social Transfer, combining several transfer programs into a block-funded program.

Moreover, the guardians established a new Expenditure Management System focused on rigorous expenditure restraint. Its features included: (1) programs were to be reviewed on an ongoing basis; (2) expenditure and deficit targets were to be achieved on a step-by-step annual basis; and (3) new expenditure proposals would be considered in the context of the tight fiscal framework and as part of the Minister of Finance's budget.

Program Review represented a temporary victory of the guardians, with the support of the priority-setters, over the spenders. The exercise was centrally directed and its focus was exclusively top-down. The objective was sole and clear – gradually to reduce the deficit to zero by eliminating or reducing expenditure programs. This was accomplished by a combination of strong political will and prudent fiscal forecasting and budgeting by the Finance Department. Budgeting became one-dimensional, focused exclusively on reducing the fiscal aggregates. Allocations were temporarily suspended because any allocation of any new money to any spender, no matter how meritorious the cause or how small the amount, would undermine the discipline of restraint and reduction required by all. Even expenditure reallocations were not considered because any flexibility in resources was destined for the government's bottom line.

The severe cuts, coupled with prudential forecasting, restored fiscal balance in 1997 and established the goal of a 'balanced budget or better'. Almost every important aspect of the budget-making process was consolidated in the Department of Finance. It reinforced and solidified the central locus of decision-making on new expenditure initiatives between the two chief guardian ministers, excluding spending ministers and the President of the Treasury Board; and along with cuts to the center, accelerated the decline in the capacity and stature of the Treasury Board and its Secretariat over departmental programs and expenditures, and in influencing the budgetary process (Lindquist 1996).

After the review these guardians and priority-setters were able to dominate the budgetary process in the event that surpluses would come available for spending. A tight collaboration of both cooperation and competition between the guardians in Finance and the priority-setters in the Prime Minister's Office (PMO) – even in the face of increasing political and personal tensions between Finance Minister Paul Martin and Prime Minister Jean Chrétien – ensured that only those contributing to the narrow range of budget priorities could participate. The PMO priority-setters ensured that new money would only go to a few priorities (for example, children, health and the new economy), and the Finance guardians controlled the design of the initiatives, consulting only with highly selected spending departments like Industry Canada and HRDC when necessary.

THE FOUR REFORM PERIODS IN PERSPECTIVE

Budget reform initiatives were introduced in each period, often responding to disappointment in and failure of previous reforms. Some were incorporated into ongoing budget practice, becoming fixtures of the process.

Others were tailored to specific challenges, soon overtaken by subsequent initiatives or fading under the clutter of ongoing budget reform. Program budgeting established the micro-level architecture for budgeting. It solidified decision structures to ensure competition among new expenditure demands, but unsuccessfully sought to induce competition between existing and new expenditures. PEMS proved too time-consuming for ministers and required heavy central machinery, but linked budget reforms with the cabinet decision-making process. The incremental reforms of the 1980s and 1990s instituted some permanent budget techniques that increased managerial and expenditure flexibility for departments and agencies and provided incentives for efficient budgeting. The one-time shock treatment of Program Review of the mid-1990s demonstrated that, with strong political will and public support, budgetary decision-making could periodically effect major structural change in the government's expenditures.

RECENT DISPARATE BUDGET REFORMS: 2003 TO THE PRESENT DAY

It is difficult to discern the meaning of budget reform in Ottawa post-2003. The political rhetoric of the Martin Liberal government (2004–06), calling for 'a continuous culture of reallocation', quickly evaporated with the reality of attempting to govern through the turbulence of the 'sponsorship scandal' and the resulting minority government. The more recent low-profile and tentative outlines of a 'new expenditure management system' of the Conservative minority government led by Stephen Harper (from 2006) predicated on the often promised, but seldom achieved, objectives to 'manage programs to clearly defined results [and] systematically review the funding and relevance of all program spending' has yet to materialize. The results of this new system were not evident in the first two Harper government budgets which announced that the growth in expenditures exceeded the growth in the economy.

Various reform remnants of the last decade can be pieced together to describe the current approach to budgeting. Although it may not seem like real budget reform, primarily because it relies on past practices, it represents 'new' reform since the announced changes promise that:

- departments and agencies will manage their programs to clearly defined results, and assess their performance against those results;
- the Treasury Board Secretariat will oversee the quality of these assessments and ensure that departments explicitly address risk as well as cost-effectiveness;

- building on these assessments, cabinet will systematically review the funding and relevance of all program spending to ensure both that spending is aligned with the priorities of Canadians and that it effectively and efficiently delivers on the government's responsibilities; and
- cabinet will undertake a rigorous examination of all new spending proposals, taking explicit account of the funding, performance and resource requirements of existing programs in related areas (Department of Finance 2006).

The current approach is best seen as evolutionary rather than dramatic reform. Mixed in with the new requirements are remnants of old initiatives or realizations of previous ambitions. Its features include: a deeply embedded mentality of a balanced budget or better; prudence in economic and fiscal forecasting; extensive year-end budgeting; budget allocations controlled by the Prime Minister and the Minister of Finance; limited administrative and operational reviews and reallocation; the strengthening of financial watchdogs; and a proliferation of departmental and whole-of-government performance reporting.

Some initiatives are reformist, like the strengthening of financial watchdogs unveiled by the Conservative minority government in April 2006 in its high-profile Federal Accountability Act. Others, like year-end budgeting, have emerged quietly as a consequence of other reforms like the commitment to balanced budgeting. Still others, like prime ministerial budgeting, are the culmination of long-standing trends and patterns.

The trajectory of recent budget reform in Ottawa is not due to some loudly promulgated grand design but reflects disparate influences emerging over time as budget players quietly react, adjust and adapt to changing circumstances and opportunities. The emerging style is quieter and promises less, finding indirect ways to change the system. It reflects the broader realities of effecting change under minority governments and the power differentials among the various actors.

A BALANCED BUDGET OR BETTER

The goal of a 'balanced budget or better' now guides all budgeting. Neither Liberal nor Conservative governments, whether majority or minority, have been prepared to return to deficit budgets.[8] Balanced budgets, and often significant (or 'surprise') surpluses, have been achieved every year since 1997. This has been accomplished not through legislative strictures and targets, but through political will supported by public opinion,[9] a seemingly sensible economic and fiscal policy. Like the lessons learned by those who experienced first hand the devastation of the 1930s Depression, citizens and politicians also remember the problems associated with the increasing deficits and ballooning debts of the 1980s and early 1990s. No one wants to go back into deficit, even though it may prove an effective fiscal policy option in the future.

Coupled with the resolve to achieve balanced budgets there is a bipartisan commitment to reduce public debt as a proportion of GDP. This has been based upon arguments that public debts are intergenerational in nature, that interest payments on the public debt consume 20 percent of total public expenditure, and that expenditure pressures will increase as demographic change takes place. Despite the inherent risks of targeting debt to GDP – a small error in projecting the path of nominal GDP could require large fiscal corrections – the Liberal government in its 2005 budget reaffirmed its commitment to reduce the debt-to-GDP ratio to 25 percent by 2014–15. The Conservative government in its 2006 budget confirmed that the 25 percent target would be reached by 2013–14, and appears on track to reach this goal in 2011–12. To show citizens that the Harper government was fiscally responsible at a time of increasing economic uncertainty, the Finance Minister, Jim Flaherty, used his 2008 budget to put the lion's share of the year-end surplus ($10.2 billion) into debt reduction rather than tax cuts or new spending.

A political commitment to a balanced budget or better represents a powerful macro-reform initiative, highly visible and understood by all. There can be little or no disagreement on whether or not it has been achieved. But not only does it determine budget outcomes, it also significantly shapes the budgetary process.

PRUDENT BUDGETING: HEDGING AGAINST UNCERTAINTY

Prudent economic and fiscal forecasting have been the hallmark of budgeting since 1994, and are essential to achieving balanced budgets (Kelly and Lindquist 2003). In recent years, finance ministers have not attempted to 'control' the fiscal framework by ensuring that projected expenditures, revenues and surpluses (or deficits) are achieved in terms of actual outlays, revenues and fiscal balances. Instead, they seek to establish and maintain fiscal credibility by hedging against the inherently uncertain economic and fiscal projections.

Finance guardians build prudence into every stage and every component of the budget, including the economic outlook, the fiscal forecasts of expenditure and revenues, the fiscal framework and its fiscal targets, the fiscal dividend and how it is to be used, and the costing of direct expenditure and tax expenditure initiatives that compete for new funding. The extent of prudence has been estimated at $6–10 billion.[10] According to one independent analysis, Canada has 'larger and more conservative fiscal forecasts errors than most other countries' (IMF 2005). The study goes on to explain that: 'the aggregate forecast error is composed of small but consistently one-sided errors in fiscal subcomponents, which appears characteristic of a conservative forecasting approach'. Prudent forecasts are not 'forecast errors',they are a rational way for officials, ministers and governments to hedge against the inevitable uncertainty they face, and to avoid the 'mistake' that actual deficits are larger than predicted or that balanced budgets turn into deficit budgets.

Prudent budget planning begins with the economic and fiscal outlook, undertaken in four steps:

1. *Economic assumptions.* Finance surveys about 20 private sector economic forecasters on a quarterly basis. It refines these forecasts to ensure prudence and consistency. From the budgets of 1994 to 1998, prudence was explicitly incorporated into the economic outlook and the fiscal projections by adopting economic assumptions more pessimistic than the average of the private sector economic forecasts, including higher interest rates and weaker economic growth.
2. *Status quo fiscal projections.* Finance officials build prudence into revenue and expenditure projections with deeply entrenched standard operating procedures. So, if junior analysts identify a range for the forecast of particular revenues with high and low limits, senior forecasters pick the lower limit. Revenue numbers are always rounded down and expenditure numbers rounded up.[11]
3. *Update status quo projections.* The fall Economic and Fiscal Update in advance of the upcoming budget presents another opportunity for building in prudence. The forecasters select more pessimistic economic assumptions and ensure that their updated expenditure and revenue forecasts are conservative.
4. *Adjusting fiscal projections for budget planning.* Achieving prudence here involves two determinations. One is establishing an annual 'contingency reserve' to guard against unforeseen circumstances and the other is building into the fiscal framework an explicit amount for economic prudence. Both decisions provide further protection against achieving a smaller surplus than projected or, worse, falling into deficit. The annual contingency reserve has been large; for a number of years it was set at $3 billion per year and, if not needed, was applied

at the year end to reduce the federal debt. Economic prudence has generally been set at $1 billion in the first year of the five-year fiscal framework, rising to $4 billion in year five. If this amount is not needed, it can fund new expenditure or tax reduction priorities.

Prudence is also built into fiscal targets. The challenge in recent years for the Finance Minister has been the same: first, how to establish both credible and achievable targets; and second, how to ensure that these targets are achieved and not underachieved. Former minister Martin established five-year fiscal projections but only set out two-year targets publicly in his budget. In 1995, instead of promising that the $42 billion deficit would be eliminated in five years, he established short-term, achievable targets by promising that the deficit would be reduced to $25 billion in 1996. Hence, with prudent fiscal forecasting the government has put in place budget practices which from 1995 to 1997 yielded fiscal deficits better than initially forecast and, since 1998, produced fiscal surpluses better than forecast.

THE ACCIDENT OF YEAR-END 'TOP-UP' BUDGETING

With a succession of year-end surpluses substantially larger than forecasted, the appetite of spenders began to increase. Finance guardians initially controlled year-end spending through such devices as 'independent foundations', used to park resulting surpluses off-budget, often to the exclusion of claims by spending departments. Pressures from spenders to expand budget priorities were successfully rebuffed by priority-setters and guardians, and the few initiatives that spread new monies to spending ministries, such as infrastructure programs, were carefully designed and controlled by the center.

Year-end budget 'top-ups' have now become an important feature of budgeting. Since 1998 a larger portion of the expenditure allocations happen at the year end as part of the regular February budget.[12] Small in proportion to the size of the entire budget, year-end surplus monies have constituted a significant proportion of the new money allocated in any budget and fiscal year. For example, in the February 1998 budget, $3.2 billion was allocated at the year end to new expenditures in 1997–98, whereas at the outset of the budget in February 1997 only $1 billion of new money had been allocated. The year-end top-ups as a percentage of total allocations made for 1997–98 were 76 percent. In the February 2005 budget $10.9 billion was allocated at the year end to new expenditures in 2004–05, whereas in March 2004 only $2.2 billion had been allocated to fund new initiatives. The year-end allocations as a percentage of total new money were 83 percent in 2004–05 (see Table 5.1).

Year-end budgeting goes hand in hand with comprehensive budgeting where all, or most, new expenditure decisions are part of budget decision-making. In this way central guardians and priority-setters increase their influence over spenders by insisting that new spending proposals are compared against all others and against government's priorities. But this accounts for a very small portion of the overall budget; less attention is given to reviewing the much larger ongoing base of expenditures.

BUDGETING FROM THE CENTER

Budgeting from the center has become an increasingly important feature (Savoie 1999), working to the exclusion of most spending ministers. On budgets, prime ministers prefer to avoid cabinet colleagues and deal exclusively with their ministers of finance. This is not simply a matter of prime ministers providing unwavering support to their finance ministers at budget time, but of increasing their direct role in determining budget priorities and the degree of flexibility in the fiscal framework, and allocating expenditures to major new initiatives.

Working closely together and assisted by their supporting agencies (the Prime Minister's Office and the Privy Council Office, and the Department of Finance), these ministers jointly determine the contents of the major expenditure initiatives in budgets (Good 2007: Chapter 4). They can ensure that the scarce incremental resources are concentrated and directed only to the most important and visible priorities of government. Again, this joint focus is not on the base of ongoing expenditures.

However, year-end surpluses have gradually declined over time, and governments have granted major tax reductions (personal, corporate and sales). Guardians and priority-setters have sought new ways to finance expenditure pressures while not relapsing into deficits. This includes not only focusing new spending towards new and important priorities, but also reallocating expenditures from old programs to new priorities.

REALLOCATION: STILL ONLY A PROMISE

Despite a litany of promises from budget reformers about reallocation, actual achievements so far have been small. The review and reallocation of ongoing expenditures has been minor and sporadic (Lindquist 2006). There have been at least three-and-a half distinct attempts.

Table 5.1 New money allocated to upcoming fiscal year compared to end-of year top-up allocated for the same fiscal year ($ in billions)

Fiscal Year	1997–98	1998–99	1999–2000	2000–2001	2001–02	2002–03	2003–04	2004–05	2005–06	2006–07	2007–08
New allocations for upcoming year in main budget	1.0	2.6	4.1	4.4	3.6	2.6	4.7	2.2	7.4	11.7	8.4
Allocations at year-end (top-ups)	3.2	5.7	6.2	2.1**	3.4***	6.4	3.6	10.9	0.8****	4.9	2.7
Total allocations for the fiscal year	4.2	8.3	10.3	6.5	7.0	9.0	8.3	13.1	8.2	16.3	11.1
Year-end top-up allocation as % of the total	76%	69%	60%	32%	49%	71%	43%	83%	10%	30%	24%

Notes:

* Excludes tax expenditure and general tax reductions.

** There was no budget in the spring of 2001, however the 17 May 2001 Economic Update indicated that an additional $2.1 billion was expended at year-end in 2000–2001.

*** 30 October 2002 Economic and Fiscal Update.

**** Excludes $4.9 billion for general tax reductions, including GST reduction. If these tax reductions are included the year-end allocation as a percentage of total allocation increases from 10% to 44%.

Source: Department of Finance, Budgets and Economic and Fiscal Updates, 1996 to 2008.

First, in 2003 Finance Minister John Manley spoke in bold terms of 'reallocation for transformation', and in his 2003 budget he announced that $1 billion would be reallocated. The results were hardly transformative. Subsequently, the President of the Treasury Board reported that the savings were largely one-off savings, achieved through: 'a number of initiatives, including reductions in some activities or lower-than-anticipated use of some services, unavoidable delays in the start-up of some others, and other measures to reduce resources that are currently allocated' (President of Treasury Board 2003).

Second, when Martin became Prime Minister in December 2003, he boldly promised a 'continuous culture of reallocation'. He announced that the Treasury Board would be 'remandated to focus on providing rigorous oversight of government expenditures' and 'be responsible for continuous reallocation and realignment of government expenditures'. However, a newly established expenditure review committee of cabinet, chaired by the President of the Treasury Board, floundered as committee ministers were unprepared to make cuts to themselves and others at the same time that most other ministers were spending.

Third, the review exercise was relaunched, this time through a cabinet committee headed by the Minister of National Revenue with support from the Privy Council Office (PCO). The expenditure reviews included departmental reviews in the 30 largest departments and agencies, horizontal policy and program reviews, and operational reviews in ten areas of government expenditure. After considerable negotiation with spending departments, the PCO put $17 billion (over five years) in proposals to ministers from which they could decide. The February 2005 budget announced nearly $11 billion in cumulative savings over the next five years, with 89 percent coming from improved efficiencies in government operations. The savings were reinvested in other priorities, with $2.1 billion in efficiency savings in employment insurance directed back to the department for either a reduction in premiums or enhanced benefits. The remaining savings, about $8.5 billion, were reallocated through the 2005 budget to other departments to fund new initiatives in defence and security, the environment, support for Aboriginal Canadians, and maintaining the integrity of core government operations.

Lastly, the March 2007 budget of the Conservative Harper government contained a low-profile announcement of its new expenditure management system, including reviews of selected departments each year. Despite some tightening of focus, early indications suggest achievements have not been significant. The most recent review of 17 organizations with expenditures of over $13 billion (15 percent of total direct spending) produced limited results. Indeed, buried in an obscure annex attached to the 2008 budget was an admission of partial progress in achieving modest administrative and operational savings of less than $400 million. A subsequent review of Ottawa's many central human resource agencies seems focused more on organizational streamlining than on expenditure savings and reallocation.

By maintaining attention on reallocation, both Liberal and Conservative governments have attempted to change long-standing and deeply entrenched incentives and disincentives affecting spenders, guardians and priority-setters. During the Martin and Harper minority governments, the promise of expenditure reallocation has exceeded actual performance. Admittedly, for a majority government this presents an invidious task. Reallocation involves transforming old expenditures into new priorities, re-examining existing commitments that have significantly hardened since the last major down-sizing exercise of Program Review in the mid-1990s.

STRENGTHENING FINANCIAL WATCHDOGS

As its first legislative priority, the Conservative Harper government unveiled the Federal Accountability Act in April 2006. This legislation greatly strengthened the scope, powers and responsibilities of financial and budget watchdogs. The measures and the language used to describe them were decidedly reformist in nature and in tone: 'ensure truth in budgeting', 'strengthen the power of the Auditor General', 'strengthen auditing and accountability in departments', 'clean up the procurement of government contracts', 'provide real protection for whistle-blowers' and 'designating deputy ministers as accounting officers'. The following seven major reforms dealt with budgeting and the management of public money:

1. The creation of a Parliamentary Budget Office (PBO), to improve the transparency and credibility of the government's fiscal forecasting and budget planning.
2. Granting new powers and resources for the Office of the Auditor General to audit any individual and organization receiving public money from the federal government, including the growing number of public, private and voluntary sector partnerships and other multi-party financial arrangements.
3. Appointing a chief audit executive in each department and agency, reporting directly to the deputy minister and reporting functionally to the Comptroller General.
4. Strengthening the independence of internal departmental audit committees by requiring that members be drawn largely from outside government.

5. Designating deputy ministers as accounting officers for their departments to make them accountable before parliament to answer questions related to their assigned responsibilities.
6. Enshrining in law a commitment to fairness, transparency and openness in the government procurement process, and appointing an independent procurement auditor.
7. Encouraging every public servant to become a watchdog by providing them with whistle-blower protection and incentives.

Such accountability reforms have the potential to affect all three budgetary functions: determining fiscal aggregates, allocating expenditures and managing programs and finances.

It is too early to determine the precise influence the PBO will have through its analysis of the fiscal aggregates and projections underpinning budgets. It will hardly compare with the influential US Congressional Budget Office, which plays an important and independent role in formulating budget projections. However, future governments wanting to maintain at least a balanced budget with prudent forecasting and budgeting may find that they are under increased scrutiny by increasingly informed parliamentarians. However, the House of Commons Standing Committee on Finance will not have anything like the influence on overall budget levels enjoyed by US Congress committees.[13]

These watchdog reforms are unlikely to have much influence on actual budget allocations. When requested by a Commons or Senate committee, the PBO can provide independent cost analysis of any expenditure or tax proposal considered by either house and to undertake research on the departmental estimates before a committee. At best, this may have some indirect effect on departments and agencies to ensure that initial cost estimates for spending proposals are not underestimated. It is difficult, however, to see how the cost analysts in the PBO will be able to compete with the cost experts in departments and agencies, in the Treasury Board Secretariat, and in the Department of Finance, all with direct experience in the running of expenditure programs.

The potential effect of strengthening external and internal watchdogs on financial management and program efficiency in government is difficult to assess. At one level these watchdogs are likely to sharpen public and political attention on matters relating to government financial mismanagement. Concern about increased public exposure of financial mismanagement could lead to improved financial management and greater efficiency in the use of public money. How this is undertaken will determine what actually happens. If guardians and spenders introduce more guidelines and frameworks, adding to the web of rules, financial compliance might be strengthened but government operations and programs will be less efficient. In the sponsorship scandal, the Auditor General said some rules were broken. She did not say there were not enough rules. Whether the government will be able to meet the Prime Minister's commitment to public servants that 'this government will not be imposing more regulations . . . [but] will look to repeal ones that inhibit [their] effectiveness' is far from certain (Harper 2006). This has proved difficult to achieve particularly with administrative and budget reforms in the aftermath of a major crisis (Good 2003).

Emphasizing these financial watchdog functions, the focus is now on 'following the money', not results; the priority is on audit, not program evaluation. Indeed, the resources for internal audits in the federal government increased dramatically from $5 million in 2005 to $56 million in 2007. In contrast, the resources for program evaluation, $6.5 million in 2005, were not substantially more in 2007. When it comes to evaluating government performance and links to budgets, the upper hand will be with the auditors who 'audit' programs and their management against a narrow set of financial management and efficiency criteria, and not with program evaluators who 'evaluate' program results against a broader set of performance and effectiveness criteria. This may contribute data and information about whether the government is 'doing the thing right', but it will not produce information and analysis to be debated as to whether the government is 'doing the right thing'.

The dramatic strengthening of internal and external financial watchdogs has changed the traditional dynamic among budget guardians. Less emphasis is put on internal reciprocity and mutual adjustment within government, and more on independent reporting to, and external scrutiny by, parliament and those outside government. Canada's budgetary systems will come to rely less on trust and informal understandings to lubricate 'village politics' over shared and competing interests, and more on a reliance on public reporting, external scrutiny and independent verification. This is part of the gradual transformation from the 'old village' with its closed expenditure community to the 'new town' with independent and increasingly influential financial watchdogs.

THE PROLIFERATION OF PERFORMANCE REPORTING

The rise of financial watchdogs has significantly increased the demand for public reporting by government, and cast it largely in terms of issues of accountability, with enhanced accountability proceeding under the guise of expanded management accountability frameworks. Performance reporting and accountability, however, are not the same thing: the former conveys results achieved, and the latter explains to an authority how conferred responsibilities were discharged. However, more public reporting, and increased political and public concern about accountability, has led to a growing tendency to treat performance reports as accountability documents.

Compared to other Westminster systems, Canada has a weak tradition of parliamentary scrutiny of budgetary and administrative matters. Reforms to improve reporting to parliament have been a never-ending process for the Treasury Board Secretariat. Over the past decade the amount and extent of reporting to parliament has increased significantly. The current 'reporting cycle' includes a host of budget, performance and accountability documents. The budget, presented about six weeks before the start of the fiscal year, sets out the government's fiscal plan and unveils the new expenditure initiatives.[14] The President of the Treasury Board also tables a government-wide performance report which attempts to link departmental performance to four broad spending areas (for example, social affairs) and 13 outcomes (for example, healthy Canadians). The long-standing Public Accounts, summarizing the government's financial transactions over the previous fiscal year, are also tabled by the President of the Treasury. And under the banner of enhancing accountability, the government now releases management accountability assessments for each department and agency. They include some 20 indicators (for example, asset management) and some 90 measures. Along with these and other documents, parliamentarians now receive well over 1000 documents each year.

The results of all this public reporting are mixed at best. Two former deputy ministers have sharply criticized the 'surreal' nature of the reports (Clark and Swain 2005). Parliamentarians have escalated criticism of the estimates process and their limited role in meaningfully reviewing departmental spending (Good 2007: Chapter 9). While there has been no comprehensive assessment of whether and how parliamentarians use these reports, all indications suggest minimal use – they do not contain information sufficiently embarrassing to the government (McDavid 2005).

CONCLUSIONS: REFORMS, RESPONSES AND REMNANTS

Canadian governments have a long tradition of reforming their budgetary systems. The changes adopted were closely associated with the particular challenges and opportunities facing governments at the time. Knowing where budgeting was going required knowing where government was going. Budget reforms were usually responses to failings of the previous reforms; more specifically, the inability to deal adequately and systematically with emerging problems and challenges of the budgetary process and its outcomes. Reform was usually triggered by dissatisfaction shown by one or more of the major budget players with one or more of the central objectives of budgeting (maintaining fiscal aggregates, effective resource allocation, and efficient service delivery and financial management). It also related to the government's policy and political objectives.

In Ottawa there has been an uneasy balance among these competing objectives and, at times, through overreaction, an imbalance. Budget reforms in Ottawa are reactive and adaptive, often partial and episodic. Governments rarely predict future budget problems and put in place comprehensive plans and strategies to address them. Instead they adapt, adjust and modify existing budget institutions, techniques and procedures as they go along. Reforms and their remnants go hand in hand.

Most recently, the elaborate architecture of system-wide budget reforms have not been promulgated with quite the same enthusiasm and high profile that accompanied previous initiatives. When efforts to reform budgeting are contemplated, governments tend to focus on one component of budgeting, such as the recent strengthening of financial watchdogs through the Federal Accountability Act. Today, reform initiatives emerge less as comprehensive pre-planned packages, with carefully integrated and precisely engineered components rooted in the traditional concerns of budgeting, and promulgated with fancy acronyms, bells and whistles, but rather emerge as responses to a broader set of contemporary issues about Canadian governance. The issues propelling gradual changes in budget reform are also driving the broader changes in government: the concentration of power at the center, accountability and transparency, declining levels of trust in public institutions, new forms of service delivery and the challenge of horizontal coordination, and concerns about the declining role of members of parliament.

The current budget 'style' must be discerned from individual pieces operating at several levels within government, a combination of remnants, current practices, recent central reforms, and future promises and challenges. These include: a strong commitment to a balanced budget or better; prudence in economic and fiscal forecasting; extensive year-end budgeting; major budget allocations controlled by the Prime Minister and the Minister of Finance; limited administrative and operational reviews and reallocation; the strengthening of financial watchdogs; and proliferating performance reporting. These disconnected and discrete elements have been grafted onto an established budget process.

To the extent that it is a 'system', it finds coherence through reaction and adaptation to a broader set of issues facing government, but not through planning, promulgation and procedure around a narrowly defined set of budget issues. However, the system has proved adaptable and resilient in the face of changing economic and fiscal pressures on the global and domestic fronts. Changes to the institutional and decision-making machinery are rarely structural and permanent. Instead, ad hoc and temporary 'work-arounds' – for example, a time-limited cabinet committee on expenditure review supported by a special Privy Council Office secretariat – are idiosyncratic decisions made by a prime minister to get on with a specific job without the time-consuming and costly requirement of comprehensive system redesign.

Resilience, however, relies on reaction and comes at the expense of developing a proactive approach. The tendency towards reaction and resilience may increase. The promise of expenditure reallocation has yet to be realized, even in part. Restoring the capacity of the Treasury Board Secretariat to play a major role in expenditure review and allocation requires significantly accelerating current initiatives. Finding a way to bridge the gap between the proliferation of performance reports and budget decision-making remains a major challenge. The balanced budget commitment is the anchor holding the system together. When this anchor loosens, as it surely will, the government will need to be prepared with a package of budget reforms and incentives which does not rely exclusively on a public consensus on prudence, but which is fully integrated with its central decision-making processes.

NOTES

1. The 'A' budget consisted of expenditures required to finance existing programs at their current level of service. The 'B' budget embraced financing for new programs or to expand existing ones. The 'X' budget focused on expenditure reductions to existing programs to finance new programs.
2. These are programs of a continuing nature not requiring an annual parliamentary vote for funds and representing over 65 percent of total federal government spending.
3. PEMS sprang from the Expenditure Management System (EMS), announced by conservative Prime Minister Clark in his 1979 minority government in an effort to strengthen the hand of guardians through multiyear fiscal planning, overall expenditure levels at the top, and specific expenditure levels by policy sector or 'envelope'.
4. Solange Denis's message to Prime Minister Mulroney was that 'if you continue with this cut to seniors' benefits, it's goodbye Charlie Brown', which everyone understood meant the Prime Minister.
5. The Glassco Commission was the Royal Commission on Government Organization (1962) which urged greater managerial and business practice in areas of public administration.
6. The five initial tests were: (a) Public Interest Test: does the program or activity continue

to serve the public interest? (b) Role of Government Test: is there a legitimate and necessary role for government in this program area or activity? (c) Federalism Test: is the current role of the federal government appropriate, or is the program a candidate for realignment with the provinces? (d) Partnership Test: what activities or programs should or could be transferred in whole or in part to the private or voluntary sector? (e) Efficiency Test: If the program or activity continues, how could its efficiency be improved?

7. These consultations built on previous reforms introduced by Michael Wilson, Minister of Finance under the Mulroney government, to regularize the budget process on the revenue and expenditure side, including more parliamentary hearings with experts (see Lindquist 1994).
8. Even the socialist New Democrat Party called for a balanced budget in its campaign promises in the most recent general election.
9. While some countries, some state governments in the United States, and a few provinces in Canada have found it in their interest to establish fiscal targets in the form of legislated rules, Canadian finance ministers have not. One exception was between 1991 and 1994 when the Fiscal Control Act imposed legislative limits on the government's ability to spend. The essence of the limitation was that any spending in excess of the legislated target could be offset by cutting spending below the target in the following two years. In addition, expenditures related to emergencies and to strongly cyclical programs such as employment insurance were exempt. According to a former Associate Deputy Minister of Finance: 'The Mulroney government's experience taught at least one useful lesson: in the end, the legislation was so complex that is failed to pass the communications test. Actual expenditures were quickly driven well below the initial targets. Rather than revising the targets down, the incoming Liberals simply allowed the legislation to lapse. Few Canadians noticed' (see Drummond 2004: 315).
10. 'To ensure a balanced budget or better', explains a finance assistant deputy minister, 'we had to build a lot of prudence and contingency into our budget forecasts by erring on the more conservative side. To ensure we do not go into the red, we need to build in \$6 billion to \$10 billion annually' (quoted in Good 2007: 150). This is confirmed in an independent review by O'Neill (2005).
11. Since the rounding on the expenditure side is to \$0.1 billion, some Finance officials quietly speak of the 'rounding reserve,' which affords flexibility for 'small imperatives' without concern that it will break the fiscal framework (correspondence to author from a former senior official, Treasury Board Secretariat, 24 July 2006).
12. This was a reform introduced by Minister of Finance Michael Wilson in the mid-to-late 1980s.
13. The Standing Committee on Finance may, however, with the analytical support of a professional and competent PBO and with its televised hearings with the Minister of Finance, be able to provoke a broader and more informed public debate about the appropriate fiscal stance for an upcoming budget.
14. The estimates are tabled a few days later and set out the spending plans in three parts. Part 1 outlines total expenditures by board category. Part 2 supports the Appropriation Act and provides detailed expenditures by department and agency. Part 3 consists of Departmental Reports on Plans and Priorities (RPPs) and Departmental Performance Reports (DPRs).

REFERENCES

Allen, R.R. and D. Tommasi (eds) (2001), *Managing Public Expenditure: A Reference Book for Transitional Countries*, Paris: OECD.

Aucoin, P. and D.J. Savoie (eds) (1998), *Managing Strategic Change*, Ottawa: Canadian Centre for Management Development.

Auditor General of Canada (1976), *Report of the Auditor General*, Ottawa: Minister of Supply and Services.
Clark, I. and H. Swain (2005), 'Distinguishing the real from the surreal in management reform: some suggestions for beleaguered administrators in the government of Canada', *Canadian Public Administration*, **48** (4), 453–76.
Department of Finance (2005), 'Expenditure review for sound financial management', accessed May 2005 at www.fin.gc.ca/budget05/booklets/bkexpe.htm.
Department of Finance (2006), *Advantage Canada: Building a Strong Economy for Canada*, Ottawa: Public Works and Government Services Canada.
Department of the Prime Minister (2003), 'Changing government' press release, 12 December.
Drummond, D. (2004), 'Do we need fiscal rule?' in C. Ragan and W. Watson (eds), *Is the Debt War Over? Dispatches from Canada's Fiscal Frontline*, Montreal: IRPP and McGill-Queen's University Press, p. 315.
Good, D.A. (2003), *The Politics of Public Management: The HRDC Audit of Grants and Contributions*, Toronto: University of Toronto Press.
Good, D.A. (2007), *The Politics of Public Money: Spenders, Guardian, Priority Setters, and Financial Watchdogs inside the Canadian Government*, Toronto: University of Toronto Press.
Harper, S. (2006), 'Accountability and the public service', Prime Minister's speech to the public servants, Ottawa, 23 March.
International Monetary Fund (IMF) (2005), 'Canada selected issues', Washington, DC, accessed at www.imf.org/external/pubs/ft/scr/2005/cro5116.pdf.
Kelly, J. and E.A. Lindquist (2003), 'Metamorphosis in Kafka's Castle: the changing balance of power among the central budget agencies in Canada', in J. Wanna, L. Jensen and J. de Vries (eds), *Controlling Public Expenditure: The Changing Role of Central Budget Agencies – Better Guardians?* Cheltenham, UK and Northampton, MA, USA: Edward Elgar, pp. 85–105.
Lindquist, E.A. (1994), 'Citizens, experts and budgets: assessing Ottawa's emerging budget process', in S.D. Phillips (ed.), *How Ottawa Spends, 1994–95: Making Change*, Ottawa: Carleton University Press, pp. 91–128.
Lindquist, E.A. (1996), 'On the cutting edge: program review, government restructuring, and the Treasury Board of Canada', in G. Swimmer (ed.), *How Ottawa Spends 1996–97: Living Under the Knife*, Ottawa: Carleton University Press, pp. 205–52.
Lindquist, E.A. (2006), 'How Ottawa reviews spending: moving beyond adhocracy?' in G.B. Doern (ed.), *How Ottawa Spends 2006–2007: In from the Cold, the Tory Rise and the Liberal Demise*, Montreal: McGill-Queen's University Press, pp. 185–207.
Lindquist, E.A. and G. White (1994), 'Streams, springs and stones: Ontario public service reforms in the 1980s and the 1990s', *Canadian Public Administration*, **37** (2), 267–301.
McDavid, J. (2005), 'Using performance reports: findings from the legislator uses of performance reports project', paper presented to the 25th Anniversary Conference of CCAF-FCVI, Ottawa, 17–18 October.
O'Neill, T. (2005), 'Review of Canadian federal fiscal forecasting; processes and systems', accessed September 2005 at www.fin.gc.ca/toce/2005/ONeil_e.html.
Organisation for Economic Co-operation and Development (OECD) (2003), '24th annual meeting of OECD session budget officials: annotation agenda', accessed at http://oecd.org/dataoecd/61/21/2633689.doc.

President of the Treasury Board (2003), news release, Ottawa.
Royal Commission on Government Organization (1962), *Management of the Public Service*, Ottawa: Queen's Printer.
Savoie, D.J. (1990), *The Politics of Public Spending in Canada*, Toronto: University of Toronto Press.
Savoie, D.J. (1999), *Governing from the Centre: The Concentration of Power in Canadian Politics*, Toronto: University of Toronto Press.
Schick, A. (1997), *The Changing Role of the Central Budget Office*, Paris: OECD.
Treasury Board of Canada, Office of the Comptroller General (1981), *Guide on the Program Evaluation Function*, Ottawa: Ministry of Supply and Services.
Van Loon, R. (1983), 'Ottawa's new expenditure process: four systems in search of co-ordination', in G.B. Doern (ed.), *How Ottawa Spends: The Liberals, the Opposition and Federal Priorities*, Toronto: James Lorimer, pp. 93–120.
Wildavsky, A. (1974), 'Some butterflies were caught, no elephants stopped: the zero-base budget, a precursor of PPBS', in A. Wildavsksy (ed.), *Budgeting: A Comparative Theory of Budgetary Processes*, Boston, MA: Little, Brown, pp. 278–96.

6. Budgeting in New Zealand after the reforms: from radical revolutionary to cautious consolidator

Richard Norman and Derek Gill*

TRAJECTORY OF REFORM

New Zealand's public sector reforms in the 1980s have been compared by a senior UK official to a 'shooting star busting onto the firmament, lighting up the night sky' of public administration and management. This chapter will explore what has happened to that shooting star. New Zealand conforms to the old adage: 'Communist at 20, Conservative by 30'. The practice of budgeting has moved from the youthful phase of radical revolution to the middle age of consolidation and planning for retirement.

New Zealand's budget reforms starting in the late 1980s were wide-ranging, and notable initially for the medium-term focus on net worth and transparency and subsequently for being the first country to introduce accrual accounting and output budgeting. After a decade of rapid and radical reforms until the mid-1990s, the pace of change has been steady and incremental as New Zealand has become a cautious consolidator. What is striking about the last 15 years is that, while priorities and policy content have changed with different administrations, the budget system has been remarkably stable. The emphasis on debt reduction during these 15 years has proved to be important preparation for the international financial crisis of late 2008. In November 2008, a newly elected centre-right government led by the National Party was able to face the effects of this financial crisis with almost no government debt and was able to offer tax reductions, a sharp contrast from the election of 1984, which prompted the wide-ranging reforms of that period.

At the macro level of budgeting, fiscal policy has shifted dramatically from an emphasis on short-term macroeconomic stabilization before 1984 to a medium-term strategy focused on sustainability, transparency and predictability. Sustained structural surpluses (averaging 4 per cent of gross domestic product over the last five years) have allowed net debt to be reduced from the peak of over 50 per cent of gross domestic product in 1992 to below zero by 2006.[1] The medium-term fiscal framework enshrined in legislation has provided a prompt to focus on the 'middle-aged' issues of providing for retirement for an ageing population.

At the sectoral level, spending on health and education has increased in real and relative terms, while the relative share of spending on welfare transfers, debt servicing, core government administration and external security has fallen. The role of government as a producer and investor in market activities declined dramatically with privatizations during the 1980s and 1990s, but more recently Air New Zealand and the rail system have been brought back into public ownership with the government re-entering the banking market through Kiwi Bank, a subsidiary of New Zealand Post. In line with other Organisation for Economic Co-operation and Development (OECD) countries, the government has had to guarantee bank deposits to stabilize the finance sector in late 2008. Accrual accounting and the introduction of a Crown balance sheet have proved effective in increasing the focus on longer-term ownership issues such as pension liabilities and the foreign exchange exposure of government foreign debt.

At the departmental or agency level, there has been a shift in the locus of responsibility away from central agencies such as the Treasury to line agencies whose managers were given considerable authority as resource managers, and in return are held accountable for achieving results spelled out through contracts and strategic plans.

IMPLEMENTING A MEDIUM-TERM FISCAL STRATEGY

Before 1984, budget secrecy was used to political advantage by Sir Robert Muldoon, Prime Minister and Finance Minister between 1975 and 1984. His National Party government borrowed heavily in an effort to make New Zealand more self-sufficient in energy, as well as to fund budget deficits in part created by generous tax-funded universal superannuation for the over-sixties and tax cuts to support incomes under the wages and prices freeze. Government net debt (as a proportion of GDP) rose from 9 per cent in 1976 to 41 per cent by 1985, and peaked at 52 per cent in 1992. When Labour came to government in 1984 and 'opened the books' it found that past budget decisions were unsustainable with a deficit of over 6 per cent of GDP. Debt levels had escalated rapidly and an economic slowdown was predicted.

Unpleasant financial surprises on coming to office prompted first Labour and then the Nationals after 1990 to introduce more transparency in budgeting, in line with the Official Information Act of 1982. These changes in budgetary practice were then reflected in the Fiscal Responsibility Act 1994 which mandated principles for responsible fiscal management and required the government to set and report against explicit medium-term targets (for fiscal balance, net worth and net debt).

This transparency has strengthened budget discipline as financial markets immediately translate changes in fiscal forecasts into interest and foreign exchange rates. The external pressures have strengthened the hand of ministers of finance in restraining the spending ambitions of colleagues. Budget forecasts and reporting based on accrual accounting have created an additional constraint by focusing attention on the government's overall financial position, prompting close scrutiny of risks, liabilities, capital spending and current spending that might reduce that net worth or increase net debt. By 2007, net debt (after the inclusion of the New Zealand Superannuation Fund) was negative, and gross debt just over 18 per cent of GDP. While there have been important differences in emphasis between administrations on the mix of expenditure control and tax increases, asset sales and capital investment, there has been a shared commitment to the medium-term focus of fiscal policy.

The three administrations between 1984 and 2008 maintained a transparent and medium-term approach to budgeting, but varied significantly in their styles of budgeting. At the time of writing, the centre-right government, elected in November 2008, had yet to establish its style. The reformist Labour government of the 1980s placed great emphasis on fiscal stabilization and consolidation and implemented a medium-term

BOX 6.1 THE EFFECT OF RESERVE BANK INDEPENDENCE ON BUDGET DECISIONS

Under the Reserve Bank Act 1989, the Central Bank was given independence to exercise monetary policy to achieve the inflation targets set by the government (1 to 3 per cent per annum). This has had a significant effect on fiscal strategy setting. The Minister of Finance needs to consider whether budget decisions will be perceived as creating inflationary pressures by the Reserve Bank or financial markets. Sustained economic growth since 1992 has paradoxically required the government to constrain new spending in each budget to reduce the risk of the Central Bank raising interest rates in its fight against inflation.

fiscal strategy aimed at sustaining net worth rather than short-term macro stabilization. During its first term (1984–87) fiscal consolidation was its priority despite forecasts of a macroeconomic slowdown. Its fiscal strategy had three parts:

- Revenue enhancement including the aggressive removal of direct subsidies and tax concessions, simplification of the overall tax system through the introduction of a goods and services tax, a flattening of the income tax scale and the removal of distortionary indirect taxes.
- An expenditure strategy that sought to improve the effectiveness of expenditure through wide-ranging structural changes, and reduced subsidies while shielding health and social security spending.
- The notional 'balance sheet' received increasing attention with a focus on improving net worth, liability management and debt reduction through asset sales.

Between 1990 and 1999, the right-of-centre National Party, first as a majority government, but then in a fragile coalition between 1996 and 1999, sought to reduce the tax burden through cuts in spending on transfers (New Zealand Superannuation and other welfare benefits) and real reductions in public spending other than in education and health. Initially this fiscal restraint occurred during a period of economic contraction with high unemployment but subsequently the economy rebounded strongly, allowing a 'Hand Up' package of tax cuts and assistance to low-income workers to be introduced in the mid-1990s amounting to 5 per cent of GDP.

Since 1999, left-of-centre coalition governments led by the Labour Party have experienced continued economic growth. With a non-indexed income tax system and an increase in the top marginal tax rate in 2000 from 33 to 39 per cent, the tax to GDP ratio increased by three percentage points to 32.5 per cent over the four years to 2006. Falling debt servicing and transfer payments and steady economic growth allowed the generation of substantial surpluses, which reached a peak of more than 5 per cent of GDP in 2006. From 2000 to 2005, this created the fiscal headroom for the creation of the NZ Superannuation Fund and selected spending increases without significantly increasing the overall expenditure-to-GDP ratio.[2]

Sectoral Shifts in Government Activity

There are four areas of spending that constitute the bulk of government expenditure. These four are health, education, pension or superannuation

Table 6.1 Key fiscal aggregates as a percentage of GDP, 1980, 1990, 2000 and 2003–10

Year	Four main expenditures	Other spending	Core revenue	Operating balance (OBEGAL)	Net debt less NZSF** assets
1980*	21.0	13.9	32.9	−2.1	16.0
1990*	25.1	15.6	39.9	−1.3	49.7
2000	24.1	7.3	31.5	1.3	19.3
2003	21.5	10.1	32.8	1.2	11.9
2004	21.0	8.2	32.5	5.1	5.5
2005	20.8	9.8	33.9	3.9	2.9
2006	22.6	9.7	35.5	6.1	−0.6
2007	23.1	9.6	33.8	4.8	−2.2
2008	23.0	9.7	34.3	2.9	−3.2
2009	22.9	9.7	33.3	0.7	−3.7
2010	22.8	9.6	33.1	0.5	−5.2

Notes:

* Note that 1990 and 1980 data are on an International Monetary Fund (IMF) GFS basis and data after 2000 are on a GAAP accruals basis so, other than net debt, the series are not strictly comparable. Data prior to 2007 are actuals while data after 2007 are Treasury 2008 budget night forecasts. The October 2008 Pre-Election Economic and Fiscal Update revised the operating balance forecasts down significantly in the light of deteriorating economic conditions. OBEGAL is operating balance excluding gains and losses, and is discussed further in the chapter. The OBEGAL figures in this table do not reflect the difference between total spending and total revenue due to rounding and different accounting treatments.

** New Zealand Superannuation Fund.

payments, and other benefits. Remaining expenditure or 'other expenditure' includes spending on administration, law and order, defence and debt financing.

During the last 15 years there have been considerable sectoral shifts across these four major areas and within the residual other spending. Spending on health, in particular, and education has grown steadily in real and relative terms since the early 1990s with increases from 4.9 per cent to 6.2 per cent, and 5.0 per cent to 5.5 per cent of GDP respectively between 1994 and 2007. Spending on superannuation and other benefits has fallen through a combination of policy changes such as the increase in the age of entitlement to superannuation from 60 to 65, and cuts to the benefit levels in the early 1990s which reduced nominal benefits by an average of 20 per cent, and which have never been reinstated. Demographics have also been favourable with reduced dependency ratios and dramatic falls in the number on unemployment benefits. With the fall in net and gross debt, there have been significant reductions in debt servicing. 'Residual government' spending declined over the 1990s by around 1 per cent. But within that overall trend there were significant shifts with a decline in spending on external security (defence) offset by increased spending on internal security (police, prisons and the justice system). Over time, however, there is evidence of considerable resource reallocation at the sectoral level.

Accrual accounting and the introduction of a Crown balance sheet have proved effective in increasing the focus on longer-term ownership issues and the management of the overall financial position and net debt of government. Preparation of the first balance sheets in the early 1990s highlighted future problems with unfunded benefits for public sector employees. As a result, the Government Superannuation Scheme was closed to new members in 1993. Foreign currency exposure of the government debt portfolio was hedged to reduce the impact on the balance sheet and the Accident Compensation Scheme moved to full funding to provide assets to match the liabilities from long-duration claims (Warren and Barnes 2003: 36–7).

Agency-Level Expenditure

To impose fiscal control, the key strategy of the Treasury in the late 1980s was to 'give away control of small numbers in exchange for control of large numbers' (Scott 1996).[3] In exchange for autonomy delegated to chief executives over the smaller numbers contained within agency output appropriations, the budgetary system sought to maintain an 'electric fence' against overspending.[4] Chief executives on performance-related contracts have been expected to manage industrial relations negotiations and fund salary increases from fixed baseline output funding which has not been adjusted for inflation. The processes for gaining additional funding to compensate for inflation or other capability pressures have put the onus on agencies to prove the need for additions to their baselines. The effect of non-indexing has placed pressures on agencies to deliver efficiency gains that Treasury officials hoped and intended the system would produce.

A key component of the 'fence' has been fixed nominal rolling baselines, a contrast from the previous 'bid and review' budgets based on inputs. At the same time centrally negotiated wage settlements were largely abandoned, and replaced by a devolved system involving around 200 line agencies. With the new system, chief executives faced a fixed budget on the one hand, and responsibility for employment relations within their own agency on the other. The employment arrangement for chief executives was based on an employment contract for a fixed term, usually for five years with the right of renewal for a further three, subject to performance.

From Inputs and Cash Budgeting to Outputs and Accrual Budgeting

In 1989 legislative reforms changed the basis for appropriations from cash inputs for programmes to appropriations for the full accrual cost of outputs. These outputs are short statements of services provided by public organizations as contributions towards outcomes. Outputs were adopted as the basis for current appropriations because outputs, in contrast to outcomes, are measurable and controllable by a single agency. Since 1992, budget appropriations for classes of outputs have been underpinned by output plans (initially termed 'purchase agreements' to emphasize a hard-edged contracting) in contrast to the programme and input funding used previously. The intention was to have government services costed in the same way as in the private sector, including applying a charge for capital (discussed below). This was expected to enable greater value-for-money comparisons to be made. Managers were given freedom to manage those costs without being constrained by centralized input and process controls. Outputs were expressed in terms of quality, quantity, timeliness and cost and monitored through Annual Reports and formal audits by the Office of the Auditor General, which reports to parliament on both the financial information and non-financial performance measures.

An analytical distinction between government as purchaser and government as owner was a major feature of the design of the budget system. Outputs were used to describe the government's interests as a 'purchaser' of services. As purchasers, governments have an interest in the lowest-cost supply and the best possible value for money, with the results of such negotiations being shown in the Estimates of Expenditure statements. As owners of organizations which deliver services, governments also have an interest in the future capacity and capability of organizations, whose financial information is shown in a balance sheet. The tension between these two sets of governmental interests, which was submerged under the previous cash accounting system, has been highlighted since the reformed system was fully implemented. As a result, questions have been raised about whether fiscal discipline (as reflected in the relative fall in share of spending on 'residual government') undermined the capability of public organizations because the pressure was greater than potential productivity gains. Schick (1996) observed that purchase interests inevitably drove out ownership interests. But in the absence of independent measures of the value of outputs or evidence on trends in public sector productivity, and given the limited information and lack of focus on ownership issues before 1989, there is little firm evidence either way.

Since the passage of the Public Finance Act 1989 and the introduction of output-based accrual accounting there have been a series of significant adaptations to the budgeting process. Key milestones have included:

- Fixed nominal baselines (non-indexed) were introduced in 1991 and used in every budget since then.
- Non-departmental appropriations were changed to an accruals basis in 1994 and the first accrual Crown financial statements were prepared and published.
- The Fiscal Responsibility Act was passed in 1994 requiring annual publication of the government's fiscal strategy (including medium-term scenarios). Under the principles of responsible fiscal management, the strategy includes a twice-yearly publication of economic and fiscal updates (also immediately prior to a general election), as well as a pre-budget publication of the government's budget policy statement.
- A three-year budgeting framework was adopted for the first time in 1996 as part of the coalition agreement between the Nationals and New Zealand First.
- The budgeting framework was extended to four financial years by the incoming Labour government in 1999.
- In the early 2000s the impact of new expenditure initiatives was linked directly to the government's primary objective of eliminating debt, rather than to previous provisions.
- In 2004 the Consolidated Public Finance Act included a new requirement for a statement of long-term fiscal position to be produced at least every four years.

Appropriation Requirements

Appropriations come in six types: (1) departmental and non-departmental outputs (classes that group similar outputs); (2) capital expenditure; (3) benefit and other transfer payments; (4) borrowing expenses (debt servicing); (5) a special appropriation for the security agencies that combines capital and operating expenditure; and (6) a residual category (other expenses). Supply provisions allow for financial authority in advance of appropriations. Budget documents also highlight new initiative allocations so it is possible to track the new money over time. Each organization then has the ability to choose how it manages each appropriation type within the amount and scope of the allocation. In some organizations, output classes and outputs are managed centrally; some are more devolved.

Expenditure is based on appropriations that relate explicitly to ministers, not ministerial departments – so in theory the minister is accountable to parliament, not the ministries. In New Zealand, as there is no requirement for a one-to-one relationship between ministers and departments, often one department has multiple ministers and hence administers multiple votes and appropriations.

Annual appropriations lapse at the end of the financial year and agencies are generally required to return 100 per cent of unused appropriations under a 'use it or lose it' rule with the predictable consequence that there exists an end-of-year spend-up as agencies attempt to use available appropriations for the approved purposes. There are three significant exceptions. One is a provision for multiyear appropriations, but these are only sparingly applied to selected programmes such as major acquisitions by the National Library. Another exception is for public bodies funded from fee revenues that are outside of the legal Crown. The third is some scope to shift appropriations between years for expenses and capital transfers, which provides an element of flexibility but also undermines some of the discipline that would otherwise exist.

CHANGING BUDGET DOCUMENTS

Budget documents have become considerably larger in order to provide transparency and details about outputs and changes in ownership values. Budgets in the Muldoon era (1975–84) included one book of narrative and a one volume of estimates. These were one-year political statements which provided minimal cash-based programme information, based on the Planning, Programming, and Budgeting System (PPBS). More recently, Treasury officials have reported that: 'while the previous regime had 56 programmes . . . the budget process now has a comprehensive schedule of 774 costed outputs' (Warren and Barnes 2003: 11). Current information includes medium-term forecasts, agency statements of intent which assess strategic issues in terms of capability and performance and the estimates which provide accrual-based analysis of expenses and planned changes in balance sheets. A review of accountability documents undertaken in 2007, which attempted to simplify the budget documents and make them more accessible to parliamentarians, is currently being implemented.

One area in which the complexity of budget information has decreased is in the supplementary estimates. Supplementary estimates were used before 1984 to introduce major policy changes to achieve short-term fiscal stimuli in line with the Keynesian economic management of the period. One such 'mini-budget' in 1981 introduced a doubling of the universal child benefit to provide a fiscal stimulus to the economy as part of a coordinated OECD-wide 'dash for growth'. Supplementary estimates are now largely a mechanical and technical report in which forecast variances are recorded and funds moved between appropriations. Overspending has become rare, given the risk to a chief executive's reputation from coming in over budget.

In contrast to 20 years ago, when almost all budget documentation was done by the Treasury and departments did minor proofreading, departments now prepare their own budgets and supporting information, within strict baseline criteria. Information is filed electronically, avoiding the error-prone double handling characteristic of the previous largely manual system. The budget is now prepared using a financial database that can be accessed by both the Treasury and departments through a secure web-based package. It has streamlined the production of Budget documents, as well as assisted with the financial monitoring of agencies. The current database (known as 'CFIS net' – Crown Financial Information System) was introduced in 1999 and is used by agencies to report on their monthly expenditure, upload spending bids, and to take responsibility for all the information that appears about their vote in the annual budget documentation. In turn, it enables the Treasury to monitor the spending of agencies readily throughout the year and during the budget-setting process to track how much money has been committed.

Several important benefits have come from these innovations. Before 1989, most budget work was done by a small group of officials working with the minister. Now, using CFIS net, agencies produce their own numbers and text and as a result have a degree of ownership of the information. In addition, there is only one source of information used by the Treasury and departments, which results in greater accuracy and efficiency – particularly as all budget documents can be produced from this database. The ability to use the database to update the Minister of Finance on the latest financial position is also a powerful tool during the initiatives phase of the annual budget when tracking overall spending.

USE OF BUDGET DOCUMENTS BY PARLIAMENTARY SELECT COMMITTEES

While the complexity of the budget documents and the amount of available information has increased considerably, by contrast, the considerations of parliamentary select committees have barely changed. Despite separating examination of estimates from the review of the previous year's annual report and increasing the availability of information about the medium-term fiscal strategy (outputs, and to a lesser extent outcomes), the underlying political dynamic remains unaltered. Under input budgeting, it was virtually impossible to have a debate about the results expected from spending, as opposed to the sums allocated for the inputs. Information on longer-term trends and performance has not changed the essential nature of the select committee game, although the release of longer-term forecasts has added transparency to budget debates. With output-based accrual reporting, however, the major dynamic of select committees is still essentially a search by opposition members of parliament (MPs) for 'dirt' to embarrass the government. Frequently that pursuit focuses on inputs such as staff numbers, processes for selecting consultants, or travel and accommodation, rather than probing into the effectiveness or efficiency of state sector performance.

The political composition of select committees has changed a little as a result of New Zealand's adoption of a proportional representation electoral system in 1996, which has resulted in a succession of minority governments. Today, governments can no longer rely on select committees being on the side of the executive, with non-government members in the majority and often with non-government chairs. This has meant that government members typically take a fairly passive role on committees, while opposition members seek information with which to embarrass the government.

BUDGET OUTCOMES: MANAGING SURPLUSES

New Zealand has achieved a record of having one of the longest runs of continuous budget surpluses among OECD countries, with surpluses in the operating balance recorded every year since the introduction of consolidated accrual accounts in 1994, but with the first significant deficit now forecast for 2010–11, based on the economic slowdown due to the impact of the international financial turbulence in late 2008. Successive finance ministers have grappled with how to maintain financial discipline in the face of these growing surpluses. The National Party, in government during the 1990s, and as an opposition party between 1999 and 2008, and in government again from November 2008, has preferred tax cuts and family assistance as strategies.

Labour-led governments between 1999 and 2008 were extremely reluctant to cut taxes after increasing the marginal tax rate for higher-income earners on coming to power in 1999, with a platform of 'investing in public services'.[5] Falling costs of debt servicing and reductions in spending on transfer payments, such as unemployment benefits, during a period of economic growth, allowed Labour to increase spending on health, selected education, social services and other developments while keeping overall expenditure-to-GDP ratios broadly stable until 2005. In the 2005 election the opposition used tax cuts as a major plank for distinguishing it from the government. The promise of a very small tax cut from Labour in 2005 was seen as so insignificant that commentators attributed this as a cause of the party nearly losing that election.[6]

Labour relied on different methods to maintain fiscal discipline. One approach adopted in the 2007 budget was to introduce a savings scheme (Kiwi Saver) which is in effect a deferred tax cut received on retirement. The major innovation, however, was the introduction in September 2003 of a New Zealand Superannuation Fund to cushion future taxpayers against the rising costs of funding superannuation for an ageing population. This has enabled a significant portion of the surpluses in the 2000s to be earmarked for investment in the 'Super Fund' to help meet the claims expected over a projected 40-year horizon. By 2008 this fund had grown to $NZ8 billion (or 4 per cent of GDP), slightly larger than the current annual total spend on New Zealand Superannuation. But by 2027, when contributions to the fund are projected to cease, it is forecast to be valued at 28 per cent of GDP.

In the run-up to the 2008 election political differences over tax cuts were no longer significant as the Labour government announced tax cuts which would largely absorb the remaining operating surplus. Indeed, once the cash required to fund capital investments is included, the projected result is a cash borrowing requirement of 2 per cent of GDP in 2009.

INCREASES IN SPENDING

Under both National and Labour governments, spending on health and education relative to GDP has increased steadily during the last 20 years while annual spending on New Zealand Superannuation and other transfers has been reduced. Both governments have sought to increase participation in work relative to staying on welfare by providing support for low-to-middle-income earners, through the tax relief and family assistance packages known as 'Hand Up' under the Nationals and 'Working for Families' under Labour. Both administrations have increased real expenditure particularly in regard to education and health, in part reflecting public expectations that such services should match the best in the OECD, or at least Australia. Alternative employment in Australia, particularly for skilled professionals such as doctors, has continued to put pressure on the costs of these services.

Differences between the political parties have been most evident in budgeting for the core state sector. Under the Nationals, between 1990 and 1999, tight fiscal control and chief executive-run industrial relations kept a ceiling on wage claims[7] and the number of employees in the core public sector was reduced. Between 1999 and 2008, Labour, a party which has strong union support, sought to address campaign concerns about a perceived run-down in the capability of public services, and as a result employment in the core public service and the wider state sector grew steadily. In addition, the government supported pay increases for well-connected unions such as those for nurses, social workers, teachers and the police. Not all unions have succeeded in avoiding the baseline funding regime in which chief executives have to manage wage costs within budgets which are not adjusted for inflation. Notably, in 2001, the government took a tough line over a strike by veterinarians by reducing the initial offer that had been on the table.

Since 2005, while operating surpluses have increased, so too has spending relative to GDP. This real spending growth has been reflected in employment growing across virtually all government agencies, and real wages in the state sector increasing in line with trends in the private sector. Both Labour when in government and the Nationals when in opposition raised doubts about the value for money from these increases in expenditure. Perhaps the best-documented example was the Treasury's attempt to measure the changes in output and productivity in the health sector in response to significant increases in expenditure (from 4.6 per cent in 1990, to 5.5 per cent in 2000, to 6.6 per cent in 2008). While measurement problems made it difficult to assess outputs and productivity in the majority of the health sector, for the 40 per cent of the sector that could be measured, 'there was little evidence of increased output . . . And indeed measured productivity fell over the 1999–2002 period' (Treasury 2005: 7). The emphasis on value for money is likely to increase during the next few years as the fiscal position tightens in response to tax cuts and the impact of an increasingly ageing population.

Impact of Accrual Accounting on Surpluses

As well as providing more transparent information focusing on the government's overall financial position, the use of accrual accounting and budgeting has affected the definition of a budget surplus. Non-cash extraordinary and abnormal items, which need to be expensed through the operating statement, can have a major effect on the extent of the recorded surplus. For example, the forecast surplus for 2007–08 had to be reduced by \$2.7 billion to allow for unrealized losses from declines in the value of the New Zealand Superannuation Fund investments on overseas equity

BOX 6.2 ANALOGY WITH THE FAMILY BUDGET

The 2004 budget used the analogy of a household budget to explain the surplus. The operating surplus was likened to a family's income after everyday expenses had been dispensed. But other commitments had to be recognized. Government contributions to the New Zealand Superannuation Fund were the equivalent of planning for the future and building up savings. Student loans were likened to a family lending to their daughter at university, with the expectation that the loan would be repaid once the daughter was in the workplace. Funding for an extension to the family home was likened to government commitment to capital purchases such as new roads and state houses. Investments in government enterprises and entities such as health boards were compared with a family investing in a small business to maintain and expand its activities. 'Taking all these commitments into account, the household's spare cash – in the same way as the Government's operating surplus – is fully committed', the budget statement declared.

markets, and increased liabilities for worker compensation and government superannuation.

Considerable effort has gone into communicating that accrual surpluses are not equivalent to a cash surplus available for spending or investment. The Fiscal Outlook in the 2008 budget, for example, contains two measures of the overall fiscal position: the Total Crown operating balance (including one-off gains and losses discussed above), and the Total Crown OBEGAL (operating balance excluding gains and losses) which gives a direct measure of the underlying stewardship. It contains separate details on Core Crown and Total Crown expenses and revenues with the latter including separate legal entities outside of but still controlled by the Crown. In addition, detailed forecasts of the Core Crown residual cash (netting out non-cash items like SOE and Crown entity surpluses), and contributions to the New Zealand Superannuation Fund and capital spending are also included.

Fiscal Discipline through the Use of Fixed Baselines

A key innovation in New Zealand's approach to budgeting has been the use of the Australian system of centrally controlled rolling multiyear baselines (or forward estimates) since 1991. This reversed the burden of proof on spending proposals as baselines were fixed in nominal terms and were only amended for explicit new initiative funding. By the early 1990s inflation had been reduced and the implicit assumption for the public sector was that some cash input costs, such as for computers, would fall and compensate for other relative price changes.

Individual line agencies were each charged with managing wage expectations within the hard budget constraint of a fixed output budget. Chief executives had to pay for any wage increases by reducing staff numbers, eliminating restrictive practices and clawing back other terms and conditions. Other public sector reforms empowered managers to manage and make decisions about their core business and which activities they would get out of. To quote one former Treasury official: 'people built their own cages'. There were few centrally imposed top-down initiatives such as the compulsory contracting used in Britain. Rather, the incentive was for managers of agencies to redesign delivery within the baseline funding and in so doing avoid external scrutiny as part of a review.[8] For example, an award-winning innovation putting the entire Companies Office registration and filing system online was all managed within baselines.

By the mid-1990s, in response to concerns about pressures on capability, a baseline review process was introduced. Agencies opting for a baseline review had to demonstrate, through benchmarking and other techniques, that a price increase was warranted as the output prices were competitive, and that efficiency gains had already been exploited. The reviews focused on the volume of outputs as well as the price. Any decisions on changes in baselines were made as part of the new initiative process so any spending increases could be assessed against competing priorities. Unsurprisingly, only a handful of organizations opted to go through a review.

Reporting Outcome Results in Budget Documents

While the move to output budgeting and accounting[9] was achieved quite quickly over three to four years, the shift to a greater outcomes-focused management, first through the Public Finance Act 1989, then a system of Statements of Strategic Results Areas (SRAs) and Key Result Areas (KRAs) and subsequently a centrally driven 'Managing for Outcomes' initiative in 2001, has not proved durable. New Zealand has largely failed to make the same progress on outcome management as it has on output measurement. Each agency prepares an *ex ante* Statement of Intent (SOI) and an *ex post* Annual Report against the expectations set in the Information Supporting the Estimates and the SOI. Unusually, compared with practice in other jurisdictions, both financial and non-financial performance measures are audited.

There has been a move to comprehensive sector reporting, starting with the environmental sector in 1997, the social sector since 2001 and economic development indicators in 2007. The need for economic reporting had been met before then by the information provided as part of the medium-term fiscal framework required under the Fiscal Responsibility Act legislation. In the 2008 budget, Information Supporting the Estimates was grouped together in ten sectoral volumes reflecting the coverage of the various select committees.

New Zealand has always lacked significant information suitable for the evaluation of programmes, contrasting with Australia for example. The limited availability of information about effectiveness is partly a legacy of the poor introduction of the Programme and Performance Budgeting System (PPBS) in New Zealand. While some agencies were readily able to access bodies of research about 'what works', often this evidence does not exist. Unsurprisingly, where evidence has been hard to find, progress in evaluation has been slow.

A Treasury review in 2007 raised concerns that information from evaluations played little part in budget allocations. It recommended government should place a new emphasis on performance information for new initiatives and sought the greater use of cost–benefit analysis (CBA) to rank alternative proposals quantitatively. However, the link between performance information and budgeting allocations remains a vexed one. Where an agency is bidding for additional resources in the budget process and every available measure of outcome performance is deteriorating, it is unclear whether one should conclude that: more resources are required (capability needs augmenting); no more resources are required (throwing good money after bad); or there is no necessary link between resources and results (lags separated in space and time). Clearly the links are not mechanical or automatic. In evaluation, New Zealand has been a follower rather than a leader.

Changes in Budget Processes

Budget processes have differed according to the preferences of prime ministers for cabinet management. National governments used annual meetings at Premier House at which cabinet ministers engaged in a reasonably collegial process to link budgeting and strategy. Labour governments have used a more top-down and centralized approach, with a relatively short strategic phase. Major strategy decisions have tended to be taken by a limited circle sometimes limited to a handful of senior players such as the

Prime Minister, Deputy Prime Minister (also the Finance Minister) and the Prime Minister's Chief of Staff.

Key stages of New Zealand's budget process are:

- The Budget Policy Statement, which provides early advice of the budget policy framework, has to be published before the end of March.
- The budget itself is presented in May, which in addition to the budget speech includes updates of the five-year forecast and the parameters for the next three budgets, while the Fiscal Strategy report provides long-range forecasts for at least ten years.
- The Economic and Fiscal Update is published at the end of each financial year (30 June).

In addition, a Statement of Long Term Fiscal Position is produced every four years to give a 40-year projection.

The credibility of any budget process relies strongly on the accuracy of forecasts. Inaccurate forecasting risks undermine the ability of the Minister of Finance to enforce spending limits. Reform of the late 1980s was in part prompted by a loss of faith in the ability of the system to forecast accurately or control spending. During that period, increasing deficits, largely driven by wage settlements in a time of high inflation, discredited the budget forecasts. While the quality of fiscal information has improved significantly, recently there has been criticism by the Prime Minister, Helen Clark, of the quality of forecasting given significant underestimates of the size of the fiscal surplus. By contrast, a reporting error by the Inland Revenue in 2008 resulted in significant under-reporting of tax revenue which reduced the size of the surplus reported for that month.

Two ways of funding capital projects are available: an explicit capital appropriation from cabinet or from funds retained on an agency's own balance sheet. Depreciation is explicitly funded in New Zealand as part of output prices, so agencies can, without further approval or explicit appropriation, purchase replacement capital assets. However, a technical innovation linked with accrual budgets was the introduction of a 'capital charge' on the net assets of agencies to encourage the efficient use of assets, or discourage 'lazy' assets. This capital charge is levied on the value of net assets at a rate based on the weighted average cost of capital facing the government. This was consistent with the philosophy of letting the managers manage, but holding them accountable through the use of incentives. Reducing asset holdings reduces the capital charge and depreciation expenses and hence frees up current revenues for the agency to allocate to other priorities. It also reduces the depreciation funding for replacement assets.

Initially the application of the capital charge was controversial in some areas, in particular for self-funded or user-pays services, where the cost of the capital charge had to be met from user fees, not a top-up from government output funding.[10] Overall the capital charge has had a positive effect by increasing management attention on asset holdings and asset management, but it has been less powerful than expected in triggering asset rationalization. Evidence for this lack of major effect is the virtual absence of agencies offering capital withdrawals in order to free up operating funds to allocate to other priorities. The capital charge has been in operation for 15 years and is a well-established and relatively uncontroversial part of the budgeting regime.

WHAT SCOPE FOR REPRIORITIZATION?

Since the introduction of output budgeting there has been complete freedom to spend on inputs, and scope to move expense appropriations between output classes as part of the budget, through Supplementary Estimates or limited end-of-year transfers. Agencies generally prefer to reprioritize resources covertly as part of a funding package, often after the year has begun, rather than offer 'savings' to the Treasury as part of the budget round with the risk that the 'savings' offered will be reallocated to other votes. There is also scope for substitution from capital to current spending. Because of the capital charge, agencies have incentives to withdraw money from their balance sheet, but historically there have been relatively few capital withdrawals. This is perhaps because agencies are unwilling to return capital for fear that they will not regain that investment when required at a future juncture.

The easiest way to move funds is still within the vote of one portfolio minister. Almost all reprioritizing has occurred within the output funds under the control of a single minister, with baseline funding jealously guarded by both officials and ministers. Cross-portfolio reallocations have been difficult. Any reallocations to existing baseline funding have required significant government-wide exercises that were centrally initiated (by central agencies or senior budget ministers) and involved blunt targets (for instance, shared pain through a straight 3 per cent cut across all baselines).

Agencies' Self-discipline to Come in Under Budget

The number of agencies breaching appropriations at the level of either the output class or the overall vote is very low, because of the reputational damage. The incentive is to come in at 99.99 per cent of budget, but not come in over it.[11] Chief executives potentially risk reputation, performance bonuses and potentially contract renewal for overspending. Techniques used by agencies to come in right on budget include explicit rationing, even in some cases for demand-driven items, through to management of overhead allocations and reassignment of overhead costs from one output to another. The final month of the financial year often results in creative accounting for the output to which the cost is attributed, gaming the timing of invoices and the time period they relate to.

If agencies come in well under budget they surrender those funds. Most agencies operate under the 'use it or lose it' rule which leads to the predictable result of end-of-year spend-ups. Despite repeated requests for better incentives, there has been no progress on dealing with agency surpluses as the concept does not fit neatly into the purchaser–ownership model. The rationale for not doing anything about this comes from a control perspective. Money has been legally appropriated by parliament for a specific purpose and so should be reauthorized (and returned). Calls to adopt an incentives approach, such as the practice in Singapore where agencies and the centre each share 50 per cent of savings, have gone unheeded.

While the Public Finance Act allows for the annual budget to be presented up until 31 July each year, a mid-May budget is the norm. One consequence of this is that the main budget process is out of synch with the business cycle of departments so that their end-of-year actual figures (final spending at 30 June) are not known until after budget decisions have been taken. The result is that departments then take ad hoc requests to cabinet around June for the use of the available funding, which – straight on the heels of an annual budget round – leaves senior ministers frustrated that opportunities to fund the highest-priority pressures from available funding are lost or weakened.

These examples indicate that whatever the rules of the budget process, gaming is inevitable given real resources are at stake. Gaming over end-of-year surpluses and internal reallocation exist at the departmental level. Gaming also exists at the political level with allocations likely to be influenced by a minister's ranking in cabinet or the political importance of the minister. Coalition formation also offers opportunities for gaming although there are strict and respected rules around public servants' engagement with politicians in this process. Yet, some agencies devote time to advising their minister prior to an election about what the future funding commitments for the sector should be.

Power and Politics in Budgeting

New Zealand's trajectory of budget reform divides into three political cycles: six years of a right-wing Labour majority government to

1990, followed by a nine-year National Party-led administration, which became increasingly dependent on coalition partners after 1996, and then a series of Labour Party-led coalition governments between 1999 and 2008. A fourth cycle may be commencing from November 2008, after the National Party was able to form a centre-right government supported by three smaller parties. Both major parties traditionally started in power running very centrally controlled budget processes with strong leadership from their respective ministers of finance, Roger Douglas (1984–88), Ruth Richardson (1990–93), Bill Birch (1993–99) and Michael Cullen (2000–2008). Initially, their focus was on bilateral negotiations with ministers responsible for departments. But as each administration progressed, more devolved and collective team arrangements evolved for determining spending priorities. Governments gradually established different forms of ministerial teams, around themes or sector groups, to take greater collective oversight of the budget process. The evolution of a more collective process has a number of advantages over individual bilateral arrangements, including making it easier to keep within the overall budget allocation, and much greater ownership of the final budget outcome (FBO) or decisions by ministers.

For example, the budgetary politics of the Labour government in its third term (2005–08) included a number of collective steps. First, the whole cabinet agreed a budget strategy paper setting upper spending limits for the annual budget, also agreeing which groups of sectors or ministers should be clustered together, and what proportion of the total budget allocation would go to each group. Second, the sector groups of ministers then convened and, supported by their own departmental officials, worked through a process of ranking, scaling, revising and deciding the total list of budget bids in their group, so that they eventually achieved a balanced package. Third, the package was then referred to Minister of Finance for review, who on the whole accepted the package recommended by the vote ministers without changing or removing bids. Fourth, the final packages were then reviewed by senior budget ministers. In the most recent budget round there was even a review across the relative priorities of the packages to ensure that the bottom priority receiving funding from one group was more important than a priority that was not able to be afforded in another group.

However, despite the advantages of collectivity, there are still inevitably trade-offs to be managed. The Minister of Finance is less able to review individual bids in a sector approach than through individual bilaterals with each vote minister, and is reliant on the Treasury acting as the Minister of Finance's agent with the sector group of ministers. That in turn places a lot of store on the relationships between the Treasury and the Minister of Finance and also the quality of the information-sharing with agencies. In sectors like Health, where there is really only one agency with a large allocation, both the Treasury and Minister of Finance are effectively removed from being able to scrutinize the prioritization of the proposed initiatives to receive funding. The unevenness in the quality of leadership by lead agencies in the deliberations of each sector is also a problem. And Treasury vote teams (vote analysts in particular) have to balance their 'assess and assist' role in the budget process. In the assist role, vote teams work alongside departments in updating baseline information and developing budget initiatives for specific votes and sectors. They provide the link between departments, other Treasury teams and the Minister of Finance. Vote teams are a department's first source of advice at any stage of the budget process. Yet in their assessment role, Treasury vote teams are responsible for providing guardian-type advice to the Minister of Finance and sometimes the sector lead minister on budget claims.

More recently the politics of the budgetary process have been significantly shaped by big 'P' party politics. With the introduction of multi-member proportionality, New Zealand has moved from a system of majority governments to a range of coalition, minority or minority coalition governments. This has allowed minor parties, in return for supporting the government on confidence and supply matters, to have far greater influence on resource allocations (through coalition agreements) or ministerial portfolios.

In the reform period under Labour in the 1980s and under the Nationals after 1990, the Treasury was the most powerful government department, with a close and effective relationship with the Minister of Finance. Successive ministers of finance have also been powerful ministers, many being seen or acting as second in charge of government. The combination of a capable and powerful Finance Minister and a capable Treasury has proven a very powerful partnership. But the power of the Treasury derived more from its capability and influence with senior ministers than from any formal power.

However, since the 1999 election and throughout the Labour government's three terms, the Treasury lacked the same effective relationship that was developed with previous ministers of finance. Although the Treasury remains a capable and effective organization, its lack of political capital with the most recent Labour administration has significantly reduced its power because of its inability to deliver its minister's position. The wider role once enjoyed by the Treasury exercised across economic policy, budgetary and finance, and public sector reform, has been somewhat circumscribed into a more traditional budgetary ministry. The Treasury's influence on government decision-making has tended to wane as an inner circle of powerful ministers around Prime Minister Clark have sought to impose their influence.

ARE WE MORE STRATEGIC IN OUR DECISION-MAKING?

Budget reforms are not an end in themselves; they were meant to enable us to make better and more strategic decisions. One of the early criticisms of the New Zealand reforms in the early 1990s was that the budget has tended to dominate strategy-setting rather than being an instrument of strategy-setting. There is some truth in this criticism. Even budget rules that were supposed to assist strategic decision-making have not been utilized. For example, the provisions in the Public Finance Act allow for joint appropriations to fund joint projects of significance, but in fact these provisions have not been used to date.

The response to this criticism in the early 1990s was to build a strategic management system around Key Result Areas (KRAs) and Strategic Results Areas (SRAs) in order to link strategy and budgeting more closely. The government's SRAs were designed to encourage chief executives to collaborate across organizational boundaries while individual chief executives developed the KRAs to help achieve the government's SRAs. National-led governments after 1994 sought to make strategic priorities explicit through this framework and held strategic planning retreats for cabinet ministers at which cross-portfolio issues could be debated.

But the results of this process were mixed. The articulation of strategy through SRAs created a new problem with the profusion of KRAs in agencies, and each agency claiming to be indispensable for achieving the government's goals as stated in the SRAs. The SRA–KRA framework also did not mesh neatly into outputs and output budgeting, but ran parallel to it. The system was revitalized under the Nationals following a change of Prime Minister, with a system of ministerial teams setting strategy and using that to drive the budget rather than the budget driving strategy. The results of the 1999 election, however, meant that the new system did not operate sufficiently long enough to be evaluated. Attempts at strategic management are closely tied to the style of the Prime Minister and the SRA network system did not survive a change of government.

The Labour government discontinued the SRA–KRA framework, but its replacement set of 'government goals' was too general and unconnected to the rest of the public management system to provide traction on the budget process. Instead, priorities were initially dominated by the government's key election platform set out in its pledge card. Subsequent attempts to integrate strategies and outcomes also had limited effect. For instance, moves to better link outputs and outcomes in the budgetary process under Labour's 'Managing for Outcomes' initiative in 2001 was expected to increase the alignment between resourcing and strategic planning. Yet, in practice it had little impact on the priority-setting process in the budget. By the government's third term, Labour began to articulate a three-pronged set of priorities based on the 'key themes' of families young and old, national identity and economic transformation. While such priorities proved a useful budget management device for allocating funding to new initiatives, strategy has generally been emergent rather than explicit.

Linking strategy to budgets has emerged as one of the more difficult challenges for the New Zealand polity. Much of the budgetary reform trajectory New Zealand adopted was intended to impose controls, strict rules, discipline and tight incentives to manage. Provisions for strategic decision-making did not attract quite the same attention. During the terms of governments between 1984 and 2008, the ways in which decisions were taken did change – usually according to the differing preferences and styles of prime ministers and their management of their cabinets or governments. Yet, on reflection over the whole reform period since 1985, the budget has continued to dominate strategy because the budget has been the only sustained consistent medium-term 'game in town'. And perhaps will always be so.

In late 2008, as a new government was preparing a response to a domestic economic slowdown and mounting international financial pressures, the value of fiscal control and strengthening the government's balance sheet during the favourable economic conditions of the 1990s and early twenty-first century became very evident. While New Zealand's external private debt per capita is among the highest in the OECD, the New Zealand government, with no net debt, no foreign debt exposure and a strong and transparent balance sheet, is well placed to respond to the economic downturn. Budget reforms, which were initially radical and then cautious in the process of consolidation, provide the new government with significantly more strategic options than those faced by the incoming government of 1984.

NOTES

* The authors would like to thank Bridget Sullivan for her input to the first draft of this chapter and to John Wanna and officials in the New Zealand Treasury who reviewed the penultimate draft. As usual, responsibility for the views, and any errors or omissions, remain the authors'.

1. All data in this chapter are expressed as a percentage of GDP unless otherwise stated.

Data before 1994 are on a Government Financial Statistics (GFS) cash basis; all data thereafter are accruals based on GAAP.

2. It should be noted that in the two years since 2005 the recurrent spending-to-GDP ratio increased by 2.3 per cent to 32.1 per cent
3. G. Scott (1996). Graham Scott was Secretary of the Treasury between 1986 and 1993, the period of major reform.
4. A comment by the Associate Minister of Finance, Maurice McTigue, *The Press*, Christchurch, 6 June 1992. Electric fences play a key role in New Zealand's livestock industry and are a significant feature in this country of just over 4 million people and 32 million sheep.
5. From 33 per cent to 39 per cent for incomes above $60 000 with no indexation of the thresholds.
6. Labelled by the opposition as 'chewing gum' tax cuts – barely enough to fund an extra pack of chewing gum.
7. The main area in the 1990s where it did not prove possible to use the budget constraint to cap public sector wage growth was in the education sector where the Ministry of Education was required to negotiate national collective bargaining agreements with teachers' unions on behalf of schools and other providers.
8. The New Zealand approach echoes the motivational lessons identified by Wilson (1989: 177) from contrasting management styles at the United States Department of Defense. Robert McNamara was Secretary of Defense during a period of significant budget increases, but extremely unpopular because of his centralizing of budget decisions. By contrast, Melvin Laird, Secretary between 1969 and 1973, cut spending by a third, yet was popular with Defense staff for allowing considerable autonomy over where cuts were made. Wilson uses the illustration to highlight the importance bureaucracies place on autonomy and control – the 'turf' to which his Chapter 10 heading 'Turf' refers.
9. It is important to recognize both the size and limits of this achievement. New Zealand was a true pioneer doing what no other jurisdiction had done before. It is also important to recognize the limits of achievement: the systems introduced produced macro costings that were adequate for external reporting purposes, but even in 2008, other than third-party revenue funded activities, few government agencies had adequate micro costing systems at, say, the project level. For example only one agency could provide information on the cost of participating in value-for-money reviews announced as part of the 2006 budget. Ironically it is not possible to assess directly whether value-for-money reviews represented value for money.
10. The most famous example of the impact of the capital charge was the decision of the Ministry of Foreign Affairs to significantly reduce its (valuable) holding of New Zealand works of art, displayed in New Zealand diplomatic missions. The art was given to New Zealand galleries.
11. In practice so as not to breach parliamentary appropriations, agency underspends of 1–3 per cent are common because of multiple line items or multiple votes.

REFERENCES

Boston, J., J. Martin, J. Pallot and P. Walsh (1996), *Public Management: The New Zealand Model*, Auckland: Oxford University Press.

Schick, A. (1996), *The Spirit of Reform*, Wellington: State Services Commission.

Scott, G. (1996), *Government Reform in New Zealand*, Geneva: International Monetary Fund.

Scott, G. (2001), *Public Management in New Zealand*, Wellington: Business Round Table

Scott, G., P. Bushnell and N. Sallee (1990), 'Reform of the core public sector: New Zealand Experience', *Governance*, **3** (2), 138–67.
State Services Commission (SSC) (1998), 'Strengthening strategic management: summary of fiscal modelling work', SSC occasional paper no. 4, accessed at www.ssc.govt.nz.
Treasury (NZ) (1989), *Putting it Simply: An Explanatory Guide to Financial Management Reform*, Wellington: Treasury.
Treasury (NZ) (1996), *Putting it Together: An Explanatory Guide to the New Zealand Public Sector Financial Management System*, Wellington: Treasury.
Treasury (NZ) (2005), 'Value for Money in Health: The DHB Sector', Treasury report T2005/344, Wellington: Treasury.
Treasury (NZ) (2008), *Budget*, Wellington: Treasury.
Warren, K. and C. Barnes (2003), 'The impact of GAAP on fiscal decision making: a review of 12 years experience with accrual and output based budgets in New Zealand', *OECD Journal of Budgeting*, **3** (4), 7–40.
Wilson, J.Q. 1989. *Bureaucracy: What Government Agencies Do and Why They Do It*, New York: Basic Books.

7. Budget reform in Japan: continuous efforts but still a long way to go

Masahiro Horie

CONTAINING DEFICITS AND DEBT: REFORM EFFORTS OVER THE LAST 30 YEARS

Japan may be considered a latecomer to budget reform, even though it can realistically claim to have made continuous reform efforts over the last three decades. Its budgetary problems have been largely structural (due to structural overspending). Hence, the main objective of these reform efforts has focused on containing and cutting expenditure. However, we must acknowledge that such efforts have been half-hearted and rhetorical, episodic and time-consuming. And results have been rather disappointing. Frequently, by the time we should have been entitled to expect results, reform programs had been suspended or postponed due to factors such as deteriorating political or economic circumstances and for other expedient reasons.

A further difficulty for the reform program in Japan is that it has been subject in effect to one-party rule. The ruling Liberal Democratic Party (LDP) dominated politics in Japan, governing for more than 50 years, except for a very short period of less than one year in 1993–94 until the spectacular change in government in 2009. The LDP could not contemplate making drastic changes to a budgetary system it had largely instituted and crafted. Having a revolving door of short-term prime ministers has also not helped the commitment to sustained reform. More recently, though, in the context of lower economic growth, Japanese prime ministers have launched structural fiscal reform programs and reforms to the budgetary system itself, which would seem rather drastic measures in the Japanese context. Furthermore, given that the present-day economic circumstances and the international credit crisis have again led to predictions for lower future growth, politics in Japan will remain volatile and unstable. As a consequence, the future of any further budgetary reform is uncertain.

Japan's Budgetary Structure

The overall budget of the national government is composed of three separate budgets: a general account budget, a special account budget and a budget for government-affiliated financial agencies. The special account budget is separately managed for specific services and enterprises such as pension and insurance programs and funded by their specifically appropriated revenue sources. There were 21 special account budgets in FY2008. The size of these budgets in FY2008 was ¥83 trillion for the general account budget, ¥368 trillion for special account budgets and ¥0.2 trillion for government-affiliated financial agencies' budgets. Excluding 'double accounted' money flow among these budgets, the net size of these combined budgets amounted in total to ¥214 trillion.

The Constitution authorizes the cabinet to make and submit the annual budget to the Diet. The cabinet submits three kinds of budgets in January together with the fiscal investment and loan program of the government. In the Diet they are deliberated en bloc usually in February and March, as the fiscal year begins in April. In addition to the 'initial' budget which comes into effect from April each year, supplementary budgets can be submitted when necessary. While the initial budget is formulated through a rigorous process under strict fiscal discipline and involves a thorough examination of the budget estimates, supplementary budgets are made more flexibly in response to the perceived needs of the time. As such there is scope for less important or less effective expenditure to appear in these supplementary budgets. Until recently, the main interest in budgetary issues shown by members of the Diet (and the mass media) was focused on the general account budget in the initial budget, not on supplementary budgets.

The government's aim in imposing budget discipline ostensibly is to ensure the soundness of fiscal condition. The issuing of public bonds to help finance annual budgets is strictly regulated by the Fiscal Law. However, Japanese governments began issuing bonds for public works from FY1966 and bonds to cover deficit financing from FY1975. By 2008, the government was chronically dependent on the issuing of bonds. For example, the initial general account budget of 2008 required a total of 30.5 percent revenue raised from bonds (see Figure 7.1). And almost 80 percent of the bond issue for FY2008 was to provide for deficit financing, not for infrastructural works (see Figures 7.1 and 7.2). In recent years the deficit problem has mushroomed almost out of control. According to the estimate by the Ministry of Finance at the beginning of the FY2008, by the end of FY2008 the total amount of outstanding bonds issued on behalf of the national government was expected to be ¥553 trillion, which equates

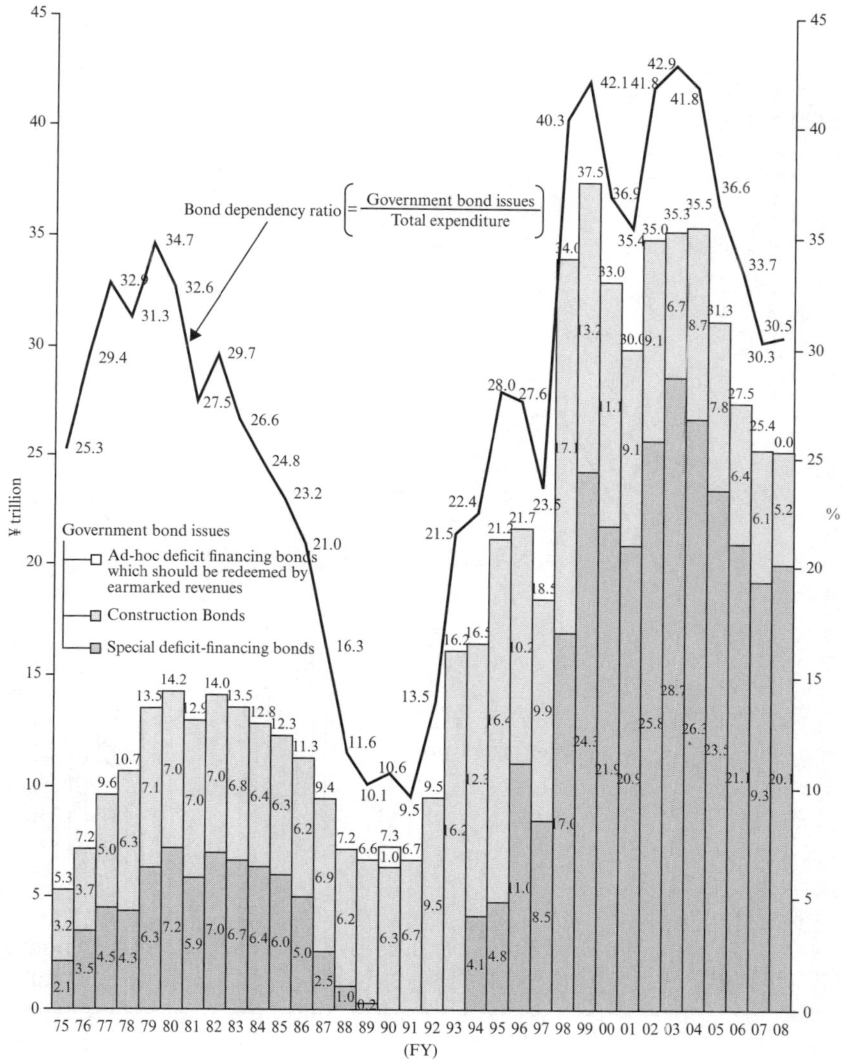

Note: FY1975–2006: settlement, FY2007: revised, FY2008: budget.

Figure 7.1 Trends of government bonds issues

to 105 percent of expected gross domestic product (GDP) for the year (see Figure 7.3). The outstanding bond issue of both the national and local governments together is expected to be ¥778 trillion, which is 147.6 percent of expected GDP in 2008.

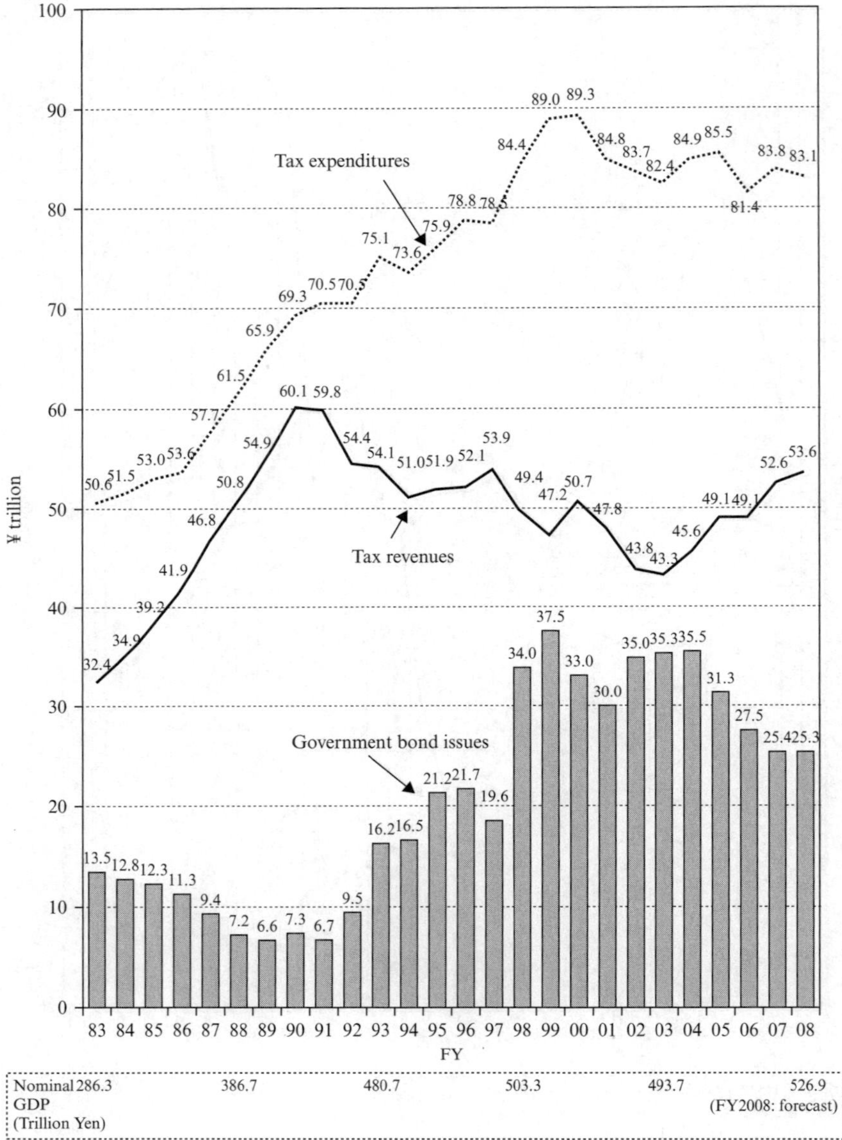

Note: FY1983–2006: settlement, FY2007: revised, FY2008: budget.

Figure 7.2 Trends of general account tax revenues, total expenditures and government bond issues

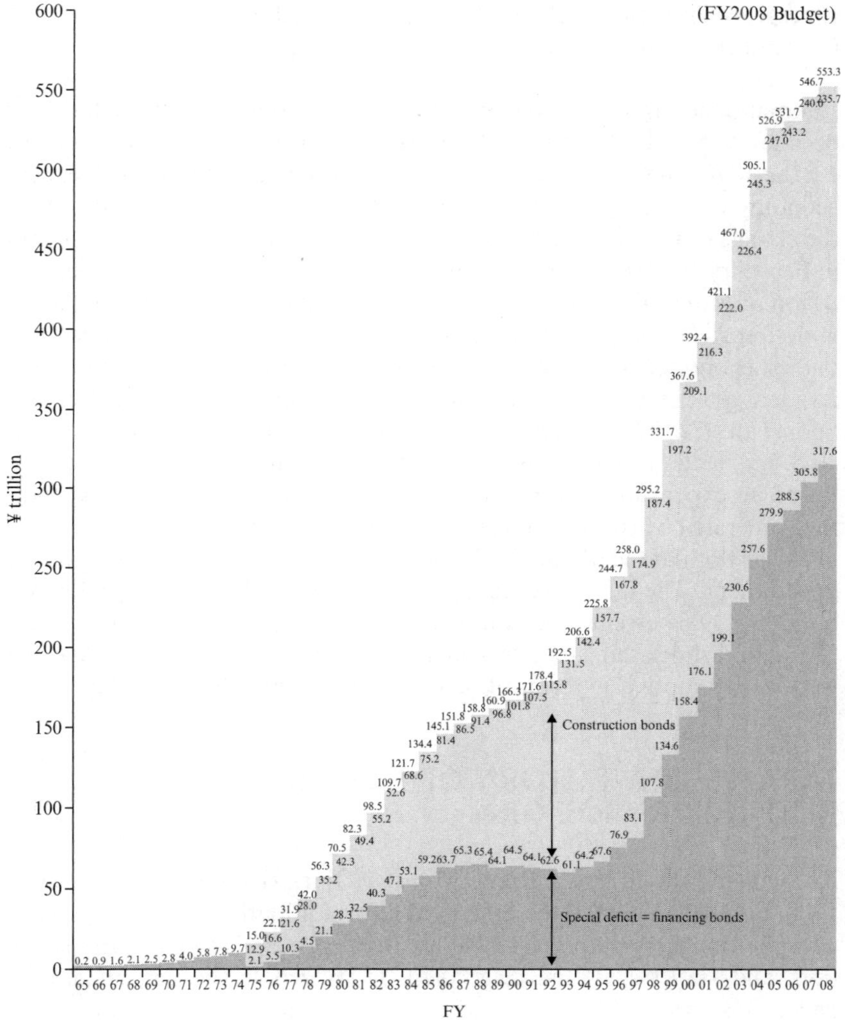

Notes:
1. FY1965–2006: actual, FY2007 and FY2008: estimates.
2. The special deficit–financing bonds outstanding includes refunding bonds for long-term debts transferred from JNR Corp.
3. The estimates of FY2007 and FY2008 excluding front-loading issuance of refunding bonds is approximately ¥527 trillion, ¥533 trillion, respectively.

Figure 7.3 Trends in accumulated government bonds outstanding

Emergence of Fiscal Problems: the Legacy of the Dollar Shock and Oil Crises of the 1970s

International crises have affected the Japanese economy over the last four decades and forced a series of reactions from successive governments. By the 1970s the days of double-digit high GDP growth in the Japanese economy were over. The 'Nixon shock' or 'dollar shock' in August 1971, the change of the foreign exchange system from a fixed to a floating system in February 1973, and the 'oil crisis' of 1973, all contributed to the deterioration of economic conditions. In Japan they brought about high inflation with 'frenzied' prices of commodities, resulting in a serious recession – the biggest economic downturn since the Second World War. In response the national government issued deficit financing bonds in the supplementary budget of FY1975 to make up for insufficient tax revenue and to spur recovery in the economy. Budget-making over the succeeding years followed an expansionary fiscal policy relying on increased public expenditure generated by issuing increasing amounts of public bonds. This caused ill effects both to the prices of commodities and to the fiscal position of the government. The initial general account budget of FY1979 depended on bonds for 39.6 percent of its total revenue. To make such matters worse, the 'second oil shock' hit Japan in January 1979. Yet, Japan still was expected to be a 'locomotive' in terms of its potential to boost the global economy.

JAPAN'S TRAJECTORY OF FISCAL AND BUDGETARY REFORM

Recognizing the urgency, Prime Minister Ohira (December 1978 – June 1980) decided to launch the first fiscal reform initiative to reconstruct the national finances, setting FY1980 as 'the first year for fiscal reconstruction' and FY1984 as 'the target year to overcome the dependency on deficit financing bonds'. Cutting expenditure was the main technique to achieve this objective. The government considered the introduction of a new value added tax, but it was not considered feasible to put it on the political agenda. Unfortunately, Prime Minister Ohira died suddenly in June 1980. The initial budget of FY1981 managed only to reduce bonds by ¥2 trillion. The cabinet of the succeeding Prime Minister Suzuki (July 1980 – November 1982) imposed an across-the-board 'zero ceiling' on the budget requests from ministries and agencies for FY1982. In addition, the Provisional Commission for Administrative Reform was established in March 1981 which made urgent recommendations in July to streamline government programs and services and to cut government expenditure.

Specific proposals to cut government expenditure were reflected in succeeding budget years. The ceiling imposed on budget requests was tightened to a 'minus ceiling' for FY1983 and after. However, the initial general account budget of FY1983 was still dependent upon bonds for up to 26.5 percent of its total revenue, more than half of which was for deficit financing. In August 1983, the cabinet of Prime Minister Nakasone (November 1982 – November 1987) was forced to postpone the target year for the end of bond dependency for deficits from FY1984 to 1990. A thorough review of government expenditure was then made with the level of general expenditure then set at equal or less than the previous year from FY1983 to 1987. Due mainly to an economic recovery producing increased tax revenue (coupled with additional revenues from a new consumption tax and extra revenues from selling the stock of the privatized Nippon Telephone & Telegraph Company), the issuing of deficit financing bonds was avoided in the initial budget of FY1990 for the first time in 15 years. Thus, the initial mid-term objective was achieved in the rescheduled target year. The dependency on bonds to fund the annual budget also gradually decreased. Yet, the government continued to issue public works bonds every year and the total amount of outstanding bonds continued to grow. Expenses related to the issuing of bonds, such as the redemption of issued bonds and interest payments, accounted for more than 20 percent of the general account budget expenditure. This greatly reduced the flexibility in government budget-making.

A Period of Brief Tranquility before a Return to Increased Borrowing

For three years, governments avoided issuing deficit-financing bonds (FY1991, FY1992 and FY1993). It was a period of brief tranquility before the Japanese economy again fell into recession, suffering the collapse of the 'bubble economy', which resulted in major decreases in tax revenue for four consecutive years. The government was forced into taking various fiscal and economic measures to stimulate the economy, including tax reductions and the adoption of a supplementary budget in 1994. The issuing of public works bonds again began to increase sharply in FY1994 and new bonds were also issued in the same year to cover the general deficit. A huge amount of bonds were issued for the supplementary budget of FY1995. In the initial general account budget of FY1996, the dependency on bonds issued jumped from 17.7 percent to 28 percent over the previous year. More than half of the bonds issued in FY1996 were in the form of deficit financing bonds, an amount that was four times higher than that of the previous year in monetary terms.

Initial Attempts at 'Structural Fiscal Reform': A Stymied Effort

Prime Minister Hashimoto (January 1996 – July 1998), who was the head of the Liberal Democratic Party which lost office in 1993 but which came back to power in 1994 as a dominant party of the new coalition, became the Prime Minister soon after the FY1996 budget was made. Winning the general election in October 1996, he organized the Administrative Reform Council to deliberate on the reorganization of government as well as other reforms. His cabinet decided in December 1996 to achieve 'fiscal soundness'. The major components of this decision were the reduction of the ratio of fiscal deficit of the national and local governments as a whole to 3 percent or lower against GDP, overcoming the government's dependency on deficit financing bonds, and decreasing the dependency on bonds in aggregate as early as possible and certainly by FY2005. He labeled FY1997 as 'the first year for the structural fiscal reform'. In the initial general account budget of FY1997, both public works bonds and deficit financing bonds were reduced in large sum. Also the amount of general expenditure, excluding the expenditure for expenses related to bonds already issued, was kept within the stipulated ceiling amount of tax and other revenues. 'Primary balance' was achieved.

To discuss more lasting and effective measures for structural fiscal reform, Prime Minister Hashimoto established the Structural Fiscal Reform Council in January 1997. It was composed of the Finance Minister and an array of other ministers, former prime ministers and ranking members of the LDP and its coalition parties. In June 1997 the council endorsed a plan to promote structural fiscal reform. Based on the conclusion of the council, the Law on Special Measures for the Promotion of Structural Fiscal Reform was submitted in September and enacted in November 1997. The major components of this law were almost identical to cabinet's decision of December 1996.

The four-point plan aimed to:

1. reduce the ratio of fiscal deficit for both the national and local governments as a whole to 3 percent of GDP or less;
2. reduce the deficit budget financing bond issue to zero;
3. reduce the dependency on bonds to the level equal to or lower than the level in the initial budget of FY1997; and
4. achieve the target level of reduction of expenditure for each major substantive policy area, such as social security, public investment, education, defense, science and technology promotion.

The first three objectives were to be achieved by FY2003, which was in effect two years earlier than had been originally intended in December

1996. The fourth objective was to be implemented during 'the intensive reform period' from FY1998 to FY2000. Fewer bonds, both public works bonds and deficit financing bonds, were issued in the initial budget of FY1998 but the reduction was minimal compared with the target level set in the 1997 law. The ratio of the fiscal deficit to GDP also decreased slightly in the initial budget by 1.2 percent (but increased from 5.9 percent to 9.7 percent if one-off factors were included). Prime Minister Hashimoto had taken the first steps toward structural reform.

STRUCTURAL REFORM COMES TO A SUDDEN END

However, the economic slowdown which began in March 1997, and growing anxieties about the financial system, affected the economy very badly. Due to these developments and for other reasons such as the increase of consumption tax rate from 3 percent to 5 percent, Prime Minister Hashimoto was forced to announce a special tax reduction in December 1997, only one month after the enactment of the Structural Fiscal Reform Law. Hashimoto also announced a comprehensive package of economic measures in April 1998, immediately after the FY1998 budget was passed by the Diet. Then, the following month, he was forced to amend the Structural Fiscal Reform Law, postponing the target year from FY2003 to FY2005. Although he had initially accelerated the schedule in 1997, he was forced to decelerate it to the original schedule just six months later.

Hashimoto was defeated in the election for the House of Councillors in July 1998, and was forced to step down. Obuchi (July 1998 – April 2000) from the same party became the new Prime Minister. His most urgent task was to boost the economy. In November 1998 Obuchi announced urgent economic measures, substantially larger than those proposed by Hashimoto. His supplementary budget provided a major economic stimulus although funded mostly from borrowings. More than half the bonds issued were for deficit financing. Together with the bonds issued in the initial budget, the total amount of bonds in FY1998 jumped from ¥18.5 to ¥34 trillion, while the government's dependency on such bonds also increased from 23.5 to 40.3 percent.

So, in December 1998, a Law to Suspend the Fiscal Structural Reform Law was enacted. In FY1999, the amount of bonds issued increased further to ¥37.5 trillion and the dependency on bonds rose to 42.1 percent. During the term of Prime Minister Obuchi, economic measures to boost the economy were given higher priority than fiscal reconstruction and structural fiscal reform. Fiscal discipline was relaxed. After the sudden death of Obuchi in April 2000, Mori (April 2000 – April 2001) became the Prime Minister. Although the rate of bond issuing decreased due to the increase of tax revenue, new ones were still issued as priority was given to economic recovery. However, there remains much argument about the effectiveness of such stimulus measures. Nonetheless, the aggregate bond liability of the national government amounted to ¥368 trillion as of the end of FY2000.

Koizumi's Tilt at a Full-Scale Structural Reform

Succeeding Mori, Prime Minister Koizumi (April 2001 – September 2006) emphasized the necessity of significant structural reform for the Japanese economy and society. Koizumi was an enthusiastic advocate of 'small government'. On his political agenda he gave the highest priority to privatization, deregulation and decentralization with the slogan: 'From government to the private sector and from the national government to local governments'. Fiscal reform was also high on his list of priorities. He immediately appointed an economics professor, Takenaka, as his Minister for Economic and Fiscal Policy to steer the Economic and Fiscal Policy Council, a deliberative body chaired by the Prime Minister. Minister Takenaka managed the council quite effectively to embrace full-scale structural reforms. Takenaka remained in cabinet for the whole of Koizumi's prime-ministership as the 'engine' promoting the reform agenda.

With regard to fiscal policies and budgeting, Takenaka attempted to change the players and processes behind budget-making, and change the frame of reference and perspectives involved in deliberating economic and fiscal policies. He tried to wrest control of the budget from the Budget Bureau in the Ministry of Finance by replacing it with his own advisory council. He wanted to change the deliberation process involved in budgetary formulation. He tried to reform not only the general account budget, but also the special account budgets and fiscal investment and loan programs. In this he was backed by Prime Minister Koizumi who said: 'There is no sanctuary in structural reform'. Takenaka was especially skeptical of the effectiveness of public works expenditure used to stimulate the economy. And on bonds, he was critical of the huge amounts that had been issued by preceding cabinets.

The first step in major structural reform was taken by the Koizumi cabinet in June 2001. It adopted basic rules for the management of the economy and government finances (referred to as the *Hone-Buto* decision, meaning a 'strong bones' policy in Japanese). Cabinet made clear its determination to restrict the bond issue to ¥30 trillion or below in the following year's budget. Although ¥30 trillion had been issued in the preceding year, it was not an easy target to meet as tax revenues were expected to decline, while demands for expenditure were increasing. Koizumi managed to keep his promise in the initial budget of FY2002, but was forced to introduce a supplementary budget adding an additional ¥5 trillion of bonds. Paradoxically, the higher level of bonds was maintained in FY2003 and FY2004, resulting in the dependency on bonds reaching its highest level in FY2003 at 42.9 percent of revenue. More than 75 percent of the bonds issued over the three years FY2002-04 were to cover the budget deficit. However, Koizumi fulfilled a promise made in January 2002 that public works expenditure would be reduced to the level of the FY1991 budget. Gradually, the dependence on bonds declined to ¥31.3 trillion in FY2005, and then continued to fall to ¥25.4 trillion in FY2007 and ¥25.3 trillion in the initial budget of FY2008.

Prime Minister Koizumi resigned voluntarily in September 2006, even though his popularity was high. His successor, Abe (September 2006 – September 2007), followed Koizumi's fiscal strategy. However, Abe resigned after suffering defeat in the election for the House of Councillors in July 2007 when the ruling coalition lost its majority in that House. And when the next Prime Minister, Fukuda (September 2007 – September 2008), could not overcome political difficulties in the Diet, he too was forced to resign, handing over to Taro Aso in September 2008. The political situation in Japan was most unstable, with political leaders hesitant to address issues unwelcome to the general public.

Three Interconnected Phases of Reform: Aiming at Financial Reconstruction and Structural Fiscal Reform

From 2001 the *Hone-Buto* policy became an annual set of commitments, consisting of various instruments (fiscal and expenditure targets, financial reforms and changes to the budget system). They gradually became consecutive targets and more integrated commitments, forming in effect medium-term fiscal plans. Such *Hone-Buto* policies are now regarded as the framework for managing government finances and budget-making for succeeding LDP-dominated coalition cabinets.

The Koizumi cabinet used these frameworks in its 'first phase of reform' from 2001 to 2006. This phase consisted of two subperiods: 'the intensive adjustment period' (2001–04), and the 'concentrated reinforcement period' (2005–06). In this latter period, the cabinet declared its intention of achieving a surplus in the primary budget balance for both the national and local governments by FY2011. The subsequent reform period, extending from 2007 and running to 2011, has been labeled 'the second phase of reform'. After this, a future reform period from the early 2010s to the mid-2010s has been flagged as 'the third phase of reform'. In this third period, the cabinet has committed itself to reducing the ratio of outstanding bond issue against GDP, something it feels it cannot achieve in the short term. But in stating its future intentions, the cabinet has not said exactly how it will address or realize the planned reductions of outstanding bonds. Its success will depend on many factors such as how far expenditures can be cut, the level of economic growth, increases in tax revenue, and possible increases in the rate of the consumption tax.

To achieve a surplus in the primary balance in the second phase, the government will have to deal with an estimated imbalance of around ¥16.5 trillion in both national and local government finances by FY2011 (assuming a nominal economic growth rate of 3 percent in this period). Most of this bid to trim ¥16.5 trillion is intended to be achieved by expenditure cuts (namely between ¥11.4 and ¥14.3 trillion). The shortfall is to be bridged by revenue increases. In 2006 the Koizumi cabinet committed itself to a tough *Hone-Buto* policy. It announced expenditure cuts in most major policy areas: ¥1.6 trillion in social security; ¥2.6 trillion in personnel expenditure; between ¥5.6 and ¥3.9 trillion in public works investment; and between ¥4.5 and ¥3.3 trillion in other areas. But in relation to revenue measures, the cabinet has not specifically declared its hand, even though its commitments imply that the consumption tax rate will be raised some time in the near future to ensure stable revenue levels for social security, which is a major cause of increasing expenditure given Japan's aging demographics.

In the following two budgets (FY2007 and FY2008), cabinet implemented the expenditure cuts announced in the *Hone-Buto* policy of 2006. However, the reduction of public works expenditure hit local economies hard, especially in rural areas where public works as a major undertaking. Moreover, the alleged ill-effects of deregulation began to catch public attention. People became impatient over the growing disparity between rich and poor, and between rich areas and poorer ones. People started to become weary of continuing the 'reform' trajectory promoted by the Koizumi cabinet.

In 2008, the Japanese economy again went into recession. This threw into doubt the 3 percent economic growth target – a precondition of the reform package. In August that year the cabinet responded with further measures to boost the economy. And the ruling coalition parties began to consider further measures to soothe the people. These measures, which will require additional public expenditure, have enjoyed bipartisan support in the parliament. Even after the power shift from the ruling LDP to the Democratic Party of Japan in 2009, it is unlikely that stringent fiscal measures will be adopted due to public expectations. So, whether or not the 'second phase of reform' goes as expected in the remaining period is becoming unclear. Achieving a surplus in the primary balance in FY2011 now appears unlikely or, as the Japanese say colloquially, 'the light before the wind' (literally, a candle flickering in the wind is easily extinguished).

CHANGES IN THE ACTORS AND PROCESSES OF BUDGET-MAKING

Enhancing the Role of the Prime Minister

Historically, Japan's budget-making process was wholly controlled by the Budget Bureau of the Ministry of Finance with its own advisory body, the Fiscal System Council. Every year each government ministry would submit a budget request to the Budget Bureau by the end of August in line with a cabinet guideline issued at the end of July. This guideline was prepared by the Budget Bureau. The Budget Bureau would then examine the budget requests and prepare a draft budget to be decided by the cabinet, usually by the end of December to be submitted to the Diet in January. In making each budget, economic forecasts for the following year were agreed in December before cabinet decided on the budget. Ruling parties would be consulted by the Budget Bureau before such decisions were finalized. The Fiscal System Council, whose members were selected by the Budget Bureau from outside government, would deliberate budget-making policies as well as specific budget items of importance, before making recommendations directly to the Finance Minister. Staff of the Budget Bureau provided support to the Fiscal System Council and would usually try to induce the council to make the same kind of recommendations sought by the Budget Bureau.

The Japanese Diet is not allowed to construct its own budget plan, but is authorized to deliberate on the budget, in contrast to the US case where the Congress makes its own appropriation Acts. It is assumed that the Diet can change the content of the budget proposed by the cabinet. But because the Constitution only gives authority to the cabinet to submit the budget, in practice the Diet is unable to make changes that affect the main spending proposals or deteriorate the comprehensiveness of the budget. Usually, by the time the Diet begins its deliberation on the budget, the approval of the ruling parties is already secured. As the fiscal year begins on 1 April, the Diet is expected to finish its deliberations by the end of March.

Fiscal conditions forced Japanese leaders to take more personal responsibility for budget settings. In January 2001 the Economic and Fiscal

Policy Council (EFPC) was established as part of Hashimoto's reorganization plan for the national government. The council was intended as a new and powerful deliberative body located within the Cabinet Office attached to the Prime Minister's portfolio. It was aimed at strengthening the leadership of the Prime Minister and the cabinet in economic and fiscal policy-making. Even though it has existed for only a relatively short period of time, the new council changed the budgeting process considerably.

The Economic and Fiscal Policy Council is composed of the Prime Minister, the Chief Cabinet Secretary, the Minister for Economic and Fiscal Policy and other ministers and non-minister members that the Prime Minister decides to appoint. The Prime Minister usually appoints the Minister of Finance, the Minister of Internal Affairs and Communications, the Minister of the Economy, Trade and Industry, the Governor of the Bank of Japan and four knowledgeable members from outside of the government. Although the Prime Minister is the chairperson of the council, the Minister for Economic and Fiscal Policy actually steers the council and is responsible for the management of the council. Other ministers are invited to the council only when the Prime Minister considers it necessary.

When the council was first created, the Ministry of Finance tried to limit its role. But after Koizumi became Prime Minister and appointed Takenaka as the Minister for Economic and Fiscal Policy in April 2001, the council became the most important organ that deliberated not only economic and fiscal policy but also almost all important substantive policy matters. The EFPC is now authorized by law to decide on the basic fiscal policy of the government including the government finances and the management of the economy. Its power derives from its power over the budget: there is no policy or program without budget. And the council can discuss any policy matter it chooses.

Adopting a Strategic Approach to Budget-making

With the strong support of Prime Minister Koizumi and in cooperation with four non-ministerial but knowledgeable members of the EFPC, Minister Takenaka convinced the council to proceed on a course of strategic budgetary reforms. Following the initial *Hone-Buto* policy of June 2001, the council decreed a further set of fiscal rules in 2002. It committed the government to issue a 'Mid-Term Perspective on the Structural Reform and Economy and Government Finance' in January, and to revise it annually. It insisted that the *Hone-Buto* policy would be revised each June or July, setting annual targets based on a comprehensive deliberation of economic and fiscal policy and substantive policies of importance. And, such frameworks would be imposed over the annual budget-making round early in December. The strategic aim of such rules is to achieve a 'primary balance', a key word in Japan's fiscal reconstruction. This objective was first articulated in the structural fiscal reform of 2001 and appeared in publications of the Ministry of Finance. But it was only after the *Hone-Buto* policy of 2006 that this English terminology became widely used in daily conversations among bureaucrats, politicians, the media and others.

The council has inserted new actors and changed the budget process. It has changed the schedule, the perspectives and the frame of reference for budget control. Economic and fiscal policy and budget matters are now discussed in detail from various viewpoints all the year round by the council. Often these meetings occur more than 30 times a year, each with the Prime Minister in attendance. Substantive policy directions for the following year are discussed by the council before any budget requests are made and before the Budget Bureau begins its examination. It is difficult for the Budget Bureau (or any claiming ministries) to assemble a budget contrary to what has been written in the *Hone-Buto* policy and the fiscal policy settings declared by the council. And to urge greater efficiencies, the council also attempts to project-manage major spending programs, setting time schedules or milestones for policy implementation and following up the progress of policies.

Information used in the council's deliberations is delivered to the mass media immediately after council meetings and also put on the Internet home page of the EFPC. The Minister for Economic and Fiscal Policy usually holds a press conference immediately after a council meeting. The press conference video is also put on the Internet. Moreover, a rather detailed summary of the proceedings of each council meeting is put on the Internet home page within a few days of the meeting, and a complete record of proceedings is made available to the public later. Such practices of openness have contributed to increased discipline, greater transparency of discussions on budgetary and fiscal policy, and wider education about the major issues related to budget-making.

The Importance of the Strong Political Leadership

During the administration of Prime Minister Koizumi and Minister Takenaka, the council was most influential. But it appears that the influence of the council has gradually decreased in the succeeding cabinets. There are several reasons for this. Succeeding prime ministers have not been as enthusiastic as Koizumi was about structural reform. They became more interested in other policy matters, rather than fiscal or budgetary reform. They could not maintain the momentum to continue with drastic fiscal reform when confronted by resistance from those affected.

The council's membership of ministers and non-minister members also gradually changed. Politicians became jealous of non-ministerial members who superseded politicians with their influence over highly critical policy matters.

The political situation in the Diet also changed. Prime Minister Koizumi had enjoyed a majority in both the House of Representatives and the House of Councillors. As leader of the ruling coalition with high popularity, he could get things done. With the strong political support of Koizumi, the Economic and Fiscal Policy Council was able to wield considerable influence. After Koizumi departed, the ruling parties lost their majority in the upper House of Councillors. Now without the strong leadership of a Prime Minister who could control both the Diet and the bureaucrats, the power of the council declined. Nevertheless, it remains important that the council managed to introduce various budgetary reforms, changed the deliberative processes of budgeting, disclosed and debated many problems in budget-making, and threw new light on the overall decision-making process.

BUT BUDGET LOOPHOLES STILL EXIST

While the annual budget is now formed through a more rigorous process under stringent financial conditions, there still exist a number of loopholes within the system which are problematic to good budgetary and fiscal performance. These loopholes provide reasons why Japan's success at budgetary control has been rather lukewarm. The main three loopholes are: supplementary budgets, the special account budgets, and the Fiscal Investment and Loan Program.

Supplementary Budgets

The government is allowed to add a supplementary budget when additional expenditure is considered necessary because of reasons that have emerged since the initial budget was passed, or when other factors have affected the initial budget. The supplementary budget is always made in response to the different necessities of the time. Budget formulators only refer to the initial budget when they make year-to-year comparisons, excluding the supplementary budget. For instance, the Budget Bureau uses the fiscal limits of the initial budget to contain the expansion of expenditure, maintain discipline and underscore its efforts of rigorous examination of expenditure requests. It assigns a strict 'ceiling' upon the budget request each ministry can submit. However, this strict 'ceiling' and other rigorous processes are not necessarily applied in formulating the supplementary budget. It is often the case that budget requests not accepted in the initial budget are then included in the supplementary budget. There are many cases where programs or projects judged ineffective, less important or wasteful in the initial budget were then accepted in the supplementary budget to boost the economy. While such cases demoralize budgetary officials, the Budget Bureau can also use the supplementary budget to soothe ministries which have complained about the excessive rigor of the initial budget.

Supplementary budgets, thus, offer governments a tactical loophole. They can appear to avoid excessive expenditure in the initial budget while committing additional expenditures in supplementary budgets. Additional bonds for deficits or public works projects can be issued as part of these packages. Any tax revenue exceeding the estimated amount may be used for additional expenditures in the supplementary budget. More recently, the problem of supplementary budgeting has been severely criticized. With unhappy memories of huge supplementary expenditures in the 1990s, the cabinet has become cautious in considering the need for making a supplementary budget. Yet, there is always the opportunity to use supplementary budgets in the name of boosting the economy or ensuring the welfare and security of the people.

Special Account Budgets

Special account budgets are allowed by law only when it is necessary to manage a dedicated account, separate from the general account, for specific services and enterprises. They are funded either from their own sources of revenue or monies transferred from the general account budget or from other special account budgets. There were 45 special account budgets in FY1967. From 1970, governments have refrained from establishing new special accounts while trying to decrease their number. At the time of the government's reorganization in 2001, there were still 38 accounts. There are now 21 special accounts in 2008. The total amount of expenditure of special account budgets is about ¥368 trillion in FY2008, although that figure drops to about ¥178 trillion after excluding 'double accounted' money flows.

Even though there is supposed merit in separating these special accounts (such as making clear the relationship between the benefit of services and the cost of producing them, or facilitating efficient management), having so many special accounts makes aggregate government budgeting more complicated and difficult to understand. They can also compromise the efficiency of the government's budget as a whole. Although each special account budget is jointly managed by the Ministry of Finance and the respective ministry in charge of the substantive programs to be funded, the Budget Bureau has been less interested in these accounts than in the general account budget. Revenues generated in each special account are retained within that account irrespective of actual needs and can often be used for apparently unnecessary or wasteful expenditure or kept as a reserve. Once revenues are secured, any incentive for efficiency is likely to be lost. Furthermore, spending ministries often transfer program expenses from the stringent general account budget to a lukewarm special account budget, often at the request of the Budget Bureau.

In February 2003, Finance Minister Shiokawa ordered a thorough review of special account budgets, saying to the Committee of the House of Representatives: 'while we eat rice gruel in the main house (the general account budget), children eat *sukiyaki* in the detached room (the special account budgets)'. The Fiscal System Council of the Finance Ministry began the review in March 2003, supported by the EFPC that was also trying to promote reform of these off-budget accounts. The Fiscal System Council made reform proposals each year, which were reflected in the annual budgets of FY2004, FY2005 and FY2006 and in the new comprehensive Law on Special Account Budgets enacted in March 2007. Under this law, the disclosure of assets and liabilities of each special account is now legally required. Services, programs and enterprises were reviewed for rationalization and efficiency. Expenditures and revenues were reviewed. Ways to reduce the transfer of funds from the general account budget to special account budgets were reviewed, as was user-charging. Financial statements were reviewed to increase their transparency. The need for separate management of special accounts was also reviewed. As a result, it was decided to reduce the number of special accounts from 31 in FY2006 to 17 by FY2011. Hollow-log reserves discovered have been transferred to the general account budget or used for financial reconstruction.

Fiscal Investment and Loan Program: the 'Second Budget'

The Fiscal Investment and Loan Program (FILP) is not officially part of the national government's budget, since it is not a gratuity or subsidy but is policy-related money provided through government-affiliated organizations or local governments. In selecting how to deliver government policies, the government considers whether to invest funds as a grant or provide a loan, usually with more favorable treatment than that provided by private financial institutions. When the budget is tight, the FILP offers an alternative funding route. With ample funds historically available for the FILP, including postal savings, it was a scheme that was widely used. This is why the FILP has often been referred to as 'the second budget' of the government. Although requests for FILP funding are examined by the Financial Bureau of the Finance Ministry, consultation is made with a spending ministry and the Budget Bureau during each budget-making round. The total FILP is submitted to the Diet together with the annual budget and deliberated en bloc. After a drastic reform of the FILP in 2001, which abolished an automatic inflow of money such as postal savings, the amount of funds available to the FILP began to decrease sharply. At its peak in FY1996, ¥40.5 trillion was invested in the FILP, but by FY2008 only ¥13.87 trillion was commissioned. Demand for FILP funding has declined as a result of governmental reorganization and administrative reform efforts. Outstanding FILP borrowing is estimated to be ¥219.9 trillion in FY2008, down from ¥417.8 trillion in FY2000.

Other Controversies over Unnecessary Reserves and Wasteful Expenditure

There is currently a heated argument about whether there still are 'unnecessary' surplus reserves in special accounts and, if so, how much. There is also controversy as to how much 'unnecessary' or 'wasteful' expenditure exists in the government's budget as a whole. These issues are related to wider debates on how best to reconstruct government finances (especially the general account budget). One argument, in essence, is to use 'unnecessary' surplus reserves in special account budgets and eliminate all 'wasteful' expenditure, to help balance the budget. This would obviate the necessity of raising the rate of the consumption tax especially if general revenues increased due to an expanding economy. The other argument is that the amount of possible expenditure cuts and 'unnecessary' surplus reserves are limited and, therefore, it would be prudent to consider raising the rate of the consumption tax as early as possible.

It is true that there is some 'unnecessary' and 'wasteful' expenditure and 'unnecessary' reserves. But it is not an easy task to decide what is 'unnecessary' or 'wasteful' and what magnitude may exist. In many cases, there are pros and cons for different arguments. And in most cases, those who are most likely to be seriously affected, even if they are small in number, are most vocal about preserving their arrangements.

REFORM OF BUDGETARY AND ACCOUNTING METHODS

The Quest for Rational, Evidence-Based Budget-making

In order to control expenditure, the government introduced annual 'ceilings' upon the budget requests each ministry or agency could make, often in the process further tightening these ceilings. If ceilings were too tight this led to inflexibility in budget-making. So, the government through the EFPC changed the methods of budget-making, expanded the frames of reference for decision-making and introduced various new perspectives and viewpoints into budget-making. Four efforts have been made to reform budgetary methods in relation to new or existing policies and programs.

The Usage of Survey Results and Inspection of Policy Execution

The Budget Bureau is authorized to inspect and survey the results of budget execution of specific policies and programs. This function is attached to the budget-making function but was often regarded as less important by the Budget Bureau. Finance Minister Shiokawa reactivated this function, considering that in the management cycle 'plan – do – see', the 'see' function is very important to ensure efficient and effective delivery. The Budget Bureau and regional offices of the Finance Ministry now choose between 50 and 70 policies and programs a year for review conducting surveys and on-the-spot inspections. The results are reflected in subsequent budget decisions. Yet, the number of policies and programs targeted for such inspection remains tiny compared to the huge amount of government activities.

The Usage of Resolutions of the Diet and Results of Audit by the Board of Audit

The Diet can make resolutions to warn the government of inappropriate or wasteful policy execution, based on its deliberation of the budget, its review of the accounts, and the results of audit by the Board of Audit. The government must pay respect to these resolutions in budget-making. The Board of Audit, an independent body, conducts audits on the execution of budgets and the processing of accounting. Auditing is not limited to the examination of accuracy and compliance, but is extended to include performance reviews of the economy, efficiency, effectiveness and even the necessity of specific policies and programs. To this end, the Board of Audit undertakes in-depth surveys and conducts cost–benefit analyses of major programs and large-scale public works projects when deemed necessary or required by the Diet. Such results are used in future budget-making.

The Usage of Analysis and Evaluation of Policies, Programs and Projects

Under the Policy Evaluation Law, enacted in 2001, every ministry is required to evaluate the policies, programs and projects under its charge. The Ministry of Internal Affairs and Communications conducts a meta-evaluation of the evaluation activities of ministries, and also carries out independent evaluations of policies and programs involving two or more ministries. Evaluations can consider the necessity of these policies or programs as well as their efficiency and effectiveness. Each ministry can choose which policy to evaluate, but is required by law to evaluate public works projects, science and technology projects and official development assistance projects. Evaluations can take place before a specific policy is decided upon or after a policy is implemented. The government, in turn, is required by law to make efforts to use the results of policy evaluation appropriately in its budget-making. Even though the Budget Bureau is not yet satisfied with the quality of the evaluations conducted by spending ministries, the budget system is gradually becoming accustomed to incorporating the results of evaluation. However, since the budgetary process is influenced by various factors, it is uncertain whether these evaluation exercises have actually improved the quality of budget decision-making and, if so, to what extent.

Greater Coordination and Clustering

Since there are similar or interrelated policies and programs involving many ministries, it is important to examine any overlapping redundancies and to coordinate the policy-making, budget-making and implementation processes. As the Budget Bureau is subdivided into analytical sections corresponding to the spending ministries, it is not necessarily effective in reviewing apparently overlapping or interrelated policies and programs. Instead, it was decided that this function should be undertaken by the Cabinet Secretariat. From 2004 the Cabinet Secretariat began to focus on coordination, selecting interagency or overlapping policies and programs for review. It considered these as 'clusters' of policies (and programs) where integration was important. By 2008 it had identified 17 policy clusters, although this approach still remains in its infancy.

Reform of Government Accounting

The importance of financial disclosure was often overlooked in Japan because most of the reform attention was directed towards fiscal controls and budget-making. Documentation on the financial position of the government was insufficient not only for disclosure but even for ensuring the appropriate, efficient and effective management of financial activities of the government. It was specifically pointed out that information on the assets and liabilities of government remained limited in comparison with private enterprise accounting.

For this reason, the reform of government accounting was grad promoted. Although Japan's budgeting and accounting system a cash-based system (as prescribed by law), the governm explore other methods to improve its financial reporting. Accrual accounting began to be introduced in areas where it was deemed to be suitable. Moreover, an integrated financial reporting system has gradually evolved over the last decade.

On the financial position of the government as a whole, a comprehensive balance sheet was produced annually between 1998 and 2002, combining the balance sheets for the general account and special accounts by using techniques adopted from private sector accounting. Then, from 2003 and after, a complete set of financial reports were prepared and made available to the public (a consolidated balance sheet, a statement of expenses of activities, a statement of the change of difference of assets and liabilities, and a statement of revenues and expenditures for each division). These documents show the flow and stock of the government as a whole. In addition, financial reports for each special account and each ministry have been prepared and made open to the public in relation to the settlement of accounts from 1999 and 2002 respectively. Financial information on special accounts is now statutorily required by the Law on Special Account Budgets of 2007 and subject to examination by the Board of Audit. Financial documents of incorporated administrative agencies, which are corporations independent from a ministry, have also been prepared and released publicly. For other government-affiliated corporations, statements of administrative costs and other disclosure documents have been produced since 2000.

BUDGETARY DOCUMENTATION AND COMMUNICATION: STATUTORY REQUIREMENTS AND PUBLIC RELATIONS

Japan's Fiscal Law, which is the basic law concerning budget-making, mandates that the government's budget submitted to the Diet must consist of a series of basic budgetary statements together with a list of supporting documents. Basic budgetary documents include:

- the general principles of the budget;
- the revenue and expenditure budget;
- the continuing budget;
- pre-approved carry-over expenditure; and
- pre-supposed Treasury's liability commitments.

The Fiscal Law also requires ten other explanatory documents be attached to the budget, namely:

1. a document about the details of revenue budget;
2. a document covering the planned expenditure requests of each ministry and agency;
3. a document about the settlements (total and net) of revenue and expenditure and a document about the revenue and expenditure budget (total and net) of the coming year in question;
4. a document detailing the state of the national Treasury;
5. a document on the scale of bonds issued and public borrowing;
6. a document about the assets of the national government;
7. a document about the assets, liabilities, profit and loss of corporations the national government has invested in;
8. a document explaining the presupposed Treasury's liability commitments;
9. a document explaining the continuing budget; and
10. other documents necessary to explain the state of financial condition and the content of the budget.

There has been almost no change in these statutory requirements since major amendments were made to the Fiscal Law in 1952. Supplementary budgets and any temporary supply budgets customarily only require the first two basic budgetary documents.

In presenting these budgetary documents, the content of the revenue and expenditure budget is presented organizationally according to the structure of government organizations (divided into ministries proper, external organs of the ministry such as agencies or commissions, and organizations attached to the ministry). Estimates of revenue are presented according to the ministry and nature of the tax. For example, in the case of the revenue of the Finance Ministry, income tax is shown as are stamp duties and other taxes, along with comparisons to previous years. Planned expenditures are also presented within this organizational framework, but show the objective of the expenditure. In addition to the amount of expenditure sought, a brief explanation is made about the requested planned expenditure.

Theoretically, there are several potential ways in which the expenditure budget could be shown. It could be presented by organizational unit, by function or objective of government activities, or by the nature of the expenses. Ideally, it should present information so that it is easy to understand the whole picture of government, to compare changes year by year, to ensure the appropriate control of budget-making and execution, and to identify organizational responsibility for specific expenditure. Japan's view is that there must also be stability in the schema of presentation to enable judgments to be made over the shorter and longer terms. This is one reason why the statutory provisions of the Fiscal Law have not been changed for decades.

Nevertheless, Japanese governments have found it advantageous to present budgetary information in other ways. Thus, additional non-statutorily required documents have been generated and these have tended to increase in number almost every year. For instance, in cooperation with spending ministries, the Finance Ministry releases additional documents when the budget is submitted to the Diet other than those statutorily required. Among these documents are: 'The Explanation of the Budget' and 'The Details of Expenditure'. These non-statutory documents are more flexible and can be changed in response to changing imperatives. For example, specific policy areas can be highlighted to show the increasing importance of this policy area.

'The Explanation of the Budget' explains the revenue and expenditure budget as well as the Fiscal Investment and Loan Program (FILP). It also presents expenditure according to the major functional areas of spending, namely: social security, education and science and technology promotion, expenses relating to the bond issue, pensions, local allocation grants, defense, public works, economic cooperation, small and medium-sized enterprises, energy, food, and others. These functional areas are subdivided further allowing brief explanations of specific policies and programs to be made with comparisons to previous years. 'The explanation of the budget' is a handy document of about 160 pages and widely used when the Finance Ministry explains the budget to those concerned. However, it mainly contains input information (amounts of expenditure, inputs to sustain government activities, and functional areas of spending) but provides very little explanation of the desired outputs and outcome of government activities. 'The details of expenditure' document shows the content of each organizational expenditure budget in more detail than shown in the statutorily required document. The Budget Bureau does this because it does not want to be too bound by the Diet on the specific details of each organizational budget. But it is necessary to provide such detailed information to the organization concerned. This suggests another reason as to why the Fiscal Law has not been changed, because it is very convenient to produce documents which are not statutorily required.

Other forms of communication strategies and public relations exercises are used to convey information about the budget. These are particularly addressed to members of the ruling parties and the mass media. Between September and December each year, budgetary submissions from the spending ministries including material used to justify the requests are made available. The evaluation results of policies, programs and projects are also released. The press often covers negotiations between spending ministries and the Budget Bureau, focusing on new policy requests or controversial policies. In the final stages of the budget process, when ministers and other top officials of spending ministries negotiate with the Finance Ministry, they will usually hold a press conference to explain the outcome of the negotiation. From its side, the Budget Bureau calls a press conference when it submits its draft of the budget to the cabinet when the negotiation stage is over, but before cabinet has approved the final budget.

When the budget is submitted to the Diet, officials of the Budget Bureau and spending ministries attend corresponding committee meetings of ruling and opposition parties. They will usually attend the offices of ranking members before these meetings. During deliberation by budget committees in the Diet, first in the House of Representatives and then in the House of Councillors, various requests or requirements are made by members of these committees. In response to such requests and requirements, additional materials are prepared and submitted. As to the requests and requirements from opposition parties, officials of ministries concerned will consult with ranking members of the ruling parties on the respective budget committee when they think it necessary. The Finance Ministry also produces various materials for public consumption to explain public finances in Japan. They are printed for publication and put on the Internet and the ministry's home page. Each spending ministry also prints various materials concerning its budget and puts them on its home page. There are now so many documents released to the public during the budget process and after the budget is presented, that Japan would rank among the most open of Organisation for Economic Co-operation and Development (OECD) countries.

CONCLUSIONS: A MIXED SCORECARD

Over the past three decades, Japan has made continuous efforts to reform its fiscal policies and government finances, as well as its budget-making processes and post-budget policy execution. Whether these efforts have been successful or effective is a matter for debate. It is at best a mixed scorecard. As this chapter has shown, there are several distinct characteristics but also several shortcomings and limitations in the reform efforts pursued by Japan.

Japan's fiscal situation has been overburdened by an enormous reliance on bonds to shore up the annual budget, resulting in a huge amount of outstanding borrowing. To address this structural difficulty, governments have most emphasized the cutting of expenditure. But it has not been easy to cut expenditures and overcome this fiscal difficulty. Rather, it has been a constant battle. Reform efforts have been episodic and time-consuming. No drastic reductions in expenditure have been achieved, and significant loopholes still exist that can be used to undermine fiscal discipline. As a consequence, cutting expenditure will continue to be the main priority in budget-making in the foreseeable future.

One of the possible reasons for this constant battle with reform can be traced to the long years of dominance by the same ruling political parties. With the exception of the early Koizumi years, the LDP has found it hard to maintain its commitment to reform. As the Koizumi period shows, strong leadership and a strong passion for reform is a fundamental prerequisite for real reform, and this commitment must be sustained for some years. While the change of power to the Democratic Party of Japan in 2009 may make it possible to review allocations free from the constraints of the past and the network of powerful vested interests, it does not guarantee that strong leadership will emerge. Japan could just as easily fall into political turmoil.

Even though a cautious reform trajectory appeared more acceptable to the Japanese electorate than a more drastic one, the mindset of the people has not changed very much. They continue to demand government spending and insist that governments intervene when something happens. For instance, each time Japan has experienced economic recession, the government has been forced to increase government expenditure in order to boost the economy, usually funded by bond issues. Reform plans announced with the best of intentions have often been suspended, postponed or given up.

Hence, the likelihood of further significant reform is uncertain if not improbable. Significant reforms to improve the quality of the budget and the process of budget-making are unlikely to be given a high political priority unless they can simultaneously contribute directly to cutting expenditure or reducing the bond issue. Although various budgetary reform efforts have been attempted over many years, some of which have proved effective, there is still a long way to go in Japan.

REFERENCES

Aoki, Masahiko and Kotarou Tsuru (eds) (2004), *Nihonn no Zaisei Kaikaku, [Fiscal Reform of Japan: Redesigning the Frame of State]*, Tokyo: Toyou Keizai Shinpousha.

International Monetary Fund (IMF) (2001), *Japan: Report on the Observance of Standards and Codes – Fiscal Transparency Module*, Washington, DC: IMF.

Komura, Takeshi (2008), *Yosan to Zaiseihou, [Budget and Fiscal Law]*, Tokyo: Shin Nihon Houki Syuppan Kabushikigaisha.

Ministry of Finance (various years), highlights of the budget for FY2008; FY2007; FY2006; FY2005; FY2004; FY2003; and FY2002.

Ministry of Finance (various years) *Nihon no Saisei,* [*Japan's public finance*] *FY1990–FY2008,* published annually by Toyou Keizai Shinpousha.

Ministry of Finance (2003, 2005, 2006, 2007, 2008), *Current Japanese Fiscal Conditions and Issues to be Considered.*

Ministry of Finance, *The Japanese Budget in Brief,* for years FY2001 and FY1999.

Miyazaki, Masato (2006), 'Framework for fiscal consideration: success and failures in Japan', *OECD Journal on Budgeting*, **6** (4) 123–48.

Organisation for Economic Co-operation and Development (OECD) (2005), 'The legal framework for the budget systems', *OECD Journal on Budgeting*, **4** (3) 1–483.

Ohta, Hiroko (2006), *Keizaizaisei shimon kaigi no Tatakai, (Battle of the Economic and Fiscal Policy Council)*, Tokyo: Toyou Keizai Shinpousha.

Savage, J.D. (2000), 'A decade of deficits and debt: Japanese fiscal policy and the rise and fall of the Fiscal Structural Reform Act of 1997', *Public Budgeting and Finance*, (Spring), 55–84.

Takenaka, Heizou (2006), *Kouzou Kaikaku No Shinjitsu, [Truth of Structural Reform],* Tokyo: Nihon Keizai Shinbun Syuppan sya.

Tanaka, Hideaki (2003), 'Fiscal consolidation and medium-term fiscal planning in Japan', *OECD Journal on Budgeting*, **3** (2).

Wright, Maurice (2002), *Japan's Fiscal Crises*, Oxford: Oxford University Press.

8. Korea's four major budgetary reforms: catching up with a big bang

John M. Kim

In 2003 the Korean government launched the 'Four Major Fiscal Reforms'. This was a package of four budget system reforms that were implemented simultaneously. The ambitious 'big bang' reform package was designed to transform almost overnight Korea's old budget system,[1] which lacked virtually all of the modern features found among Organisation for Economic Co-operation and Development (OECD) countries' systems, into one which incorporated most of their best practices. Following several years of design and provisional implementation, the reforms were finalized with the passage of the National Fiscal Act 2007, which replaced the decades-old Budget and Accounts Act[2] as the law that formally defines the government's budget system.

Widely viewed as a successful attempt, some weaknesses have nonetheless come to light in the short time since the reforms were introduced. This chapter will offer a reassessment of the Four Major Fiscal Reforms and identify factors and processes that account for the more successful outcomes compared to those that ultimately resulted in potential defects. Before doing so, the chapter argues that Korea's reforms are noteworthy for several reasons.

First, 'big bang' reforms that redesign the entire budget system are rare enough. The Korean reforms merit special attention because the country undertook a major transformation in one go. Second, the Four Major Fiscal Reforms attempted to graft features usually found in countries with parliamentary systems to one that followed the presidential system of government. The Korean reforms illustrate how the nature of the political system can impact on the outcomes. Third, the Korean reform package was arguably the first instance claiming to have transplanted Western reforms successfully onto Asian soil.[3] They were viewed with great interest in the region and among developing countries. Fourth, the Korean reforms also present a good case for leapfrogging. This raises the question of whether requisite stages of development in public administration can be bypassed without significant problems occurring.

The 2003 Fiscal Reforms consisted of:

1. the National Fiscal Management Plan (NFMP), a five-year multi-annual budget modeled after Sweden's Spring Fiscal Policy Bill;
2. the introduction of top-down budgeting;
3. implementation of performance-based budgeting (PBB); and
4. building the Digital Budget and Accounting System (DBAS).

The reforms were designed and launched early on in the Roh Presidency (2003 to 2007), with the Vice-Minister of Planning and Budget as the main proponent, who then quickly rose to become Minister, and was subsequently appointed to an arguably more influential post in the Presidential Office. From inception to implementation, the reforms proceeded at a rapid pace, reflecting the political constraint imposed by the fact that the President, an important supporter of the Vice-Minister's reform drive, was limited to a single five-year term by the Constitution. This meant that the reforms skipped the process of building widespread consensus, even within the budget ministry. Instead, they were designed and implemented in a top-down fashion by small team within the budget office (the Ministry of Planning and Budgeting – MPB), aided by expert advice from World Bank specialists.

BACKGROUND AND MOTIVATION

The ambitious scope and intense pace of the reforms naturally begs the question: why? The official rationale was that Korea needed to get its budget system in better shape before long-term pressures on public finances built up to an intractable level. The principal source of this mounting fiscal pressure was population ageing. With rapidly falling mortality, fertility hovering close to half the level required for a stable population, the proportion of the elderly (aged 65 and above) among the population was forecast to jump from 7.2 percent in 2000 to 14.4 percent by 2019. Since a similar aging of the population had taken most Western countries a century or two, compared to a mere two decades in the Korean case, fiscal pressures were expected to build up much more quickly than they had in other developed countries. This required urgent action now to streamline the budget system. Besides population aging, it was also noted that the secular rise in living standards and a maturing democracy were adding to spending needs as well. A gradual breakdown of traditional homogeneous values and social norms was unleashing a greater demand for diversity and improved quality of life.

Table 8.1 General government fiscal balance (% of GDP)

	1991	1992	1993	1994	1995	1996	1997	1998	1999	2000
Australia	−3.8	−6.0	−5.6	−4.6	−3.7	−2.2	−0.5	0.6	1.6	0.1
Canada	−8.3	−9.1	−8.7	−6.7	−5.3	−2.8	0.2	0.5	1.6	3.2
Denmark	−2.4	−2.2	−2.9	−2.4	−2.3	−1.0	0.4	1.1	3.2	2.5
Korea	1.8	1.4	2.5	3.1	4.2	3.8	3.6	1.9	3.1	6.9
Netherlands	−3.2	−4.4	−3.6	−4.2	−4.2	−1.8	−1.1	−0.8	0.4	2.2
Sweden	−2.0	−7.8	−11.4	−10.8	−7.7	−3.1	−1.6	2.1	1.3	3.7
United Kingdom	−3.1	−6.4	−7.9	−6.7	−5.8	−4.4	−2.2	0.4	1.1	1.6
OECD	−3.7	−4.6	−5.0	−4.2	−3.9	−3.2	−1.8	−1.4	−0.9	0.0

Source: OECD (2002), Annex Table 28.

While this official rationale had some validity, it is also true that reforms, especially big ones such as Korea's Four Major Fiscal Reforms, rarely take place merely because of some anticipated future pain, however serious. Rather, reforms themselves are typically painful enough that they will not be attempted unless there is an immediate and even greater gain. Table 8.1 shows that budget deficits in many OECD countries had reached crisis levels before these countries were forced to introduce reforms for fiscal consolidation that were strong enough to return their budgets to balance or surplus within several years. Canada introduced the Expenditure Management System in 1994, Sweden adopted top-down budgeting in 1996, The Netherlands implemented prudent economic assumptions in 1994, and the UK began enforcing its two fiscal rules in 1997.[4]

In contrast, the table shows that Korea maintained an exemplary surplus throughout the 1990s, even in the aftermath of the Asian financial crisis of 1997. In fact, Korea's public finances had enjoyed more than two decades of balanced or surplus budgets since the early 1980s, and national debt in 2003 was just 23 percent of gross domestic product (GDP), which again compares quite favorably with a much higher 76 percent average for the same year among OECD countries. A small deficit in 2006 (−0.1 percent) was replaced with surpluses in 2007–08 despite expenditure rising by around 7 percent. What other factors, then, can help to explain the reforms?

Personal ambition was perhaps the most important factor. The Vice-Minister who initiated the Four Reforms was an exceptionally ambitious person, even by the competitive standards of Korean officialdom. The Four Major Fiscal Reforms certainly met the bill for a significant achievement commensurate with his towering ambition. They were also a satisfying solution to his long-standing frustration, that 'There must be a better way to do budgeting!' This was a thought shared by many former budget examiners who had experienced seemingly haphazard budgeting decisions year after year, reached only through exhausting negotiations with line ministries and agencies over mind-numbingly small details. Furthermore, an overarching project like the Four Reforms would cement the Ministry of Planning and Budgeting's status as the undisputed premier ministry with 'ownership' of the national policy agenda, giving the clear upper hand to budgeting in the perennial rivalry with the Finance Ministry.

Politics was another factor that spurred the reforms. To push through with the challenging task of the reforms, their proponents sought the new President's imprimatur. In the process, budget reform was to some extent sold as an effective vehicle for promoting some of the core causes of the newly elected government.[5] These core causes included increasing public spending to assist the society's disadvantaged groups, and dismantling Korea's centralized, monolithic authority in pursuit of a more grassroots, democratic society. The Four Reforms were meant to contribute to these causes by providing an effective medium-term framework for reallocating budgetary resources toward social policy and by decentralizing the budget formulation process. It is not difficult to deduce that the pace of the reforms would be increased to achieve as much as possible while the reformers had the blessing of the President and those in the most influential political circles.

In addition to these factors, the nature of the Korean civil service also influenced the implementation of the reforms. Korea has a long tradition of a well-developed centralized system of public administration which goes back at least several hundred years. This means that decentralized government and the delegation of authority were quite alien concepts to government officials. Moreover, Korean civil servants are similar to their counterparts in some continental European governments in that they form an elitist bureaucracy that embodies a strongly legalistic mindset. There is a tendency to value form over substance and tight *ex ante* logic over pragmatic *ex post* results. As will be explained later, these traits affected the choice of the Swedish model for the new medium-term expenditure framework (MTEF), and also influenced the implementation of top-down and performance-based budgeting. Finally, a peculiar feature of the Korean civil service is that there is a regular rotation of civil servants to different positions (as also occurs in Japan). This reassignment takes place almost annually and at all levels. Although the newly reassigned official will usually be within the same ministry or agency, the position will often have little or no connection to their previous post. While this practice discourages corruption and produces a steady supply of well-rounded middle or higher-level managers, it works against the accumulation of genuine expertise and institutional memory. It also makes it easier to succumb to pressure from above or from the outside ('I won't be here next year, anyway') and thus works against professionalism and accountability. On the positive side, the imperatives of rotation give rise to a mentality of 'do first, fix later' which can also make it easier to initiate a bold change such as the Four Reforms.

MEDIUM-TERM AND TOP-DOWN BUDGETING

Dubbed the National Fiscal Management Plan (NFMP), Korea's new multiyear budget system, or medium-term expenditure framework, is a direct adaptation of the Swedish model. It is a five-year medium-term fiscal plan,[6] updated annually, that specifies annual spending ceilings for both total government expenditure and sectoral (ministerial) expenditures, which are enforced during annual budget formulation through top-down budgeting. But why the Swedish model? After all, Korea's centralized, authoritarian culture of government is an almost polar opposite of Sweden's decentralized, consensus-oriented government.

The principal appeal of Sweden's Spring Fiscal Bill was that it satisfied the needs of the Korean bureaucracy's legalistic mindset for a very well-defined stand-alone plan. The ceremonial aspect of a senior ministerial 'retreat', a special cabinet meeting over a weekend to finalize spending ceilings, was likewise appealing and was copied, not least because of the prestige conferred on the organizers by an overnight meeting chaired by the President, which would give the budget ministry (MPB) the power to enforce the ministerial spending ceilings. The format and content of Korea's NFMP, like Sweden's, include forecasts for the economy and government revenues, targets for the budget balance and national debt, annual spending ceilings and sector-by-sector plans (discussion points) of key issues that the government intends to address.

The appeal of the Swedish model is perhaps better explained by considering how Korean officials would have reacted to other models of multiyear budgeting, especially those that included financial projections but which were not tied to plans. A case in point is the US budget system. The Office of Management and Budget (OMB) requires that departments include ten-year projections of expenditures for their programs in their annual budget requests, which makes multiyear considerations an integral part of the budget examiner's decisions in the annual appropriations process. But this kind of multiyear forecasting, without a clearly defined and separate multiyear plan, was simply too vague for Korean tastes, especially because there would be no tangible output or document to show as the end-product of a major reform.[7] On the other hand, the UK's Spending Reviews, which implement biennial budgeting through Annually Managed Expenditure and biennially updated Departmental Expenditure Limits, would be too complicated for Korea, although clearly they are well-defined stand-alone medium-term fiscal plans. The UK system would also cede too much budgetary authority to the line ministries, which the Korean budget ministry was not quite prepared to do, despite having announced this as a key feature of top-down budgeting. Finally, the Dutch model, where a coalition agreement on a fiscal plan is usually binding and without revision throughout a government's four-year term, would have been considered too inflexible.

Besides the advantage of being a separate, well-defined plan, another reason for choosing the Swedish model was the fact that it is tightly coupled with top-down budgeting. Two earlier attempts by the Korean budget ministry to introduce medium-term fiscal plans, in 1982 and 1998,[8] were abandoned because the plans were ignored in the annual budget formulation. The budget office was, therefore, keenly aware that the success of its new NFMP would depend crucially on making the plan binding upon the annual budget. The Swedish model provided the perfect solution, as it made top-down enforcement of the multiyear spending ceilings the crucial link between the medium-term plan and the annual budgets.

The other rationale given for adopting top-down budgeting was that, in return for accepting the spending ceilings imposed on them, line ministries would be allowed greater discretion in formulating their own budgets. This would yield the dual benefits of eliminating the unproductive rounds of repeated negotiations with the budget ministry, and allowing the line ministries to utilize the expertise they had in their respective areas to come up with the most efficient use of their expenditure envelopes. It was considered that each ministry would know how to make the best use of budgetary funds for its own policy area, and would be trusted to come up with a budget to do exactly that. Such devolution of budgetary authority dovetailed very nicely with the political priorities of the new government, which were touted as the main rationale for top-down budgeting. However, it is doubtful whether the MPB ever seriously entertained the possibility of relinquishing its control over the line ministries' budgets. It did not fully trust them to do their budgets properly and believed in any case that it could enforce the ministerial ceilings unilaterally. In short, the budget ministry took advantage of the top-down reform to impose the spending ceilings to save time on budget negotiations with the ministries, but it neglected to loosen the review process for budget requests from the ministries. It invested hardly any effort in building a consensus over top-down budgeting within the government (and even in the MPB itself), relying on the centralistic mindset of the budget officials to prevail in the end.

The Korean model that tightly couples its medium-term NFMP with top-down budgeting is by 2008 in its fifth year,[9] allowing enough time for a more objective reassessment. Overall, the NFMP has successfully laid the basic framework for multiyear fiscal management. Nevertheless, it appears that the NFMP skipped over some crucial elements during its implementation, which may undermine the medium-term plan's effectiveness over a longer period of time.

First, Korea's NFMP still lacks a mechanism or procedure to ensure that it starts with prudent economic assumptions. In particular, the growth forecast essentially remains an ad hoc decision by the budget office, making it susceptible to an optimistic bias. Second, there is room to improve transparency in the NFMP, and more generally the budget system. Neither the NFMP nor other budget documents show a proper reconciliation between forecasts or plans from the previous NFMPs and the actual, realized figures reported in the current version. An accounting of errors in forecasts and targets, if properly done, would provide for an easy check against perpetually optimistic projections of the economy's performance, which in the experience of many countries have often led to chronic deficits and rising national debt. Third, despite the outward resemblance, the NFMP is designed to be much less binding than the Swedish Spring Fiscal Bill. Whereas total government spending is fixed by parliamentary approval three years ahead in Sweden, in Korea it can be revised annually (and actually is) with each successive NFMP, and is finalized only together with each annual budget. Even then, the total spending ceiling is effective only in the *ex ante* sense for budget formulation purposes, in contrast to Sweden's total ceiling, which is also binding *ex post* on actual expenditures.

Each of these three weaknesses in Korea's NFMP in effect grants the government some leeway to modify its medium-term plan continually, especially to suit the spending demands of the annual budget. It would therefore appear that the integrity of the NFMP depends almost solely on the budget ministry's self-discipline. Whether this will be strong enough is a question that is implicitly answered in the decision of the reform architects to omit these safeguards against lapses in fiscal rectitude. This decision, in turn, perhaps accurately recognizes the political reality of budgeting in Korea, where the Ministry of Planning and Budgeting is unfortunately still in a considerably weaker position than its Western counterparts to uphold principles and *ex ante* fiscal rules against pressure from politicians and the public for expedient spending proposals.

Another weakness that poses a potential threat to the long-term health of public finances in Korea is mandatory expenditures. Good budgeting in this field requires the ability to produce and understand long-term projections, which is why actuaries, demographers or other kinds of specialists can often be found among budget reviewers for this field in many countries. However, the regular annual reassignment of Korean civil servants makes it impossible to fill these positions with reviewers who have the required qualifications, and nor does it allow them enough time at a position to build up adequate experience. The practice of frequent reassignments further compounds the problem because budget officials have little incentive to devote resources to projects that construct or augment longitudinal micro-level datasets, which would allow them to improve long-term projections. But, such datasets take at least several years or even more than a decade to yield meaningful results, by which time virtually everyone involved would long since have moved onto different positions and not be able to reap the fruits of their investments.

The experience with top-down budget reform has been the least satisfactory among the Four Reforms. The top-down reform was implemented unilaterally without securing support from the front-line budget examiners. Except in early blueprints of the Four Reforms, the reform proponents did not stress the importance of devolving budgetary authority. The MPB officials continued to conduct reviews and negotiations with line ministries the old way, although they were quick to demand that ministries observe the NFMP spending ceilings in their annual budget requests. The reluctance of the budget examiners to move away from their centralized, control-oriented mindset was reflected in the number of spending ceilings in the NFMP, which exceed 200. Ideally, the total number of ceilings should be 30 to 60 at most in order to give spending ministries enough room to make their own budgeting decisions. Acknowledging this significant shortcoming, however, the top-down initiative has some positive aspects. It has significantly reduced the workload of both the budget examiners and their counterparts in the line ministries by eliminating the customary overbidding in the latter's budget requests.

Even as a means of enforcing spending ceilings, however, not everything has worked perfectly. Several ministries have continued to submit budget requests that still exceed their respective ceilings, although not by as much as before.[10] The two most common excuses given by the non-complying ministries were that they found it impossible to make the call on which of their equally important programs had to be reduced or eliminated and therefore preferred to leave the final decision up to the budget ministry, or that there was some important last-minute new addition that had the President's approval. One of the 'delinquent' ministries even came up with a new way to play the budgeting game. Although the respective ministry's excess budget request was reduced significantly, it still contained as many new program requests as before. These claims were now reduced to a relatively small size in order to fit them within the reduced total request.[11] This actually made for a heavier burden on the central budget reviewers responsible for that ministry. Finding themselves unable to simply throw out the abnormal requests for newly proposed programs, they had to review the same number of cases as before, but the smaller requested figures would now often obfuscate rather than inform their decisions. Its inability to put an end to such aberrant behavior revealed that the budget ministry was not as powerful vis-à-vis the line ministries as it had thought. In fact, most budget officials canvassed about this problem at OECD experts meetings, stated that it would be unthinkable in their own governments, virtually all of which have parliamentary systems, for line ministries to go against directives from the Finance Minister in this manner.[12]

In summary, what the NFMP and top-down budgeting actually accomplished together was to establish an effective budgetary framework for reallocating resources into social policy spending. With a change of government in early 2008, such priorities then changed but the NFMP and top-down budgeting still remain a good framework for steering spending into priority areas. The combination of NFMP and top-down budgeting has not performed as well for controlling aggregates such as the budget balance and government debt,[13] mainly because of the lack of prudent assumptions and inadequate transparency in budget documents. It is unclear whether these measures have contributed to efficiency in annual budget formulation, other than by lightening the budget office's workload considerably. And, not much has been accomplished in terms of giving ministries greater autonomy over their own budgets or inducing them to utilize their expertise in their own fields.

PERFORMANCE-BASED AND PROGRAM BUDGETING

Performance-based budgeting is widely regarded as the most successful component of the Four Reforms. It was implemented in four distinct phases, with the first phase actually beginning before the Four Reforms began, during the Kim Dae-jung administration. In contrast to the successful phases that would follow, the first phase took some time to get started and even then was launched only as a tentative pilot project during 2000–2002. The problem was that performance budgeting was simply too vague for Korean officials to accept readily. At the time, despite several years of research by the MPB, the budget ministry could not discover a way to have performance information (even were the indices to be somehow well-defined and measured) fed back into budgeting decisions in a well-defined formulaic manner, which is what the Korean bureaucracy expected of a sensible action plan. In the end, the ministry decided on a small-scale trial experiment – an unusual step in Korean government.[14] Entitled 'Performance Budgeting', the new performance-based system was designed to reflect the US Government Performance Results Act (GPRA), with some modifications. A total of 22 divisions from the line ministries were selected to participate in this project, and were required to develop annual performance plans.

Building on this experience, the second initiative began as one component of the Four Major Fiscal Reforms in 2003. The 22 ministries and agencies were invited to submit annual performance plans to the MPB along with their annual budget requests. This initiative was also inspired by the GPRA example but implemented only a limited subset of GPRA features. While the GPRA requires each agency to submit their strategic plans, annual performance plans and annual performance reports for every single program, the Korean version required only a performance plan and was limited to only major budgetary programs over US$1 million in size. In 2005 this second initiative, now called the Performance Management System of Budgetary Programs, was expanded to cover all 26 ministries and agencies.

Although slow to start, once begun performance-based budgeting had the advantage of being able to show continual, clear-cut progress through distinct phases. This is usually a career-enhancing attribute in any bureaucracy. Soon a specialized performance unit had set down firm roots in the MPB. At the next, third step of its evolution, the performance unit introduced the Self-Assessment of Budgetary Programs (SABP) in 2005. The SABP was designed to copy the US Program Assessment Rating Tool (PART) with some modifications.[15] Similarly to PART, the SABP asks ministries and agencies to conduct self-assessments by filling out a checklist developed by the MPB that covers questions on planning, management and results. The SABP is designed to cover roughly 500 programs every year, a pace which would allow MPB to review every major spending program in three years.

The SABP became the first time that spending programs were systematically rated. The MPB saw this as a good opportunity to attempt to solve the as yet unclear problem of how to relate performance information back into budgeting decisions. In conjunction with the first SABP, the MPB announced that programs with poor ratings would be subject to budget cuts of up to 10 percent. Although rather crude, this has proven to yield effective results. It has made ministries and agencies pay closer attention to performance management. Analyses of subsequent budget requests submitted to the MPB show that it has also led ministries to reallocate their budgets pre-emptively in favor of programs with higher marks by reducing the size of poorly-rated programs even before the budget ministry intervened.

Finally, the fourth initiative attempted to complement the self-assessed ratings with a more in-depth, objective evaluation. Introduced in 2006, the Budgetary Program Evaluation exercise enables teams of third-party experts to conduct in-depth assessments of a small set of problematic programs each year. In contrast to the SABP, which produces program scores that can be loosely compared against one another, this latest evaluation system produces a detailed review for each individual program that identifies weaknesses and problems to be addressed.

Despite its rather rushed implementation, Korea's performance-based budgeting has been successful enough that it now counts among the leading countries in recent meetings of OECD senior budget officials. What factors account for this success? To a large degree, three key innovations that went against conventional wisdom explain this success. All three maintained a common and tenacious focus on making performance management actually matter to the managers of the evaluated programs. First, there was the SABP, enhanced by the novel twist of a potential threat to cut budgets by 10 percent, an innovative experiment that proved to be effective precisely because it was such an inelegantly crude mechanism of feedback into budgeting. Second, performance-based budgeting was meant to focus budgetary decision-making on the program level, but to date the Korean budget ministry has instead focused on the sub-program or the activity level as the basic unit of evaluation. This practice has helped maintain the attention of line-ministry middle managers by emphasizing details and specificity, as opposed to the somewhat abstract objectives and measures at the program level. Third, the budget ministry decided early on to reassign the main burden of performance review and management to a separate, specialized unit, rather than leaving it to the budget reviewers. Although there is debate about which approach is superior, the first SABP was conducted by the budget examiners, with the performance unit acting as a separate control tower within the budget ministry. This method was quickly abandoned after one year as placing an impractically heavy burden on the budget examiners. In particular, given that they were likely to be assigned to a different position the next year, it would have been too much to expect them to have or invest in a level of expertise in their fields that would allow them to engage in more than a perfunctory attempt at performance-based budgeting. Since then, performance-based budgeting has been administered entirely by a separate, specialized unit within the budget ministry.[16]

Generalizing from these points, it is the sustained focus by the budget ministry's performance unit on practical outcomes rather than the specific decisions themselves that accounts for the success of performance-based budgeting in Korea. Instead of holding onto abstract principles and lessons derived in a different environment, the performance unit was quick to recognize the practical constraints of the Korean situation and implemented a series of timely measures to ensure that middle and higher-level managers in line ministries would take performance-based budgeting seriously.

There are some remaining challenges for performance-based budgeting, but before discussing them, it is necessary to introduce the last of the Four Reforms: the Digital Budget and Accounting System (DBAS). The ultimate objective of this reform was to build a computerized network system through which all budgeting activities would take place. In itself this was a relatively straightforward engineering exercise and therefore not likely to be of much interest to the student of budget system reforms. However, the DBAS reform also had a list of intermediary objectives that are relevant, since they aimed to streamline the budget classification system before building that into the new DBAS.

The most important of these sub-objectives was the consolidation of programs into one-line budgets, which began to transform the existing line-item budget classification system into a program-oriented classification. The old line-item budget structure followed classifications by organization (ministries and agencies) and then by budget account (revenue source). As a result, program- or activity-level expenditures were fragmented over different accounts, and sometimes across multiple ministries or agencies. This worked against budget transparency as it was practically impossible to see how resources were allocated to different policy functions. The new program budget classification aimed to simplify the budget structure and thereby establish a clear systematic linkage among policy, organization and spending programs.

Following advice from a team of World Bank consultants, the program budget reclassification followed several principles. First, the primary purpose of the budget structure would be to serve as the basis for resource allocation, meaning the government could plan ahead and set spending priorities in the NFMP and top-down ceilings using the new program classification. Second, the new program classification was aligned to organizational structures in order to ensure accountability. Third, the program was adopted as the basic unit to which performance management would apply and be monitored. The latter two principles meant that, ideally, there would be no overlap in policy functions between ministries or among performance objectives of expenditure programs.[17]

These principles also meant that the other reforms could not be completed independently of the program reclassification. This put considerable pressure on the program budget reform, with the result that it was completed within about a year. In turn, this meant that some parts of the new program budget classification would have ended up following the existing organizational structure, since one year is too short a period to allow for adequate restructuring of organizations or responsibilities to satisfy the 'no overlap' principle. Indeed, a recently conducted comprehensive review of all performance objectives revealed that numerous activities and even programs in different ministries or agencies had identical objectives. This is thought be a problem of misspecified performance objectives. However, most of these appear to be cases of incomplete program or organizational restructuring. Apparently, cosmetic restatements of program objectives to make them look different from one another did not successfully survive the translation into specific performance objectives. Instead, the remedy will involve organizational restructuring and reshuffling of responsibilities between ministries, which will require much more time and effort than simply fixing the problematic performance plans.

Another sub-objective of the DBAS reform was to establish a government cost-accounting system, which would take performance management to the next step by allowing managers to compare the costs of programs and organizational units against their output or outcome measures. This aspect of the DBAS reform has been put on hold because no decision could be reached on how to allocate indirect costs among different units or programs, for which there is no obvious or logical solution. Although, in the experience of other governments, it should be a relatively simple exercise to adopt a rule-of-thumb method commonly used in corporate accounting to allocate overhead expenses, it appears that the cost-accounting project has lost momentum and must await a subsequent opportunity to be completed.[18]

THE FINAL HURDLE

For several years, the Four Reforms proceeded quickly and smoothly within the executive branch, at a pace that was reminiscent of Korea's 'telescoped' economic development that had occurred from the early 1960s. The first sign that something could go wrong surfaced when it became time to clear the final hurdle, which was to obtain the formal approval of the National Assembly, Korea's unicameral legislature. Although the existing Budget and Accounts Act did not preclude a multiyear fiscal plan and performance management as complementary supporting systems for the annual budget,[19] the budget ministry wanted to revise the law to reflect the Four Major Fiscal Reforms and mandate the key features of the new budget system. The end result was the National Fiscal Act, which required that, together with the annual budget proposal, the government transmit the NFMP and performance information to the legislature. During the negotiations with the National Assembly to legislate the new law, it became increasingly clear that the Four Reforms had proceeded executively without much thought for a significant role for the legislature in the budget process. Because the reforms rested on executive commitment and political will, there was no apparent method to make the key features of the Four Reforms (for example, expenditure ceilings) binding upon the legislature or underscored by law.

In 2004, the first year of the Four Reforms, the National Assembly committees thought expenditure envelopes were an interesting novelty and took care to observe them as they worked on amendments to the government's budget proposal, but recently there has been a marked drop in the legislature's attention to the NFMP and its spending ceilings. It is important to note that the legislature still does not have any self-binding mechanism or rules to protect budgetary integrity. However, the national Constitution offers some protection in this regard, as it explicitly states that the legislature may not increase but only lessen the executive's proposed budget.[20]

Similarly, it is doubtful whether performance-based budgeting has significantly influenced budgetary scrutiny by the legislature. The National Fiscal Act requires that performance reports be submitted by the government, but neither the Act nor other laws or rules specify that the National Assembly ought to do anything with the performance information so delivered. Committees or staff members may choose to utilize the information as it suits them, but other than that, it seems fair to say that the National Assembly's interest in performance information has been characterized by the same tepidity as in legislatures in other OECD countries.

The clearest instance of the National Assembly's reluctance to follow the budget ministry's reform drumbeat arose over the content and format of budget documents. The budget ministry took great care to prepare new budget documents that contained much descriptive narration at the program level, after having studied the budget documents of Australia and other Commonwealth countries. However, since the old budget documents had contained much more detailed budget figures at activity and sometimes subactivity levels, the new ones were judged to be 'very pretty' but too sparse in informational and especially numeric content to satisfy the National Assembly. This forced the government to revert immediately to the old format.

In sum, the overall assessment of the Four Reforms to this point in time is that much progress was made rapidly but they stumbled at the final hurdle. Despite the earlier achievements in modernizing the executive's budget process, the reforms failed to take root in the legislature, which somewhat limits their effectiveness. The single most important reason for this setback at the final stage was that the reforms were without exception copied or adapted from parliamentary systems. Until the legislation of the National Fiscal Act, the reform architects had not given much thought as to how the legislature would be involved in the new budget system, but belatedly realized that budget reforms worked differently in a presidential system where the legislature has the actual final say over the budget.[21] It could be argued that the changes within the executive in Korea's reforms, right up to the legislation of the National Fiscal Act, would have been counted as a successfully completed reform in many parliamentary systems, and in particular, Westminster systems. But having a presidential system meant that Korea's Four Reforms had one additional hurdle to clear.

This does not mean there were no shortcomings along the way, especially related to the introduction of major reforms in one big bang. Korea attempted to 'leapfrog' many sequential stages of public administration reform in pushing ahead with its Four Reform strategy. The top-down reform in Korea provides an example that suggests limitations with leapfrogging. Many line ministries were unable or unwilling to make difficult final decisions on their own budgets, and those that dealt with mandatory expenditure programs did not have adequate capacity for long-term budget projections. Neither did the spending ministries have strong internal controls. These shortcomings in managerial capacity at the line ministries comprised a major hurdle to the effectiveness of top-down budgeting, which was supposed to delegate budgetary authority to the ministries and agencies. The budget ministry was well aware of this obstacle, which was another reason besides its simple reluctance to relinquish control that explains its decision not to decentralize the budget formulation process.

As a final observation, Korea had good budgetary performance even before the recent reforms. As explained earlier, the budget has been mostly balanced or in surplus for nearly three decades, and government debt is markedly lower than the OECD average (under 25 percent of GDP with net debt under 5 percent). Surpluses were recorded in 2007–08 despite major increases in defense spending. But, while Korea's fiscal performance has been good, it has not directly been related to the Four Reforms. What, then, explains Korea's success at managing its budgets?

Not surprisingly, a tradition of strong political will to uphold budgetary integrity was the most important factor. In the early stages of Korea's economic development, from the 1960s to the 1970s, the budget suffered from chronic deficits and large debts. In the 1980s, President Chun, an authoritarian leader from a military background like his predecessor President Park, placed controlling inflation and budget deficits at the top of his economic agenda. Publicly professing ignorance in economic matters, he delegated economic policy wholly into the hands of a few superb technocrats. The budget ministry took this opportunity to firmly establish the principle of 'spending within revenue'. This effort to firm up budgetary discipline was aided by a string of exceptional performances by the economy, thanks to a confluence of low exchange rates, low interest rates and low oil prices.

The administrative culture of the civil service has also played a role in maintaining good budgetary performance. In the 1990s, the political system finally began moving toward a full democracy after decades of authoritarian rule by former generals, and spending needs increased somewhat. However, the budgeting process still remained quite centralized and the culture established in the budget ministry during the 1980s that values fiscal integrity still prevails even to this day. Even in more difficult economic times, this policy remains strong in Korea.

The lack of a substantial welfare state and less popular demands for spending compared to other OECD nations also helped the effort to maintain budgetary discipline. Somewhat perversely, the introduction of nationwide welfare programs has actually helped the budget balance, but may contribute to undermining discipline in the long run. This is because the National Pension has been running huge surpluses which count toward the budget balance. These surpluses have helped immensely to offset the spending increases, especially after the Asian financial crisis of 1997. However, in an accrual accounting sense the pension surplus was not a true surplus and actually masked a likely deficit. What has seemed like a blessing for the budget balance may end up as a heavy burden to later generations, because the current pension surpluses create some room for the budgetary authorities to relax their guard against deficits.

In sum, Korea's good budgetary performance since the 1980s is explained by a strongly authoritarian political leadership and a centralized and disciplined civil service culture that strove to uphold fiscal discipline. Since the 1990s and especially after the Asian financial crisis, the transition to democracy and a rapidly aging population has encouraged more vocal demands from different groups for greater social spending. Both the political leadership and the budgetary authorities are much more vulnerable to these pressures that affect public finances than before. Although Korea did not depend on a good budget framework to produce good budgetary performance, with the emergence of a more democratic and aging society the budget ministry is likely to find that a good fiscal management system, such as the modern budget system built through the Four Reforms, will prove essential to protect the budget's integrity from such pressures.

NOTES

1. Korea's traditional budget system maintained the traditional bottom-up line-item budgeting model. It had been used since 1948 when the Republic was founded. Budget reforms in the 1980s and 1990s mostly focused on cleaning up the numerous special accounts and trust funds (off-budget earmarked funds), which had a tendency to proliferate and thus required some major effort by the government to simplify and consolidate them every few years. Arguably the only significant attempt to reform procedures for budget formulation and execution took place in the early 1980s, when zero-based budgeting and medium-term fiscal plans were introduced. These were, however, one-off exercises that were abandoned quickly after their primary purpose was served, which was to bring chronic inflation and budget deficits under control. The reforms of the early 1980s have nonetheless had a lasting impact, which was to establish sufficient budgetary discipline to keep Korea's budget balanced or in surplus. One effective internal procedure that survives to this day is the review panel, composed of all senior officers in the budget office, before which an examiner responsible for reviewing new proposals from line ministries must defend any decision to approve new requests.
2. The new budget system as envisaged by the Four Major Fiscal Reforms differed from the budget system described by the existing Budget and Accounts Act, which explicitly defined the national budget as strictly annual in scope and specified a budget classification system that was initially understood to be preclude program budget classifications. The National Fiscal Act mandated the National Fiscal Management Plan (multi-annual budget) and performance plans as integral parts of the budget process.
3. Singapore and Hong Kong may be exceptions, where innovations are followed with considerable interest. However, the Korean case may offer a more useful comparison for most countries because of the size and complexity of its economy. In fact, currently (2008) only six countries are larger than Korea in terms of both per capita GDP (US$20 000 as of 2007) and population (slightly under 50 million): the US, Japan, the UK, France, Germany and Italy.
4. They are the well-known 'Golden Rule' and 'Sustainable Investment Rule'.
5. This was the second of two successive governments that, for the first time since the Republic was founded, could be characterized as leftward-leaning. Earlier administrations had espoused a government-directed growth-first philosophy in which a strong centralized state favored a few large business conglomerates, or the Korean 'chaebols', as the vanguards of economic growth. After several decades of such developmentalism, it took a disaster of unprecedented severity in the Asian financial crisis of 1997 to usher in the Republic's first left-leaning government. The ensuing backlash against developmentalism included more public spending to assist society's disadvantaged groups during President Kim Dae-jung's administration. The next government, led by President Roh Moo-hyun, continued to increase welfare spending and added the devolution of central authority to its priority agenda.
6. Strictly speaking, both the Swedish and Korean multiyear budgets are three-year plans, since the first two years correspond to the past and the current year.
7. On the legislative side, the US budget resolution somewhat resembles the Swedish model, as it gives five-year ceilings for spending. However, the Korean budget ministry

tends to avoid occasions to highlight the powerful role of the legislature in the US budget process.

8. Establishing a medium-term fiscal plan was one of the stipulations that came with the emergency loans by the International Monetary Fund (IMF) and the World Bank to help Korea cope with the Asian financial crisis. The Korean government accordingly produced a Medium-Term Fiscal Plan, but this quickly ended up as a 'pretty document on the shelf' that was ignored in annual appropriations. It was not binding on the annual budget, and political expediency quickly overrode the MTEF plans, especially in the form of emergency measures to overcome the immediate crisis at hand.
9. The NFMP top-down model was first applied in 2004 to the FY2005 budget.
10. Before top-down budgeting was introduced, ministries' initial budget requests on average asked for an increase of about 30 percent over their previous budgets. Top-down budgeting brought this figure down to 11.7 percent in 2004 for the FY2005 budget and further to 7 percent in 2005. The latter figure is close to the average increase allowed in the top-down ceilings, which means most of the spending ministries observed their respective expenditure limits.
11. Since increases were also requested for the ministry's existing programs, only a minor portion of the smaller increase requested by the ministry over its previous budget could go to the new requests. For the FY2006 budget, however, the ministry asked to have almost 40 new programs approved in addition to the 90 existing ones. This meant that on average the size of newly proposed programs were minuscule in comparison to the existing ones.
12. Budget officials from several Asian countries have told the author that they would probably encounter the same problems as Korea did, which suggests that the limited influence of the budget or finance minister could possibly stem from differences between Asian and Western cultures, rather than from forms of government. However, this is far from conclusive, since it is also true that all of the Asian countries in question follow the presidential system of government.
13. Somewhat misleadingly, the official budget balance has shown a long series of surpluses, thanks to huge surpluses in the National Pension. The pension is still relatively immature and has been taking in contributions from practically the entire workforce since 1988 but has only just begun making payments to the first cohorts to meet the minimal 20-year contribution requirement for pension eligibility. The real budget balance after deducting the pension surplus, called the 'managed budget balance', has been mostly in deficit since the Asian financial crisis, resulting in a steady growth of government debt.
14. This in itself was a precedent-setting move, since pilot projects were unheard of in the Korean public sector back then. Rather, the norm was to implement any new plan or reform uniformly across the board without any exceptions. Any hint of tentativeness or partial implementation would likely have been construed as a strong signal that the plan in question had not been fully thought through, or that it was only a temporary stop-gap measure that the authorities would abandon later at some convenient point.
15. Korea's SABP was the first instance where the US PART was adopted for use in another country. A few other countries have since followed suit and introduced similar self-assessed checklists.
16. This unit itself is vulnerable to the same kind of negative influence from the regular reassignments, but has managed to preserve continuity and build up expertise by outsourcing much of its work to the Center for Performance Management at the Korea Institute of Public Finance, a government-sponsored think-tank that specializes in public finance and management.
17. The program was defined as a comprehensive set of all government activities that contribute to the same policy objective, and they had to be clearly differentiated from one another.
18. Similarly, other DBAS projects to introduce accrual accounting and to unify the accounting system of subnational governments have been postponed for later implementation.
19. At the beginning of the Four Reforms, the budget ministry initially thought that the

budget system as envisaged by the reforms would violate the letter of the law, and began working on a bill that would reflect the budget system reforms and replace the Budget and Accounts Act. This later became the National Fiscal Act. Subsequently closer examination showed that the new system would still be compliant with the Budget and Accounts Act, but the budget ministry still wished to have the new features mandated by law.

20. Unlike parliamentary systems, without the constitutional restriction, the legislature would be free to add its own spending items, as in the US system. France, which has a semi-presidential system like Korea, has a similar constitutional prohibition against budget increases by the legislature.
21. Previously, decades of authoritarian leadership meant that the legislature had almost no influence over the budget process. In effect, similarly to Westminster systems, decisions by the budget ministry were final. However, Korea's transition to full-fledged democracy during the 1990s had changed the political landscape and gave greater influence to the National Assembly.

REFERENCES

Blondal, J. (2003), 'Budget reform in OECD member countries: common trends', *OECD Journal on Budgeting*, **2** (4), 7–25.

Diamond, J. (2003), 'From program to performance budgeting: the challenges for emerging market economies', International Monetary Fund working paper WP/03/169.

Jung, M.K. and I. Lienert (2004), 'The legal framework for budget systems: an international comparison', *OECD Journal on Budgeting*, Special Issue, **4** (3).

Kim, J.M. (ed.) (2005), *From Line-item to Program Budgeting: Global Lessons and the Korean Case*, Seoul: Korea Institute of Public Finance.

Kim, J.M. and C.K. Park (2006), 'Top-down budgeting as a tool for central resource management', *OECD Journal on Budgeting*, **6** (1), 87–125.

Kim, J.M. and N. Park (2007), 'Performance budgeting in Korea', *OECD Journal on Budgeting*, **7** (4), 1–11.

Organisation for Economic Co-operation and Development (OECD) (2002), *Economic Outlook No. 71*, Annex Table 28, June, Paris: OECD.

Schick, A. (1990), 'Budgeting for results: recent developments in five industrialized countries', *Public Administration Review*, **50** (1), 26–34.

Schick, A. (2003), 'The role of fiscal rules in budgeting', *OECD Journal on Budgeting*, **3** (3), 7–34.

World Bank (1998), *Public Expenditure Management Handbook*, Washington, DC: World Bank.

9. Budget reforms in Denmark: unheralded but nevertheless effective

Lotte Jensen and David Fjord*

Budget reforms? We haven't seen any since the 1980s.
(Ministry of Finance Official)

The epigram of this chapter captures the reaction of experienced budget specialists when asked to describe the trends in Danish budget reforms over the past 20–30 years. If budgetary reform is system-wide, comprehensive or programmatic, and aimed at transforming the principles by which the system as a whole operates, then it has been rare in Denmark. There has been only one explicit reform program, simply referred to as 'the budget reform' in common parlance. It occurred in the mid-1980s and is the last example of such a reform. It also constituted the only occasion when the budget system was systematically and publicly scrutinized (BRU 1983) and the only occasion where politicians were engaged in defining and promulgating reforms to the budget system.

Denmark's narrative of budget reform suggests that a severe economic crisis, and change of government in 1982, led to a brief period of budget reform in the mid-1980s, tailored specifically to strengthen aggregate fiscal discipline via fixed targets, top-down processes and enhanced leadership responsibility at ministry and agency level. The reform elevated the Finance Ministry from a sidelined position to the center of government decision-making. After the next regime change in 1993 back to a social democratic government, the interpretation of crisis management changed; Keynesian fine-tuning was reintroduced, but in a firmer variant than in the 1970s. Expenditure politics receded to the back-burner and the attention of Finance drifted toward macroeconomic policy. Budgetary reforms became fragmented, concentrating on issues of operational efficiency and budget implementation. When a new Conservative–Liberal government came to office in 2001, it opted for a tax freeze, while simultaneously accepting the former government's economic medium-term expenditure plan to 2010 calling for a restrictive budgetary stance. Initially, the strong business cycle, and an escalating competition for voters over welfare policy, placed the government in a dilemma: maintaining a firm fiscal policy while expanding welfare benefits. This situation focused attention on the operational efficiency of the public sector, which was seen as a prime target when reallocations were politically unfeasible. Current reforms have targeted cost structures, strengthened performance and sought economies of scale in cross-cutting administrative reforms. While attention to results has increased, in general initiatives concerning output performance remain detached from budget decision-making.

If we adopt a more modest definition of 'budget reform' we can identify a number of changes to Danish budget practice. We therefore start with a chronology of the reform trends affecting government budgeting over the last 30 years.

The 1980s were characterized by a concern with budget inputs, aggregate fiscal discipline and top-down steering based on targets supplemented by incentives to comply with them. The key initiatives of the 1985 budget reform were: annual targets, budget ceilings, net appropriations, integration between national and local government finances, introduction of carry-forwards, budgeting in current prices, across-the-board cuts ('the lawn mower'), devolution of budget responsibility to ministries and agencies, relaxed personnel regulation and the introduction of state-owned enterprises. Activity-based budgeting was introduced in university funding by 1981 and extended to secondary and tertiary education during the 1990s.

In the 1990s the reform focus became more bifurcated but moved away from input controls. One reform strand was concerned with throughput and output while the other addressed contextual conditions affecting the budget. The former stressed internal incentive structures and better internal control devices in the search for ways to optimize the efficiency of state agencies. Where the 1980s devolved responsibility to agency heads, the 1990s enhanced the accountability dimension and introduced more control of them. The key initiatives were agency performance contracts, performance payment, enhanced control and annual reports from agencies. The concept of the 'contract chain' expressed this development. The latter strand explored structural policy and macroeconomic policy that provided a backdrop for budgetary outcomes. It emphasized labor market and tax reforms, the introduction of medium-term fiscal and economic frameworks, and extended use of so-called 'special studies' of selected policy areas. The two strands largely mirrored two separate communities in the Finance Ministry.

After 2001 attention again returned to outputs and outcomes. A growing dichotomy between voter preferences for welfare services, labor market pressures, and a government policy toward tax freezes, all heightened demands on public institutions to deliver desired outcomes according to political targets and the quality expected by end-users. At the same time the cost of public provision has remained central to Finance's work in terms of cost information, incentives and increasing efficiency in specific areas of the public sector. Accrual accounting and budgeting were introduced for operating expenditures and associated capital spending, and some centralization of administration for large-scale projects has occurred along with cross-cutting efficiency gains.

In broad terms, reform attention has progressed down the budget chain from inputs via throughputs to performance outputs and outcomes. However, the Danish case mirrors Pollitt's (2001) observations of the weak integration between financial and performance management in general. As attention moved away from the early stages of the budget cycle, reform activity became detached from budget formulation although it still used the language of cost-efficiency. The majority of reform activities concerned performance, control and auditing. These are seen as attachments to the budget process rather than budget reforms per se. Hence, budgeting and reforming tend to connect primarily in matters of operational efficiency.

THE POLITICAL AND ECONOMIC CONTEXT RELEVANT TO BUDGET REFORM IN DENMARK

Denmark is a multiparty political system with a tradition of coalition or minority governments. With no Crown financial initiative, the budget is never stronger than the consensus that arises out of the composition of parliament. Annual budgets are often the result of 'patchwork' deals where different parts of budget agreements depend on different political parties. Since 2001 the Liberal–Conservative government has managed to build a stable budgetary majority with its support party but the price of this stability has been an impetus to improve welfare services to the government's core support base.

Denmark has an institutionalized welfare state with public expenditures well above 50 percent of gross domestic product (GDP) – the second-largest public sector in the Organisation for Economic Co-operation and Development (OECD) (Blöndal and Ruffner 2004). It was built up from the 1960s with the bulk of welfare services decentralized to local government through the 1970s. The national government had no control over local government spending, and its contribution to the deficit, until 1979.

The expansion of the welfare state was initially covered by taxation. But, between 1975 and 1984, Denmark amassed a substantial debt burden, which was accelerated by interest payments. Debt servicing became an increasing imposition on the economy from 1975 (Mørch 2000: 399; Andersen and Christiansen 1991: 61). The Minister of Finance proclaimed that the country was 'heading towards the abyss' in October 1979. From then on, budgetary policy became center stage in political debate. A 'responsible' economic policy became the benchmark of political competence and legitimacy. The Conservative coalition that came to office in 1982 after the voluntary step-down of the sitting government nominated public expenditure as its key policy problem and paved the way for the budget reform package in 1985, which Finance bureaucrats had wanted for several years.

Throughout the 1980s the size of the public sector became politically controversial. Right-wing parties conceived it to be a structural impediment to economic growth and proclaimed a 'zero-growth' program compared to 1984 (Christiansen 1990, 1999). The government did not stick to this ambitious plan, but the focus on budget discipline and the discourse around responsible public spending lowered the average level of public consumption remarkably over the 1980s compared to the decade before (Nielsen 1988; Andersen and Christiansen 1991; Christiansen 1999; Kieler and Gaard 2005). Fiscal policy did not manage to solve the unemployment problem and a new controversy emerged between the Conservative government's supply-side arguments of tax relief and lower unemployment benefits versus the opposition's case for a demand-driven 'kick-start', an active labor market policy and 'controlled' expenditure growth. A new Social Democratic government took office in 1993, redefining 'economic responsibility' from budgetary policy to structural policy, and promoted an interpretation of the public sector as a solution rather than a problem (Jensen 2008). The 'small state' ideas of the 1980s were supplanted by a 'smart state' discourse. The role of the public sector was to stimulate growth and 'get the wheels going' to expand revenue generation further and pay down the public debt. The stimulatory policy fuelled the economy such that unemployment declined – as did costs of providing benefits (Kieler and Gaard 2005).

As summarized in Figure 9.1, public debt has decreased; the budget balance has improved and the annual growth in public consumption is lower than in previous decades. Since 1998 the state budget balance has been in surplus. The fiscal position, prior to the 2008 international financial crisis, was caused by decreased unemployment benefits, lower net interest payments due to the reduced public debt, and higher revenues from the corporate tax and the oil and gas exploration activities in the North Sea. The surplus was estimated to be 3.6 percent of GDP in 2008 and 3 percent in 2009, with a deficit of 1.2 percent forecast for 2010; but these were made before the effects of the financial crisis were apparent (Finansministeriet 2008).

The strong budgetary position was more due to exceptionally high revenue levels than to expenditure control. Medium-term expenditure

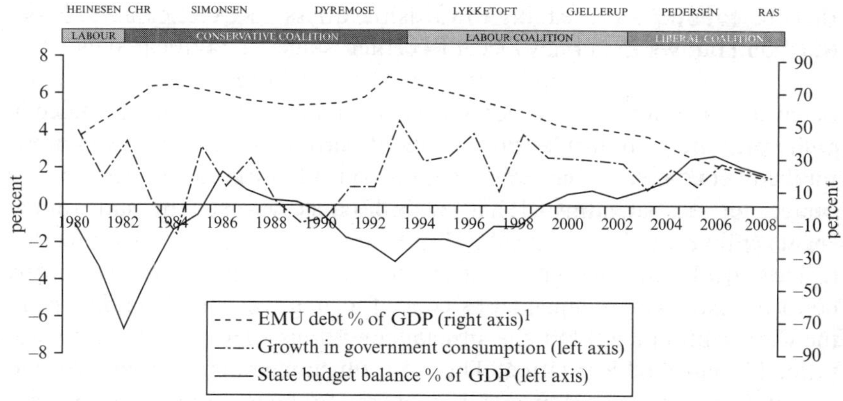

Note: 1: The EMU debt is compiled in accordance with the EMU Growth and Stability Pact. The EMU debt is compiled at nominal value on a gross basis and comprises the debt of the central, regional and local governments as well as social security funds.

Figure 9.1 Public sector budget balance, consumption growth, and debt, 1980–2007

plans generally impose soft targets in the present budget year while setting tougher but fictional limits in out-years. When revisions occur, they consistently allow higher growth rates in the current and following year, offset by firmer expenditure control in later years. This fiscal slippage is opposite to what occurred in the 1980s when tough limits in the present year were compensated by prospects of softer targets in the future. Hence, a planned annual growth rate in spending of 0.5 percent set in 2004 was revised upwards to 1 percent in 2006. This reflects the so-called 'welfare agreement' of 2006 between the government and the main opposition parties, according to which long-term labor market policy has allowed increasing public consumption in the short term (front-loading) on the expectation of future expansion in the workforce. Only in 2003 and 2007 have the growth ceilings not been broken. It is also the case that declared targets tend not to be actually met in practice. These observations suggest that even for a Conservative–Liberal government with a stable operational budget majority, the pressure for welfare services and other new initiatives leads to budget slippage. This is exacerbated even more so in a context of massive budget surpluses where additional resources are readily available. Denmark is also locked in a welfare-providing trap, where increased private prosperity leads to further demands for expanded public services.

BUDGETING DEPENDS ON DECENTRALIZED AND MULTILEVEL NEGOTIATIONS

Local and regional governments play an important role in the Danish polity and are responsible for around 70 percent of general government spending (DKR302 billion out of DKR434 billion in 2007). Around 63 percent of this spending (DKR132 billion) is financed by state block grants (Finansministeriet 2007). Grants are the only financial source for regions, while for local governments consumption can be supplemented by local taxes. The independent status of local government is affirmed in the Constitution (§82) but the specific conditions they operate under are framed in national legislation. There are thus recurring tensions between national and local governments in interpreting the nature and boundaries of local autonomy. Local government organizes and delivers services within the large (and voter-sensitive) areas of social welfare and education, covering around 70 percent of all public consumption expenses.

A complex system of annual central–local budget negotiations, known as the 'agreement system', has evolved since the 1970s to meet the challenge of multilevel budgetary management. The system basically consists of negotiations between the Finance Ministry and the peak organizations Local Government Denmark (LGD) and Danish Regions (DR) covering the sector. Negotiations are weakly institutionalized, largely governed by informal rules and expectations. Agreements are not legally binding for the individual municipalities or regions. Moreover, agreements on tax levels and expenditure targets are collective across the sector. A given local government is, thus, allowed to raise expenditures and taxes beyond the terms of the agreement, provided the excess is offset by restraint in other jurisdictions. Finally, the system also contains a so-called 'extended total balance principle' which compensates local governments if national decisions lead to local expenditure increases, and expects them to reimburse any 'savings' that are due to decisions at the national level.

Growth rate targets for the municipal sector (both LGD and DR) are set by political agreement in June each year. This defines the terms of local government budgeting, which concludes in October. Usually, conflicts emanating from the summer debates resurface at this point in time when proposed budgets cannot meet the targets. Since 2005, the national government has begun reducing block grants in order to punish exceeding spending ceilings (Regeringen 2008). This move is controversial since it violates the principle of municipal autonomy.

However, budgetary slippage has taken place each year, constituting a problem for the Finance Ministry as the guardian of expenditures and macroeconomic policy. Latest figures indicate that under current agreements in 2008 growth rate targets have been overtaken by real growth in the municipal sector (Finansministeriet 2005; Indenrigs and Sundhedsministeriet 2007).

It is impossible to explain the Danish budgetary process without taking local government budgeting and the respective negotiations into account. However, for the purpose of this chapter, we will focus on the national budget system and consider local government finance as an important contextual feature with its own dynamics and substantive influence on budgetary outcomes.

LIMITED FORMAL REGULATION OF THE BUDGET PROCESS

Legal stipulations applying to the national budgetary procedure are intentionally sparse. The Constitution (§§ 43, 45, 46 and 47) merely states that all expenditures must be decided through ordinary or extraordinary budget legislation procedures; that no taxes can be levied without legal mandate; that the budget proposal must be presented to parliament no later than four months before the budget year; and, finally, that the accounts must be presented to parliament no later than six months after the budget year. Auditing is formally carried out by six 'state auditors', nominated by parliament. In practice the audit is performed by the Audit Office, which until 1991 was a part of the Ministry of Economics, but subsequently became independent under the auspices of parliament with the right to initiate analysis on its own behalf. The annuality of the budget is hence a function of the Constitution, as is the duty to report back to parliament.

The budget itself is a law of parliament. Further regulation of the budget process takes the form of government circulars issued by Finance or its Economic Agency. The first budget 'rulebook' was published, discretely, by Finance in 1972, deliberately keeping its legal status inexplicit and thereby preserving room for maneuver. In general, Finance has the power of interpretation in budget matters where no formal rules are specified or where ambiguities leave room for interpretation.

THE CORE ROLES OF THE MINISTRY OF FINANCE

According to §§ 14–16 in the Constitution, the Prime Minister appoints all ministers and distributes portfolios between them. After that, each minister assumes full responsibility for their ministry politically and legally. Traditions of ministerial independence support a culture of ministerial sovereignty, but formal roles are left open and unspecified.

The Ministry of Finance has no constitutional role or formal position on which to base its influence and role. Rather, it has devised its own core roles from institutional practices and the imposition of its authority at crucial times. How far Finance is able to exert such influence is dependent on many factors such as political backing, power relations with other ministries and local governments, the changing policy orientations of central agencies and the general economic situation. Moreover, Finance performs many economically related functions, such as macroeconomic policy, government budgeting and administrative oversight, and these can rival each other for influence over time. Over the past 20 years, Finance has steadily grown into a leading player at the center of government, largely due to its ability to play bureaucratic politics and demonstrate the worth of its advice to government. It has deliberately expanded its role as an analyst and coordinator of government policy, gradually changing from a reactive veto player to a proactive policy-maker engaging itself in policy development in other ministries.

Finance's position as the 'first among equals' in the core executive depends fundamentally on support from the Prime Minister. It also stems from wider perceptions across government of its intra- and interorganizational capacities and legitimacy (Jensen 2003). Historically, individual ministers could apply directly to the Finance Committee of parliament for supplementary appropriations in the budget year, without consulting Finance. Often supplementary appropriations could be twice as high as the original budget. This led to the adoption of an institutional rule whereby the Minister of Finance insisted that no ministry was allowed to approach the committee without prior approval from Finance. After some initial criticism, this rule has been accepted, helping to preserve Finance's authority until today (Østergaard 2007: 75, 108; Jensen et al. 2008). Under the present (2008) government, in-year supplement appropriations due to new unfinanced policy initiatives from line ministries have been marginal.

In response to public sector growth and the difficulties faced by the budget agency in trying to integrate three-year forecasts into the political debate, Finance advocated the establishment of a series of 'planning centers' in the 1970s coordinated by a Central Planning Center collecting information from local and national government to support on various policy issues. One such center was the Center of Expenditure Politics (Østergaard 1998: 270; Jensen 2003). Although the complete plan was never realized, Finance positioned itself as the de facto Central Planning

Center to integrate national and local government finances. It used this position to increase its influence over government policy-making in the 1980s and particularly the 1990s. It also developed into a combined think-tank and chancellery, heading up a number of key government committees (Jensen 2003).

One important institutional feature of Finance's core roles is the historical split between its budgetary responsibilities and the wider administrative efficiency responsibilities it took on. Budget-related activities were dealt with by the specialist Budget Department (BD) within the ministry. However, there was no similar organizational underpinning for its administrative reform activities until 1970 when a separate Administrative Department (AD) for policy was formed (with personnel management subsequently included). The AD was created in order to 'enhance appropriate, effective and economic behavior and organization' in the state bureaucracy (Smith and Dehn 1995: 92).

These two departments were fused in 1994, which was widely interpreted as a hostile takeover by the BD. There was considerable public debate over the future of administrative reform. Some felt the 'soft' organization consultants would be 'eaten' by the 'budget roughs', or that administrative policy would soon become the manservant of expenditure politics (Beck Jørgensen 1995; Dehn and Smith 1995). Against these fears, the administrative reform group consolidated its position internally and began developing and publishing proposals for public management reform. However, many of these administrative reform initiatives remained detached from the budget process. Partly, this was because the leadership of Finance at the time was more concerned to link budgeting with overall economic management and structural adjustment. Economists rather than managerial reformers were implanted into the Budget Department in order to facilitate a more policy-oriented and macroeconomic take on budget settings and processes.

Administrative policy became a mere appendix to this development and internal career paths largely followed the momentum. Finance primarily regarded administrative policy reform in terms of performance management, and as an issue best dealt with in the control relations between line ministries and their agencies. Although reforms were generally framed in the discourse of enhanced operational efficiency, they were never meant to be integrated into the overall budget process and be used for reallocative purposes. Only recently have direct administrative savings been collected by Finance in the budget process, due to targeted administrative reforms – most noticeable expected savings following the establishment of shared service centers and from efficiencies generated from the better coordination of cross-cutting projects after 2001.

THE SOLE INCIDENCE OF SYSTEMIC BUDGET REFORM, 1984–85

The reform process in the 1980s was shaped by the change of government from Social Democratic to Conservative–Liberal in 1982. For several years economic and fiscal conditions were steadily aggravated. Public expenditure climbed by 14.5 percent per year between 1971 and 1981, whilst annual taxation also grew by 10.5 percent (BRU 1983: 245). On the political side, different schools of thought were struggling over whether the country should invest or save to avert the crisis. Organizationally, Finance was severely weakened by the strong dependency of the social democratic government on the labor movement, which permeated into the government machinery and elevated the Ministry of Labor to the de facto powerhouse of government, relegating Finance to the role of spectator. The Finance Minister resented this position and tried to improve the organizational and structural conditions for Finance to gain more say. One of the initiatives adopted was the so-called Budget Reform Committee (BRU), which was inspired by British and Swedish budget debates and the OECD's public management PUMA project the Capacity to Budget. The author of this project, Allen Schick, was invited to speak to a prominent audience of budget actors, including a number of then junior officials who would later occupy leading positions in the ministries (BRU 1983: 213f; Østergaard 1998: 311; Heinesen 2006).

The 1984–85 budget reform was based on critiques of the existing budget system, which was seen as inflexible, confusing, informed by irrelevant formalities and lacking incentives to economize. Notably the proportion of annual expenditures handled through the budgetary process had declined to about 20 percent. A saying developed that staff members spent 80 percent of their time on 20 percent of the expenditures (Østergaard 1998: 310). The most significant criticism concerned the fact that staff appointment controls consumed enormous bureaucratic energy as did the implementation of the 'gross principle' that prevented agencies from covering their expenditure by revenue from their own activities and which acted as a disincentive to do more. Four main principles guided the work: budget ceilings and devolution; incentives to economize and enhance efficiency; simplification of procedures and systems; and, finally, increasing use of information technology.

During the preparation phase, the incoming Liberal Finance Minister took the lead and involved himself personally in working out what would later be referred to as the Modernization Program. Consequently, budget reform activities were energized by a rare political commitment and became integrated into a much broader and more radical attempt to

Table 9.1 Key elements of the 1984–85 budget reforms

Reform instruments	Key features
Budget ceilings	• A 'total ceiling' for each ministry encompassing all expenditure types, including entitlements • No 'back-stage' reserves to cover additional expenditures • Inclusion of consequences for local government – the so-called 'extended total balance principle' • Net-based budgets introduced
In-year monitoring	• Ministries must report status of ceilings in May, September and December to the Finance Ministry • Ministries obliged to take steps to counteract upward deviations from the budget ceiling
Savings and carry-forwards	• Unspent appropriations carried forward up to 4 years, provided anticipated use specified • Appropriations carried forward to the following year do not count in the budget ceiling for that year
Staff controls	• Detailed scrutiny of single appointments replaced by frame-based system where controlling only the higher-level appointments • A system based on time and wage ceilings

Source: Finansministeriet (1984a).

change public sector organization and management. The change of political regime facilitated the reform process, and removed the impediments placed on Finance by the Social Democratic party. A reform committee member expressed it like this:

> Suddenly, it was legitimate to talk about concepts like outsourcing, deregulation, marketization and privatization. In FM, years of frustration was replaced by a new self-esteem, bordering on a know-all attitude . . . There was a feeling that everything FM ever wanted was now possible. (Østergaard 1998: 313)

The BRU report of 1984 was thus adopted completely by the political system over the next period and driven even further than the BRU had dared to hope. The key elements of reform implemented are given in Table 9.1.

Budget reform preoccupied Finance throughout the 1980s. Although, partly due to changing ministers, the explicit ideological overtones of the reform complex faded somewhat over the decade, its agenda remained closely connected to expenditure politics and the enhancement of aggregate fiscal discipline (dubbed 'zero growth'), debt reduction and a firm concern about operational efficiency (Finansministeriet 1990, 1991, 1992). While there were many aspects to the reform initiative, we here present the overall principles and assess their effects on the budget system.

The cornerstone of the reforms was that annual aggregate targets for gross government expenditures were set in February–March and announced to the Finance Committee of parliament. The goal was a 'zero growth' regime, measured against the government expenditure level in 1984 (Christiansen 1999: 46; Finansministeriet 1984: 61). Once the aggregate target was set, it was broken down into so-called 'total ceilings' for each ministry, encompassing running costs as well as mandatory appropriations and capital investment. Once a portfolio received its envelope, the distributional conflicts were in principle internalized to a struggle between the parts of the ministry and the ministry and its agencies. The 'deal' in the system was more autonomy for ministries within a less-specified envelope in return for keeping strictly within it (Finansministeriet 1984: 56).

The envelope was 'fenced' by the lack of central reserves in the system; by the equilibrium-mechanism between state and local government which made it impossible to offload costs on local government; and by the principle of current prices, which made developments in salaries and costs of acquisitions an internal problem for the ministries. Moreover, since entitlements were also inside the allocated envelope for each ministry, it was the ministry's own problem to compensate for increases, either by changes in legislation or by cutting other parts of the budget (Finansministeriet 1984: 57). If the ministry wanted to expand beyond the given envelope, net appropriations made it possible to earn money and spend them on new initiatives. Also initiatives that saved money at the municipal level could avail the ministry with resources for new initiatives (Finansministeriet 1984: 59). If the ministry was able to economize resources or earn more money than it could spend, it would not be punished, but rewarded through the carry-forward system. In-year compliance with the total frame was monitored by Finance through a reporting system after which line ministries should regularly report budget performance, and according to which they were obliged to take steps to prevent or repair breaches.

In sum, the systemic changes worked from the assumption that once the annual target was fixed and envelopes distributed, the combination of incentive structures and monitoring systems would make aggregate fiscal discipline self-implementing. These premises were later termed 'a macho system for majority governments', since it did not allow for the inevitable conflicts, bargains and adjustments in a minority government or coalition situation. In terms of allocative efficiency, the global reallocation between government priorities would take place at the beginning of the process. Once envelopes were distributed, allocation and reallocation was in the hands of the single ministries and agencies. The philosophy was that decisions on allocation should be based on concrete knowledge of the given policy area.

Although the budget reform was generally well received among commentators (Melander 1988; Christensen 1990; Christiansen 1990; Andersen and Christiansen 1991) and was initially considered a successful disciplining device by Finance (see Analysenotat 1999) criticism was also mounted.

The 'zero growth' regime signaled an ambitious ideological goal to which considerable political prestige was tied. According to calculations from Christiansen (1990: 49), the ambitions were met in the first couple of years at the national level, even though public expenditure as a whole was 19 percent higher in 1989 than in 1983. However, revenues also grew due to improved international economic circumstances, and budget deficits turned into surpluses for a couple of years (Nielsen 1988: 314). An evaluation of government's track record depends on measuring standards. Measured against its grand proclamations, the policy did not meet its goals. But from a longer time perspective, the 1980s was a significant breaking point with public expenditure decreasing as percentage of GDP for the first time in 20 years (Andersen and Christiansen 1991: 28–30). Opinion polls showed the 'crisis consciousness' initially enjoyed broad public acceptance in the early 1980s but then waned subsequently (Andersen 1988: 163). Core executive actors believed this notion of economic crisis influenced the political climate for two decades (Jensen 2003). Hence, from a more macro-oriented perspective, the reforms were successful if the ambition was to bring the economic situation of the country to the front of the political agenda and break a long-standing deficit problem.

But from the perspective of steering the budget process, a number of shortcomings were recorded by critics. First, as the cornerstone of the new system was fixed annual targets set prior to the budget process, it depended on political determination and a willingness to stick to the initial targets when confronted with expenditure demands from ministries, organizations and voters. Government had invested a lot of political prestige in the targets and went far to comply with them, but this proved difficult after the first few years. For a minority government, it was increasingly difficult to find parliamentary support for a firm fiscal policy. To mask its inability to meet self-imposed targets, the government used different kinds of 'blue smoke and mirrors' as Meyers (1994) puts it. For example allowances for families with children was booked as negative income instead of expenditures; state-owned enterprises were declared off-budget; and unrealistic expenditure cuts were built into budget proposals to meet the annual targets but then seeped out again during the political budget negotiations in parliament. Commentators concluded that no budget system is any stronger than the actors using it – a standard conclusion also formulated by Schick (1998). And once politicians relaxed, the message to the rest of the system was that ceilings were not as fixed as they seemed. In practice, the new budget system was criticized for stimulating institutions to increase public consumption (Christensen 1990: 430–35).

Second, reallocation across organizational entities was not aided by the budget reform. The ceiling system tended to breed a perception of envelopes as 'properties' of the single ministries. If reallocation between areas was desired, it had to be undertaken at the beginning of the process as a collective decision at the highest level of government. A retrospective internal memo argued: 'In practice, however, the frame-setting process became a cutting exercise, where the clue was to find addresses for cuts that were generous enough to last the whole year' (Analysenotat 1999: 22). Incentives to stay under the ceilings and reallocate underneath them were most significant at the bottom of the hierarchy. But these incentives were undermined by lack of self-discipline at the top of the budget chain – among politicians – who also lacked good information about the real costs of programs and therefore the evidence to be able to reallocate from less effective to more effective programs or toward political priorities. The general *stimmung* [mood] at the end of the 1980s was that there was again a need for tighter monitoring of the single ministries. Around 1990 Finance sought to get back to the initial rigor of the early 1980s and to focus on the size and efficiency of the Danish public sector as a key structural problem.

In sum, critiques of the 1984–85 reforms were directed against the vulnerability of soft targets as the foundational logic of the system and against the lack of incentives to keep underneath the allocated ceilings. Two types of remedies were aired (Christensen 1990: 438). One was to imbue targets with formal authority through legislation. Another was to strengthen incentive structures and minimize information asymmetries through principal–agent-oriented steering systems. Governments responded to these challenges in the 1990s.

PIECEMEAL CHANGES IMPACTING ON BUDGETS IN THE 1990s

The idea of a budget law was judged to be politically unrealistic (Christensen 1991: 438) and in the higher echelons of the core executive it never gained ground (Østergaard 2008). Especially after the change of government in 1993 that strengthened Finance's political backing, the judgment was that, apart from the absence of legalistic traditions in Denmark, the informal and pragmatic system was a better platform from which to manage public spending. Moreover, fixed legal targets could expose governments to the risk of not sticking to self-imposed limitations. Finally, governments of the 1990s were less prepared than their predecessors to lock themselves into a straitjacket of fixed growth measures. Instead of pegging public expenditure growth to an index year or to the year before, it was tied to GDP with the instruction that it 'must be clearly below the GDP growth' (Jensen 2008). This indicated that the focus was on macroeconomic growth and economic structures, rather than the minutiae of expenditure control.

Finance pursued two different routes in the 1990s. On the one hand, its budgeting was integrated with the government's structural and macroeconomic policies. Consequently, the budget process became a vehicle for a more policy-driven style of governance. The budget sections of Finance became more analytical and evidence-based. Finance defined itself as the biggest think-tank in Denmark and as the leading economic research community (Østergaard 1998). After the fusion of departments in the mid-1990s, administrative reform agendas were seen as promising alternatives. These included the adoption of agency performance contracts and business accounting principles. As one permanent secretary stated: 'If this is administrative policy, there is nothing wrong with administrative policy' (Eldrup 1994). But the connection between budgeting and administrative reform was weak. Budget staff were tied to the annual routines of budget formulation or playing devil's advocate by analyzing policy operations (Jensen 2003: Chapter 6). The administrative policy staff expanded steadily as did the amount of publications they produced. The department literally became a 'reform factory', increasingly oriented toward the international reform community and serving to import, translate and adapt the shifting waves of OECD ideas to the Danish context. The functional split between administrative reforms and budgetary practice remained a feature of the reform efforts of the 1990s.

Instead of formalizing new rules for the budget process, Finance established itself as a central player in government decision-making and coordination processes in order to influence the substance of agenda-setting and policy development (Jensen 2003, 2008). Important elements in its toolbox became 'special studies', multiyear agreements and medium-term targets. Special studies had been around since the mid-1980s (Østergaard 2008; Blondel and Ruffner 2004) but gained a more prominent position. A special study could take the form of an analysis carried out either bilaterally between Finance and a line ministry, or across several portfolios if the policy problem or field influenced more than one ministry, typically with Finance as chair. Topics were typically selected by Finance in areas where efficiency gains and possible savings were expected. This gave these studies a bad reputation with line ministries who saw them as pre-emptive strikes. One line ministry remarked that 'special studies are a particular kind of studies where the conclusion is written from the start'. Often cross-cutting analyses made it easier for Finance to break down the fences of ministerial sovereignty. Line ministries were conscious that these studies provided Finance with influence over their subject matters. The most proactive ministries managed to use the studies to demonstrate their need for further resources. But the main idea was to feed the analyses into the budget process to identify an economic buffer for political reallocation (Budgetdepartementet 1991; Økonomistyrelsen 1996; Jensen 2003, 2008).

Multiyear agreements were introduced in the 1980s, inspired by the so-called 'free municipality' experiment and the UK 'free zones'. It was promoted as an efficiency-enhancing tool in 1994 (Regeringen 1993). The agreements would typically be for three- to five-year horizons, covering policy areas like the police, defense, primary schools or a specific institution such as the Royal Opera or the railways. Prior to an agreement a thorough special study would take place to identify the needs for future years as well as potential for savings and enhanced efficiency. After that, the budget would be agreed for a number of years and would not be affected by further cuts or claims. The agreements could involve political deals (providing a way for parties outside government to make sure that money was allocated to specific areas), or be managerial in nature, representing a contract between a ministry and one or more of its agencies. Over the years, most agreements have been political deals.

Although intended as an efficiency-enhancing tool, the agreements developed into asymmetrical arrangements in which ministries or agencies were allowed additional funding when they could argue that their portfolio had expanded. However, funding envelopes were not reduced even in the case of shrinking tasks. It also added a dimension of inflexibility into the budget preparation phase given that cuts and savings had to be extracted at this point in time. As a result Finance's stance toward multiyear agreements became less enthusiastic than during the first years, but still a substantive amount of running costs remained subject to the arrangement – well over half (Jensen 2008: Chapter 5; Finansministeriet 2003).

If fixed legislated targets were eschewed, an alternative medium-term fiscal framework was adopted in 1997, the first year of surplus. Public expenditure control could no longer be legitimized by the 'sins of the past', but instead looked to the future. The annual growth rate in public consumption became deducted from future economic requirements, primarily in terms of debt reduction, which in the 1990s was built into the annual economic planning. The requirements were supported by fiscal rules derived from the Economic and Monetary Union (EMU) criteria. The first medium-term expenditure framework, Denmark 2005, forecasted economic projections to 2005. However, the status of the annual growth targets was not formal as they were never built into the economic planning system as hard annual targets. The ensuing frameworks are best understood as political agreements to commit government and parliament to future sustainability in broad terms. Thus, they depended on a general political acceptance of a sustainable future, future demographic changes and taxation requirements. The frameworks provided guidance, but did not prevent slippage in the actual budget years, as the requirements had not been calculated into the three-year budget forecasts for the ministries. The targets remained at the macro level and had to make their way into the budget through the ordinary battles each year. Typically, the lack of discipline in a current year was explained as necessary investments or spending which would offset future consumption. Revised calculations and graphs were frequently issued showing future discipline strengthening in return for current largesse (compare Finansministeriet 1997: 51; 2003c, 2006b, 2007a, 2008a).

Internally, a 30-page review of existing budget procedure was produced in September 1999 which was critical of the system and painted a rather dark picture of budgeting as a steering process with waning significance. The main claim was that the budget system had been left largely untouched since the 1980s reform, although new challenges had evolved and the preoccupation with expenditure control had given way to a greater policy focus. But if the intention was to make a case for a second wave of budget reform, it did not eventuate. By the late 1990s, Finance did not see budgeting as the key to its influence so no reinvention was deemed necessary. Budgets remained targets, envelopes and nominal number games.

The 30-page review made several criticisms of existing practice:

- The envelopes of ministries had developed into an institutionalized 'property right' of ministries and agencies, shielded by the tradition of ministerial responsibility as well as the principles of decentralization. This worked as a serious impediment to cross-cutting reallocation.
- Finance was restricted to marginal budgeting, when ministries wanted additional funds or were asked to cut. Thorough analysis of individual budgets, their cost structure and effectiveness, was outside the realm of action. The timing of the process also prevented Finance from engaging in such analyses.

- Annual targets were set in nominal terms, and ministries, when asked to contribute to cuts and savings, could deliver nominal savings from a variety of sources, which were in effect defined as 'anything but construction' (produced through cuts in transfers, running costs, sale of assets, creative bookkeeping for the following year).
- The envelope system did not correspond to the evaluation of government policy, which was based on the development in public consumption. This meant that Finance could demand ministries deliver cuts, but had no way of ensuring the impact on consumption.
- Annuality meant agencies could push problems ahead to next year, without being impeded by multiyear targets. Simultaneously, the decentralized cuts had enabled considerable savings and carry-forwards: DKR 16 billion in 1999.

The report made some suggestions, big and small, which would strengthen both the role of Finance and the significance of budgetary policy. Among the suggestions were firmer multiyear budgets (not just extrapolated forecasts), and a revised definition of envelopes which would prevent ministries from delivering budget improvements from sources without impact on the indicators on which government would subsequently be measured. It recommended a process in which government priorities were incorporated more explicitly from the start of the process, whilst Finance should have more space and time to conduct analyses on which government's final decisions of allocation were made.

SUPPLEMENTARY REFORMS TO MANAGEMENT: CONTRACTS AND OUTPUT CONTROLS

New management philosophies developed in the ministries, stressing the management of the ministry as an enterprise. It was believed that the budget regime of the 1980s had focused too much on keeping within ceilings and too little on substantial goals and results. An enhanced results orientation entered the scene with the introduction of so-called 'free agencies' in 1991, based on the idea of quid pro quo. In return for demonstrated improvements in results in terms of enhanced productivity, service and quality measures, agencies were granted more autonomy in terms of personnel recruitment, results-based payment, the ability to carry forward surpluses created through internal rationalization and, finally, a budget guarantee protecting the agency from general across-the-board cuts (Finansministeriet 1996: 92). The underlying philosophy was that agencies would improve their performance if given more autonomy and rewards. The change of government in 1993 renamed these bodies as 'contract agencies', whose responsibility was to meet certain targets over a fixed period of time in return for budget security. In the first phase attention was directed toward goal-setting and the negotiations between purchaser (the ministry) and provider (the agency).

But the increased use of individual performance payments and business methods, together with the decentralization of budget competence, led the government to develop a framework with more focus on organizational results and managerial accountability. An independent factor fuelling this interest in enhanced visibility and control of results was the realignment of the National Audit Office from the executive to parliament. Once the auditor became external to the system, it was seen as imperative to create internal systems to prevent cases of mismanagement, some of which had already attracted criticism from the auditors (Finansministeriet 1996a: 7, 19). This led to a new 'internal controller' function which was implemented in almost all ministries (Finansministeriet 2001). The focus changed from setting targets to showing results. A related initiative was the 'enterprise account system' introducing a consolidated reporting document for all agency spending and results. Gradually an increased focus was placed on goal-setting and reporting in the agencies. Contract management developed into a coherent 'contract chain', where cascading goals were defined, procedures and incentives for reaching them worked out, and ways of measuring and reporting their fulfillment were introduced. Agency performance contracts became ingrained in the management of the public sector at large – a development generally seen as a positive contribution to improved resource management and transparency (Ejersbo and Greve 2005: 91).

There were also criticisms of the push to embrace management techniques. One strand of criticism concerned accounting procedures. In 1997, 134 enterprise accounts were produced, some of them reaching 100 pages. Although using a common format, the reports varied enormously in the data presented and results reported. The format and volume generated a heated debate, with some holding that the accounts were useless to parliament and a resource-consuming ritual, while others argued that a communal format was essential. Subsequently, in 2002, the format was reduced to a concise 'annual report' which should be 'more simple, brief, more accounting-oriented and closely linked to the performance management system' (Finansministeriet 2002). Although more focused and cut down to 25 pages, the 152 reports delivered in 2004 amounted to 3800 pages, but by now the reports were considered of negligible use to parliamentary deliberation. The initial ambition of using the accounting information for comparison and reallocation across ministries in the budget decision phase had disappeared, and the use of these reports became restricted to the control of individual agencies, primarily inside their own ministries.

Another strand of criticism concerned the nature of the agency goals in the performance contracts. As a consequence of the focus on internal management, a large proportion of the goals were internal and managerial, rather than oriented toward end-users. In effect, agencies spent a considerable amount of time telling the world how they organized themselves and what they did, but very little about the results of their endeavors. Performance management and budgeting were not sufficiently linked in the contracts, which inhibited cost calculations. These shortcomings led Finance to revise the guidelines for the performance contracts to stress the output orientation (Finansministeriet 2003b).

So, what can be defined as budget reforms of the 1990s represented a shift from input controls toward throughputs and outputs with the aim of enhancing efficiency and transparency of agency operations. However, the ambition of creating a governing system based on measurable goals and performance results, which in turn could be used as input information in the budget procedure, foundered due to several problems. One was the problem of finding a format of reporting which was both sensitive to individual agency management needs, and digestible for external actors and comparable. Another was to develop output measures of relevance for external stakeholders and users. Whilst the management of individual agencies became the object of more intense attention, the contract format failed to connect to the overall budget process. They remained two distinct sets of activities.

REFORMS POST-2000: SQUEEZING PUBLIC MANAGEMENT BETWEEN WELFARE PRESSURES AND A TAX FREEZE

A Liberal–Conservative government took office in November 2001, and in contrast to its liberal predecessors of the 1980s, accepted that a high level of welfare services had become a general preference in the electorate. Moreover, although the strength of the business cycle increased public revenue, it also fuelled rather than dampened welfare expectations. A political manifesto, based on a tax freeze, was introduced as a strong signal that the creeping taxes of the previous decade would be supplanted by rationalization and enhanced efficiency in order to gain welfare service improvements. The initial attitude of the new government was that it was possible to cut budgets both selectively and generally. In 2003, deep cuts were made in the Ministry of Environment and the Foreign Office. In terms of budget reforms, the change of government marked a shift of accent toward a more market-oriented discourse, contracting out, comparing costs with private providers and stressing the importance of end-user outcomes. The government revitalized the Modernization Program of the 1980s, with the belief that there was considerable potential for efficiency dividends to be taken from the 'cold hands' of public bureaucracy that could be invested in the 'warm hands' of direct service providers. The title of the first program, 'With the Citizen at the Wheel' (Regeringen 2002), was a part of a broader government discourse of 'putting people before systems', signaling that government was on the side of the taxpayers and service users against systemic forces.

The previous government's medium-term expenditure plan for 2010 with its built-in budgetary restraints was retained (but subsequently renegotiated to allow the growth rate of public consumption to rise from 0.5 to 1 percent per year). Together with the tax freeze, the commitments placed government in the 'new politics of the welfare state' dilemma, between popular welfare demands and economic limitations. Hence, the focus on budgetary gains from managerial efficiency was reinvigorated under three initiatives. First, accrual accounting and budgeting was adopted to enhance businesslike efficiency and total cost comparability. Second, an attempt was made to drive contract management toward output and outcome-oriented measures. And third, the administration of information technology (IT), as well as the management of large-scale projects and procurement, were all centralized to harvest efficiency gains.

Denmark was hardly enthusiastic about accruals. It came onto the agenda as a consequence of the 'free choice' model in the local government service delivery, which allowed cost comparisons between public and private providers. Eventually, Finance agreed to transfer state agencies from cash to accruals as part of the government's Modernization Program in 2002, and all central government departments and agencies moved to the new format in 2005 and 2007. The reform rationale was to improve economic decision-making in the agencies and cost-efficiency through new incentives for administration of asset, investment planning and enhanced scope for comparability of costs (Finansministeriet 2003a).

Contrary to most other countries converting to accrual principles, the aim in Denmark was solely to improve micro-management and performance in agencies, and not to enhance transparency of the government's entire macroeconomic actions by establishing a new accrual-based state balance. Individual balance sheets were constructed for ministries and agencies, but only operating expenditure and associated departmental capital spending was changed into the accrual format. The major parts of the budget – capital spending on infrastructure, military assets and national heritage, as well as grants and transfers such as old-age pensions – remained on a cash or commitment base. In total, appropriations transferred to an accrual basis constituted only around 10 percent of the 2007 state budget.

Finance expected improvements alongside these reforms. Agencies and departments were provided with increased managerial freedom, multiyear budgets running out to several years and incentives to expand investments (Finansministeriet 2006). Each agency and department was entitled to a 'loan ceiling' within which new capital acquisitions could be initiated. It allowed agencies to initiate desired investments (loans) if other operational activities could be cut or if investments were paid back by future cost reductions. The accrual reform also delegated the financial responsibility for investments to the agencies, which needed to find space within their budgets to cover depreciation and interest caused by new capital acquisitions. Failed investments, putting an immediate burden on the budget due to write-downs, must be covered within the agencies' existing appropriation.

Additionally, the accrual reform provided agencies and departments with a better platform to calculate the real costs of products and services delivered by the state. This included cost transparency, improved planning and use of existing production factors, and better benchmarking possibilities with other agencies and private firms (Finansministeriet 2003a). The reform also changed the carry-forward procedures by distinguishing between funding appropriated to unaccomplished tasks and remaining net capital. Agencies must 'reserve' appropriations to solve unaccomplished tasks the following year, making their backlogs visible in financial terms. The procedure identified delayed tasks and their cost, and at the same time isolated net results in the agencies. A positive net result could be spent on other relevant purposes while a negative result had to be balanced in the following years. Any net capital was likely to be 'vacuumed up' by Finance on a regular basis.

Thus, the accrual reform was initiated with the objective of improving the microeconomic management in agencies and departments. An evaluation in 2008 examined the change of behavior and procedures in the agencies. Most agencies had indeed taken some action in accordance with the opportunities and incentives embedded in the reform, scanned the existing assets or engaged in new capital acquisitions. Agencies were also using accrual accounting and budgeting to engage in long-term planning of investments (Økonomisk Fokus 2008). The new cost information, however, does not seem to have changed the strategic economic decision-making or the ministries' performance management. Few agencies have analysed their organizational cost set-up and fewer have changed it. Most agencies have not compared their cost structures with those of other agencies or private sector companies.

The annual budgetary game has only been affected by the accrual reforms at the level of detail. For example, the sale of assets can no longer be used 'invisibly' to sponsor new spending in the coming fiscal year, which was a widespread practice over the years. On the other hand, the fact that appropriations fund the cost of asset depreciation over several years has meant that Finance has lost some control over decision-making commitments.

Finally, after 2000, the contract philosophy of the previous decade was subject to revision. In 2003 a new publication, 'Effective Management in the State' (Finansministeriet 2003b) was published in which several previous instructions were 'canceled' and a new, coherent framework was presented, combining mandatory ministerial 'efficiency strategies' (especially focusing on policies for contracting out and coordination of procurement across agencies in the ministry) and agency contracts as well as special targets for end-users. Instructions to display written efficiency strategies was meant to put pressure on agencies to organize rationally through exposure to external stakeholders and the general public.

The guidelines for agency contracts have remained voluntary. However, since 2003 Finance has continuously stressed that targets should be set at the output and outcome level – to which agencies have complied. Agencies report on their specific performance on each contract goal in the annual report. They also report the share of an appropriation used to achieve a goal. Moreover, efficiency targets in the contracts were initially another way to put productivity pressure on the agencies. Nevertheless, Binderkrantz and Christensen (2008) show that the focus on efficiency targets in the contracts was largely subsumed within wider political agendas and policy settings. Contracts may still have an internal budgetary significance in the game between line departments and their agencies, but targets in the contracts are rarely linked to resources and in general the contracts have remained unconnected to the budget. Finance does not include performance information in the budget decision phase (OECD 2007: 136). Thus, agency contracts are solely an intra-ministerial performance management tool. Finance has never seriously sought to enable decision-makers to allocate and reallocate resources on the basis of operational efficiency data. The persistent lack of progress or achievement in linking performance and budgeting shows the barriers to such ambitions.

TAKING OVERALL STOCK OF DANISH BUDGET REFORMS

Only one transformational budgetary reform has taken place: the mid-1980s reform that drew on elements already launched in the 1960s. The 1980s reform was prompted by a crisis consciousness that evolved into a cultural and attitudinal change enabling decision-makers to impose a policy of budgetary restraint. A further budget component was added in the mid-1990s, when medium-term fiscal frameworks were installed under the headings of 'Denmark as Spearhead Nation' and 'Denmark 2005'. These initiatives bred a broader political and cultural acceptance of using future challenges as a benchmark for economic policy now that past problems were solved.

Top-down restraint exercises have come in two forms: in the crisis management years in the early 1980s when a 'zero growth' dogma was adopted that paved the way for the across-the-board (or 'lawn mower') cuts intended to achieve aggregate fiscal discipline; and in the shape of the tax freeze in 2001, the aim of which was to restrain expenditures via the revenue side. Subsequently, the 2005 Act enabled the national government to punish municipalities that break budget and tax agreements. It is worth noting, however, that none of the exercises have fundamentally changed budgetary behavior or eliminated unintended consequences. The 'lawn mower' was restricted in scope by multiyear agreements; the restrictions built into the tax freeze were counterbalanced by unprecedented revenue levels; and the 2005 Act is still subject to annual political confrontations between state and sub-state actors, the outcome of which depends on the political power relations at a given time.

Internal procedures and informal rules have been changed in a variety of ways over the past 30 years, the most significant being the frame budgeting embedded in the 1980s reform, including the internal in-year reporting system, the introduction of special studies in the 1980s and enhanced use of them in the 1990s. The enterprise reporting system, originally thought of as a vehicle for enhanced allocative decision-making by parliament, ended up as primarily an internal steering device in the ministries. The most spectacular technical reform is the accrual budgeting and accounting reform from 2005 to 2007.

Over the past ten years the culture surrounding budget formulation has been ambivalent. On the one hand, the strong business cycle has fostered a perception of 'no limits' which, alongside the weaker political standing of the traditional guardian role in government, has made budgetary policy hard to promote. On the other hand, there is a simultaneous awareness of resource pressure which has promoted market regulation and business methodologies to squeeze out resources for the allegedly insatiable welfare demands. The result has been a coexistence of 'burning platforms' hindered by a lack of authority and legitimacy to insist on the significance of tough budgeting. However, the recent global financial crisis has led the Finance Minister to a change of discourse: from open-ended national economic prosperity to the imminent need for fiscal caution. Judging from the budget negotiations of 2009, it has proved difficult to impose restraint measures or a more cautious *stimmung*. The global financial crisis has reopened a debate between actors who argue for an economic stimulus (enhanced public investments) and actors who argue for structural supply policies (tougher measures on the labor market to expand the workforce).

It is true that the frame of reference for legitimate budget policy-making has shifted to one of preparing to meet the challenges of the future. However, spending plans and medium-term frameworks have been continually adjusted, pushing demands ahead and with no fixed annual targets set as a result of the plans. Politicians care more about the future, in ways they did not 20 or 30 years ago, but at the end of the day they care most about the preferences of current voters, and there is no formal system or rules that prevents or 'criminalizes' this. Danish governments produce a variety of budget indicators, but are not held systematically and formally to account for them. The budget procedure is inevitably complex due to the multiparty and multilevel system and the political phase that can always disrupt carefully worked-out budget plans. In recent years, the parliamentary situation has produced a budgetary majority and the government is now able to sanction municipalities breaking budget agreements. This, however, does not automatically ease the job of maintaining aggregate discipline or reallocating across sectors or portfolios. They remain politically sensitive tasks, especially as the major part of the budget covers voter-sensitive welfare services. Reforms in these areas tend to work on a long-term horizon far away from the next election. In the meantime squeezing the public sector bureaucracy has become the default option for greater 'juicing' of resources. Reforms have increasingly been oriented toward operational efficiency. Budget reform over the past decade has tended to affect budget implementation more than budget decision-making, and more changes have taken place in the relationship between ministries and their agencies than in the aggregate budget decision procedure.

For more than ten years, Denmark ran budget surpluses, although currently the surplus is rapidly diminishing. After the introduction of medium-term fiscal plans in 1997, a consensus developed around debt reduction in accordance with EMU demands, and creation of sustainable economic planning for future generations. This created demands on the annual budget process to produce appropriate surpluses to pay off debt.

Given the strong business cycle, the task was fairly manageable over the past decade, as annual revenues and the ensuing surpluses consistently exceeded the forecasts until the present financial crisis. The ability to pay down debt did not demand any restraint in the short run. On the contrary, surpluses have been communicated politically as successful fiscal governance, and bred the interpretation among all groups of spenders that there was ample room for considerable welfare expansion.

With welfare and tax relief central electoral concerns, the government has sought to deliver on both sides: to cut taxes and provide visible welfare investments. Repeatedly there has been discussions as to whether or not the 2015 medium-term fiscal plan is realistic and sustainable and whether or not welfare investments are real or 'blown up' – that is, presenting figures and numbers today to create an impression of grand investments, whilst cutting welfare in the longer term. Either way, the discussions reveal that surplus-bred expectations, and yesterday's need to mask government overspending with different kinds of tricks, has been supplanted by a need to demonstrate a high level of growth in public consumption along with the ability to keep within self-imposed limitations. These exercises have hardly made it easier for the public at large to judge the state of the economy. The presentation of the budget proposal for 2009 was widely criticized for speaking with two tongues. A revealing comment from a leading newspaper captured the situation well: 'How is Danish economy at the moment? Hard to say after more than a full hour of press briefing with the Finance Minister' (*Berlingske Tidende* 26 August 2008)

NOTE

* The authors would like to thank Mogens Pedersen of the Danish Ministry of Finance, Hans Henrik Østergaard, formerly of the Danish Ministry of Finance, and our research officer, Frederik Hjorth.

REFERENCES

Analysenotat (1999), *Oplæg til møde om budgetreformen*, internal memo, Copenhegen: FM.

Andersen, Jørgen Goul (1998), 'Vælgernes holdninger til den offenlige udgiftspolitik,' in Karl-Henrik Bentzon (ed.), *Fra vækst til omstilling*, Frederiksberg: Nyt fra Samfundsvidenskaberne, pp. 191-216.

Andersen, J.G. and Christiansen, P.M. (1991), '*Vælgernes holdninger til den offentlige udgiftspolitik*', in Bentzon, K.H. (eds), *Fra vækst til omstilling*, København: Nyt fra Samfundsvidenskaberne, pp 145-191.

Beck J. (1995) 'Hvor gik forvaltningspolitikken hen, da den gik ud?', in Lægreid, P. and Pedersen, O.K. (eds), *Nordiske forvaltningsreformer*, Frederiksberg: Danmarks forvaltningshøjskole, pp 117–38.
Binderkrantz, A. and Christensen, J. (2008): 'Delegation without agency loss? The use of performance contracts in danish central government' University of Århus working paper.
Berlingske Tidende, (26.08.2008), 'En tur i skoven med finansministeren'.
Blöndal, J. and Ruffner, M. (2004), 'Budgeting in Denmark', *OECD Journal on Budgeting*, **4** (1), 49–79.
BRU (1983), *Rapport fra arbejdsgruppen vedr. budget og bevillingssystemet.* København: FM.
Budgetdepartementet (1991), *BP-afdelingen: en evaluering*, København: FM.
Christensen, J. (1990), 'Budgetreformer og udgiftsadfærd: om émbedsmænd og politikeres manipulationer og mulighederne for at manipulere dem', *Politica*, 4, 422-41.
Christiansen, P. M.(1990), 'Udgiftspolitikken i 1980'erne. Fra asymmetri til asymmetrisk tilpasning', *Politica*, 4, 442-56.
Christiansen, P. M. (1999), *Ej blot til pynt. Om budgettets politik og politikernes budget.* Ålborg: Ålborg Universitetsforlag.
Ejersbo, N. and Greve, C. (2005), *Moderniseringen af den offentlige sektor*, København: Børsens Forlag.
Eldrup, A. (1994), *Talemanuskript til årsmøde i Nordisk Administrativt Forbund*, internal memo, København: FM.
Finansministeriet (1984), *Budgetredegørelse 1984*, København: FM.
Finansministeriet (1990), *Udgiftsanalyser 1990*, København: FM.
Finansministeriet (1991), *Udgiftsanalyser 1991*, København: FM.
Finansministeriet (1992), *Udgiftsanalyser 1992*, København: FM.
Finansministeriet (1996), *Budgetredegørelse 1996*, København: FM.
Finansministeriet (1996a): *IKR rapporten*, København: FM.
Finansministeriet (1997), *Finansredegørelse 1997*, København: FM.
Finansministeriet (2001), *Organisation og ledelse i centraladministrationen*, København: FM.
Finansministeriet (2002), *Aktstykke om ny rapporteringsordning*, København: FM.
Finansministeriet (2003), *Budgetredegørelse 2003*, København: FM.
Finansministeriet (2003a), *Omkostningsprincipper i staten*, København: FM.
Finansministeriet (2003b), *Effektiv opgavevaretagelse i staten*, København: FM.
Finansministeriet (2003c), *Kommunale budgetredegørelser 2003*, København: FM.
Finansministeriet (2005), *Kommunale budgetredegørelser 2005*, København: FM.
Finansministeriet (2006), *Introduktion til et omkostningsbaseret bevillingssystem*, København: FM.
Finansministeriet (2006a), *Aftale om fremtidens velstand og velfærd*, København: FM.
Finansministeriet (2007), *Budgetredegørelse 2007*, København: FM.
Finansministeriet (2007a), *Mod nye mål – Danmark 2015*, København: FM.
Finansministeriet (2008), *Den økonomiske situation oktober 2008*, København: FM.
Finansminsiteriet (2008a), *Budgetoversigt 4,* København: FM.
Heinesen, K. (2006), *Min krønike*, København: Gyldendal.
Indenrigs and sundhedsministeriet (2007), *De kommunale budgetter.*

Jensen, L. (2003), *Den store koordinator – Finansministeriet som moderne styringsektor*, København: Jurist og Økonomforbundets Forlag.

Jensen, L. (2008), *Væk fra afgrunden: Finansministeriet som økonomisk styringsaktør*, Viborg: Syddansk Universitetsforlag.

Jensen, L., Andersen, T. S. and Henneberg, S. (2008), 'Statens budget – processer, rammer og aktører', in P.M. Christiansen (ed), *Budgetlægning og offentlige udgifter*, Academia.

Kieler, M. and Gaard, S. (2005), 'Two decades of structural reform in Denmark – a review', working paper. København: Finansministeriet.

Melander, P. (1988), 'Budgetreformen – et paradoks mellem finanspolitisk sikkerhed og organisatorisk forandring', in Bentzon, K.H. (ed), *Fra vækst til omstilling*, København: Nyt fra Samfundsvidenskaberne, pp 259-95.

Meyers, R.T. (1994), *Strategic Budgeting,* the University of Michigan Press.

Mørch, S. (2000), *24 statsministre,* København: Gyldendal.

Nielsen, C. (1988), 'Den borgerlige regerings styring af den offentlige økonomi', in Bentzon, K.H. (ed), *Fra vækst til omstilling*, København: Nyt fra Samfundsvidenskaberne, pp 295–333.

Organisation for Economic Co-operation and Development (OECD) (2007), *Performance Budgeting in OECD Countries*, Paris: OECD.

Økonomisk Fokus (2008), Desillusion over nyt statsligt regnskabsprincip.

Økonomistyrelsen (1996), *Brugerundersøgelse – Finansministeriets Departement*

Østergaard, H.H. (1998), *At tjene og forme den nye tid*, København: FM.

Østergaard, H.H. (2007), *Den røde bygning*, København: FM.

Østergaard, H.H. (2008), memo – written communication with authors.

Regeringen (1993), *Ny kurs mod bedre tider,* København.

Regeringen (2002), *Med borgeren ved roret,* København.

Regeringen (2008), *Justering af aftalesystemet for den kommunale økonomi,* København.

Schick, A. (1998), *A Contemporary Approach to Public Expenditure Management,* Washington DC: World Bank Institute.

Smith, M. and Dehn, J. (1995), 'Mellem rationalitet og retorik', in *Nordisk Administrativt Tidsskrift* 1.

10. Budget reform in The Netherlands: sadder but much wiser now

Jouke de Vries and Ton Bestebreur

Reforms to the public sector and budget processes in The Netherlands have followed a particular international trend. Being a small European country, with an open economy, The Netherlands is oriented toward the Anglo-American world. It has drawn many of its ideas about public sector reform from such sources, sometimes labeled as new public management (NPM). It has also looked to ideas circulating within the Organisation for Economic Co-operation and Development (OECD) more generally, but in all cases it has 'translated' and implemented these initiatives in the Dutch institutional context.

The Netherlands is a constitutional monarchy embedded within a bicameral parliamentary democracy. The Dutch political system can be characterized as a multiparty democracy based on proportional representation, a party-list system of election and a single national electorate. Thus, government in The Netherlands is, almost by definition, coalition government. Coalitions come in various compositions and majorities depending on the election results and the subsequent formation processes. Dutch politics is more recently characterized by the growth of populist parties of the extreme left and right, and as a consequence there has been pressure on the political parties of the center also to move in these directions.

The Dutch political and administrative system is driven by a unitary state, albeit highly decentralized. The national welfare state implements policy in cooperation with the 12 provinces and 443 municipalities. These decentralized entities receive their budgetary funding directly from the Province Fund and the Municipality Fund respectively. Provinces and municipalities also have autonomous tasks and duties in joint government.

The Dutch bureaucracy functions as a merit system compatible with a multiparty democracy. Accordingly, there is no major change in civil service personnel when a new government takes office. The Netherlands has 14 central departments (ministries). Each ministry is led by a minister, usually aided by one or more junior ministers. The ministers are part of the

Council of Ministers where the influence of the Prime Minister ('Minister-President') is modest. He is *primus inter pares*, although the integration of The Netherlands within the European Union (EU) has slightly enhanced the position of the Prime Minister within the Council of Ministers. One of the most important relationships within this Council is that between the Prime Minister and the Minister of Finance. The Ministry of Finance has a strong position within the network of central departments.

As with other advanced democracies, the politics of the Dutch budgetary process forms an important part of politics in general. The budget shows the connection between political goals and financial means. The budget provides an important part of the answer to the central question of politics: who gets what, when and how? In the budgetary process various actors with different roles or powers operate. In the past it was possible to use Heclo and Wildavsky's 'village life' metaphor (1974) to describe the various relations in the Dutch budgetary process. There were close connections between the Ministry of Finance, the financial world (the Dutch Central Bank) and the Standing Committee of Finance in the Dutch parliament. The Ministry of Finance maintained close ties with the other two departments of the so-called 'social-economic triangle': the Ministry of Social Affairs and Employability and the Ministry of Economic Affairs. Within the overall budgetary process a complex interaction existed between the Ministry of Finance and all the spending departments. It is our hypothesis, based on the more recent work of the Canadian budget specialist David Good (2007), that the financial village has developed into a modern metropolis. Among the new inhabitants are the Prime Minister who has become an important budget actor, the relevant institutions of the EU, and a number of emancipated internal and external watchdogs that have recently asserted their positions in the political power game.

In this chapter we evaluate the ways in which consecutive Dutch governments have pursued budget reforms from 1989 onwards. But before we make a closer examination of these periods there are three overarching budget reform trends worth mentioning.

First, Dutch budgetary policy was focused on achieving a balanced budget, or as near to balanced as possible. The Ministry of Finance was guided by the Economic and Monetary Union (EMU)-centered target-setting of the EU. In order to introduce the euro successfully as the new currency for enhancing European integration, the financial coordination between the member states of the EU became an essential priority. The respective member budgets needed to be balanced, otherwise the euro would most likely become a weakened currency against the US dollar. In Holland the EMU criteria were particularly helpful in forcing governments to achieve a (nearly) balanced budget, although there were differences in the speed of implementation across the EU member states.

Second, budget processes gradually focused more and more on accountability. Both chambers of parliament and the National Court of Audit (NCA) stressed the importance of accountability and increasingly became the internal watchdogs for the taxpayers. Accountability was further enhanced through the transition from input to accrual budgeting and the changeover to performance management in agencies. There were demands that budgetary documents should become more informative. In order to make well-informed assessments these documents needed to be transparent and readable, otherwise there could be no satisfactory discussion about the budget and the evaluation of its results. Parliament asked for the third Wednesday in May each year to become a so-called 'Accountability Day', on which a goal-oriented set of statements from departments would be introduced so that parliament could discuss questions of effectiveness and efficiency of governmental policy. This transformation was called 'From Policy Budgeting to Policy Accounting' (Van Beleidsbegroting tot Beleidsverantwoording or VBTB). In the process, independent agencies and semi-independent agencies needed to work efficiently because they became the actual service delivering units within the government bureaucracy.

Third, like all OECD countries, there continued to be some important off-budget activities. The revenues of the Dutch gas production and some asset sales were put into a so-called Economic Structure Enhancing Fund (ESEF). Investments from this fund can be used to strengthen Dutch infrastructure such as high-speed rail links, and for the stimulation of 'knowledge economy innovations'. The objective of the fund is twofold. First, it intentionally removes such revenues from the debates around the general budget and thus their expansionary impact. Second, it guarantees that significant money will be spent on improving the country's economic infrastructure.

Apart from these trends we should acknowledge that an understanding of budget reforms would be enhanced by a perspective on the broader questions of public sector reforms. They include the privatization of various tasks of the welfare state, the creation of independent agencies (*zelfstandige bestuursorganen*) and executive agencies (*agentschappen*), the introduction of market forces and competitive tendering (rail, energy and water), the decentralization of policy implementation to local government (for example social security measures), and the introduction of a decentralized bargaining process to deal with public sector labor relations. However, a systematic elaboration of such a perspective is beyond the scope of this chapter.

BUDGET REFORM IN THE NETHERLANDS, 1989–2008

Dutch budget reform has followed a closely connected trajectory, particularly over the past two decades, driven by the need to comply with the fiscal targets of the EU. In the following section we divide these decades of budget reform into five chronological periods. These five periods are: 1989–94, 1994–98, 1998–2002, 2002–07 and 2007 and beyond. They correspond with the terms of various Dutch cabinets and their reform initiatives from prime ministers Ruud Lubbers (1982–94), through Wim Kok (1994–2002) and to Jan-Peter Balkenende (from 2002). We analyse each period by focusing on three themes indicated below:

- budgetary policy and fiscal control;
- changes to budget processes, especially attempts to enhance accountability; and
- the impact of budgetary reforms on policy delivery, especially on independent agencies.

In the third period (1998–2002) we also discuss changes to budgetary documentation which occurred only in this period.

Meeting the EMU Targets: the First Period of Reform, 1989–94

During the 1980s, the principal objective of budget policy in The Netherlands was to reduce the large budget deficits that had increased considerably in the preceding years. From 1983, a strict norm was introduced to reduce the deficit through a schedule of annual targets. Regardless of the economic cycle a stipulated norm established prior to each budget year had to be attained. However, in the 1980s the policy was only partially effective as the budgetary process was characterized by much turbulence.

In the early 1990s economic development stalled and economic growth declined. This resulted in diminishing tax revenues. In combination with the higher interest payments caused by increasing national debt, this led to considerable budgetary problems. In order to be able to realize the deficit objective, additional cutback measures had to be adopted and successive budget cuts were deemed necessary. The actual deficit did decline despite disappointing economic growth. This was due to stringent discipline requiring frequent and recurring cutback rounds. The new objective of the third Lubbers cabinet (1989–94) in regard to budgetary policy was to seek to comply as soon as possible with the requirements laid down in the Maastricht Treaty of 1992 for countries wishing to participate in the Economic and Monetary Union (EMU). From this point on, the budget politics of the Dutch government were no longer solely subject to national considerations, but to a stipulated European framework. The EMU was about to commence and The Netherlands wished to be part of it.

The concept of strict budget discipline brought the cabinet almost to a state of conducting permanent budgetary negotiations. These lasted from early spring to late August, ending just in time for the traditional budget presentation on the third Tuesday of September. To underscore the seriousness of budget discipline, the cabinet members agreed to impose additional cuts to compensate any unforeseen budget overruns. This became a key characteristic of Dutch budgeting and even parliament effectively adopted these unwritten rules of budgetary decision-making. The effect of this policy was to limit parliament's opportunity to amend the budget successfully. In this period, the overall average of budget amendments by parliament dropped below 0.2 percent of the annual budget. However, to preserve some scope for latitude, the Ministry of Finance allowed some uneconomic 'back-door' investments to occur, mainly to satisfy social expectations for new public investment. In this way the government accepted off-budget expenditures like financial leases for new prisons and private financing using toll payment mechanisms to fund expensive tunnels.

To improve service delivery in this context the government turned to agencification in two important ways: establishing 'independent agencies' and a new form of 'executive delivery agencies'. By the early 1990s the government returned to an old idea by establishing 'autonomous governing bodies' (AGBs). Such agencies have a long history in The Netherlands, but the number increased markedly in the last decade of the twentieth century. These independent public entities were defined as: 'organizations which . . . are charged with the implementation of one or more public policies, and which are funded publicly, but which operate at arm's-length of government'. Most AGBs were established as statutory bodies, founded by a specific Act of Parliament. As autonomous agencies they were legally separate from government departments and independent of ministerial authority, with no direct hierarchical relationship with ministers. Many public bodies were reshaped as independent agencies, some financed through the national budget, others financed by individual contributions of citizens demanding services (such as the issuing of driving licenses, number plates for cars, and the registration of property). Essentially they operate off-budget even if they receive recurrent funding, and operate independently which is sometimes seen as problematic with respect to democratic accountability.

A further reform was proposed to parliament in 1991–92: the introduction of regular or 'executive delivery agencies'. Such organizations have a separate corporate identity but were placed under direct ministerial control and subject to supervision and instruction by their core ministry. Agencies operated and published separate financial accounts and their managerial freedoms were negotiated with the parent ministry. Ministers maintained control through a 'steering' relationship and retained some managerial discretion and responsibility for the management of the agency. Each agency was able to keep and redirect some of the gains from efficiency savings accumulated to a maximum of 5 percent of annual turnover, thus providing some small further incentives for improvement. Performance management was considered part of the steering model.

Budgetary Renewal: the Second Period of Reform, 1994–98

Qualification for the EMU was the leading policy goal during this period. By 1994 The Netherlands had not yet complied with the convergence criteria for the EMU that had been agreed in 1991. In particular, the Dutch budget deficit was too high. The national deficit was almost 4 percent of gross domestic product (GDP) (while the EMU allowed a maximum of only 3 percent) and the debt level fluctuated around 80 percent of GDP (while only 60 percent was allowed). The magnitude of public debt resulted in substantial interest expenses. In short, there was much work to be done.

The key development in budgetary policy in this period under Prime Minister Wim Kok (1992–2002) was the introduction in 1994 of 'trend-based budgetary policy' or 'Zalm norm' as it is sometimes called after the long-serving Finance Minister Gerrit Zalm (1998–2002 and 2003–07). This policy was characterized by four interrelated components: the adoption of cautious economic premises; a stricter separation between revenues and expenditure; the imposition of an expenditure framework with ceilings; and the adoption of 'one principal moment' for budgetary decision-making. Many of these reforms, which we detail below, were derived from the Anglo budgetary world.

It was soon apparent that previous predictions regarding the rate of economic growth had been too optimistic. In order to diminish the chance of setbacks, the new trend-based budget policy was based on cautious economic predictions. This cautiousness on the part of the cabinet reduced the chance of discovering unexpected deficits. After years of ad hoc recurring cutbacks, this new policy introduced by Finance Minister Zalm led to political and administrative calm around decision-making with regard to the expenditure and revenues of the government.

A second characteristic of trend-based budgetary policy was the imposition of a strict separation between revenue and expenditure. Windfalls on the revenue side could no longer be used to spend more than was originally budgeted. If additional expenditure was sought within one policy area (for example more funds for education) it could only occur if less matching expenditure was spent within another policy area (for example less funds for benefits). Unexpected increases in revenue returns could only be used for reducing the budget deficit or for relieving the financial burden on citizens (tax cuts).

Expenditure was controlled by using fixed expenditure ceilings with which spending ministers had to comply. Expenditure limits were bound by a ceiling covering a period of four years. Upon the start of a new cabinet the ministers decided on the medium-term expenditure framework. These multiyear agreements for expenditure control were intended to fit within the four years of a parliamentary term, taking economic growth and inflation into account. Each annual budget had to be prepared within this framework, and if priorities changed and potential increases in expenditure were intended, then various compensatory decisions had to be taken to remain within the ceiling.

Previous budgetary negotiations in cabinet had been fraught and time-consuming. Cabinet deliberations became, in the words of a former Minister of Finance, Jelle Zijlstra, 'a slightly neurotic pattern of budget composition, budget implementation and frequent interim adjustments'. In order to bring more calm under the trend-based budgetary policy, decisions about the main features of the budget were only rendered once a year – in the spring. So, within the medium-term framework, annual budget decisions were taken at 'one principal moment' each year rather than dribbling out across the year.

Together these restrictions on budgetary decision-making became known as the 'Zalm norm' and the Liberal Finance Minister gained widespread political, professional and public respect for this policy. During his period as Finance Minister he gradually shifted the focus of budget-making from a narrow concern with avoiding the annual deficit, to one of sustainable public finances and balanced budgets which nevertheless allowed some year-to-year variation. He was also prepared to relax budgetary rules where such changes could prove more efficient and accountable. For example, from 1994 he introduced an 'end-of-year flexibility scheme' that aimed to avoid the frantic December spending spree which was widely seen as inefficient and wasteful.

During this period, parliament sought to exercise more influence in regard to budgetary control. It tried to reinvent its role by focusing more on the quest for control through such means as parliamentary committees, budgetary investigations and informational support from budgetary experts similar to that provided in the US by the Congressional Budgetary Office. It also demanded better information about the annual accounts of government, and worked closely with the National Court of Audit (NCA) on efficiency studies of government expenditure. The NCA increased its scrutiny of independent agencies and gained much respect for this work.

Executive agencies began to proliferate. By the end of the 1990s, 40 agencies had been created accounting for approximately 60 percent of all government employees. Agencies created included the prison service, the public works agency, the government housing service and agencies handling subsidy requests. Accrual accounting and budgeting was introduced for all agencies, but only covering their running costs; program budgets still remained in traditional cash commitments held in the ministry. As a result, all agencies had to administer their budget and report on it using two different systems. Furthermore, parliament had to authorize two different budget types, a development which was criticized by the NCA for its complexity and potential threat to the transparency of the budget process.

During these years, discussion also started on the optimal extent of autonomy for independent agencies. This was partly because of a perceived lack of effective political control and transparency in performance, but also because of problems caused by their relative financial autonomy. Criticism grew with indications that the salaries of the executives of independent agencies had increased enormously. The savings of these agencies had also grown substantially. Yet, the number of independent agencies continued to grow mainly due to the perceived benefits for the responsible departments.

Toward Abundance: the Third Period of Reform, 1998–2002

The EMU officially commenced on 1 January 1999. It was premised on agreements made in the Stability and Growth Pact of 1997. This pact stressed the vital importance of permanent sound finances for the stability of inflation, interest rates and the euro. It also insisted that member states maintained budget discipline once they participated in the EMU. The most important agreement required countries to pursue a budget balance or surplus in the middle–long term. This rule should prevent a country from exceeding the maximum deficit of no more than 3 percent of GDP in times of economic adversity. While EMU countries themselves remain responsible for their national budget policy, they were subject to certain European preconditions and sanctions under the agreed framework.

The Netherlands qualified relatively easily for the EMU. The national debt had dropped from over 60 percent of GDP to just above 50 percent, and in 2000 for the first time in 40 years the country realized its first budget surplus. The successful separation of revenues and government spending helped enforce discipline under the strictly kept spending ceilings. Fluctuating revenues were mostly higher than estimated, primarily due to the Zalm-inspired conservative economic forecasts. However, a clear policy on maintaining the surplus once it was achieved had not been implemented, resulting in massive demands from spending ministers after the first surplus had been reached.

As the importance of the EMU grew, other forms of European-centered consultation reinforced this trend, such as the so-called 'Ecofin' (Economic and Financial Affairs Council) meetings of European finance ministers. As a member of this epistemic community, the Dutch Ministry of Finance gained new powers by arguing that domestic budgetary policies should be kept within the framework of Ecofin policies, which were aimed at delivering annual structural surpluses and were extremely critical of off-budget expenditures and budgetary 'back doors'. With its own house in order, the Dutch government also tried to enforce EMU rules on other jurisdictions, and for a while Finance Minister Zalm was praised as 'Il Duro' ('the hard one') after he had sought conflict with Southern European countries that failed to meet the EMU deficit standards.

Parliament had long been supportive of the various reforms introduced to the budget process. In cooperation with the Ministry of Finance and the NCA, it introduced the practice of making the third Wednesday in May the day each year when the accounts of government departments were to be presented to parliament, together with the conclusions of the NCA after auditing the annual reports. This resulted in the much earlier availability of these accounts, meaning that they were then much more useful in decision-making and in the succeeding budgetary debates for the upcoming budget year. They allowed for more serious parliamentary scrutiny of the results of government spending. And they allowed members of the lower house of parliament to begin consulting with individual ministers in June, on the basis of the annual reports and the Court of Audit reports. But parliament's interest in these integrated reports soon evaporated due to a lack of sustained interest.

During this third phase, the government also introduced a major redesign of the budget documents. In May 1999, the Ministry of Finance announced to parliament that the government intended to introduce an outcome-based budget system to replace the present input-based one. The new structure was called 'From Policy Budgeting to Policy Accounting' (VBTB) and it promised an explicit emphasis on results. The first official

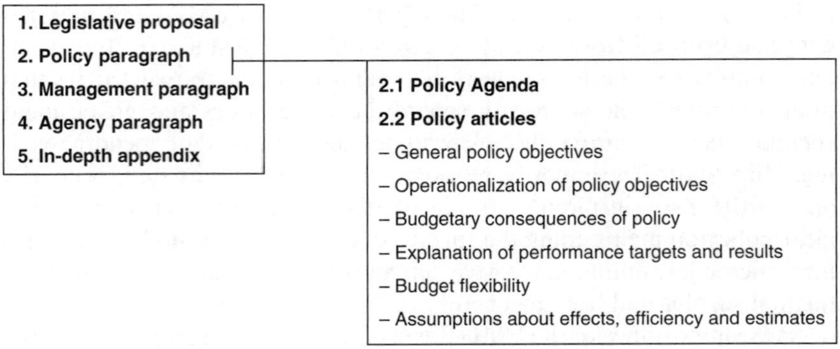

Figure 10.1 The new structure of the budget and accounts

outcome-based budget was presented to parliament in September 2001. The objective of the documentary redesign was to make the budget more transparent while linking policy, performance and resources more closely. In spring 2003, the first restyled *ex post* annual reports, including performance information, were sent to parliament, after being audited by the NCA.

According to the VBTB initiative, (Figure 10.1) each departmental budget should be able to elaborate:

- What do they want to achieve?
- How do they want to achieve it?
- What should it cost?

Then, the following Annual Report of each department should focus on the corresponding accountability questions:

- Has the department achieved what they wanted?
- Has the department done what they should have done in achieving it?
- Did it cost what was expected?

Beyond this development, Finance Minister Zalm pursued the government-wide introduction of accrual budgeting, even though the costs of implementation were estimated to be high and there was some doubt about the added value of such a system for the remaining ministries. Already, the organizations responsible for the delivery of services and execution of policy had been transformed into agencies with accrual systems. However, after the demise of the Kok government in 2002, later cabinets have deprioritized this initiative. Although accrual budgeting was seen as promising, it was considered too costly to entertain.

Despite the best of intentions, the VBTB initiative to provide results-oriented budgetary documentation and accounts did not enjoy great success. Parliament continued to feel dissatisfied by the lack of clear relationships between goals, budgets, policy instruments and performance data. Parliament was critical of the lack of meaningful performance information and remained dissatisfied with the evaluations and the performance information in the accounts as well. The new budgetary documentation also reduced the amount of detailed budget information, due to the aggregation of expenditures (spending articles) into outcomes. On the other hand, spending departments have clearly benefited from VBTB, because the change to outcomes and the increased average size of spending articles gives them much more discretion vis-à-vis the Ministry of Finance and parliament.

The VBTB initiative thus had major shortcomings. The relevance and reliability of the performance information produced was questioned. The quality and impartiality of evaluations was queried. The real 'need' for a particular policy was never questioned and there were not enough *ex ante* evaluations of whether the chosen policy would actually work. And there was no discussion of causal factors, such as had outcomes been achieved because of or despite a given government policy? So, in the end, the once promising idea of budget presentation redesign (VBTB) did not deliver what was anticipated, and no longer seemed to be a key issue for either the Ministry of Finance or the parliament.

Figure 10.2 indicates the level to which spending departments have been able to report performance data against their total budget, shown as a percentage. The range is between 25 percent compliance (for the Ministry of Housing, Spatial Planning and Environment) up to 90 percent of total expenditure (for the Ministry of Agriculture, Nature and Food Quality).

After the proposed implementation of accrual budgeting for ministries came to grief, parliament succeeded in ensuring that at least one spending department (Agriculture, Nature and Food Quality) would test the concept as a pilot. But across government there were few expectations that the idea would be reintroduced again.

There were serious attempts made to evaluate the performance of executive agencies. But the results indicated mixed findings. Some had shown improvement in the quality of services provided or had managed to provide the same quality of service for less money. But others indicated less positive results, and some had difficulty in even demonstrating clear results at all.

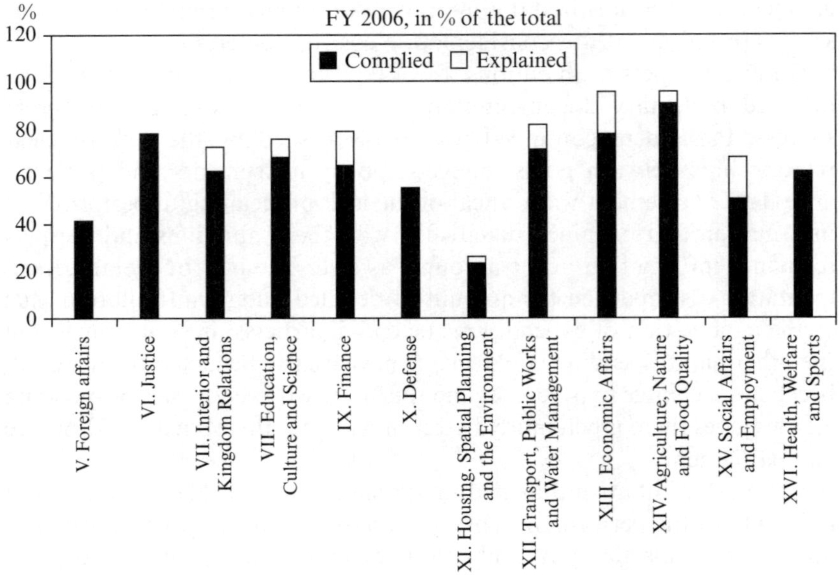

Source: AR (2006).

Figure 10.2 The VBTB conformity of performance indicators (2006, in % of the total)

Return to Sadness: the Fourth Period of Reform, 2002–07

From 2002 The Netherlands again faced more difficult economic times that naturally affected its financial position. In 2000 The Netherlands had managed to achieve a budget surplus of 1.5 percent of GDP. In 2001 this surplus shrunk to 0.1 percent of GDP. In later years the country suffered a loss of reputation in Europe when it recorded a deficit greater than 3 percent to GDP (see Figure 10.3). As a result the Ministry of Finance forced through new, and even stricter, budgetary policy rules which made it possible to limit the spending of provincial and local authorities in the event the country was in danger of exceeding the 3 percent EMU criterion. This was an unprecedented law in which the central government exerted its power to overrule other government authorities. After this temporary failure to meet the EMU criteria, the Balkenende cabinet re-established control over public finance with some highly debated budget cuts. Increasingly, the national budgetary policies were brought in line with the European policies of the EMU, leaving less flexibility for spending ministries and adding power to the Ministry of Finance. By the end of its

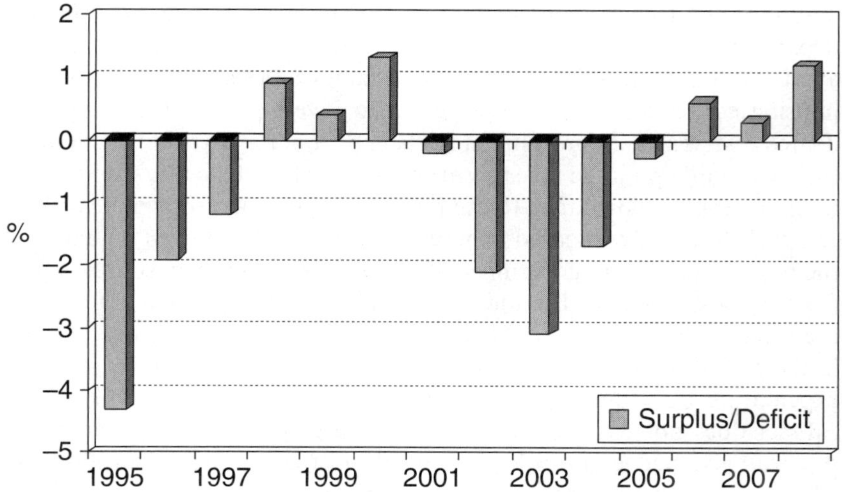

Source: Dutch Ministry of Finance, Miljoennota 2009, the Hague.

Figure 10.3 The annual surplus deficit of The Netherlands 1995–2008 (% of GDP)

first term in 2006 the government managed to finish with relatively good results, adding to the reputation of Zalm who had become the longest-serving Minister of Finance in The Netherlands.

Parliament again tried to improve the quality of information it received in regard to reviewing public finances. But its experiment with the Council of Economic Advisors (REA) turned into a painful failure. Parliament felt it needed greater analytical expertise and independent support to help cope with the massive overload of information from the Ministry of Finance and spending departments. So, it established a council of five well-known economists supported by a secretary. However, the new council members began formulating their own agendas, straying into taboo areas, with reports on sensitive issues such as tax deduction on mortgage payments. Within two years, after much parliamentary criticism, the members of the REA resigned and replacements have not been appointed.

Commencing the Fifth Period of Reform: from 2007 to the Crisis of 2008 and Beyond

The main focus of Dutch budgetary policy has shifted now toward sustainable budgets that are robust in the long term. In particular, additional saving measures have been implemented to help reduce the debt such as additional budget cuts on running cost budgets for central government departments. However, there have also been new calls to spend to help avert the financial crisis of 2008. For example, the largely autonomous housing corporations have been asked to invest part of their unprecedented reserves in new housing projects in the poorer parts of the country, thus speeding up public investment through 'extra-budgetary' funds. The level of debt has now fallen to the high forties as a percentage of GDP, a relatively low level compared to other OECD countries. Given the aging of the population, future governments will be able to use the resources freed from interest payments for additional healthcare and pension schemes. It is estimated that the number of people aged 65 or older will almost double in the period to 2040 to more than 4 million. This will cause increases in expenditure on old-age pensions and aged-care which the Balkenende cabinet does not wish to leave as a tax burden for future generations. Accordingly, budgetary policy is aimed at creating future surpluses to allow future governments to be better able to adapt to the higher costs associated with an aging population. The existing goal is still to reach a structural surplus in 2011 of 1 percent of GDP.

The attempt to provide integrated performance and financial reports to parliament on the third Wednesday in May has not yet turned into a success. Annual reports typically lack proper information, or are too technical, and some political leaders or cabinet ministers avoid the debates. Even after seven years of attempts, parliament is still struggling to make the concept function properly, although it has established a small parliamentary research unit of eight people to assist its efforts. Moreover, in the fall of 2008 the Balkenende government decided no longer to pursue the costly implementation of accrual budgeting and accounting beyond the existing running cost budgets of agencies.

When the financial crisis hit the markets in 2008, it heralded a new episode in the increasing role of the Dutch Ministry of Finance. Almost overnight the Dutch Ministry of Finance felt it necessary to take over the Dutch activities of the threatened Fortis/ABN-Amro Bank from its Belgian owners at a cost of €16 billion. Taking the initiative, the Finance Ministry opened credit lines for other banks of up to €10 billion and provided strategic guarantees for the financial sector up to €200 billion. Simultaneously, after local governments reported substantial losses of savings in failed banks like Lehman Brothers and the Icelandic banks, the Ministry of Finance announced even sharper prudential rules for local governments and claimed a central role in the negations with the foreign authorities in an effort to reclaim some of the savings of local government and Dutch citizens. The government chose to be proactive.

There are enormous risks and potential pitfalls associated with these actions, but we must also acknowledge that in the financial crisis it was again recognized that the state is the bastion of last resort. However, we can make two observations from the initial attempts to stave off economic catastrophe. First, the Minister of Finance, Wouter Bos, took the lead in the rescue operations, in close cooperation with the Central Bank of The Netherlands. It soon became apparent that in the midst of the financial crisis the Minister of Finance, supported by professional experts, played a dominant role in the policy initiatives. Government responses to the crisis were technocratic in nature. Second, parliament was only informed about the multimillion bailout operation after the newspapers had widely debated this unprecedented government action. It was left behind as a spectator on the sidelines. Parliamentary requests for greater scrutiny or wider debate, led by the opposition parties, were neglected. Hence, in addressing the financial crisis, this effectively left the Minister of Finance in a crucial, unique and unprecedentedly dominant role in reshaping the country's financial system.

FINDINGS AND CONCLUSIONS

Dutch cabinets have been prepared to implement significant budgetary reforms, tending to add new reform efforts onto previous iterations of reform. Different coalition agreements and compacts have paved the way for budget reforms to be implemented during the tenure of the cabinet. Most of these reform initiatives have gained bipartisan or even multi-partisan support from the political parties. Although fiscal policy is political, governments of different complexions have developed shared objectives as they have sought to contain expenditure and move toward balanced budgets. Fundamentally, the budget process is technocratic and not disturbed by partisan politics. Reformers have also benefited from international ideas that were incorporated within the financial subsystem. By contrast, other public sector reforms have been driven by partisan politics. For instance, center-right coalitions tended to be protagonists for the free market, while center-left coalitions abandoned privatization, choosing independent agencies or executive agencies as their preferred delivery means.

It is impossible to overstate the importance of the European Union in enhancing the attempts of the Dutch government in achieving fiscal discipline. Following the signing of the Maastricht Treaty, the EMU framework became a powerful tool for the Ministry of Finance in target-setting. Moreover, the growing importance of the EU has tended to underscore the influential position of the Prime Minister in relation to fiscal discipline.

National attempts to control deficits were reinforced by the existence of the EMU criteria (see Figure 10.1). All member states joining the EMU had to bring their budgets into line with the published targets announced at Maastricht. In The Netherlands case it would not have been possible to replace the national currency of the guilder with the Euro if these EMU targets had not been met. Institutional support from the EU made the coordination of the budgetary process somewhat easier.

Gradually, budgetary policy has become less expedient and crisis-ridden and more future-oriented. In the near future, once the financial crisis has abated, Dutch governments will have to tackle substantial problems such as their aging population, climate change, a rising sea level and the energy predicament. These political problems demand long-term policy and financial solutions. Nowadays while much spin or symbolic language is used in budget briefs, real money has to be set aside to tackle these significant problems.

Parliament has traditionally accepted a small role in target-setting and budgetary allocations. Formally speaking, control over budgetary appropriations is the most important right or power of parliament. However, it is difficult for the members of parliament to have a clear sense of what exactly is going on in the budget process. Parliament can appear impotent and far removed from the process. Increasingly, it became aware that the monitoring and review of the budget process was deficient. Consequently, parliament requested the installation of the Accountability Day on the third Wednesday in May. This day of budget responsibility has thus far not proved a great success, mainly because the information presented has been too general and at an aggregate level. There is some evidence that parliamentarians have shown a lack of real political interest in pursuing this initiative. Parliament also established a special council of top economic advisors (the REA), but the experiment failed, partly due to its penchant for undertaking eccentric and one-dimensional economic analyses, but also because of the problematic relationship between an independent think-thank and the various political parties in parliament.

Spending departments benefited most from the results-oriented VBTB initiative. One consequence of this reform was that, on average, the expenditures on policy outcomes are shown to be three times as high as before. Departments can move money around without being checked by the Ministry of Finance or the parliament. The policy discretion enjoyed by the spending departments has become much wider.

The move to form special delivery agencies was a complementary innovation. Many executive agencies under ministerial direction improved their management and may have benefited from the switch to accrual budgeting. But agencification did not produce the anticipated improvements in performance and the adoption of accruals has not proved as useful as was intended because not all costs tend to be counted.

A consequence of assuming a neoliberal reform direction was that privatization and marketization of policy areas became possible. One of the discovered paradoxes here was that governments found they needed more not less regulation and monitoring when they introduced market values into public provision. The banking sector was probably the major exception to this trend, until the financial crisis of 2008 brought a new wave of financial regulation and intervention. So, next to the edifices of the old bureaucrats, new towers were built, inhabited by regulators and controllers of the market providers. Public servants and street-level bureaucrats began complaining of the burden of control, excessive monitoring and accountability overload.

Attempts to demonstrate greater accountability have also been disappointing. The 'third Wednesday in May' initiative failed because the members of parliament were not really interested in this difficult subject. And the attempt to augment the expertise available to the legislature, by establishing a Council of Economic Advisors, ceased functioning after only a few months.

Finally, from the above evidence, we can draw two important theoretical conclusions. The first builds on the research finding of David Good (2007), who states that Heclo and Wildavsky's classic metaphor of 'village life' can no longer be used as a precise description of the present-day budgetary process. The second conclusion counterposes the technocratic part of the budget process with the more symbolic side of politics in order to explain why several new budget reform initiatives did not work. These proposals were largely written in symbolic language, but the actual implementation turned out to be difficult.

In 1974 Wildavsky and Heclo introduced the metaphor of 'village life' to explain the politics of the budgetary process. They stated that the politics of the budgetary process was dominated by a small, influential and closed network. Budget policies were made within this closed and technocratic subsystem, without intervention of other outside actors or partisan politics. Of course, within the financial subsystem, there has always been a struggle between the Ministry of Finance and different spending departments. The spending departments would use their constituencies to help improve their bargaining position. In the past the pressure from these spending departments was one of the causes of inflation. Such behavior was criticized by economic-based theories such as public choice theories, which assumed that the behavior of politicians, public servants and interest groups was based on self-interest. After the fiscal crisis of the welfare state, budgetary behavior became less predictable, especially the relations between guardians and spenders and the spending departments and their associated interest groups. New coalitions emerged between politicians and top public servants aimed at containing or cutting overall public spending. Such cooperation between politicians and bureaucrats can be analysed in terms of the so-called 'bureau-shaping model' (Dunleavy 1991). Significantly, this model can explain behavior which would appear to be contrary to the self-interest of bureaucrats. Budget deficits suddenly became unacceptable and tougher fiscal discipline had to be imposed often when social expenditures were still increasing due to demographic pressures. Not only did deficits become smaller and fewer in number, but surpluses were achieved. The internal behavior of the state was changing.

Our study confirms the hypothesis that the close-knit 'village' has been transformed into a modern international cosmopolitan city. This new metaphor implies that budgetary politics is more open to changing influences and that new actors have entered the system, for instance the European Union, international organizations and a growing number of internal and external watchdogs. This process of transformation has been gradual and largely technocratic in nature. But into the future other critical voices will have impact. Citizens with rising expectations of service delivery, more critical watchdogs and critical media, are all likely to find a stronger voice in the new, more open, metropolis of budgeting.

The second conclusion deals with the symbolic use of information in politics. According to some commentators, such as Niskanen (1971), there exists an asymmetric information relationship between the bureaucracy and parliament. However, largely due to the symbolic importance of the budget to parliament, there has been a massive increase in the provision of information to the parliament – mainly from the Ministry of Finance. Because of the growing importance of transparency and the performance revolution, the asymmetry would appear to have been reversed. Today, members of parliament are drowning in a pool of detailed information. But while the monitoring of the budget is ostensibly one of the most important parliamentary functions, it is also difficult to perform well. Budgets and financial reports are complex and technical. Also, the presentation of the budget has changed from focusing on the input side of administrative resourcing to focusing on the output side of performance and results. But due to the high aggregation of such outcome information and a lack of causality this information can be more opaque rather than transparent.

Unless parliament can interrogate such budgetary and performance information it is failing in its responsibilities. Citizens feel there ought to be a relationship between the level and quality of public services and the levels of taxes that they pay. When citizens are dissatisfied with the level of public service delivery they become more critical and distrustful. In the

Western world this is one of the causes of declining trust in established political parties and public organizations more generally. This decline in trust is perhaps one of the unintended consequences of the performance revolution. The Dutch parliament has tried, with considerable difficulty, to reinstate its position and hold governments more to account for their performance. But various ambitious attempts have failed in recent times and we have had to rely on other watchdogs to pursue questions of value for money. It is an unfortunate paradox that the generation of more performance information may in reality lead to lower levels of confidence in public provision.

REFERENCES

Algemene Rekenkamer [National Court of Audit] (2008), *Staat van Beleidsinformatie* [The state of policy information], Den Haag: National Court of Audit.

Bestebreur, T., A. Kraak and K. van der Burg (2003), *Modern Financieel Management bij het Rijk* [*Modern Financial Management at State Level*], Den Haag: SDU.

Blöndal, J. and J. Kromann Kristensen (2002) 'Budgeting in The Netherlands', *OECD Journal of Budgeting*, **1** (3), 43-80.

Dunleavy, P. (1991), *Democracy, Bureaucracy and Public Choice*, London: Pearson Education.

Good, D.A. (2007), *The Politics of Public Money: Spenders, Guardians, Priority Setters, and Financial Watchdogs Inside the Canadian Government*, Toronto: University of Toronto Press.

Heclo, H. and A. Wildavsky (1974), *The Private Government of Public Money: Community and Policy Inside British Politics*, Berkeley, CA: University of California Press.

Kam, de C.A. and A.P. Ros (2003–08), *Jaarboeken Overheidsuitgaven* [*Public Finance Yearbooks*], Den Haag: SDU.

Kraan, D.J., 2004. 'Typically Dutch', *OECD Journal of Budgeting*, **4** (4), 103–25.

Niskanen, W.A. (1971), *Bureaucracy and Representative Government*, Chicago, IL: Aldine Atherton.

Nispen, Frans K.M. van and J.A. Posseth (2006), 'Performance budgeting in The Netherlands: beyond arithmetic', *OECD Journal of Budgeting*, **6** (4), 37-62.

Oosteroom, van R. (2002), 'Distributed public governance: agencies, authorities and other autonomous bodies in The Netherlands', *OECD Journal of Budgeting*, **2** (1), 103-20.

Tijsseling, I.C. and P.G.J. van Uden (eds) (2004), *Made in Holland – Dutch Public Finance: Lessons and Experiences*, National Academy for Finance and Economy.

11. Budget reforms in Spain: anything else beyond budget discipline?

Xavier Ballart and Eduardo Zapico

Spanish governments started the reform of the budgetary process during the first half of the 1980s with the introduction of program budgeting. But internal budgetary practices did not change significantly. The budgetary process remains under the control of the Ministry of Economy and Finance (Ministerio de Economía y Hacienda or MEH), the agency in charge of controlling public expenditure, setting taxes, managing borrowing and setting overall economic and fiscal policy. This main central budget actor did not pursue a policy of broad managerial reform or change the system to make it more managerial or businesslike, as some other Organisation for Economic Co-operation and Development (OECD) countries did (OECD 2001). However, Spain has been a success in terms of budget stability, comprising the imposition of fiscal discipline, the attainment of budget surpluses and the achievement of debt reduction. All this has been achieved in a decentralized system of government where more than 50 percent of public spending depends on regional and local governments. In a rather traditional, pragmatic, incremental and bureaucratic fashion, Spanish governments, including both the Socialist and the Popular parties, progressively reduced the deficit until 2005, when they achieved the first of a series of consecutive surpluses maintained over the past three years (MEH 2008). So, budget stability arrived, annual budget outcomes improved, documentation partially changed, but Spain did not change the budget decision-making process nor embrace with enthusiasm reforms to deliver meaningful information presented together with the budget.

From the 1980s Spain's disaggregated public sector experienced profound transformations in public finance, especially in the volume and composition of revenue and spending. However, it was external pressure which was critical in forcing Spanish governments to make serious efforts to achieve fiscal consolidation after 1994. In particular, Spain's agreement to join the euro and abide by the conditions of the Economic and Monetary Union (EMU) empowered governments to impose and maintain fiscal discipline. Successive ministers of economy and finance, representing Socialist and Popular Party governments, were proud to leave public finances in better shape than they had found them on reaching power. The European pressure justified a policy of top-down control over the budgetary process, but more in the area of budget stability and aggregate public spending than in the areas of spending management or the redistribution of resources. In its macroeconomic policy, Spain approved tough fiscal rules in 2001 and 2006 (see Ley 2001, 2006a), which can be interpreted as the national version of the European Stability and Growth Pact. With regard to the micro-management of resources, Spain also passed two pieces of legislation with the Budget Law of 2003 (Ley 2003) and the Agencies Law of 1996 (Ley 2006b), but their impact on public administration has not yet been so profound.

This chapter presents, in the first place, an overview of the Spanish trajectory in budgetary reform. It considers initiatives taken in the area of fiscal discipline and stability, and reports changes to budget processes and resource management, particularly with the gradual adoption of a performance budget framework. Second, it provides an analysis of changes introduced in budget documentation and in the budget cycle, including changes in the relations between the MEH and spending ministries. Budget reform in sub-central governments has not been considered. Finally, discussion turns to an evaluation of the main outcomes of the reforms attempted, including the use of an output–outcomes framework and the extent to which a performance-oriented perspective is present in Spain's policy-making.

SPAIN'S TRAJECTORY OF BUDGETARY REFORM

The Spanish trajectory in budgetary reform has been gradual and adaptive, since there were no big bursts of change or innovation. Spain followed the path of earlier reforms in the US and in other advanced European countries with a partial introduction of program budgeting in the 1980s. More recently, Spain has adapted to the requirements of the European EMU by declaring its intentions to eliminate annual budget deficits. It has also begun discussions to adopt a form of output–outcomes management as advocated by the OECD, the IMF and other international institutions. Hence, Spain is no newcomer to budgetary reforms. It has followed a long path of reform, from the first attempts to rationalize spending decisions until the recent reforms to ground budgetary policy in a wider European framework while governing a decentralized system which is all but in name a federal state.

One can distinguish at least four distinct, although somewhat overlapping, phases of budget reform:

- a phase of improved planning techniques and technical improvements from 1976 to 1979;
- a program budgeting phase from 1984 to 1994;
- a belief in the zero deficit phase over the period from 1994 to 2006 leading to the enactment of budget stability laws; and
- a recent phase of a return to the performance management philosophy from 2003 to 2008.

These four phases are examined in turn.

Better Planning and Technical Improvements, 1976–79

Spain did not introduce any of the initiatives that were taking place during the 1960s in the main European countries with regard to the review of public spending (Gunther 1980). The main concern of the post-Franco regime before the adoption of the democratic Constitution in 1978 was with fiscal growth and with the main policy instrument being major 'development plans'. Those plans not only committed substantial resources to projects, but also induced the application of methodologies for the *ex ante* assessment of public investment and the cost–benefit analysis of projects, particularly in areas of public works and infrastructure.

The introduction of these planning techniques was limited in scope to economic projects. It was not applied to wider social programs (Ruiz-Huerta et al. 2007). The innovations of this phase can hardly be considered as major budgeting reforms. Furthermore, there was almost no correspondence between cost estimates obtained in the process of evaluating projects and final executed budget allocations. There was also no coherent policy to improve spending management, nor was there the institutional capacity to monitor and manage the budgeting cycle on the basis of better information on outputs and effectiveness.

Program Budgeting, 1984–94

The first Socialist government after the democratic transition came to office in 1982 with the political promise of change. While many of its big spending plans were conditioned by the severity of the industrial crisis in Spain, the charismatic President Felipe González (1982–96) put great emphasis on reforming public administration and making the machinery of government work better.

Fascinated by the US and French experience with program budgeting, the MEH invited some spending departments to produce a new budget format based on programs. In 1984, the Council of Ministers officially required all departments and public organizations to present their expenditures according to program classifications. The order from the ministry established basic rules on setting objectives and devising indicators for every program. Since then expenditure information in the Spanish budget has been presented according to three basic criteria: by economic function, by organizational allocations and by program structures.

The aspiration of the then government was to add rationality to a budgetary process in which decisions were often taken on the basis of incomplete information. Reforms were introduced from a results-oriented perspective, intending to link funding decisions with results, effectiveness or impact. However, the program reforms did not prove useful in budgetary coordination, nor in providing a more coherent view of public spending across all areas of government. The focus on programs did not improve the motivations or the actions of the various spending departments or agencies. The broad definition of programs was often criticized (Zapico 1989) and public administrators had trouble in setting objectives, finding adequate and relevant indicators and, in general, connecting their activities with social impacts or the overall statutory strategic plan of the government. Also, for presentational purposes ministries and agencies grouped their programs into one multiyear program that included long-term information on the activities of public enterprises and other public entities with a functional dependency on the ministries. It was hard to see demonstrated performance. But within this phase we also saw the introduction of intense computerization of budget administration within the public sector and of changes in auditing techniques to make spending controls less obstructive while enabling auditors to look into performance activity beyond the control of compliance with legal requirements (MEH 1983, 1985).

The volume of resources managed by the public sector increased considerably during the second half of the 1980s through to the beginning of the 1990s until the economic crisis of 1993 hit the Spanish state. Previous assumptions about the levels of economic growth were overly optimistic, and decentralized public administrations, particularly the autonomous communities, had problems in meeting the increased demands for public services in the areas of education, health and public infrastructure. The inevitable result increased deficits and added to the growing burden of public debt at the regional and local levels.

Believing in the Zero Deficit and Budget Stability Laws, 1994–2006

The reform emphasis on results lost some ground in the mid-1990s because the utility of program budgeting was questioned and because political attention now turned toward the European EMU integration process. Spain began a period of continuous growth from 1994 until 2008 which provided robust increases in revenues. As in the Australian and New Zealand cases included in this book, the combination of increased tax receipts and expenditure discipline made it possible to produce an almost balanced budget by the year 2000 and to achieve annual budgetary surpluses from 2005 to 2007.

The accomplishment of budgetary surpluses encouraged the government to formalize balanced budgets through the imposition of budget stability laws. While the Spanish budget remains authorized on an annual basis, since 1998 the public sector has been expected to work with long-term economic scenarios and multiyear programming as the main reference for the preparation of the annual budget. Then in 2001 the Spanish parliament passed legislation on budgetary stability. This first law was subsequently amended in 2006 after it was considered that the original definition of 'stability' was excessively rigid. Moreover, it was also felt that autonomous communities had to participate in the discussion of the general budget framework as they are also responsible of the final budgetary results of the whole country.

The amended stability law of 2006 linked the principle of budget stability to the economic cycle. It stipulated the obligation for governments to budget for a surplus when economic circumstances were favorable, while allowing the possibility of incurring in a deficit during the low phases of the economic cycle with the aim of achieving an average position of equilibrium (Iglesias 2007). The Council of Ministers, on the basis of the reports of the MEH, was responsible for determining budgetary goals and the upper and lower stability limits for a three-year period. The proposed budget of the central government was then presented to the Fiscal and Financial Policy Council where the autonomous communities met and deliberated with the central government. Once finalized, the proposed budget thereafter needed to be approved by both chambers of the parliament.

The stability legislation introduced in 2001 and amended in 2006 includes a few other mechanisms that make the system less vulnerable and more coherent with the decentralized nature of the Spanish state. Most noticeably:

1. There is a combined limit of a 1 percent deficit of gross domestic product (GDP) for the three levels of jurisdiction with the following maximum relative composition: not more than 0.20 percent for the central government; 0.75 percent for the autonomous communities; and 0.05 percent for the local entities.

2. There is a possibility of an additional deficit to spend on investments that may help to increase the productivity of the system during the low phase of the economic cycle. This 'investment deficit' also has an upper limit of 0.5 percent of GDP for all three administrations, made up of: 0.20 percent for the central government; 0.25 percent for the autonomous communities; and 0.05 percent for local governments. Together with the latitude for the general deficit, this brings the total deficit to a maximum of 1.5 percent of GDP which is still only half of the limit established by European EMU rules.
3. The budget has to include the information necessary to calculate the deficit or surplus according to the European system of national and regional accounts.
4. In order to avoid deviations during budget execution, the government has to include in the annual budget a 2 percent contingency fund or reserve which may only be spent on emergency needs such as catastrophes or extraordinary events that could not have been forecast when the budget was approved.
5. The stability law does not permit the government to use the surplus from the social security funds to compensate the deficit of the state. Moreover, each regional or local government is also treated as an independent entity and it is not possible to compensate individual deficits among themselves.
6. The central government can issue warnings to other administrations if there is a serious risk of them not complying with the overall stability objectives.

One of the main questions to be asked is to what extent those laws were necessary, since the government had already achieved historic successes in the management of public finance without them. The answer to that question may be that, in the first place, the Spanish government accepted from the very beginning of the negotiations of the various European fiscal treaties that stringent rules on fiscal discipline were absolutely necessary to avoid falling into deficit and debt. Second, President José M. Aznar (1996–2004) and his Popular Party announced that they intended to be 'the first in the class' of Europe in fiscal policy and set 'the zero deficit' as one of their main goals. This objective was later made more flexible but not abandoned by the Socialists who returned to government in 2004, since they also wanted Spain to be perceived as a 'good European'. In the third place, both the Popular and Socialist governments understood that establishing fiscal rules in statutory law approved by the parliament was the best way to impose budget discipline across the system and avoid the tendency of present or future political authorities resorting to uncontrolled public spending.

The stability reforms were the eventual outcome of a long process of progressive consolidation occurring over more than a decade in the context of sustained economic growth. Certainly, the stability laws have made budgetary negotiations easier for the MEH (Iglesias and Morano 2008). The imposition of caps on spending departments allowed the MEH to contain the initial budgetary demands of ministries and agencies. And the central government was able to impose European stability and accounting rules on autonomous communities and make regional and local administrations comply with fiscal rules in the general context of Spanish public finances.

Overall, the laws of fiscal stability have proved useful in creating a certain culture of spending discipline across government. They have been particularly effective in building consultation and achieving fiscal compromises at the level of the regional governments. Into the future there may still be the need for some further adaptations of these procedures to make them more realistic (for example a less tight calendar for the targets).

However, given the onset of the financial disaster that arose in 2008 and the following economic crisis, the efficacy of such types of fiscal laws has been the subject of much recent debate. Governments consider that they must respond expediently, meaning they cannot maintain budgetary stringency against external shocks. In the current crisis, expected to be both deep and prolonged, governments have already presented public deficit scenarios to the European Commission. Most European countries are in the process of presenting corrections plans. Moreover, after the amendment of the Stability and Growth Pact in 2005, exceptional cases of a severe reduction in economic activity are accepted as a justification for presenting public deficits beyond the limits established by the EU.

In the case of Spain, the reduction of the public debt during the years of economic expansion (from 50.9 percent of GDP in 2000 to 34.3 percent in 2007), now allows a margin for maneuvering to incur larger public deficits to finance emergency action plans to stimulate the economy.

A RETURN TO PERFORMANCE MANAGEMENT, 2003–08

Two initiatives in 2003 and 2006 indicate a certain philosophical return to performance management, that had been inaugurated in the 1980s with program budgeting. Steps were taken to try to overcome the earlier informational shortcomings of the initial trial with program structures.

For instance, the General Budget Law was reformed in 2003 to emphasize budgeting by objectives and output–outcome measures, including new rules and principles for micro-management (Espadas 2005). After this reform, it was expected that a relatively sophisticated system would be developed on the basis of: (1) setting objectives for multiyear programs; (2) a reliance on results-oriented management; (3) a close alignment between objectives and expenditures; (4) improved performance reporting and the preparation of management reports with detailed information on expenditures; and (5) a broad evaluation of results and outcomes. The same reform introduced an evaluation procedure for all public policies. The MEH initially played a catalytic role in the coordination of the evaluation effort of program spending, although a new specialist agency was to be created with this specific mission.

The second initiative in 2006 opened the way for greater agencification with the passing of the State Agencies Law. There were already various types of entities with different degrees of managerial autonomy, some of them with the term 'agency' in their name. But from this time, the State Agencies Law opened up the possibility of creating up to 11 agencies with the idea of granting more managerial autonomy, in exchange for control with four-year contracts, accountability by results, external auditing and the responsibility of directors for the results achieved. The first agency created in 2007 was the State Agency for the Evaluation of Public Policies and the Quality of Public Services under the authority of the Minister of Public Administrations (CECAEE 2004). Between 2007 and 2008, six other units of the central administration were transformed into agencies in the areas of official government publishing, research, international cooperation and development, meteorology, air traffic control and security, and anti-doping in sport.

From a budgetary perspective, agencies now have greater flexibility since managers negotiate directly with the MEH over their general funding levels and have full discretion to use the resources except in the area of personnel. Agencies will be able to sell a relevant share of their services or encourage sponsors to assist in funding their activities. Agencies are able to change the management culture of the organization to develop a deeper sense of responsibility among public managers for the resources they use and the results they achieve. The MEH has to date been nervous about the establishment of agencies because of uncertainties on the revenue side and the loss of control over spending. According to various interviews made at the MEH, budget officials believe the development of agencies should be reserved only for those areas where, by the nature of the services provided, there is a greater chance of improving the quality of management and of services for citizens.

BUDGETARY DOCUMENTATION REFLECTS THE REFORM INTERESTS OF GOVERNMENT

The structure and format of the budget papers have not changed much since the mid-1980s, but there have been considerable changes in the way information is presented. Some changes sought to adapt the Spanish national accounts to European public standards and norms. Other changes attempted to offer greater transparency to the public, making the budget more readable and accessible. Each year various versions of the budget are posted on the MEH website, offering varying degrees of detail. However, the annual budget continues to be organized on the basis of three traditional classifications. Both the government and the parliament discuss the budget on the basis of the organizational allocations and the economic classification of revenues and expenditures. The budget also presents information on the basis of expenditure 'areas', 'policies' and 'programs' which still are very much determined by the organizational structure of the government.

For example, in the case of the Ministry of External Affairs, the programs identified are General Administration, Diplomatic Action, Cooperation for Development and the Promotion of Spanish Culture Abroad, which correspond with the main operational divisions of the ministry. Two budget documentation series – one with more detail, the other for presentation to the parliament – provide a narrative explanation of the policies of the ministry and each of the main divisions, including some data on expenditure effort but little information on past performance. In the case of the program Cooperation for Development, the narrative section of the 2008 budget emphasizes the goal of progressing toward spending 0.7 percent of GDP on external aid but does not give details on activities or outcomes of the development division in the past. To find such information we need to look elsewhere in the budget documentation where ministries are presented according to their basic action plans. In other cases, like in Public Works or Transportation, the budget provides a good picture of activity and output since it includes all the financial information on investment plans or transportation subsidies – with detailed statements for each project or line of action – but again there is little information on the existing policy rationale or its intended effects, which are seen as the responsibility of the ministry.

Budget documentation also reports the government's fiscal and economic policy intentions. It is in this area that the most significant changes in documentation took place, given the external and internal pressure to make European governments accountable for their fiscal and economic policies. The 2006 stability law reform regulated with detail the economic reports that the state, regional and local governments have to produce with regard to budget and economic cycles. The main responsibility for these reports lies with the MEH, which sets the overall budget objectives on the basis of the economic performance of the country. The report of the MEH has to take into account the diagnostics of the European Central Bank, the European Commission, the Central Bank of Spain and the National Institute of Statistics. The legislation also stipulated the range of economic and social variables and the kinds of analysis that these reports have to include.

The autonomous communities and local governments also participate in the deliberative processes involved in setting budgetary objectives for the cycle. They produce reports to, and for consideration by, the Fiscal and Financial Policy Council and the Local Administration Council – where these subnational governments meet with the central government to seek approval for their financial strategies. Such reports are mandatory and they are passed on to the national parliament with the rest of the government documentation.

Spending ministries are also required to produce budgetary documentation. They are supposed to group the programs delivered by their operational divisions, including those performed by agencies, corporations or public enterprises with a functional dependency on the ministry. The multiyear action program of each ministry is the basic document where the main priorities, policies and programs in each area are presented.

A different kind of new documentation has also been introduced by the internal auditing unit within the MEH. The General Controller of Central Government (Intervención General de la Administración del Estado – IGAE) has been active in producing documents that were thought to facilitate the task of managers with regard to the follow-up of programs, their objectives and performance. This is one of the instances where the MEH has assumed the role of an agent of change in the area of management beyond the organization frontiers of the ministry.

THE BUDGET PROCESS: INSTITUTIONAL PLAYERS AND THE DEVELOPMENT OF A PERFORMANCE PERSPECTIVE

Each year the budget preparation processes starts in January when the MEH prepares a three-year budget outline and draft expenditure ceilings for the following year, and submits these to the Council of Ministers. The MEH then draws up the Multi-year Budgetary Scenario in accordance with the various budget laws of 2001, 2003 and 2006. Then the Directorate

General of Budget (DGP) in collaboration with the budget offices of spending ministries and agencies prepares long-term projections within the scenario for each ministry and submits them to the MEH. The DGP adds revenue projections and sends them to the MEH which then presents the full scenario to the Council of Ministers. The MEH then prepares the draft budget along with its spending recommendations for the Council of Ministers according to the 'budget stability objectives' for both the national and regional governments.

The preliminary draft budget is discussed and approved by the Council of Ministers in September, including a multiyear macroeconomic framework contained in the Stability Program drawn up in accordance with the EU Stability and Growth Pact. The draft budget is then submitted to the lower chamber of the parliament (Congreso de los Diputados) by 1 October. Parliament scrutinizes and discusses the draft budget in October and later reviews the projected budget scenarios and approves the aggregate expenditure ceiling during the first quarter of the next year. However, neither the Congress nor Senate discuss program performance.

Budget execution is a highly regulated process with a particular concern for legal compliance. The functions of auditing and control are vested in two institutions, namely: internal audit is performed by the General Controller of Central Government (IGAE) while external audits are undertaken by the Court of Auditors (Tribunal de Cuentas).

There are four main groups of institutional players that are influential in budget deliberations and in the budget preparation process. First, the Revenue Commission, chaired by the Secretary of State for Finance and Budget, is responsible for coordinating the preparation of the revenue forecasts. Second, the Spending Policy Commission is chaired by the Minister of Economy and Finance with the assistance of the Secretary of State for Finance and Budget and with the participation of spending ministers or, by delegation, other top officials representing spending ministries and agencies. The role of this commission is to reach agreement on an initial allocation of budgetary resources consistent with government priorities and its aggregate fiscal policy. The commission sets ceilings within which each spending ministry and agency prepares their budget proposals.

Third, the Ministerial Budget Commissions are composed of representatives from the relevant units in each department, chaired by the department's deputy secretary. The task of these commissions is to make proposals for the preliminary draft budget, formulate priority criteria, review existing programs and monitor their execution. And, fourth, the Program Analysis Commissions exist, with at least one in each department. These are chaired by the Secretary of State for Finance and Budget, and their functions include the analysis of the adequacy and validity of spending programs and whether they are consistent with priorities defined by the Spending Policy Commission.

INSUFFICIENT CONSIDERATION OF PERFORMANCE INFORMATION

One of the key forces behind the Spanish budgetary reform process was the macroeconomic and European pressure to restrict public spending and comply with economic stability objectives. Such demands were meant not only to control aggregate spending, but also to improve the quality of spending (Pollitt and Bouckaert 2004). However, the twin dimensions of budget stability and performance budgeting have not been addressed in a coherent and complementary manner in the Spanish case.

The potential synergy between these dimensions was well captured in the four basic principles articulated in the reforms, namely: budgetary stability; multiyear projections; transparency; and efficiency in the allocation and use of public funds. The reformed budget law incorporated these principles in 2003. As observed by one commentator:

> the substance of the new law shows a keen interest in establishing an appropriate normative framework, making it possible to apply efficiency approaches into budgeting and to develop a management by results culture in respect to expenditure. (Sánchez Revenga 2005)

This statutory reform required multiyear programming and the definition of objectives on a regular basis. It attempted to establish a systematic link between budget allocations and main objectives for spending ministries and agencies through the adoption of management by objectives, performance monitoring and policy evaluation. So, in theory and according to the law, public managers are required to be effective in attaining their objectives and to focus on results in the planning and implementation of their action programs. For each initiative, spending management units are required to specify a relevant set of objectives appropriate to their organization. These objectives must be included in their annual multiyear program.

Beyond that, the management and control systems of public spending must be oriented toward results as well as financial compliance. Operational spending units are required to prepare an annual report on the achievement of their objectives, which is to be included in their annual reports and in the multiyear programming of the ministry. Then, in theory, the MEH, in collaboration with spending ministries and agencies, leads and coordinates the evaluation of budget programs with the purpose of ensuring that spending policies achieve their strategic and socio-economic objectives.

However, the reality is somewhat different. The capacity of the Program Analysis Commissions to facilitate performance information sharing and debate on results in the budget process remains quite limited. The Program Analysis Commissions were supposed to play the role of analyzing the adequacy and validity of spending programs in relation to their objectives; allocating resources within the budget ceilings for each ministry or agency; and ensuring that proposed allocations are consistent with priorities set at the political level. It was also intended that these commissions reviewed and took into consideration program results in the preceding year.

But they have not been very successful in fulfilling these roles due to both technical and political factors. For instance, there are shortcomings in the instructions received from the Spending Policy Commissions. Often, these instructions are neither concrete nor effectively communicated. There is a tendency to avoid or hide conflict rather than deal with it in a transparent manner. It appears that communications are difficult and collaboration is low between spending ministries and the Directorate General of Budget. There is sometimes a major imbalance between the volume of information requested by the DGP and that received from the spending management units. This information also often arrives at the very last minute. The capacity to process and analyse this information is profoundly limited. Most of the information is financial in nature and the amount of relevant performance information remains sparse. Often, spending units do not have sufficiently accurate information about the budget implications of departmental plans, reform programs or legislative proposals, complicating oversight of the adaptation of annual plans to the medium-term budget scenarios.

Furthermore, there is insufficient use made of the analytical capacities of the various institutional players, and usually weak preparation of the starting positions for negotiation on both sides. Analysis lacks sufficient depth, with most budget commitments being considered unavoidable (for example personnel costs). The scope for discretionary decision-making for budget corrections is perceived as narrow. While this may be valid in the short term, it is not necessarily the case over a medium- or longer-term horizon. Finally, there is limited scope for serious debate in the Program Analysis Commissions. Discussions are mainly focused on the projections of spending line items according to expected variations in inflation, or to new legislation or government initiatives. There is not enough time for debate or systematic analysis of programs. Debates are incremental and, frequently, focused on the maximum percentage increases authorized for budget chapters. There is scarcely any systematic debate about spending policies or ministerial priorities, and past or expected performance. There is also no debate on interdepartmental programs. So far, budget scenarios have been mainly considered as a formal exercise adjusted to the annual budget, instead of the other way around. Annual budgeting should be an extension of the budget scenarios. As one of the authors of this chapter has written before:

> The efficient allocation of resources in the framework of budgetary scenarios prepared with transparency – better knowledge on sector programs and information on performance – and with the active participation of spending managers, would be much more effective and relevant than the current annual program budget negotiations which focus on chapters or line items expenditures. (Zapico 2005)

But it would be wrong to consider that the Program Analysis Commissions do not add value to the budget process. The symbolic and relational role played by the Commissions in the process of preparing the budget has again been underlined by (Zapico 2005), who found:

> They significantly facilitate direct relationships among senior officials and shape expectations and standards of behavior or decision-making style facilitating progress toward reaching budget agreements. The commissions make it possible for technical specialists to obtain direct information on agreements or disagreements at the policy levels.

Some general suggestions for improving the functioning of the Program Analysis Commissions involve: incorporating a more strategic and selective approach into the budget negotiations; introducing a multiyear perspective in the debates; and taking into account information sensitive to the institutional and political context.

More specific recommendations to improve the work of the DGP and the Program Analysis Commissions would include the following suggestions. First, there should be some modification of the role and competencies of the DGP in relation to the Program Analysis Commissions. When preparing for program analysis meetings, the DGP should reorient its efforts and resources toward the analysis of selective strategic spending. Debates at the commissions should focus on the long-term effects and impacts of spending.

Second, the application of management by objectives and of adequate criteria in resource allocation should be encouraged. One of the main concerns of Program Analysis Commissions should be to ensure the consistency of budget programs with sector plans of spending ministries and government priorities. Other types of analysis (for example assessment of the socio-economic and environmental impact of policies or cost-effective analysis) could be prepared in collaboration with external experts.

Third, the Program Analysis Commissions require new aims and a revision of their composition and size. Four types of meetings could be considered: (1) preparatory meetings with experts from the ministries' budget offices and the audit office in spending ministries; (2) interface meeting between the DGP and spending ministry officials; (3) follow-up and compliance meetings; and (4) final meetings, at the top level, after which no changes should be accepted unless accompanied by offsetting proposals from the same department. The composition and size of the commissions should be adjusted depending on the type of meetings in order to ensure their flexible and efficient functioning.

Fourth, the commissions need to improve their decision-making capacities. To achieve such improvement the DGP should adopt a more proactive attitude during the preparation of new sector plans and programs in spending ministries. Officials of the DGP should be searching for information in the early stages on the potential budget impact of the main policy initiatives. This would allow them to anticipate possible risks of excessive spending, and to ensure sound programming (that is, relating resources to objectives and actions; choosing relevant indicators; making subsequent monitoring and evaluation feasible).

Fifth, better incentives should be introduced for coordination and collaboration between the DGP, budget offices and management operational services. Reports from the OECD (such as OECD 2001), the United Kingdom (UK Cabinet Office 1999) and the Chilean government (Chile National Budget Office 2003) present various examples of policy options that would enhance collaboration among budget and management officials. Some examples include:

1. Sharing the 'profits' from performance budgeting between the Ministry of Economy and the spending ministries and agencies; rewarding savings resulting from cutbacks or from efficiency gains; or granting flexibility to allocate a portion of the profits in accordance with predetermined criteria.
2. Creating a 'reserve fund' for innovation and productivity, to be distributed on a competitive basis.
3. Signing budget agreements specifying the information required on resources, objectives and activities while allowing more flexible spending management controls.
4. Using indicators of outcomes or impacts that require the cooperation of several services.

5. Focusing evaluation efforts more on recognizing and promoting desirable management styles than on the identification of spending misbehavior or non-compliance.
6. Making the provision of funds contingent on meeting the information requirements.

THE MAIN OUTCOMES OF BUDGET REFORM AND SOME FINAL CONSIDERATIONS

After several decades of budget reform in Spain, it is generally accepted that budgetary policy has been effective in introducing budget stability and fiscal discipline. The Spanish deficit of 0.98 percent of GDP in the year 2000 translated into a surplus of 1.3 percent in 2007, while public debt was reduced from 50.9 percent of GDP to just 34.3 percent over the same period. In terms of budget management, new budget documentation offers an improved structure and more transparency to parliament and the public in general, while the budget process is now better structured, involving more orderly interaction between budget officials and spending managers in the Program Analysis Commissions.

There have also been significant efforts to introduce a performance management perspective in the preparation and execution of budgets. However, the budget process in Spain still needs further improvements to consolidate an effective and sound performance budgeting system. Several weaknesses have been identified, namely: the lack of quality of the non-financial information produced; that budget programs follow organizational structures; that there is no time in the budget cycle for analysis and deliberation; a neglect of incentives to increase effectiveness and efficiency; and a lack of capacity within the DGP to process information.

Additional efforts are gradually being made to maintain budget discipline and further develop intended financial management reforms focusing on performance monitoring and program evaluation, both at the MEH and in spending ministries and agencies. However, the combination of stringent discipline norms together with formal requests for more performance-based budgeting, have proved insufficient. Going forward, attention should now be paid to the cultural values and administrative behavior of main budget actors, which seem to limit the effectiveness of further reform.

One of the main obstacles to advancing the performance budgeting agenda was that budget authorities were not clear about the distribution of roles and responsibilities between the MEH and spending entities in the framework of performance budgeting. The main focus of the MEH was on expenditure control and fiscal discipline while simultaneously they expected ministries to develop the tasks of devising and revising outputs and outcomes.

To achieve a substantial and relevant qualitative improvement in performance budgeting there are several conditions and factors to be considered. First, a high degree of credible, well-built and sustained political support is necessary. One explanation for the limited success of performance budgeting to date is the inadequacy or lack of continuity of political support. There was once a strong commitment and political will in the MEH to start the implementation of program budgeting. However, this interest has not been maintained over time. The political power of the Finance Minister might not be sufficient to get an active collaboration from spending ministries and agencies without the explicit support of the President of the government.

Second, budgeting cannot be assumed to be a neutral, technical exercise providing economic and financial predictions, or a mere legislative process. Some of the problems identified in this chapter relate to the attempts to impose reform processes from the center on the basis of an ideal technical solution. A non-participatory approach to budget reform might result merely in formal compliance, some 'creative budgeting' or even the rejection of performance initiatives. Conflicts and negotiations in the process should not be perceived as dysfunctional, to be avoided at all costs or solved by 'objective or neutral' analysis followed by 'automatic' or uncontestable decisions. Uncertainty, conflict and interdependence are part of the reality of the budget process. Specifying objectives, measuring performance, analyzing options and structuring the budget by programs may facilitate stability and predictability in budgeting, but will not eliminate the need for budget negotiation and conflict management.

Third, respect for the norms and legal traditions of a nation should be complemented with the development of a 'management by results' culture. There is an emerging sentiment that the legal perspective toward public budgeting is incompatible with a management approach, or that trade-offs between the two are necessary. On the contrary, we would argue it is necessary to complement the concerns about the legality of spending with a new emphasis on performance.

Fourth, formal rules and norms are insufficient in themselves to achieve effective adaptation to change in the real political, economic and social context. There is often a normative assumption that once new rules are announced they will be accepted and adopted. Legal and hierarchical traditions are deeply rooted in the Spanish system. New laws are proposed in the belief that success will be achieved once the 'perfect' norm is established and strictly applied. This was the case of the first wave of fiscal discipline laws and the performance budget-oriented laws. However, amendments to these stability laws proved necessary to allow for greater flexibility while still preserving a culture of fiscal discipline in government.

Although the importance of formal procedures should not be underestimated, they are not sufficient by themselves to ensure the successful development of performance budgeting. It is necessary to apply the same model – 'management by results' – to the implementation of new reforms. The efforts of the MEH have been based primarily on introducing new legislation and guidelines for implementing changes in budgeting, auditing and evaluation. The application of the 'management by results' perspective to the process of budget reform has not been systematically considered. The evaluation of the reforms has been neglected. A continuous effort is required for assessing the impact of the reforms to date and for searching for reform improvements.

Fifth, a capacity to learn about 'spending management' must be developed. Performance budgeting represents an idealized or idealistic budget model, supposedly facilitating improvements in public management. It is sometimes perceived as the 'only' alternative to manage public spending. Yet, the applicability of this model to different contexts or types of public organizations has not been questioned in the Spanish context. Abstract models are often regarded as the state of the art by central players. But while spending managers will adapt their information systems and financial procedures to the requirements of the MEH, they do not necessarily regard them as genuinely valuable for their own management interests. By contrast, performance-based models are often perceived in the MEH as useless for overall fiscal discipline. This may explain the difficulties identified when it comes to learning how to introduce the model, how to adapt it to a specific organizational context and how to link it with macro-budgeting. This entails consideration of the viability, validity and relevance of the reform model; where it is appropriate or inappropriate; whether there is sufficient capacity to managing the reform; or whether prevailing administrative norms (such as a hierarchical or legalistic culture) may affect the effective completion of the reform.

In conclusion, the development of performance budgeting and 'management by results' will substantially benefit from sustained political support; from an enhanced learning capacity; and from the introduction of the right incentives (for example, accountability for results). Cross-cutting these three success factors, important efforts should be made in the Spanish public sector to increase the interaction and cooperation between the various reform stakeholders so as to overcome the risk that adverse behavior will undermine efforts to adapt budget reforms to specific contexts or block collective efforts to move forward with a performance budgeting. We await the next steps.

REFERENCES

CECAEE (2004), *Informe para la creación de la Agencia Estatal de Evaluación de la Calidad de las Políticas y Servicios Públicos*, Madrid: Comisión de Estudio de Creación de la Agencia Estatal de Evaluación.

Chile National Budget Office (2003), *Systems of Management Control and Results-Based Budgeting: the Chilean Experience*, Santiago de Chile: Ministerio de Economía, División de Control de Gestión.

Espadas, L. (2005), 'La Gestión Presupuestaria por Objetivos en la Ley General Presupuestaria', seminar on La Política Fiscal en España: Retos y Perspectivas, Universidad Internacional Menéndez Pelayo, 4–8 July, Santander.

Gunther, R. (1980), *Public Policy in a No-Party State: Spanish Planning and Budgeting in the Twilight of the Franquist Era*, Berkeley, CA: University of California Press.

Iglesias, J. (2007), 'La Presupuestación en un Doble Contexto de Descentralización e Integración: la nueva regla fiscal Española', *Boletíon Económico de ICE*, 2906 (March), 37–49.

Iglesias, J. and M. Morano (2008), 'La Técnica de Presupuestación en la Administración Central Española: estabilidad presupuestaria y asignación de recursos', *Presupuesto y Gasto Público*, **51**, 107–31.

Ley [Law] (2001), Ley General de Estabilidad Presupuestaria, Ley 18/2001, December 12, BOE 298, December 13 2001; see also, Ley Orgánica, 5/2001, December 13, BOE 299, December 14.

Ley (2003), Ley General Presupuestaria, Ley 47/2003, November 26, BOE 284, 27 November.

Ley (2006a), Ley de Reforma de la Ley General de Estabilidad Presupuestaria, Ley 15/2006, May 26, BOE 126, 27 May; see also, Ley Orgánica, 3/2006, May 26, BOE 126, May 27.

Ley (2006b), Ley de Agencias Estatales, Ley 28/2006, BOE 171, July 19.

Ministerio de Economía y Hacienda (MEH) (1983), *Normas de Auditoria del Sector Público*, Madrid: Intervención General de la Administración del Estado.

MEH (1985), *Guía para el Control Operativo de Programas*, Madrid: Intervención General de la Administración del Estado.

MEH (2004), *Elementos Claves en el Fortalecimiento de la Presupuestación por Programas, Notas Técnicas de la Dirección General de Presupuestos*, Madrid: Subdirección General de Análisis y Evaluación de las Políticas del Gasto.

MEH (2005), *Guía para la Elaboración de Programas Presupuestarios*, Madrid: Dirección General de Presupuestos, Subdirección General de Análisis y Evaluación de las Políticas del Gasto.

MEH (2008), 'Presupuestos Generales del Estado', accessed at www.sgpg.pap.meh.es.

Organisation for Economic Co-operation and Department (OECD) (2001), *Outcome Focused Management and Budgeting*, Paris: OECD.

Pollitt, C. and G. Bouckaert (2004), *Public Management Reform: a Comparative Analysis*, New York: Oxford University Press.

Ruiz-Huerta, J., E. Zapico, J. Loscos and T. Takahashi (2007), 'Three decades of reforms for performance budgeting in Spain', unpublished paper.
Sánchez Revenga, J. (2005), 'El Presupuesto por Programas en España', *Economistas*, **105**, 29–38.
Schick, A. (2003), 'The performing state: reflection on an idea whose time has come but whose implementation has not', paper prepared for the 24th Annual Meeting of Senior Budget Officials, Rome, 3–4 June.
UK Cabinet Office (1999), *Next Steps: Moving On*, Cmd 2450, London: HMSO.
Zapico, E. (1989), *La Modernización Simbólica del Presupuesto Public*, Oñate: IVAP.
Zapico, E. (2005), 'Comisiones de Análisis de Programas y Asignación Eficiente del Gasto Público', *Economistas*, **105**, 39–51.

12. Budget reform in Italy: importing 'enlightened' ideas in a difficult context

Francesco Stolfi, Chiara Goretti and Luca Rizzuto

Two parallel reform threads have characterized Italy's path of budgetary reform: one affecting the procedures and documentation of the budget process; and the other the role and institutional strength of the executive and especially the central budgetary agencies. On the one hand, starting in the early 1960s, there have been successive waves of mandatory 'enlightened' reforms that have affected the budget process significantly, progressively modernizing the tools of economic policy. These statutes focused mainly on the parliamentary approval process while substantially neglecting the important games played within the executive itself. On the other hand, starting in the late 1980s and accelerating in the 1990s there has been a gradual empowerment of the executive vis-à-vis the parliament and in particular the central budget agency called the Ministero dell' Economia e delle Finanze (Ministry of Economy and Finance or MEF). This reform process has strengthened the political executive, the core financial staff of the MEF, and the standing of the bureaucracy.

The two threads are interconnected, but their different nature and paths followed makes it difficult to find immediate correspondences, with some notable exceptions such as the merger of the economic ministries in the 1990s. Statutory reforms have tended to be 'big pushes' initiated by a relatively limited number of reform-oriented experts. The strengthening of the executive and MEF, by contrast, has been a gradual process, reflecting the changing political context and the increasing political weight of the Finance Minister within the executive, as well as the increasing professionalization of the ministry. There have been few instances of dramatic change, but the accumulation of gradual changes since the 1980s has consolidated the position and power of the MEF.

Correspondence between the two threads lies in their common backdrop: namely, the country's persistent fiscal problems, the precarious political context and the impact of international (and especially European) pressure. Italy's fiscal problems began in the 1970s when, in the absence of an adequate budgetary rule framework, massive deficit spending was the answer to the decade's economic problems. While other Organisation for Economic Co-operation and Development (OECD) countries – similarly affected by the stagflation of the 1970s – proceeded to put their house in order in the 1980s, Italy's fiscal profligacy continued. The ratio of government debt to GDP hit 60 percent in 1980, then exceeded 100 percent in 1990, threatening not only Italy's participation in the process of European monetary integration, but also its very financial sustainability. Although the 1990s was a decade of fiscal tightening, the country to this day must deal with its huge stock of accumulated debt – 104 percent of GDP in 2007 – and with the costs of servicing it. This makes Italy one of the few OECD countries that in the past 30 years has never had the luxury of having to deal with fiscal surpluses. The fiscal balance continues to be imperative, not least because of the fiscal requirements imposed by the European Union. This goes some way towards explaining another feature of Italian reforms especially from the 1990s onwards, namely, the alternation and sometimes coexistence of two different policy goals: (1) control of the fiscal aggregates through top-down measures; and (2) the use of budgetary reforms as a tool for the broader reform of public administration along market-oriented lines.

Italian politics is a fundamental factor in this trajectory, affecting both the fiscal outcomes and the trajectory of the reforms. The peculiar features of the Italian political system in the Post World War II period – proportional electoral rules, high party fragmentation and no government alternation – significantly contributed to fiscal deterioration in the 1980s. In the 1990s, the ineffective party system was swept away by corruption scandals, and in its place a new and increasingly bipolar party system evolved. The demise of the old party system, and the adversarial nature of the new, affected the pace if not the content of both threads of reform. The current situation still produces fragmented majorities while harsh conflict between the two opposed sides sometimes prevents the implementation of reforms that should enjoy bipartisan support.

Finally, the international context has played an important role, above all via the European fiscal framework and the multilateral surveillance of the European institutions and member states. The timing and the content of the reforms have often been significantly affected by such international pressures. In the following section we retrace the trajectory of budgetary reform, beginning with the statutory reforms of the budget procedures and documents and then considering the more gradual development of the power and role of the MEF.

ITALIAN BUDGETARY REFORM: MANDATORY PUSHES AND THE STEADY STRENGTHENING OF THE CENTRAL BUDGET AGENCY

Over past decades, Italy has repeatedly modified its fiscal institutions with the aim of modernizing its budgetary system. In a country notorious for its inability to introduce reforms to address its political, economic and social problems, the budget has been one area in which reforms have succeeded each other with regularity since the 1960s. These reforms have often sought to apply internationally *au courant* ideas on budgeting and budgetary goals; for instance, the use of the budget process as a tool for economic planning in the 1960s, and then as part of a broader reform of public administration in the 1990s. However, the actual implementation record remains rather checkered. The overall feature of many Italian reforms is their ostensible 'enlightened' character. In Italian public discourse the term 'enlightened' usually has a negative or cynical connotation. It refers to legal initiatives or ideas for reform that construct brilliant edifices but which subsequently do not translate into the more pedestrian aspects of implementation.

The conceptual cornerstone of the Italian annual budget is section 81 of the 1948 Constitution that stipulates that the budget law authorizing the government to spend and raise revenues (*bilancio di previsione*) cannot introduce new spending or new taxes. This provision reflected the night-watchman vision of government that prevailed in the immediate post-war period, and was meant to prevent parliament from rashly altering existing legislation.

However, as the role of government in the economy and society expanded, the limitations of this constitutional constraint increasingly became evident. Given that the formal budget mostly takes stock of revenue and spending decisions already taken, it cannot really be used for framing fiscal policy in any coherent or unified manner.[1] For several decades after the Second World War the budget process was characterized by an utter lack of structure. Budget decisions were made outside any coherent framework by the individual government departments. The voting of the budget by parliament became a 'useless rite' (Cassese 1974: 263) in which parliament was called to ratify the decisions already made during the year. Accordingly, the subsequent trajectory of budgetary reform largely reflected efforts to ensure greater coherence to fiscal decision-making and to create a unified framework for budgetary policy.

The 1980s: a Time of Learning

The recent history of budgetary reform began in 1978 with the introduction of a new legal instrument, the *legge finanziaria* (known as the *finanziaria*), modeled after the French *loi de finance*. The *finanziaria* reform aimed to concentrate new decisions on spending and taxation in a single document, which would be connected to a multiyear budget document. It framed and modulated the annual economic program of the government, subject to the approval of parliament. The reform was not only inspired by foreign experiences but was also the child of the peculiar spirit of the times. The commonly held tenet in the late 1970s was that a strong parliament constituted the ideal form of democratic government – an idea especially espoused by the Communists who enjoyed strong parliamentary representation but were not part of the executive.

The decade that followed this reform was one of institutional learning. Reform advocates had not allowed for the less-than-virtuous behavior of both government and parliament. In practice, the *finanziaria* became an omnibus law where new spending was accumulated without regard to the overall aggregates. As such, the goal of a multiyear budget was never realized, and the original idea of setting binding overall fiscal targets in the *finanziaria* was undermined by expedient practice.

Members of parliament drove further attempts to patch up the budget process in the 1980s – especially the left wing of the Christian Democrats and the non-Communist left. They introduced dedicated budget sessions for parliament in the early 1980s and started to experiment with a medium-term financial framework inspired by the United States experience with the First Concurrent Budget Resolution. In this period the executive was largely a passive bystander. The government's attitude, however, changed in 1988, immediately after the decision – made at the European level but opposed by Italy – to eliminate all barriers to capital mobility within the European Community by 1990. As the Treasury Minister, Giuliano Amato, reported to parliament, it became clear in the new capital regime Italy's rapidly mounting debt would be unsustainable. With the government's support, and after an especially disastrous budget session in which the projected deficit set by the *finanziaria* exceeded the government's proposed budget by 13 percent, a new reform was passed in 1988.

The 1988 reform (law 362/88) established the foundations of the current budget system. It institutionalized the medium-term financial framework, the Documento di Programmazione Economica e Finanziaria (Economic and Financial Plan or DPEF), that sets the aggregate fiscal target which the *finanziaria* cannot violate. The DPEF sought to limit the omnibus nature of the *finanziaria*. It reduced the scope of the *finanziaria* to the annual authorization of tax rates and the amounts of spending originating from the multiyear framework or permanent spending legislation. If the government wished to change its fiscal plan, through increased spending or revenue measures, new legislation had to be introduced and debated in parliament. It also set a balanced budget requirement 'at the margin', namely for new current spending and revenues. It increased parliament's responsibility for the overall balances by strengthening the gatekeeping role of the speakers of the two chambers and of the budget committees in determining the admissibility of parliamentary amendments to the government texts. Finally, at long last, it introduced a quantification mechanism to evaluate the cost of new measures proposed by the government.

The 1988 statute aimed to establish a system of mutual constraints between executive and parliament, but in practice it worked to strengthen the executive. This reflected a mounting unease at the inability of the executive to control even its own majority, which had contributed to the deteriorating fiscal situation of the 1980s. At the same time, the political mood was changing, as the Cold War headed toward a permanent thaw. In the same months as law 362/88 was passed, parliament also approved a reform that almost entirely eliminated secret voting in the legislature, which had been the rule until then and served to exacerbate the porosity of the government's majority.

The Changing Political Context of the 1990s

Law 362/88 worked relatively well. The time required for the approval of the budget was sharply reduced. Most years before 1988 the deadline of 31 December was not met, but afterwards it was always achieved. The limit set by the DPEF on the overall balances has worked well, and parliament no longer acted to increase these limits from the government's proposal. The difference between the borrowing requirement intended by the government at the beginning of the legislative process and what finally transpired has dropped dramatically, and on occasion parliament has actually improved the balance originally proposed by the government.

Given that the 1988 budget law limited the content of the *finanziaria*, substantive consolidation measures were included in supplementary laws, the so-called *provvedimenti collegati*. These laws were connected to the *finanziaria* and examined in the budget session. However – just as some observers had feared – such supplementary laws themselves became omnibus laws. Moreover, the quantification process has been only partially successful. Its efficacy was limited by its lack of transparency and often superficial implementation on the part of the financial bureaucracy charged with providing the relevant cost estimates.

Even more dramatic changes occurred in the political sphere after 1988. Italy had participated in the evolving European Monetary System (EMS) since 1979. Yet, its fiscal situation continued to worsen, increasingly becoming a matter of concern for voters. By the early 1990s a combination of high debt, relatively high inflation, and fixed exchange rates in the context of the newly implemented capital mobility, led to a massive outflow of capital and Italy's eviction from the EMS in 1992. This happened at exactly the same time as the judiciary launched a wide-ranging investigation into corruption which involved most of the parties. The combination of the EMS debacle and the corruption investigation destroyed the electoral support for the old parties (Ginsborg 2003). In 1993, a popular referendum did away with the proportional representation electoral system – widely considered to be a contributor to corruption. In 1994 the first elections with the new electoral system (plurality with a proportional correction) saw the disappearance of most of the parties that had ruled Italy for 40 years. Since 1994 the party system has evolved toward bipolarization, with two blocs (center-right and center-left) confronting each other. Even the return to proportional representation (but with a seat premium for the winning coalition) from the 2006 elections has not dented the new bipolar nature of the party system.

The political upheavals of the 1990s had significant consequences for the reform process. The gradual transition to a bipolar party system strengthened the core executive (including the Treasury) vis-à-vis the rest of the executive and the majority parties. It improved the cohesion of the government majority,[2] thus making the passing of reforms easier. Finally, it opened the door to government alternation, which had implications for the character of reforms, with left and right governments adopting different reform agendas.

The crisis of 1992–93 gave the executive, which now included important academics with long-standing interests in administrative reform, unprecedented leeway from its own party majority.[3] Between 1992 and 1994 the Amato and Ciampi governments laid the foundations for what was going to be the overall reform drive of the decade. These governments attempted to bring together budget reform with broader attempts to reform public administration. The main measures passed in this period included: the reform of employment contracts in public administration; increased autonomy for the public managers in the management of the public resources; connecting the salaries of public managers to their performance; and the replacement of legality controls with performance controls.

In 1996, with the first center-left government of the new bipolar era, the pace of reform picked up again. Experts in public administration and budgeting returned to government, many of whom had driven the reform efforts in parliament in the 1980s or proposed the 1992–94 reforms. One of the major planks of the new government was administrative reform, and budget reform was meant to be part and parcel of this broader reform drive. Inspired by new public management (NPM), the goal of administrative reform was to move public administration toward a more managerial ethos, emphasizing accountability for results rather than legalistic compliance to rules (Stolfi 2008). At the same time, the government moved to reduce the number of government departments as a way of improving coordination at the top. The key elements of the reforms of 1997 were a new classification structure for the budget documents based on a relatively limited number of items and the merger of the economic ministries. The new classification aimed to give parliament more control on the broad policy choices, allowing at the same time greater flexibility for public managers in the use of the resources assigned to them, consistently with the new managerialist approach.

On the executive side, the Budget Ministry was merged with the Treasury Ministry in 1997, and the construction of an economic 'super-ministry' was completed with the further merger of the Finance Ministry in 2001, to create what is now the Ministero dell' Economia e delle Finanze (MEF). These developments were the last steps of a process begun in the late 1980s. The Treasury was always the most important economic ministry, in particular because it included the General Budget and Accounting Office (Ragioneria Generale dello Stato – RGS), which controlled both the formulation and the implementation stages of budgetary spending decisions. However, for most of the post-war period its influence had been limited by the strong role of parliament, political fragmentation in the executive, and by a lack of technical skills that made it dependent on the technical expertise of other institutions, mainly the central bank (Bank of Italy).

In the late 1980s, when it became increasingly obvious the government parties were incapable of dealing with the fiscal problems, the Treasury turned to the personnel of the Bank of Italy for help. The bank began to colonize the higher echelons of the Treasury. Since this time the Treasury and MEF ministers have also been disproportionately drawn from the central bank: former presidents (such as Guido Carli, 1989–92, and Carlo Azeglio Ciampi, 1996–99) or high officials of the Bank of Italy (such as Tommaso Padoa Schioppa, 2006–08).

The need to deal with these fiscal problems and in particular with the cost of government debt also led to the reorganization of the internal structure of the Treasury in 1991, with a concentration of tasks related to the management of debt, to economic forecasting and to the preparation of budget documents (and in particular the DPEF).[4] The first head of this enhanced institution (the Direzione Generale det Tesoro or Directorate

General of Treasury) was Mario Draghi (currently the president of the central bank), an economist trained in the United States, who immediately proceeded to staff his organization with new cohorts of often foreign-trained PhDs in economics, especially from the United States and Britain (Quaglia 2005a). A similar reorganization, however, did not occur in the main department involved in budgetary policy, namely the RGS, which remained a large bureaucratic entity with about 5000 staff, mainly with legal-accounting training.

The pressure of fiscal constraints heightened in the 1990s, and threatened to keep the country out of the Economic and Monetary Union (EMU). But this only served to increase the political power of the Treasury/MEF minister. By the mid-1990s the Treasury/MEF minister was safely ensconced alongside the Prime Minister and above the rest of the executive in terms of political standing.

In the 1990s the executive exploited the fast track enjoyed by the *provvedimenti collegati* as part of the budget session to reform important policy areas such as social security, public employment and health services. In the period 1992–98 a major fiscal consolidation was achieved by complex 'budgetary packages'. Fiscal decisions adopted in the state budget and in the *finanziaria* were integrated and complemented by additional measures contained in one or more *collegati*.

Many saw this practice as weakening the sovereignty of parliament, as these measures were used to introduce broad delegations to the government. Accordingly, in 1999 the content of the *finanziaria* and of the *collegati* was further regulated.[5] The scope of the *finanziaria* was widened to include either measures that would modify legislation in order to improve the balance (reducing spending or increasing revenues), or measures worsening the balance, though limited to those directly aimed at stimulating the economy. Micro-sectoral policies and regulatory provisions were excluded from consideration. The *collegati*, on the other hand, were meant to be examined by parliament outside the budget session, to regulate and modify the structure of specific policy areas, consistently with the overall economic policy targets. The tightening implied a specific control on the scope of the *finanziaria*; performed by the chairmen and speakers of each chamber. However the parliamentary gatekeepers have not always been able to limit financially irrelevant and micro-distributive amendments (De Giorgi and Verzichelli 2008).

The 2000s: the Alternation of Hierarchy and Flexibility

When the center-right returned to government in 2001 this marked a change of tack with regard to the general approach to budgetary decision-making. The fiscal position, as in other EU countries, deteriorated again. Consolidation policies pushed by the EU institutions bolstered the power and centrality of the MEF. Even though the new Finance Minister, Giulio Tremonti, a professor of tax law, had eventually to resign in 2004 over disputes within the governing coalition, it was only after he had subjected them to three years of stringent control over government resources (his opponents would say dictatorial).[6]

With the center-right government (2001–06) the emphasis was more on hierarchy than on flexibility, as had previously been the case with the managerial reforms of the center-left. The centerpiece of the new approach was the so-called *legge 'taglia-spese'* (or 'expenditure freeze law') of 2002 (246/2002). The new rules required that all expenditure legislation must indicate the 'authorized expenditure' and, depending on the type of law, this was either the maximum ceiling of disbursements or an expenditure forecast. In the latter case, legislation had to contain a specific 'safeguard clause' – inspired by the automatic cuts used in the United States with the Gramm–Rudman–Hollings Act of 1985 – to compensate for possible expenditure in excess of these forecasts.

The 'freeze law' also introduced provisions for 'emergency action' during budget execution, which empowered the MEF to intervene in cases of 'significant divergence' from the overall budgetary objectives of the DPEF. The government could issue a decree containing general guidelines to secure more effective expenditure monitoring and control. The MEF was also empowered to limit overall budget appropriations, by imposing across-the-board cuts on expenditure, excluding wages of public sector employees, pensions, and other fixed or obligatory expenditures.

However, in the six years since the adoption of the 'expenditure freeze' law, the measure has proven unsatisfactory. The only implementation of across-the board cuts was in 2002, suggesting that it was a one-off exception. Moreover, such cuts did not allow selective action (since expenditure cuts were proportionally applied to all expenditure) or lead to permanent reductions (since it could not prevent cuts being reinstated in the following fiscal year).

Furthermore, the implementation of the 'safeguard clause' has been equally unsatisfactory. The law aimed to discourage unrealistic *ex ante* expenditure projections from departments by applying a more stringent application of surveillance procedures and the threat of *ex post* action. Unfortunately, due to poor implementation this measure failed to improve the *ex ante* incentive to provide better forecasts when the budget was being drafted. In fact, in 2005 Italy incurred the EU's 'excessive deficit procedure' (EDP), because it breached the 3 percent limit required by the Stability and Growth Pact.

In terms of documentation, the program classification reforms introduced in 1997 were interpreted in a rather conservative fashion. New budget items were still connected to cost centers within the existing directorates-general of the ministries. Given the very broad scope of the directorates' activities, this minimized the connection between budget and programs that some reformers had hoped to achieve. Moreover, the RGS maintained tight control on the actual disbursements and its persisting legalistic attitudes to the controls on administrative activity minimized the actual impact of the reforms on decision-making within public administration.

The return to power of the center-left (2006–08) gave renewed energy to the managerialist attempts of the 1990s. Some actors who had inspired the 1997 classification reforms coincided with its revamping in 2007, when the MEF issued new instructions on the drafting of budget documents. In particular, the budget classification was now restructured to give greater emphasis to the connection between budgetary choices and government programs. Another area of innovation was opened by launching the first 'spending review' ever performed in the country, an experimental activity extended to five line ministries with the support of a technical committee composed of outstanding academics and experts of public finance.

It is difficult to evaluate the results of these attempts as parliament was dissolved early and the 2008 elections brought in a new majority. As the center-right returned to government, Giulio Tremonti once again became Minister of Finance (2001–04, as from 2008). And once again the reform of the budget process was included in the government's agenda as one of the main points on which a bipartisan consensus was deemed to be necessary and possible.

In sum, the 'enlightened' edifice of budget procedures and documents remains in flux, with different governments keen to make changes according to their visions of what they think budgetary policy should achieve. If there has been a constant over the decades, it has been a critical relationship between the government and the parliament on budgetary matters. During the 2000s, both center-right and center-left governments have made extensive use of confidence voting on the budget and on the *finanziaria* to overcome the decisional stall of fragmented majorities and to minimize the possibility of undesired parliamentary amendments.

THE BUDGET PROCESS: THE UNFINISHED QUEST FOR GREATER EFFICIENCY

A few main observations can be made regarding the budget process as it stands at the end of three decades of reform. First, the budget process is still more focused on the broad fiscal aggregates than on issues of efficient allocation and prioritization of resources. This is partly due to the opposition of the line bureaucracy (which has an interest in minimizing reallocation based on performance) and of the financial bureaucracy (which wants to maintain control over disbursements). It is also partly due to the fact that government debt remains extremely high, threatening Italy's participation in the EMU. It places an obligation on the country to abide by the fiscal constraints set by the Stability and Growth Pact, although the stringency of this obligation has been interpreted differently by the center-right and the center-left.

Second, despite its rationalization since the 1988 reform, the parliamentary passage of the budget remains difficult. Today the government is able to defend its aggregate fiscal targets, but still has problems defending the composition of its fiscal packages. As a result, both center-right and center-left governments have had to resort to measures (in particular confidence votes) curtailing the amendment powers of parliament, even when they enjoy comfortable majorities. Third, budget execution, in spite of the managerialist reforms of the last decade, still privileges control over minute disbursements rather than a more outcome-oriented use of resources.

The budget process starts in spring each year, with the MEF and in particular the RGS playing the key role. Since the budget cannot introduce new spending or revenues (being based on existing legislation) its draft is more of a bureaucratic than a political affair. Line ministers will often not know what the bureaucracy is asking for. The RGS begins the process when it issues a circular to every ministry with instructions regarding the drafting of the budget. The line ministries prepare a first draft, but in fact the RGS is responsible for the final draft of their budgets, often introducing significant changes from the first drafts. These final drafts are the outcome of bargaining between the RGS and the line ministries over the extent of spending increases for the expenditure authorized by existing legislation. As a result, the budget is produced incrementally rather than, as the 1997 reform intended, through a yearly re-evaluation of priorities.

In negotiations, there is no conception of the overall availability of resources (this aspect is however made clear in the second phase of budget negotiations, the one devoted to the *finanziaria*). Sectoral bureaucracies behave irresponsibly, always asking for additional funds. The RGS's action is focused on controlling the amount of resources appropriated; it shows no interest in the evaluation of current programs.

The second phase of the annual budget process is based upon the Economic and Financial Plan or DPEF, presented in June and examined by parliament before the summer. Being a document for multiyear planning, it presents macroeconomic estimates in parallel with fiscal policy baselines and targets. Fiscally, it sets four-year targets in a flexible and rolling framework for the budget balance, the public sector cash balance and the borrowing requirement for the general government (aggregates relevant with regard to EU rules).

In September the targets fixed by the DPEF constitute the fiscal limits relevant for the determination of the *finanziaria*, the law devoted to introduce new legislation affecting spending and revenues. Given the deficit that frequently emerges from these baselines (built on current legislation), the *finanziaria* has to modify expenditure and revenues in such a way as to drive budget baselines to the targets set by the DPEF.

The construction of the bill for the *finanziaria* is more contentious than for the budget. The draft is prepared by the MEF,[7] and negotiations are more political, as the spending ministers want to attempt to gain additional resources or defend their departments from any cuts. In this phase, fiscal limits fixed in the DPEF bind negotiations within the executive and, for this reason, the MEF listens to requests, negotiates with its colleagues and has the last word on the draft to be presented to the Council of Ministers. Negotiations on new initiatives are carried out between the RGS and sectoral bureaucracies.

In constructing the *finanziaria* the discretional power of the budget agency charged with collecting and preparing the figures is enormous (Pisauro and Visco 2008). Most of the time, the RGS does not distinguish among the expenditures of various departments. Its main tool of reduction is across-the-board cuts, which it exerts in a non-transparent way, not clearly presenting the criteria adopted for budget prioritization.

Before they are presented to parliament, the budget documents (budget and *finanziaria*) must be approved by the government as a whole. For the budget, the relevant meeting of the Council of Ministers is almost a formality. In the case of the *finanziaria* the council meeting is much more contentious, as spending ministers tend to wrangle again with the MEF over the allocation of resources to their departments. The Finance Minister is alone against all other colleagues. The necessary information to prevent this occurring is often unavailable, even to the Prime Minister. In addition, the latter sometimes avoids taking a position on politically sensitive, contentious subjects in order to keep open the possibility of introducing changes during the parliamentary examination of the proposed budget. Changes and corrections are often introduced by the Council of Ministers, but only a limited number of participants really know what the council has voted on. The meetings of the Council of Ministers over the *finanziaria* are conducted at the political level only, while meetings on the budget (*bilancio di previsione*) are open to the bureaucracies who are tasked with recording any changes and with translating them into technical formulations.

Parliamentary passage occurs during a dedicated budget session, which starts with the presentation by the government of the budget bills and the *finanziaria* by 30 September and ends by December. Detailed procedures regulate the parliamentary passage, mainly concentrating on preserving the overall fiscal aggregates. The first article of the *finanziaria* presents fiscal targets as defined in the DPEF. As a consequence of the voting sequence, these fiscal targets become constraints for subsequent scrutiny, as they were for the budget preparation at the executive level. According to the rules, amendments need to be neutral on the overall balance and therefore parliamentarians must propose compensating spending cuts or revenue increases for any additional request. Other parliamentary rules have been created to block the size of any proposed amendments in budget deliberations, though their implementation has not been effective at all.

Accordingly, the parliamentary approval process remains open to budgetary amendment. There is no clear difference in the Italian system between parliamentary and government responsibilities during the examination of the budget, as the latter usually becomes involved in changing its own text in order accommodate pressures coming from its fragmented majorities. Furthermore, parliamentarians present amendments and proposals emanating from line ministries that were not accepted in earlier negotiations or by the Council of Ministers. The parliamentary process also provides a chance for individual legislators to introduce changes to benefit specific constituencies, even though the financial size of these changes is usually small.

In line with new public management prescriptions, Italy has adopted tools to increase flexibility during the budget execution phase. In the early 2000s, for example, generic funds devoted to general aims have been created within the budget, consolidating previous fragmented appropriations for infrastructure, territorial development and incentives to firms. Parliament votes on these one-line funds, while the resources are then distributed by the executive.

The problem with such ad hoc reprioritization is that it does not accord with a coherent management of the government's priorities. Behind the scenes, inadequate resource planning on the part of line bureaucracies, underfunding by the RGS (which has traditionally been jealous of its ability to regulate the flow of government spending through administrative means) and the use of across-the-board cuts, have all combined to give the financial bureaucracy greater influence over reprioritization. Under the guise of flexibility, governments have shifted resources from railways to the universal mail service, or from one body dealing with labor market initiatives to another with the task of developing legislation on immigration. Flexibility was intended to provide fluidity, to shift resources away from items that could wait until next year. This practice has clearly gone against the grain of the attempts to focus budget discipline on the definition of broad policies and to increase the responsibility of public managers for the achievement of relevant outcomes.

Furthermore, the way in which control activities operate does not help in steering the system toward a greater outcome orientation. An external agency (that is, not controlled by either the executive or parliament) tasked with auditing the budgetary decision-making and the implementation of the budget decisions is the Court of Accounts (Corte dei Conti). Among the most important audits of the court is the assessment of the year-end financial statement (*rendiconto*) reporting on the activities of all government departments. These audits, although potentially important, have limitations. They continue to be based more on the fulfillment of legal requirements rather than on the assessment of a department's performance in achieving the desired results.

The problem of making public administrators accountable for the results they achieve is compounded by the persisting lack of performance indicators, despite being required by the administrative reform laws of the 1990s. In fact, the connection between performance and salary introduced for public managers in the 1990s has been perverted in a paradoxical manner: the objectives for the bureaucracy have been so devised as to ensure they receive the performance bonuses.

Fiscal Outcomes: Still Tottering on the Precipice

The first thing that strikes even a causal observer of Italian public finance is the gargantuan size of the country's debt. The second thing is the massive turnaround that occurred in the 1990s. Even though government debt remains the highest in Europe and the country still struggles with the high cost of servicing the accumulated debt, primary balances have remained in surplus since the early 1990s despite a certain relaxation in the fiscal stance following the country's entry to the EMU.

In the face of this extraordinary evolution of fiscal outcomes one might ask: what has been the contribution of budgetary reforms to this circumstance? The answer is that they have probably been effective, but they are also conditional on several other factors, in particular the degree of political commitment and international peer pressure.[8]

In the fiscal explosion of the 1980s, the government's annual borrowing requirement generally exceeded 10 percent of GDP and public debt skyrocketed from 60 percent of GDP in 1980 to 100 percent by 1990. The lack of political resilience and a lower-than-average tax pressure exacerbated the problems. In 1980 tax revenues were 34 percent of GDP compared to

44 percent in the rest of Europe. The rising cost of interest on debt represented 80 percent of the annual budget deficit by 1990.

At the time, the budget process did not help solve the fiscal problems, allowing parliament to worsen the fiscal balances proposed by the executive. Hence, the 1980s as the last decade of sustained economic growth Italy has seen were a wasted opportunity. During the decade some short-term 'maneuvers' to help reduce the deficit were attempted. But the main determinants of budget overspending, interest payments and social spending (pensions, health services and public employment) were not touched.

The real turnaround in Italian public finance occurred with the crisis of 1992. Buttressed by the sense of emergency created by the financial crisis of that year, the Amato government not only achieved a significant primary surplus, but finally went beyond one-off measures to introduce structural reforms in a number of areas fundamental for public finance: health services, local finances, social security and public administration. In the following years, governments were consistently able to achieve significant primary surpluses.

This achievement of primary surpluses was largely the result of the pressure exerted by the goal to ensure that Italy would join the EMU at the same time as its European partners. The fiscal criteria set by the Maastricht Treaty required a fiscal adjustment of unprecedented scale by 1997 – the benchmark year to assess the fulfillment of the fiscal conditions to join the EMU. Like the other European participants, Italy had to meet the stringent targets with an annual deficit of less than 3 percent of GDP and a maximum 60 percent of debt to GDP. By 1997, the government deficit was down to 2.7 percent of GDP and although the debt-to-GDP ratio was still at 115 percent it had been declining for two years.[9]

Few would have believed such a result possible, and some European partners would not have shed many tears over the country's exclusion from the EMU. But the result was achieved by a combination of pluck and luck. The story is partly one of consistent primary surpluses, as higher taxes and spending cuts were justified to voters as the price to 'enter Europe', exemplified by the 'tax for Europe' introduced by the Prodi government in 1996. Temporary measures were introduced too (such as administrative mechanisms to limit cash payments or one-off taxes) in order to meet the European deficit requirements in the short term, betting on the 'windfall' likely from the reduction of interest rates in the longer term. Finally, the story is one of decreasing debt costs. As the financial markets began to accept the idea that Italy might indeed make it into the EMU, the interest on Italian debt began to drop. The difference between Italian and German government bonds plummeted from a 7 percent gap to zero as the Prodi government committed to join the first wave of EMU

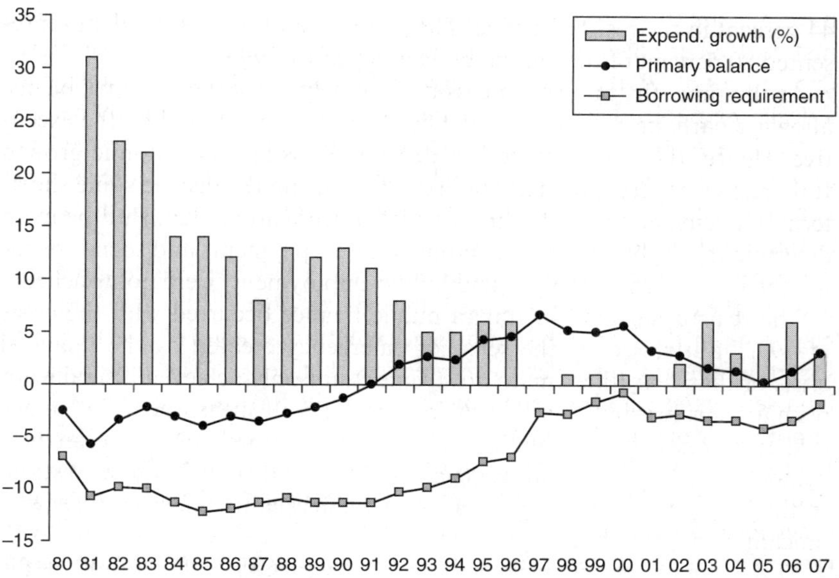

Source: MEF, Rome.

Figure 12.1 Italian budget book figures, 2007–8

participants (Spaventa and Chiorazzo 2000: 98). Moreover, the new technical staff brought to the Treasury in the early 1990s were able to restructure the debt so as to reduce interest payments significantly.[10]

The EMU goal, in reality, strengthened the position of the Treasury within the executive and the position of the executive vis-à-vis parliament. The executive used the legal instruments of the budget session to obtain from parliament delegated powers to reform important policy areas such as social security. In society at large, the EMU goal provided added legitimacy to the required sacrifices.

The period to 1997 underscored the success of the strategy of using the Maastricht criteria as 'external constraints' to force the Italian political system to accept a more prudent fiscal attitude (Dyson and Featherstone 1999). However, after the entry into the EMU there has been a decline in the drive to achieve fiscal stability (see Figure 12.1). The EMU lost its potency as an external constraint; and even though the attendant Stability and Growth Pact still calls for fiscal prudence by incorporating the Maastricht criteria into a European framework of financial reporting and sanctions, its bite is clearly limited for the countries that are already in.

The subsequent fiscal outcomes have reflected the willingness of various governments to be constrained by these European-level fiscal rules. The first center-left government achieved consistently high primary surpluses (5.5 percent of GDP on average between 1996 and 2000) and presided over a declining public debt (from 121 percent of GDP in 1996 to 109 percent of GDP in 2000). Between 2001 and 2006, due to the fragile international economic situation, the center-right opted for a supply-side economic approach based on tax cuts, and at times relied on financial measures such as the securitization of real estate.

Respect for the European fiscal constraints has been made more difficult as the country has proceeded toward new forms of fiscal federalism, beginning in the late 1990s with the devolution of control over regional spending and tax revenues to the regions themselves. The requirements imposed by the Stability and Growth Pact at the European level have been imported domestically to ensure the regions maintain these constraints. Every year since 1999 parliament has passed a Patto di Stabilità Interno (Domestic Stability Pact) setting fiscal constraints for the regions and other local governments. These constraints, consistent with the different fiscal policies of the center-left and center-right governments, have taken different forms: for the center-left constraints on the balances (thus allowing local governments to make their choices regarding their preferred combination of spending and taxes); and constraints on the rate of growth of spending for the center-right. Superficially, the pacts have been successful as most local governments have respected the requirements (Goretti and Mercuri 2004). The problem emanating from this is that the rules for subnational entities are not incorporated in a transparent way into the medium-term planning developed by the DPEF (De Ioanna and Goretti 2008). Therefore, the financial rule binding regional and local governments is not necessarily consistent with aggregate targets for the national government, and their responsibilities are not clearly connected with aggregate outcomes.

BUDGETARY DOCUMENTATION: A PATCHWORK BLANKET THAT STRUGGLES TO COVER THE ENTIRE PUBLIC SECTOR

One of the main features of Italian budget process is the plurality of budget documents: the DPEF, the budget bill, the *finanziaria* and the *collegati*. These documents provide a patchwork picture of public finance, not easily readable due to accounting differences between the different documents. As an example, the state budget's significance for the management of public resources is limited, since it only covers the central government, an aggregate that has been losing importance for the governance of public finance. Increasingly, government functions are carried out by government-owned corporations (such as the railways or the postal service), by foundations and by lower levels of government. The state budget includes only transfers to these actors; it does not disclose the links to the matching items in the budgets of other entities receiving the resources.

Another aspect of budget documentation is the limited connections between the various accounting principles adopted by public entities (De Ioanna and Rizzuto 2006). Various 'languages' characterize the fiscal rules that bind policy decisions. The state budget is drafted using two parallel accounting systems (cash and legal commitments). The 1997 reform, as part of the attempt to move from incremental to zero-based budgeting, also introduced an accruals format. However, the accruals version is only produced on an experimental basis and is not part of the budgetary decision-making process. Also, subnational budgets are compiled in cash terms and according to a different structure and classification. An additional element of complexity is evident by the unsatisfactory transparency of the budget structure with respect to central-level allocative decisions.

As already mentioned, budget reporting was revamped in 2007 to reflect a program classification again. This classification was intended to complete the 1997 reforms. It aims to emphasize the connection between government spending, policies and government programs. The broadest level of aggregation is the 'mission', each mission corresponding to a strategic goal for the government (there are currently 34 such strategic goals). Government departments may be involved in several missions. Below them are 169 'programs', or broad policies each connected to a strategic goal; in most cases programs are carried out by a single department. Each program is further articulated into so-called macro-aggregates or functional categories of expenditure (for instance, investment spending or operating costs), which are the basic items voted by parliament.[11] The current classification presents significant areas of overlap among programs and thus among government departments. As with other countries which have adopted program-based classifications, the broadness of the programs raises the question of how useful the classification really is for the actual assessment of the results achieved.

Finally, transparency issues have emerged in the planning phase. The present system based on annual decisions constrained by targets set within a medium-term planning framework has worked well in the sense that parliament no longer worsens the balance presented by the executive. The prescribed rules, however, have not prevented *ex post* breaches of the government's stated fiscal goals (De Ioanna and Goretti 2008). These goals, as set in the DPEF and then adopted by the *finanziaria*, are based on the government's own economic estimates, which have at times been criticized as being non-transparent. In particular, public finance projections and their connections with macroeconomic projections are insufficiently explained in public documents, often hiding non-prudential assumptions that jeopardize the quality and reliability of financial planning. Moreover, the practice of winning approval for the *finanziaria* by means of a confidence vote has limited the overall transparency and readability of the fiscal choices that emerge from the budget process. Rules about votes of confidence require that they can only be undertaken on a single article. The consequence is that the *finanziaria* then consists of only one article with thousands of paragraphs, making it inaccessible.

CONCLUSIONS: UNENDING BUDGET REFORMS, STRONGER FINANCE MINISTERS, YET PERSISTING FISCAL PROBLEMS

The landscape of budget reform in Italy is complicated. On the one hand, there is a pattern of constant flux, with succeeding waves of procedural and documentary reforms. These reforms have greatly improved the original fragmentation of the budget process, but have achieved less than the reformers hoped, in terms of both the overall transparency and the efficiency of resource allocation and service provision. A decade-long quest to improve the coherence of budget documentation and of the budget process has therefore been only partly successful. While the budget, DPEF, *finanziaria* and *collegati* constitute a more coherent decision-making framework than existed before the 1980s, but the main documents are difficult to read even for experts let alone interested citizens.

On the other hand, the last decades have seen a marked rise in the power of the Treasury/MEF through a combination of European pressures and domestic political changes. Such political and bureaucratic strengthening has still not been able to fulfill the needs of a modern budget process, in terms of fiscal discipline, allocative efficiency and operative efficiency. In spite of repeated reforms, and contrary to best practice, the Italian budget process still combines a very fragmented bottom-up budget preparation and a tightly centralized budget execution.

In terms of fiscal outcomes, the view is equally complex. On the one hand, Italy was able to achieve laudable fiscal control the 1990s; on the other hand, it still struggles with the crushing debt accumulated in the

1970s and 1980s and with the fiscal constraints imposed by the European Union. Control of the overall fiscal aggregates remains the main concern of the executive. But in order to achieve it, short-term measures and across-the-board cuts remain the order of the day, even though it is widely recognized that these measures do not affect the structural dynamics of public expenditure and exempt politicians from taking responsibility for potentially unpopular cuts. The challenge today is to achieve a stronger capacity to identify priorities and evaluate efficiencies in order to guarantee the sound dynamics of fiscal management.

NOTES

1. We say '*mostly* takes stock of revenue and spending decisions already taken' because the budget can modify the spending connected to entitlements based on the development of predetermined factors such as the inflation rate or contractual obligations.
2. Although the cohesiveness of Italian governments continues to be undermined by their coalitional nature, it has improved from the First Republic. The average length of government has increased from 316 days before the 1993 electoral reform to 529 days after it.
3. For instance, law 412/92, the first of the reform measures taken in this period, was forced on parliament by the executive through the imposition of a number of confidence votes. In the context of the time, when a significant number of the members of parliament were under investigation for corruption, the risk of new elections and the possibility of losing their parliamentary seat, and thus their parliamentary immunity, was an especially convincing threat.
4. With the 1997 merger between the Treasury and the Budget ministry a further reorganization turned the DGT into the Dipartimento del Tesoro (Department of Treasury). Its head retains the title of Director General of the Treasury.
5. The last systematic reform of budget procedures occurred in 1999. It was introduced by law 208/99, which focused mainly on a revision of the set of instruments of the budget process.
6. Tremonti returned to the head the MEF with the new center-right government that was inaugurated in spring of 2008.
7. For simplicity's sake, in this chapter we refer to the political head of the Treasury and later of the MEF as the Finance Minister. It should however be noted that until 2001 – when it was absorbed into the MEF – in the Italian system there existed a separate Finance Ministry in charge of taxation.
8. Fiscal sustainability is one of the functions of budgeting, although the literature has expressed doubts on the fact that specific budget institutions might give more than a marginal contribution (Schick 2004). For the opposite view see Hallerberg et al. (2009).
9. In 1992 the government deficit was 10.4 percent of GDP and debt was 108 percent of GDP and increasing.
10. Italy, like many other members of the EMU, has been accused of using a few accounting tricks to come eventually under the fiscal bars for entry. A little sleight of hand was undertaken at the time of the country's entry into the EMU. The government tried to convince financial markets it met the criteria, thus enabling it to enjoy the windfall of the drop in interest payments.
11. In addition to the formal budget there is also an identified administrative budget, and below these administrative aggregates there is a further level of detail, the *capitoli*.

REFERENCES

Cassese, S. (1974), *La formazione dello Stato Amministrativo*, Rome: Officina Edizioni.

De Giorgi, E. and L. Verzichelli (2008), 'Still a difficult budgetary process? The government, the legislature and the Finance Bill', *South European Society and Politics*, **13** (1), 87–110.

De Ioanna, P. and C. Goretti (2008), *La decisione di bilancio in Italia. Una riflessione su istituzioni e procedure*, Bologna: Il Mulino.

De Ioanna P. and L. Rizzuto (2006), 'Armonizzazione dei bilanci e autonomia contabile delle aree regionali con divari di sviluppo economico', *Rivista giuridica del Mezzogiorno*, **20** (4), 665–86.

Dyson, K. and K. Featherstone (1999), *The Road to Maastricht*, Oxford: Oxford University Press.

Ginsborg, P. (2003), *A History of Contemporary Italy*, New York: Palgrave Macmillan.

Goretti C. and M.C. Mercuri (2004), 'Vincoli finanziari, decisioni di bilancio e azione amministrativa', *Quaderni Formez – Note e commenti sul sistema amministrativo italiano*, **38** (2), 13–34.

Hallerberg, M., R. Strauch and J. von Hagen (2009), *Fiscal Governance: Evidence from Europe*, Cambridge: Cambridge University Press.

Hopkin, J. (2005) 'The Berlusconi government at mid-term', *Mediterranean Politics*, **10** (1), 109–15.

Pisauro, G. and V. Visco 2008. 'Note sulle procedure di bilancio', *Politica economica*, **24** (2), 141–58.

Quaglia, L. (2005a), 'Civil servants, economic ideas, and economic policies: lessons from Italy', *Governance*, **18** (4), 545–66.

Quaglia, L. (2005b), 'Europe and the Right in Italy: an ambivalent relationship', *South European Society and Politics*, **10** (2), 277–91.

Schick, A. 2004. 'Twenty-five years of budget reforms', *OECD Journal on Budgeting*, **4** (1), 81–102.

Spaventa, L. and V. Chiorazzo (2000), *Astuzia o Virtù*, Rome: Donzelli.

Stolfi, F. (2008), 'The Europeanization of Italy's budget institutions in the 1990s', *Journal of European Public Policy*, **15** (4), 550–66.

13. The work in progress of budgetary reform

John Wanna

> Budgeting is a work in progress. The process is never quite settled because those who manage it are never fully satisfied.
>
> (Allen Schick 2002)

The 11 Organisation for Economic Co-operation and Development (OECD) nations surveyed in this book have considerable experience with budget reforms often dating back 20 or even 30 years. Their trajectories and reform agendas vary considerably in terms of local adaptation, timing or sequencing, the political complexion of the perpetrators, institutional motivations and the scope and chosen instruments of reform. No two countries have similar trajectories or reform pathways, and there are still great dissimilarities in the ways budgets are framed, assembled and presented. Across these case studies we see trajectories, not a unilinear trajectory. It is not true to claim (as Blondal 2003 suggests) that there has been a single direction of reform along which countries have been inexorably heading (but see also Schick 2000 and 2002 where he sketches out some common budgetary trends from 1980 and tries to predict a range of future reforms). As we have seen, political and institutional differences largely account for these dissimilarities, as do the nature of the pressures experienced by governments from period to period.

Three dimensions in particular appear to divide these OECD countries: speed, scope and thematic emphasis. Some countries have attempted rapid progress with budget reform, making substantial changes in close proximity or in 'one big bang' (Australia, The Netherlands, New Zealand and Korea). Others have been much more circumspect, episodic or slow to adopt reforms (Canada, Denmark, Japan, Italy and the US). The scope of reform has also varied. We see countries that have attempted major changes to their budgetary processes, sometimes even changing the entire basis of decision-making or appropriation, while others have made relatively few changes or only sought to reform limited components of the 'systems'. Furthermore, there are different thematic emphases apparent.

In search of greater control, some have decentralized decision-making within top-down limits, while others have tried to centralize or recentralize decision-making. Some have focused on controlling inputs and limiting expenditure, others on producing results and showing value for money. We see nations that have used statutory means to enforce change as opposed to those that have relied on executive fiat. Some countries have engaged in extensive planning and review exercises, while others have been content to impose arbitrary cuts or variations without much analysis.

And yet within these substantial differences there are strands of similar narratives describing the reform endeavours that share related elements or resemblances. There are stories of partial reform replication involving degrees of policy transfer and policy learning interspliced through these country accounts. Governments have learned from each other's experiences, borrowed ideas and templates of reform from one another, and clarified to themselves the reform directions or initiatives they did not want to adopt from the international smorgasbord of ideas and practices. Some have scanned the international scene with a highly inquisitive radar looking for what might be regarded as best practice or successful models to apply.

There is certainly by now an active international epistemic community interested in budgetary reforms – mainly but not confined to budgetary officials and practitioners. They create and share stories, embroider the architecture, peddle new solutions and proselytize about their own innovations. They share secret problems and present intended solutions. But by and large these people are the victors of the process and the agents or mechanics of change. It is hard to find voices lamenting failure, admitting shortcomings, or revealing how difficult issues have been ducked or avoided. Instead, their sanctioned stories have a descriptive and prescriptive immediacy. Some narratives are laced with triumphalism and a sense that yesterday's problems have been dispensed with and today's can be solved. At various times the key messages associated with these stories have been codified and issued as 'best-practice guides' by such bodies as the World Bank (1998), the International Monetary Fund (IMF) (1999) or the OECD (2001). Yet, when subsequent officials or commentators from these countries subsequently meet there is a sense that the proclaimed solutions did not work out as intended, have been superseded, or even discontinued.

As mentioned in Chapter 1, budgetary officials are more likely to make presentations about the new or latest reforms they are about to undertake, rather than to present analysis of why previous reforms did not meet expectations (see Schick 2004: 90–91). There seems much evidence for this in our 11 countries. Governments are interested only in 'going forward' and typically show little interest in investigating the limitations of the reform practices already attempted. This may indicate why, when looking at budgetary reforms, there tends to be a fascination with immediacy, and with positive appreciations of their promise, leading only to frustration at the lack of apparent progress or implementation a few years later. The interest of most governments appears to be asymmetrical vis-à-vis the known past and the expected future.

Moreover, the existence of policy transfer has not produced conformity or uniformity. Officials may explore novel approaches and peruse the state-of-the-art documentation, but they do not directly copy, and even if they attempt to do so in part they invariably make local adaptations. Consequently, the international narratives of budgetary reform resemble national calibrations or distant echoes that may have once had some points of connection but which remain different and exist in parallel dimensions.

There have also been national examples of deliberate resistance to reform agendas, supposedly endorsed as best-practice and 'must-do' techniques. For instance, Denmark was pressured to consider introducing a fiscal responsibility Act (or charter of budget honesty) setting out in statute the fiscal strategy principles of the government; but it resisted such demands, considering that such an Act did not add anything of value to Denmark's system. New Zealanders have proudly boasted of their pioneering edifice of reform, but refused to adopt end-of-year flexibilities. Retaining such 'old' rules means that any unspent annual budgets still lapse and return to the Treasury, and so traditional wasteful spending by departments and agencies continues to occur. Korea resisted changes to its traditional line-input budgetary practices for decades until a reforming president and supporting clique seized the initiative in 2003. From the international catalogue of reform experiments, Korea became interested in the Swedish government's expenditure ceilings reforms, but refused to propose or accept that the limits would be statutorily imposed, thereby following more in the path of Australian and Canadian experience by default. These divergent examples, coming out of left field, suggest adaptation rather than policy transfer – but this is not the perception of the epistemic community.

THE KEY FINDINGS

The specific findings of this study have been grouped under six headings or topics, which are:

- What were the rationales and trajectories of budget reform in each country and were they made explicit?

- What were the triggers and catalysts for particular reform endeavours?
- How might we classify the nature, scale or scope of reform exercises?
- What common pathways and approaches have been followed?
- How far have divergent reform practices become apparent?
- How have the reforms affected budgetary politics, patterns of legislative oversight and public scrutiny?

RATIONALES AND TRAJECTORIES

With perhaps only one notable exception (Italy), these OECD governments have pursued relatively ambitious budgetary reform agendas or reforms to resource management in the public sector. In most cases governments have been relatively open and genuine over their intentions with budget reform. Major reforms have been formally declared in statutes, giving them mandatory status and, perhaps even more importantly, wide publicity. Governments have been keen to use public sanction to underscore their own accountability for adhering to the reform objectives. Even reform initiatives emanating purely from within the executive have usually been accompanied with ample documentation and statements of reform intent. In all cases governments have been concerned to make the rationales and expectations explicit, largely as a way of imposing a form of self-discipline upon themselves into the future.

Overall, two principal rationales stand out as being the primary motivations of nations to embrace reform: imposing fiscal discipline over aggregate budgets (elimination of structural deficits); and improving resource management across the public sector (enhancing technical efficiency). In practice, governments have tended to emphasize one or other of these rationales; so for example the US and to some extent Italy and Spain have largely stressed managerial reform and performance, while the UK, Korea, Denmark, The Netherlands and Japan (somewhat unsuccessfully) have emphasized fiscal control (usually producing a pattern of fiscal surpluses in these countries up to 2008). A couple of nations have zig-zagged between fiscal discipline and managerial improvements, such as Spain and Canada as they have attempted to impose 'budget stability', while Australia and New Zealand attempted to do both simultaneously for brief periods (imposing cuts to outlays while pushing a significant reformist managerial agenda across the public sector). But in these latter countries the central budget agency (CBA) had strong pockets of support for the take-up of managerial and business practice across other line agencies even though they mainly prioritized fiscal discipline.

This suggests that governments and their CBAs face a choice: they can choose to be active in imposing budget discipline or in reforming the management of their public sector – but are usually not successful in sustaining both over a longer period of time. This was true even among the one-time 'hard-line' disciplinarians such as Australia, Canada, The Netherlands and New Zealand where overall fiscal discipline was relaxed as they pursued market-based and agency-oriented reforms. Italy, alone, even though it made public commitments to introduce both strategies, does not appear to have managed to impose either.

In the reform process, less emphasis has been placed on reallocation, perhaps because it is fundamentally more difficult to impose. Expenditures have continued to grow as a proportion of gross domestic product (GDP) (especially social expenditure), and in the past governments relied on economic growth to produce surpluses which obviated the need to attempt significant reallocations. Contrary to Kraan and Kelly (2005), governments can produce very limited evidence of reallocation (or even of their desire to do so) and have no real incentive to disclose such measures even if they do manage to reallocate some resources.[1] We find evidence of reallocation being minor and sporadic (as in Canada) or at best 'covert' as in New Zealand, or involving ill-planned 'generic' allocations as in Italy (executive slush funds). Some nations have reallocated functions or responsibilities between levels of government (offloading) but not necessarily accompanied such transfers with the required level of funding or revenue powers.

There has also been much talk of making budgets more responsive to political priorities (the ostensible 'holy grail' of the reformers) – although such sentiments were not usually articulated in statements of reform intent, nor were they made open to subsequent evaluation. Certainly, politicians are now much more involved in setting and imposing aggregate fiscal controls; but is this evidence of responsiveness or contingent toughness? From our countries the evidence is slight that budgets are now more politically responsive, especially as in some nations up to 80 per cent of the budget is in the form of standing appropriations, transfers or entitlement benefits. Countries that have stressed that budgets ought to be more politically responsive have tended to interpret this as code for reducing political priorities (that is, through compacts, 'golden rules', fiscal agreements between political actors, rationing by senior ministers and edicts reducing the scope for new policy). Arguably, politicians have become more responsive to budgetary priorities and imperatives, rather than the other way around.

Two further observations can be made. First, the rhetoric and claims surrounding budget reform have usually been extravagant. There has been much posturing and bluster about budget reform (almost becoming an initiation rite for many countries to be able to sit at the table of senior budget officials). Yet often we find that not much has changed under the surface, despite the changes in nomenclature, realignments, the new procedures and reform narratives. This suggests that a 'coaching effect' is apparent, and that the language of reform is important to the robustness of budgetary systems. But language does not necessarily translate into actual changed practices – the stated intent of budgetary reform does not always align with subsequent reality. The language of revision may be crucial to system maintenance. Reform narratives and revised nomenclature may have contributed to cultural and attitudinal change (especially in relation to the expectations of participants) rather than to the ways the budget is made or how decisions are taken. Institutional politics and arbitrariness are still powerful imperatives driving public budgeting.

Second, stated rationales have tended to be expressed as generic aims and broader preferences, rather than specific targets or measurable indicators. Governments have been reluctant to establish specific criteria against which they would subsequently be judged. They seek credibility and reputation. They have preferred to be prudent, cautious, responsible or sound financial managers, aiming to balance budgets. On the rare occasions when they have been highly specific they have tended to be burned by the experience.[2] They have, therefore, to varying degrees, all preserved and institutionalized a measure of flexibility in their fiscal and budgetary policies. Some slippage is an institutional necessity.

TRIGGERS AND CATALYSTS FOR REFORM

Three trigger or catalysts for reform stand out across the 11 countries: a sense of crisis or urgency generated by circumstances; the imposition of international rules and requirements on national governments; and the changing nature of the 'budgetary problem'.

Most significant experiments with budget reform have taken place under a sense of urgency or crisis. Some of these crises have been genuine economic or fiscal crises (Canada's meltdown and austere Program Review of the mid-1990s), while others appear to have been manufactured or invented to create a certain 'space' to act (Korea under President Roh). The crisis imperative was perhaps strongest in Japan, Canada, The Netherlands, New Zealand and, originally, the UK when they undertook their major reforms, but far less significant in Spain, Denmark, Korea or Australia. By contrast, two countries – the US and Italy – have been faced with massive fiscal crises and have not been able institutionally to use such circumstances to reform their budget processes fundamentally. Japan also appears to have fallen into this category in recent years.

Significantly, the fiscal crises in Italy and New Zealand were both accompanied by political crises resulting in major changes to their political and institutional arrangements (especially to their electoral systems and party structures). No other country has changed their political institutional configurations in response, although some have witnessed wild political fluctuations in the complexions of governments (Canada, Spain, Korea, Japan and The Netherlands). One further frequent response to dealing with crises has been to concentrate arbitrary power for budgetary decisions further in the President or Prime Minister and or Finance Minister, especially in parliamentary systems, and sometimes almost to an idiosyncratic degree as in Canada under Jean Chretien, the UK under Gordon Brown, and Australia under John Howard.

The sense of crisis also permeates the scope for fiscal discipline. It appears from most country case studies that it is possible to impose major budgetary discipline and to undertake budgetary reforms in times of crisis, and that this will recur in the future as governments readjust their fiscal policies after responding to the present financial crisis. But, historically, countries seem to wrestle constantly with the issue of how to impose or keep budgetary discipline when the sense of crisis diminishes.

The imposition of international edicts and rules became powerful catalysts for national governments to take strong budgetary action. They provided external reference points to governments mandating fiscal responsibility and imposing real limits on their policy latitudes, sometimes with clear sanctions readily apparent. In continental Europe the effect has been most pronounced with Spain, The Netherlands, Denmark and even Italy curtailing their fiscal plans to fit within the Maastricht agreement of 1991, the Stability and Growth Pact (1997) and Economic and Monetary Union (EMU) rules from 1999. Such rules were not merely influential on EMU member states, they were seen as binding. Moreover, they were also persuasive in some other non-EMU nations such as the UK and Australia; indeed, when the first fiscal targets were announced after Maastricht, Australia boasted that it was then the only OECD nation to qualify for entry. The effect of these 'sound' financial international impositions assisted national governments to contain their spending in times of sustained economic growth. The efficacy of these rules in times of economic crisis will be tested in the years ahead.

Other international forces have also prompted reform action. The World Bank, the IMF and the OECD have all embraced normative models of good budgetary behaviour. Their policies are generally regarded as authoritative; and their country assessments generally find receptive elite readerships. The interchange of staff encourages analytical conversations and reinforces prevailing technocratic mindsets. Credit rating agencies and their independent assessments of financial performance also play a part in encouraging reform efforts. In time, the 2008–09 global financial crisis, with its associated credit squeeze, will impose new international pressures on governments especially as their burdens of debt increase – some perhaps to unsustainable levels.

A third trigger has been the changing nature of the perceived 'budgetary problem'. In the 1980s and 1990s, the main budgetary problem for most of these OECD nations was balancing the budget and using political discipline to impose cuts for the sake of the bottom line. Their intentions were often to reduce or contain expenditure growth, attempt to achieve balances in the immediate term, and allow small surpluses to appear, usually generated by increased revenue and other income growth. By the 2000s the budgetary problem had changed to focus more on how to maintain sustainable finances into the future, faced with demographic pressures, the ageing of the population, rising health and nursing home costs, tensions over social integration and entitlement cost. Many of the budgetary reform instruments adopted to cope with the former problem were ineffective against the second, larger set of problems. Funding long-term welfare provisions was of a magnitude far greater than the adoption of medium-term expenditure frameworks, and involved considerably more policy sector inputs than merely budgetary solutions. Governments had just begun to take seriously the implications of long-term sustainability when the global financial crisis hit in 2008; despite concerns over increased deficits in the immediate period, the salience of the longer-term problem is only going to increase in the future.

THE NATURE AND SCALE OF REFORM EXERCISES

What can we conclude about the nature and scale of the reforms attempted across these countries? Of the seven categories of reform outlined in Chapter 1, some have attracted few adherents while others have resonances with each case. The main evolving pattern of reform was not comprehensive, cumulative or even incremental, but one of punctuated stability: periods of some intensity followed by stability, perhaps relaxation and complacency. It is arguable whether any nation attempted a truly transformational set of reforms, although New Zealand (the 'shooting star') might claim it came closest to this category. Most countries attempted some reforms to selected components of their budgetary systems or processes. In general, countries have attempted to place top-down rules and processes over budgetary behaviour to limit actor volition (such as with medium-term expenditure plans), but to allow greater scope for volition within the new structural frames. Perhaps the main component reform we can identify has been to move budgetary attention from inputs to outputs and results over the past two decades.

All countries have experimented with restraint exercises involving top-down cuts to base budgets, designed to reduce spending demands in the immediate budget year and to reduce forward claims. Some nations still prefer periodic cutting or review exercises (Denmark, The Netherlands, the UK and New Zealand), while others such as Australia and Canada have instituted regular clawbacks or 'dividends' back to the budget. Agency-based management and better information systems have tightened in-year controls so few go 'over budget'. Less well reflected in country experiences is the prevalence of reallocation techniques. Over time there has been a trend to contain general government expenditures while allowing social spending to grow (or accepting that it will). This is, at best, a form of quasi-reallocation, as much of the growth is caused by increased entitlements rather than budgetary reprioritization. Some nations have had more success with pushing reprioritization within departments and agencies under tight ceilings ('covert reprioritization').

Reforms to internal procedures and informal rules occur with routine predictability, but there is no clear direction of momentum. Micro-rules are often revised to tighten controls, ensure the ongoing 'integrity' of the process, or to change internal permeabilities (for instance, on bidding or weighing rival claims). The main dynamic here is whether the rules work to constrain desired managerial behaviours or provide flexibility and incentives to manage better. Similarly, all governments have significantly improved their technical and specialized knowledge reforms, bringing in better planning techniques, information sources, real-time information and communication, accounting techniques and financial skills.

Finally, governments have attempted cultural and attitudinal changes through changing budgetary discourses and managing actor expectations. Governments have proselytized the need for budgetary restraint, improved financial management and sought various contributory payments from the community. However, these cultural disciplines appear to have had greater resonance inside government rather than with the outside community. The notion still abounds that government is the provider of last resort, and sometimes even of first resort.

COMMON PATHWAYS AND APPROACHES

Allowing for some variability, we can identify some common elements in the reform histories of these countries, and common themes that have emerged, providing logics to the reform efforts. But it is dangerous to overexaggerate the degree of convergence. Even close neighbours that might be regarded as following similar pathways or achieving a similar rate of progress (such as Australia and New Zealand) are in practice very different in the composition of reform.

The first two common themes have proved very important to budgetary management but may seem prosaic or mundane. All governments have generally moved to integrate their budgetary systems into their wider policy and planning processes. Annual budgets are not simply separate processes, compartmentalized from the routine workings of government. They are no longer once-a-year, one-off gatekeeping functions rationing resources to agencies followed by allocative announcements. Rather they are primarily ongoing resourcing discussions. The budget and the processes of budgeting are now continually integrated and incorporated in the decision-making cultures of government (strategic planning cycles, discussions over policy adjustments, new policy design, programme review and policy evaluation). As a result of this, we can see evidence of some countries running their budgetary processes continually (not just the annual cycle, or the 'one single moment'). In short, the era of 'continuous budgeting' has occurred (or returned; see Caiden 1989). It must be recognized, however, that much of this integration is internal and not necessarily made transparent to the public.

Second, governments have massively increased their information capacities and integrated financial information systems so that they are aware momentarily of any variance to projected spending or anticipated revenues. This information is amassed across government and used instantaneously by line agency management in decision-making and by central agency overseers. It is constantly generated and available inside government, but again much of it is not made public. Financial reports can be generated almost at will inside organizations and across sectors; in some jurisdictions they are reviewed every 24 hours, and monthly financial reporting to the management boards of agencies has become common practice. Mostly, governments are using cost information as a form of 'in-year' control, and are much better at the internal monitoring of costs (although, again, not necessarily publicly disclosing them). However, financial management information remains less well integrated and shared between governments (central government to municipalities in unitary systems, or between jurisdictions in federations).

In terms of fiscal discipline, governments have generally adopted and published aggregate fiscal ceilings and medium-term expenditure plans, although how 'fixed' or firm they are for the present budget and over the 'out-years' is variable (for example Japan's *Hone-Buto* or 'strong bones' policy is consecutive but can be juggled annually). Budgets are regularly updated and many countries now produce half-yearly updates of budgetary information (such as Australia's Mid-Year Economic and Fiscal Outlook – MYEFO) including reporting on changed economic assumptions and on policy changes affecting the budget balance. They provide a rolling, integrated set of plans (ceilings) against which governments can control and manage. Within this context governments have tightened up their estimates and costing processes, and many have adopted artificially 'prudent' assumptions on which the plans are based (intentionally conservative estimations). Prudent budgeting (most severely practised in Canada) has had the pronounced effect of framing annual budgets well below likely economic expectations, as well as serving to dampen down claimants' expectations.

Nations have also tended to present their budget in terms of intended results, social outcomes or deliverable outputs. The results orientation is clearly evident in budget presentation if not in formulation. Governments do not formulate their budgets by determining or purchasing their preferred volumes of results or outcomes. They still decide options according to the comparable costs of programmes or agencies, the variable levels of activity considered appropriate, and how much can be afforded. But then, once decided, budgets can be aggregated into results packages for presentational purposes and to provide direction to delivery agencies. Agencies then had to develop sound methodologies for attributing costs to individual outcomes or outputs, as well as develop certain performance indicator measures to show achievement. Nevertheless, despite broad acclaim for transferring to results-based frameworks, jurisdictions that adopted broad social outcomes for presentation have been frequently criticized for labelling that is vague, immeasurable and subjective.

When nations have implemented a results-based framework (or even programme-based presentations), three features tend to accompany this move. First, outcomes and outputs tend to be compartmentalized solely to individual agencies for budgetary purposes. One-line budgets provided to agencies tend, therefore, to become glorified base budgets for agencies. Outcome or output budgeting is code for organizational budgeting (where we agree a budget base and expect the respective agency to be performing according to some declared activities). New Zealand calls this the 'electric fence', where agencies are given fixed nominal rolling baselines instead of the previous bid and review input formulation. Agencies then have the flexibility to use their generic resources (which can be lapsing or non-lapsing) towards any designated outcome or output. Second, most governments have greatly reduced the amount of input budget data they once routinely produced. They tend to see an outcome–output framework and an input presentation as mutually exclusive or problematic entities to combine. We have gone from a situation where asymmetrical information was presented only on the input side, to one where only asymmetrical information is presented on the output side. This may be because it is too difficult to reconcile detailed input data with broad outcome frameworks – so governments do not provide detailed reconciliation. Third, despite the presentational emphasis on results, there is scant evidence that governments are using performance information or evaluation assessments to shape ongoing resource allocations. The outcomes approach has not augmented the tenuous links between performance and budgeting, and there is evidence that many CBAs do not have the analytical capacities in-house to undertake such evaluative work.

As governments have gained the capacity to impose tighter overall fiscal constraints over their budgets (although they have not always chosen to do so in practice), they have become a little more relaxed over the annuality of budgets, allowing greater end-of-year flexibility. Medium-term expenditure plans provide multiyear planning horizons. Some jurisdictions make provision for multiyear budgets to selected agencies or programmes. And many (though not all) countries have relaxed end-of-year controls. In some jurisdictions appropriations are non-lapsing (they are retained by the organization into the future if not spent in the budget year). In others, various carry-over provisions allow small amounts of departmental expenses to run into the next period. It remains the case that unspent entitlements, grants or 'administered items' automatically return to the CBA if not spent within the budget year.

In times of surplus budgeting, many nations made provision for forward liabilities by establishing various off-budget funds and foundations in which to 'bank' monies and earmark them for future use (Australia, Canada, Japan, The Netherlands). The popularity of these funds represents a return to the old ways of managing resources off-budget for ad hoc reasons. In some countries such funds are the main budget; for instance, Japan's special funds are now four times the size of the general budget. There has been a steady growth in these various off-budget funds and special foundations, both in the number of funds and in the resources allocated to them. But their uses vary enormously. Some are designed to separate major items of social spending from the general budget (for example, the Canada Pension Plan fund); others are designed to provide for future infrastructure and information technology (IT) needs (for example, the Dutch Fund for Economic Structure Enhancement); while others are top-up funds or 'slush funds' that can be drawn down in budget years as extra funds for departments and agencies for new initiatives. These funds effectively break previous notions of good budgetary practice, but provide political executives with additional latitude within the prevailing tighter budgetary rules.

DIVERGENT PRACTICES

So much of the recent experience with budgetary reform has divergent qualities. Here we focus only on the more substantial differences. One major difference is the degree to which nations adopted a statutory route to propel reform (New Zealand, the US, Spain and Italy) versus an almost absence of statutory guidance and reforms promulgated by executive fiat (Australia, Canada, the UK, The Netherlands, Denmark, Korea). Those that adopted a statutory route sought to mandate how budgets were presented in order to constrain executive behaviour; they were often premised on a distrust of executive government by the legislature (or by influential budgetary officials). Those that followed the executive policy route were perhaps less certain of their reform intentions at the outset or were unsure of the consequences of their reform endeavours (deciding to follow a pragmatic approach). They also intended to preserve a flexibility of action (or wiggle-room) to cope with future contingencies. The same points can be made about statutory versus executive declared fiscal targets.

There is no pattern of unity or consolidation of budgetary decision-making over time. Indeed, practice has seemed perverse. Some nations, commencing from a fragmented multi-window tradition of resource decision-making, appear to have tried to restrict budget decision-making to one single 'moment' (in the past Australia, New Zealand, the UK with its 'unified budgets' in the 1990s; and now Korea) whereas others have trickled out decisions throughout the year when circumstances (and revenues) are better known (Canada, Japan, the US). We tend to find that fiscal stress encourages or forces governments to consolidate their budgetary decision-making (to stop leakage, double-dipping or sequential supplementaries), whereas in more profligate times and with budgets in surplus governments allowed greater fragmentation in resource decision-making throughout the year. Canada is the big exception here. The Canadian government allocates only around 70 percent of the budget in the main budget round and then parcels out additional spending in various supplementary budgets as the year unfolds. The government claims the procedure called 'top-up budgeting' allows it to gauge more accurately what resources are available for allocation as time and contingencies develop.

The flirtation with accrual accounting and accrual budgeting also separates the nations. Some remain implacably opposed to accrual budgeting (cashing agencies for full accrual liabilities), such as Canada and the US.

Others have adopted modified accrual adjustments for some components of their budgets (for example, Denmark, Japan, The Netherlands and the UK). Two nations (Australia and New Zealand) have both introduced full accrual practices for budget-making and consolidated financial reporting across the entire government sector. However, Australia has indicated that it may step back from its full accrual model and not provide individual agencies with cash for depreciation (calculating it centrally), moving to a 'cash requirements' system for agency appropriations.

There have also been major divergences in relation to debt reduction strategies across the OECD. To some nations, debt reduction (even elimination) was the pre-eminent goal, especially among the Anglo jurisdictions (Australia, Canada and New Zealand in particular) but also to some extent in Denmark, Spain and The Netherlands. These nations all significantly reduced their public debt as a percentage of GDP over the two decades from 1988 to 2007. Italy (with debts of more than 120 per cent of GDP) and Japan (with escalating debt levels of close to 200 per cent) were the antithesis of this pattern, and belatedly the US followed in their wake (with public debt rising to around 70 per cent of GDP). Similarly, the way debt appears in budget statements varies, as does the accounting for payment of interest on debt structures. Some countries keep all their debt and interest payments on-budget (consolidated and represented in balance sheets), while others have partitioned these off-budget. In the latter case, when budget balances are shown in documentation they will only refer to the general government sector and not provide a fiscal balance of the entire resource claim of the public sector on society (liabilities to future generations).

Outsourcing, as a means of containing public expenditure costs, has received a mixed take-up and reception to date. While the UK and New Zealand have eagerly outsourced much of their policy delivery, other nations have been reluctant to use market-based delivery providers. Many nations have adopted halfway or hybrid models using various constellations of executive agencies (Australia, The Netherlands, the UK) to deliver services according to quasi-contractual payments.

BUDGETARY POLITICS AND LEGISLATIVE OVERSIGHT

Budgetary politics were once 'high executive politics' in most OECD nations, but perhaps no more. Budgetary politics have not been the principal preoccupation of executive governments in most nations since the mid-1990s. Even in the context of the 2008–09 global financial crisis, economic management rather than budgetary politics is far more germane to these governments, and occupies their collective attentions more profoundly. Periodically, budgetary crises have crystallized 'political moments' when governments have been impelled to act to make major corrections or introduce institutional changes. But after these intense periods have passed, budgeting again subsides to a state of routine normalcy.

Budgeting has been largely depoliticized because there is far less to fight about and a high degree of bipartisan support for fiscal policy settings. Larger and larger portions of public expenditure are now in the form of non-discretionary items running mainly on autopilot. Budgetary decision-making has become more mundane, involving lower-level politics and more technical small 'p' politics between officials and officials, departments and departments. One consequence of decentralization in most countries has been for line agencies to take far more responsibility for their own financial management, thereby lessening conflicts with central agencies and contributing to the depoliticization of budgeting. CBAs are also playing a less confrontational or challenging role while emphasizing *ex post* accountabilities in their oversight functions. We can note, as well, that there have been some moves to centralize top-level decision-making power in economic ministries (or with prime ministers) at the expense of budget preparation ministries.

The major exception to this is the US, which continues to have major political fights over budgets in the context of mounting deficits and debt levels. This has pressed budgetary issues constantly back onto the vacillating relations between the President and Congress. The separation of powers serves to underscore the salience of budgetary politics, while creating institutional inertia and preventing either side from substantially reforming the processes. The US case may be explained by 'hyper-pluralism inside government' or 'shared but separated government' in which resourcing issues are still big 'P' politics.

To satisfy legislative scrutiny, increased information has been produced for accountability purposes. These reports tend to focus on outcomes and results. Moreover, many nations have adopted integrated financial reporting with required periodic reporting instruments providing greater consistency of aggregate information over the medium term. They provide results-based information in multiple but integrated sources, from overall annual budget documents to agency or portfolio budget statements, updated half-yearly reports, final budget outcomes reports and agency annual reports. In many jurisdictions these information reports are presented on the same basis with consistency over time (or variations reconciled), which had not occurred in previous decades. Some jurisdictions have devolved responsibility to agencies themselves for producing their own budget documentation, financial information and performance information (meaning that the CBAs are less involved in compiling such materials).

However, the contributors to this volume find that the involvement and role of the legislature varies in the different budgetary reform trajectories. In some of the nations the legislature has been closely involved in the reform directions and in budget oversight; in others the legislature has been or remained essentially marginalized. The degree of involvement seems to be correlated to the legislative cultures and traditions of the country concerned rather than to the immediate political situation of whether the government exercises control over the legislature. Some legislatures have not shown a great deal of interest in budgetary scrutiny despite attempts by the executive to inform them better (for example, Canada, or the 'third Wednesday in May' exercise in The Netherlands).

It is true that many legislatures have been disappointed as executive governments have opted to present their budgetary information in outputs or outcomes formats. They have complained that the information is unclear, too highly aggregated, does not give a clear sense of what is happening, and suffers from multiple measures that can change from year to year. Some nations have been accused of producing less meaningful information to the legislature than previously occurred with input-oriented budgets. Three main problems have been identified. First, categories of outcomes and outputs can be redefined or adjusted from year to year to change their scope or meaning, making longitudinal comparisons impossible. Second, results-based budgetary information may not be closely related to actual performance of the agency or programme. Parliamentarians are usually looking to get their teeth into the government over some questionable activities, and outcome labels are often opaque and innocuous. Third, results-based appropriations do not give legislatures a clear idea of what they are being asked to authorize under those appropriations, and it may not be possible to drill down into budget documentation to discover sub-outputs, details on associated programmes or activities.

Finally, the onset of the global financial crisis – with its associated fiscal implications for governments – does not imply budgetary mismanagement or that the reform trajectories of the previous decades have been undermined. Arguably, most OECD nations were in a much better position to withstand the financial crisis precisely because they had put their budgetary houses in order over the preceding period. The changes in fiscal conditions brought on by the crisis, and the political imperatives to spend as a means of stimulating their economies, will undoubtedly see all OECD nations incur greater levels of debt than they enjoyed in the mid-2000s. This will place additional constraints on annual budgets into the foreseeable future, especially as interest repayments grow as a proportion of annual expenditures. But this in itself is not a measure of how well the budget reforms have worked or how effective they are as additions to decision-making. Many of the reforms introduced were designed explicitly to assist with fiscal discipline and produce surplus balances. How well they are able to achieve this in the future will be a measure of their robustness and salience in times of economic recession. If they are up to the job they will be retained and consolidated; if they are not then the history of these countries suggests that further experimentation will occur, and that they will be replaced with reform measures more effective in a different context.

NOTES

1. Kraan and Kelly (2005) argue that reallocation is increasingly important but do not really demonstrate that it is. Their study, in reality, discusses external pressures on spending (structural and demographic), new spending patterns and priorities, and changed administrative arrangements. None of these involved governments reallocating in the previous era of economic growth. Programme review functions (or cutting exercises) can lead to some reallocation but need not necessarily. It will be interesting to see in terms of the recent financial crisis and its aftermath whether governments are more able to reallocate given that the structural pressures on spending are unlikely to dissipate.
2. Two examples will suffice. The Australian Labor government committed itself to a 'Trilogy' of fiscal constraints over three years (1984–87 – not to increase taxes or spending, and to reduce the deficit as a proportion of GDP over the government's term – but found it extremely difficult to manage within these constraints as the years developed. Second, Australia's Liberal Treasurer, Peter Costello, made an explicit commitment to reduce central government outlays from 27 per cent of GDP in 1995–96 to just 23 per cent by 2001. He insisted on hard medium-term targets but was unable to meet the target (expenditures were still 25.6 per cent in 2001). His insistence on hard targets saw the government resort to various forms of disingenuousness with the national accounts; in particular, not counting a major consumption tax as federal income to try to show that central outlays were declining.

REFERENCES

Blondal, J.R. (2003), 'Budget reform in OECD member countries: common trends', *OECD Journal on Budgeting*, **2** (4), 7–27.
Caiden, N. (1989), 'A new perspective on budgetary reform', *Australian Journal of Public Administration*, **48** (1).
International Monetary Fund (IMF) (1999), *Code of Good Practices on Fiscal Transparency*, Washington, DC: IMF.
Kraan, D.-J. and J. Kelly (2005), *Reallocation: the Role of Budget Institutions*, Paris: OECD.
Organisation for Economic Co-operation and Department (OECD) (2001), 'OECD best practices for budget transparency', May, Paris: OECD.

Schick, A. (2000), 'Opportunity, strategy and tactics in reforming public management', in E. Lau (ed.), *Government of the Future*, Paris: OECD.

Schick, A. (2002), 'Does budgeting have a future?' *OECD Journal on Budgeting*, **2** (2), 7–48.

Schick, A. (2004), 'Twenty five years of budgeting reform', *OECD Journal on Budgeting*, **4** (1), 81–102.

World Bank (1998), *Public Expenditure Management Handbook*, Washington, DC: World Bank.

Index